John Nash
Rulers of the Sea

De Gruyter Studies in Military History

Edited by
Jörg Echternkamp and Adam Seipp

Volume 8

John Nash
Rulers of the Sea

Maritime Strategy and Sea Power in Ancient Greece, 550–321 BCE

ISBN 978-3-11-221555-5
e-ISBN (PDF) 978-3-11-134293-1
e-ISBN (EPUB) 978-3-11-134316-7
ISSN 2701-5629

Library of Congress Control Number: 2023944686

Bibliographic information published by the Deutsche Nationalbibliothek
The Deutsche Nationalbibliothek lists this publication in the Deutsche Nationalbibliografie;
detailed bibliographic data are available on the internet at http://dnb.dnb.de.

© 2025 Walter de Gruyter GmbH, Berlin/Boston
This volume is text- and page-identical with the hardback published in 2024.
Cover image: Naval Battle of Arginusae 406 BC near Lesbos © Grafissimo / DigitalVision Vectors / Getty Images
Typesetting: Integra Software Services Pvt. Ltd.
Printing and binding: CPI books GmbH, Leck

www.degruyter.com

Notes on spelling, names, and translations

All translations are my own unless otherwise noted. I have attempted to be as literal as possible, somewhat at the expense of readability.

All dates used throughout are BC/BCE, unless otherwise specified.

All ancient references are cited as per the *Oxford Classical Dictionary* (4th ed.), except for the Old Oligarch's *Constitution of the Athenians*, which is cited as 'Old Oligarch' as opposed to '[Xenophon] Ath. Pol.' or 'Pseudo-Xenophon'.

All distances are measured in nautical miles (nm), all elevations and depths of water in metres (m), and all speeds in knots (kts) unless otherwise specified.

Acknowledgements

This book is the culmination of many years' work. It started as my PhD thesis at the Australian National University, research that was supported by an Australian Government Research Training Program Scholarship. Since then, I have been fortunate enough to continue work on it.

There are many people I would like to thank for their support during my PhD studies and since then: the staff at the Sea Power Centre – Australia, especially Greg Swinden, Dr David Stevens, and Dr Ben Herscovitch; the Centre for Classical studies at the ANU, Professor Elizabeth Minchin, Dr Greta Hawes, Dr Paul Burton, Dr Chris Bishop, Dr Sonia Pertsinidis, and of course my office-mate Adrienne White, puzzling over ancient Greek passages and sharing memes and dog photos. My supervisor Dr Peter Londey provided great support and advice throughout my studies at ANU. He has guided me well through the years, providing sound advice, tolerating my constant proselytising of sea power theory, and tempering my more vociferous criticisms of those who did get 'maritime'.

While finishing the manuscript I had the great privilege of working with an excellent team of historians at the Australian War Memorial, a monumental project writing the Official History of Australian Operations in Iraq and Afghanistan, and Australian Peacekeeping Operations in East Timor. It was a fantastic environment to work in, as a full-time historian, under the leadership of Professor Craig Stockings. Once again, I get to thank Dr David Stevens for enlisting me in the project and supporting my extra-curricular Classics writing. A great many thanks are due to Emeritus Professor Peter Dennis, who provided tireless advice and encouragement and pushed me to get this manuscript over the line, even if it was so that I could start on a second manuscript.

Not least, a big thanks to my friends and family for putting up with long hours and rants about obscure pieces of scholarship, historiography, and tortuous passages of Thucydides in Greek.

Finally, it is to Adelaide and my dog and cat helpers that I dedicate this book. Adelaide, Grozny, Temperance, Mika, Nyx, Fenris, and Zeppelin, this one is for you.

Contents

Notes on spelling, names, and translations —— V

Acknowledgements —— VII

Introduction: 'sea power' and other concepts —— 1
    Structure —— 5

Chapter One
Setting the scene: geography, environment, navigation, and fishing —— 9
    Geography —— 9
    Environmental conditions —— 11
    Weather —— 14
    Navigation —— 17
    Sailing season —— 22
    Natural resources —— 29
    Conclusion —— 32

Chapter Two
Wooden walls: ships and naval organisation —— 34
    Naval organisation —— 34
    Ships and ship design —— 38
    Personnel —— 43
    Infrastructure —— 46
    Finance and wealth —— 48
    Conclusion —— 51

Chapter Three
The ship of state: Greek maritime consciousness —— 52
    Myth and epic —— 53
    Tragedy —— 61
    Comedy —— 64
    History and philosophy —— 67
    Herodotus, Xenophon, and Diodorus —— 68
    Dissenting voices —— 71
    Conclusions —— 77

Chapter Four
The birth of navies – sixth-century Greece —— 78
    Thucydides —— 83

Chapter Five
Divine Salamis: the Persian Wars —— 87
    The Ionian rebellion —— 87
    The (Persian) empire strikes back —— 90

Chapter Six
Rulers of the sea: Athens and the Delian League —— 101
    Walls of wood and stone —— 101
    The 'Old Oligarch' —— 104
    The *pentekontaetia* —— 108
    Athens and the Delian League —— 112
    Conclusion —— 115

Chapter Seven
The great war: the Peloponnesian war from Corcyra to Sicily —— 117
    Crisis in Corcyra —— 117
    War at sea —— 119
    The strategy of Pericles and his successors —— 121
    War in the east and west —— 131
    Pushing the limits —— 135
    The 'Peace' of Nicias —— 138
    Conclusion —— 140

Chapter Eight
The triumph of sea power: Sicily and the Ionian War —— 141
    The Sicilian expedition —— 141
    Spartan strategy 413–404 —— 146
    Conclusion —— 159

Chapter Nine
No easy thing: the fall of Spartan sea power and Athens' return —— 161
    Spartan strategy 404-370s —— 161
    Sicily and Italy —— 171
    Maritime Athens in the fourth century —— 174
    Conclusion —— 180

Chapter Ten
Aegean awakening: Thebes, war in the North, and the rise of Macedon —— 181
    Epaminondas and the Theban navy —— 183
    Athens, the Second Athenian League, and northern Greece —— 187
    Athens and conflict with Philip —— 191
    The economic dimension —— 197
    Conclusion —— 200

Chapter Eleven
The lessons of sea power —— 202
    Non-hegemonic sea power —— 202
    Corinth —— 203
    Corcyra —— 205
    Leucas —— 208
    Aegina —— 210
    Chios —— 211
    Enablers and the trinity of maritime operations —— 213
    Military operations —— 215
    Diplomatic operations —— 218
    Constabulary operations —— 220

Conclusion —— 222

Appendix 1
Glossary of terms —— 225

Appendix 2
Database of maritime operations —— 231

Bibliography —— 251

Index —— 265

Introduction: 'sea power' and other concepts

The ancient Greeks were, by and large, a maritime people. Such a statement seems obvious; yet aside from such broad statements of generalised wisdom, not a great deal of work exists on what this means in the context of classical Greek history. Are we talking about the Greeks' wonderful seaside homes and cities? Of scraps of myth that we remember about the sea god Poseidon and god of love Aphrodite, born from the foam of the sea? Of the Greeks crossing the ocean to besiege Troy and of Odysseus' tortuous journey home? Perhaps we remember stories of the Persians invading Greece in 490 with a large fleet, giving us 'marathon' as more than just an obscure beach but rather a term of modern athletic contest. Perhaps it goes so far as the next Persian invasion ten years later, where an even greater Persian force crossed by land and by sea and the land force was met at Thermopylae, the brave last stand of Leonidas' 300, though nothing is remembered of the naval clash at Artemision, only that of Salamis, a great naval battle to begin historical lists of famous and important naval battles, to be followed by the likes of Lepanto, Trafalgar, Jutland, and Midway. From there the fleets of Greece are obscured by the conquests of Alexander 'the Great', the petulant conqueror of Persia who heralded the next age of Western history, the Hellenistic Age. It is in such simplistic ways that the role of the sea in Greek history is often viewed. To be sure, there are many studies of specific aspects of Greek maritime history, from reconstructions of Greek ships through to the various aspects of the navy in Athens. Yet there is little study on **sea power** in Ancient Greece. We will return to the somewhat vexed term 'sea power' momentarily.

Similarly, a great deal of maritime strategic thought has developed over the nineteenth and twentieth centuries to consider lessons from history, but this consideration rarely stretches back farther than the age of sail, roughly the sixteenth century onwards. This appears to have two primary causes. The first is due to a pessimistic view of ancient technological capabilities and a view that the Greeks were so restricted by technology that little can be learned from maritime warfare of the time. This is a result of the tendency towards a determinist view of history by many scholars examining issues of maritime strategy, seeing naval warfare and subsequent lessons learnt as determined by technology. Second, there is seemingly a lack of interdisciplinary subject matter expertise by modern scholars dealing with certain aspects of ancient history. This has led to a dearth of works dealing with maritime strategy and sea power in the ancient world. Herein lies a gap in the existing scholarship. Using an adapted theoretical framework derived from modern maritime strategic thought, this book aims to explore how Greek city-states – a polis (singular) or poleis (plural) – used sea power.

Much like the term 'strategy', sea power is a broad concept, with many definitions building upon one another over the last few decades. The early theorist Admiral Sir Herbert Richmond is the first to explicitly give a definition of sea power:

> Sea Power is that form of national strength which enables its possessor to send his armies and commerce across those stretches of sea and ocean which lie between his country or the countries of his allies, and those territories to which he needs access in war; and to prevent his enemy from doing the same.[1]

Richmond's definition is simple and timeless and does not reduce the concept to any spatial or temporal restriction, letting it stand as a general theory of sea power. Perhaps the simplest one-line definition of sea power is provided by Geoffrey Till: 'the capacity to influence the behaviour of other people or things by what one does at or from the sea'.[2] As both of these definitions allude to, sea power is not just naval power but refers to a state's use of the sea in general. So when Athens used its extensive maritime trade networks to create a prosperous city, able to import whatever goods it could want or need, and cut off such trade to other poleis if desired, it was utilising its sea power. Though the threat of naval force might be implicit, or often explicit, Athens' maritime dominance on purely commercial terms was regularly sufficient to accomplish political and economic goals, without a single trireme in sight. The maritime law courts of Athens were widely respected, and judgements obeyed, and this perfectly illustrates one of the non-naval aspects of sea power, rather than naval power. Something worthy of explicit attention is the fact that neither of these definitions restricts the possession of sea power to large or hegemonic states. Sea power is not just something for hegemonic superpowers, it is a relationship with the sea that transcends mere military or political might. As we shall see, it was not just all-powerful Athens or Sparta who possessed sea power in the ancient Greek context.

Geoffrey Till in *Seapower: A Guide for the Twenty-First Century* lists four attributes of the sea: as a resource, as a medium of transportation, as a medium of information, and as a medium for dominion.[3] These attributes are not only applicable to the modern world but also intrinsic attributes which can be exploited – or not – as any nation throughout time might decide. A cursory examination of the Greek world shows that these four attributes are readily identifiable. As a resource the sea provided fish and salt. Vast trade networks across the Mediterranean and into the Black and Red Seas from early history onwards demonstrate the sea's utility as a medium for transportation, unsurprising given the rough ter-

---

1 Richmond (1946): ix.
2 Till (2013): 25.
3 Till (2013): 6.

rain of mainland Greece and its long coastline. Vast numbers of archaeological finds, as well as written evidence such as from the Athenian law courts, attest to the sea being used prolifically as a medium of transportation. As a means of information, 'network theory', as examined by Irad Malkin and Christy Constantakopoulou, helps show how this was the case in Greece.[4] Greek language and culture spread throughout the Mediterranean basin, and the sea was the primary means of basic and complex information dissemination. For example, news of family dramas at home in Athens was able to reach a trierarch on campaign in the Aegean.[5] The wars of the Greeks, from the Ionian Revolt through to the wars of the *Diadochi,* amply demonstrate that the sea was regularly used as a medium for dominion. By using such general principles to examine maritime operations in the Classical period, we can view this world in a new light and recognise that the sea played a central and not merely a peripheral role in Greek affairs.

A large part of this book will focus on the naval operations. Notwithstanding the above caveat that maritime means more than just naval, navies are one of the largest users of the maritime space. This is true of the ancient world, especially inasmuch as ancient sources are notoriously prejudiced towards covering matters of war and politics over social and economic matters. In the modern world, naval operations are commonly divided into three main categories: **military**, **diplomatic**, and **constabulary** (or policing).[6] These categories will be used as a guide and are not intended to force Greek naval operations into a rigid classification system. They will be used to inform this study on to what extent Greek powers thought of and enacted any kind of 'maritime strategy' and how they took a deliberate approach in the employment of maritime forces over the long term. By examining what Greek naval forces actually did, we can see just how pervasive these operations were throughout this period of Greek history. A database of these operations has been created and included in an appendix, though it is not intended for use in any kind of statistical analysis, but merely as a reference point to the multitude of maritime operations from this period.

Firstly, it is necessary to offer clear definitions of some key terms. One of the main issues is in the conflation of 'naval' and 'maritime', two terms which do not

---

4 For example, Malkin, *Myth and territory in the Spartan Mediterranean* (1994); *Greek and Roman networks in the Mediterranean* (2009); *A Small Greek World* (2011); and Christy Constantakopoulou, *The Dance of the Islands: Insularity, Networks, the Athenian Empire, and the Aegean World* (2007).
5 Dem. 50.62.
6 The span of maritime operations, or tasks. I prefer the term 'constabulary', and this is used throughout. Originally elaborated by Ken Booth and Eric Grove and subsequently modified by different navies. See Booth (1977): 16; Grove (1990): 234. See Figure 1.

refer to the same concept and which should not be used interchangeably. Naval strategy commonly refers to the purely military aspect of naval power: a navy develops a strategy to defeat another navy and thus develops a naval strategy. A maritime strategy on the other hand is 'the direction of all aspects of national power that relate to a nation's interests at sea'.[7] As John Hattendorf elaborates, this involves diplomacy, the safety and defence of merchant trade, fishing, and coastal defence.[8] Navies obviously have a central role to play in any maritime strategy, but there is more to it than only warships. A naval strategy is how one navy will defeat another – it is restricted to the military realm.[9] In the Greek context, a maritime strategy such as that of Athens involved many different aspects of national power, from setting up colonies and cleruchies through to maintaining good relations with Egypt and kingdoms in the Black Sea region from where the Athenians imported grain critical to their food security and thus their very survival. This involved the use of both hard and soft power, and the instrument used was often the navy. At the same time, it is important to make the distinction between the navy being used against another seaborne military force (naval) and being used to further the nation's larger goals such as better diplomatic relations or the protection of trade (maritime). A maritime strategy such as Athens' during the Peloponnesian War might involve the conduct of amphibious operations, with the bulk of the fighting on land but supported by a naval force. In such a case, the navy is an enabling force, allowing for the conduct of operations ashore by providing support, cover – protecting the landing force from enemy interference by sea – reinforcements, tactical manoeuvrability, or even evacuation. This is one way in which a navy can be used in a maritime strategy. This work will examine naval campaigns, not as campaigns in and of themselves, but rather as campaigns as part of a larger strategy.

Secondly, it is necessary to pin down a general definition of 'strategy'. Lawrence Freedman's book on strategy makes the point that it is a word for which the meaning has become diluted through promiscuous and often inappropriate use.[10] Both Freedman and Hew Strachan accept and are satisfied with strategy as a term to describe the relationships between means and ends, concerned with

---

7 Hattendorf (2013): 7.
8 Amongst many other issues related to the modern world such as border security, environmental conservation, and the protection of a nation's Exclusive Economic Zone (EEZ). Hattendorf (2013): 7.
9 Not to be confused with 'military' in a purist sense of referring only to the activities of armies. This work uses military in the broader sense of meaning the actions of any force engaged in armed conflict, be it on land or at sea.
10 Freedman (2013): x.

identifying national objectives as well as the resources and methods available for meeting such objectives.[11] Critically, strategy comes into play where there is actual or potential conflict between opposing powers. Strategy is much more than a 'plan' because it is required when an opposing force's own interests and objectives must be considered, perfectly illustrated by the Mike Tyson quote with which Freedman opens his book: 'Everyone has a plan 'till they get punched in the mouth'.[12] Tactics are not a concern of this book, save for how they might have influenced strategy – Athenian tactical superiority leading to bolder strategic manoeuvring, for example. This is not to denigrate tactics, but this is a topic that has been thoroughly covered in the extant scholarship on the sea and ancient Greece. Too often scholars are liberal with their usage of 'strategy', or especially 'grand strategy', and a detailed examination is required, lest the place of sea power within any 'grand strategy' becomes oversimplified or missed altogether. This is often the mistake of scholars who like to take their sweeping studies of grand strategy back to the age of Pericles and the wars of the Greeks to give their work *gravitas*, at the risk of mixing cultural metaphors.[13]

Structure

There are two main elements in the examination of sea power in the Classical Greek world. Before exploring the operations conducted by maritime forces, it is necessary to examine the core factors that enabled these operations, practical and conceptual. To begin with, practical considerations such as environment, navigation, ship design, personnel issues, and finance are fundamental to understanding what a polis could or could not do at sea. The first two chapters deal with these issues, first on geography, environment, navigation, and fishing. Chapter Two looks briefly at ships, naval organisation, and the vexed issue of piracy in the ancient world. Chapter Three explores the less tangible issues that govern maritime operations – the ways in which poleis thought of the sea and their rela-

---

11 Freedman (2013): xi; Strachan (2013): 211.
12 Freedman (2013): ix, xi.
13 For example, John Lewis Gaddis' work on Grand Strategy reduces the Persian invasion of Greece of 480 into the simple parable of the Hedgehog and the Fox, erasing all examination of actual strategy from the equation. Gaddis (2018): chapter 1. The most egregious example of this is the use of the so-called 'Thucydides Trap' construct. Convinced of by the International Relations scholar Graham Allison, the premise attempts to make a modern war between the United States and China 'inevitable' because of Thucydides' theory on the cause of the Peloponnesian War. For a rebuttal, see Kirshner, 'Handle Him with Care: The Importance of Getting Thucydides Right', 2018.

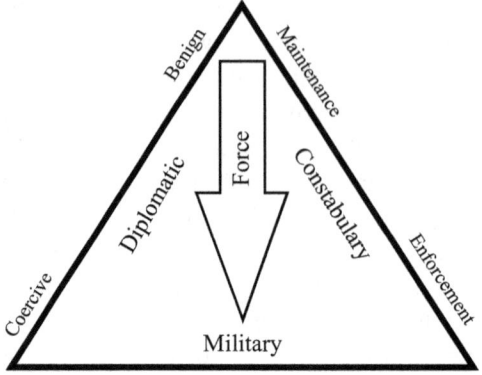

Figure 1: Span of maritime operations.[14]

tionship to it. The development of a 'maritime consciousness' – or not – is something for which examination is required. These intangibles are, arguably, more important than practical considerations. Maritime operations are complex, capital-intensive endeavours, and there must be popular will and/or strong leadership in order to devote large sums of time and capital to maritime and especially naval endeavours. Themistocles' and Pericles' lament over Athens not being an island, juxtaposed with Plato's and Aristotle's view of the sea, or more specifically the navy, as corrupting, demonstrates the complexity of Athenian perceptions of the maritime realm. Philosophical and historical writings as well as speeches and plays form a great body of evidence with respect to determining the extent to which a 'maritime consciousness' developed throughout the Greek world. This is, unfortunately, an examination held captive to the sources, and the sources for the Classical period are heavily biased in favour of Athens and Athenian matters. Nevertheless, older sources and the Athenian ones do give us glimpses of the maritime world outside of Athens, especially in the myths and stories told by the Greeks.

The chapters that follow examine the operations carried out by maritime forces in the Classical period, in chronological order from the sixth century down to 321 BCE. It is at this point that modern maritime strategic thought can help inform the study of these operations and reveal to us the extent to which sea power was present in different places at different times. Strategic concepts such as 'sea control', 'sea denial', and 'maritime power projection' are modern terms to be

---

14 Australian Maritime Doctrine (2010): 100.

sure, but they are nevertheless eminently useful in discussing what naval forces *actually* do and their impact on the strategic level. The conceptual framework for studying naval and maritime operations in the Greek world is readily available through an adapted model of modern maritime strategic thought. This is not to pose some new theoretical construct on a specific 'way of warfare' for the Greeks as some have done – most notably Victor Davis Hanson – or any other such grand concept. Such sweeping generalisations are unhelpful and can only distort the nuances of how wars were fought throughout history.[15] As Cathal Nolan has pointed out, 'the practice and history of war in the West, or anywhere else, does not reduce to some Rosetta Stone of a single cultural model'.[16] The Athenians, Spartans, and other Greeks fought wars in many different – and many similar – ways throughout the period. Sea power was important in these conflicts, and it was not a 'way of warfare' but an integral part of conflict in either a direct or a supporting capacity.

The chronological limits set in this book are somewhat outside the traditional boundaries of the 'Classical' period. A starting point of approximately 550 allows for a brief discussion of the early establishment of state-controlled warships: navies in the traditional sense. This is not to say that they did not exist before this, but as evidence from Athens, Sparta and other places indicate, we can trace a solidifying of proper naval organisation in this time period. The Athenian navy did not spring into existence with Themistocles, but had antecedents in the 500s. A chronological end date of 321 has been chosen since the defeat of Athens at sea at Amorgos spelled the end of any mainland Greek polis with the status of major sea power as the Hellenistic period was ushered onto existence. I will not examine Alexander's use of sea power, such as it was, as this would be to delve into an entirely different set of sources and problems. This naturally raises the issue of Athens as determining the period and the risk of focusing too much on Athens, a criticism I raised at the beginning. Athens provides us with the most evidence, and it was the dominant sea power for much of the period, so from a purely practical perspective it is impossible to not discuss sea power without a heavy focus on Athens. Large parts of this book focus on Athenian sea power. However, all attempts are made to examine sea power in other Greek poleis as much as possible, and many maritime operations from these other poleis are included in the Appendix and used as examples throughout the book and discussed on their own in Chapter Eleven. More than this, my aim is to open a new way of conceptualis-

---

15 As in Victor Davis Hanson's influential work, *The Western Way of War. Infantry Battle in Classical Greece*, originally published 1989.
16 Nolan (2017): 9.

ing ancient Greek maritime operations, and by applying this lens to Athens, this allows for smaller navies to be studied in light of this new framework. Notwithstanding this, it is worth noting that much as with today, sea power in the ancient world was not necessarily a universal. As Till says, sea power 'is a relative concept, something that some countries have more than others'.[17] This is true of the ancient context, where possession of warships or a navy did not necessarily equate to the possession of sea power.

A great deal of theory concerning maritime operations throughout history and in the modern day has developed over the last hundred years. With modification, this theoretical framework can be used to inform the study of naval operations and maritime issues in the Classical Greek world. Modern theorists have been too dismissive of naval history before the age of sail, and Classicists have often been unwilling or unable to use modern maritime strategic thought to inform their study of Greek history. By combining the two fields, I aim to offer new insights into the workings of naval and maritime forces in the Classical period. The sea was obviously an important factor in Greek history, but a deep examination of sea power and strategy remains lacking. Through the methods outlined above, I will address this gap in the literature and in doing so enhance the visibility of sea power and maritime strategy in the Greek world. It does not seek to prove the dominance of sea over land power, or any such revisionist notions. Rather, it seeks to demonstrate that the sea and sea power should not be viewed as of secondary importance or as a realm on the periphery of events, but of great significance in shaping the events of the fifth and fourth centuries of Greek history.

---

17 Till (2013): 25.

Chapter One
Setting the scene: geography, environment, navigation, and fishing

When looking at the Greeks and their interactions with the sea, it is important to first consider the sea itself: the geography and environment of the Mediterranean, Adriatic, Aegean, and Black Seas. Geography and environment, especially weather, helped define how maritime operations were conducted, whether it be military operations, fishing, or trade. Much has been made in the past of the limited ability for Greeks to sail the seas, either because of pre-modern navigational constraints – no compasses, charts/maps, or sextants – or because of the notion that the onset of winter somehow closed the seas entirely. This 'primitivist' view of sailing in the ancient world held little water and has slowly been overtaken by a more sensible view, at least by Classical scholars. Unfortunately, this view often pervades in the realm of strategic studies or modern naval studies, where the 'galley age', that is, anything before the age of sail, is viewed as if limited value to study or skipped over entirely.[1] This chapter aims to dispel any remaining doubt over the pervasiveness of Classical Greek maritime operations and highlights some of the complexities in naval organisation.

Geography

The first consideration is the extent to which ancient geography differs from the modern, especially factors such as sea level change. Notwithstanding some local variation due to silting and erosion, the geography of the Mediterranean as it relates to seafaring has not significantly changed from the late Neolithic period: the fifth millennium BCE onwards.[2] From that time, coastlines and island formations would have increasingly resembled the geography of the present-day Mediterranean. It is important to highlight that this is an insignificant change with respect to maritime operations in general. There have been few dramatic changes which would impact the strategic level. While local variation can seem dramatic, such as the silting at Thermopylae, this would have had an impact mostly at the tactical level of operations. The core features of the coastline and presence of islands has not changed enough that geostrategic considerations would have been so dif-

---

[1] Witness some chapter names in more modern works dealing with this era: 'Land warfare afloat' and 'the pre-naval era'; Palmer (2005): 19–38; and Cable (1998): 15–16, respectively.
[2] McGrail (2001): 88–9.

ferent from what we see today. Perhaps the biggest impact is on modern archaeology, since many port facilities and, crucially, shipsheds are now underwater through even moderate sea level rise.

The Mediterranean extends approximately 2,000 nautical miles (nm) from east to west and between 400 and 215 nm north to south, covering an area of some 2.5 million square kilometres/965,000 square miles.[3] Within this area are the Adriatic and the Aegean seas, as well as the Black Sea, the latter area covering 461,000 sq. km/178,000 sq. mi., an area roughly the size of the north-eastern United States.[4] It is physically divided into two basins, connected north and south of Sicily by the Sicilian channel in the south and the Strait of Messina to the north.[5] The two basins have notable geographical and biological differences.[6] The continental shelf is quite narrow, between 40 and 5 nm,[7] and the seabed generally drops off steeply to depths of over 900 m.[8]

An obvious but often overlooked aspect of Mediterranean geography is the length of its coastline and just how much of Greece is accessible from the sea, and vice versa. Of note is the length of the coastline represented by the Aegean Sea area: one-third of the total length of coastline in the entire Mediterranean, with 9,835 islands in Greece alone.[9] This represents a rich operating environment for maritime and especially naval forces, particularly given the availability of landing spots and sheltered areas.

Terrestrial geography is also of significance when discussing Mediterranean maritime operations. This is especially relevant to Greece, which aside from a long coastline has quite mountainous and difficult landward terrain. The fact that Greece has no significantly navigable rivers also increased the importance of seaborne trade for the movement of goods and people.[10] This difficulty was due to

---

[3] McGrail (2001): 87; Broodbank (2013): 55. Nautical Miles are a precise way to measure distance but are not generally used to measure area, hence km^2 and mi^2 used here.
[4] Broodbank (2013): 55; roughly speaking, the land area of the states of Delaware, Pennsylvania, New Jersey, New York, Rhode Island, Connecticut, Massachusetts, Vermont, New Hampshire, and Maine.
[5] McGrail (2001): 91; NP 136: *Ocean Passages of the World* (2004): 87.
[6] In some cases, the two basins are referred to as a western 'Atlanto-Mediterranean' and an eastern 'Ponto-Mediterranean'. Blondel et al. (2010): 5.
[7] Narrow compared to other places, such as Australia, where the continental shelf can exceed 300 nm.
[8] McGrail (2001): 87.
[9] About 123 of which are inhabited at present day. It is difficult to know how many were inhabited in Classical period. For more on this, see Hansen and Nielsen (2004): 732–3; Blondel et al. (2010): 10; Broodbank (2013): 75.
[10] As Horden and Purcell argue about the basic modality of goods and people in the Mediterranean, discussed in Chapter One. Horden and Purcell (2000): 365.

not just the physical terrain but also the political geography. Soldiers and merchants going by land faced not only physical obstacles but also political ones in needing to pass through the lands of different poleis with the accompanying negotiations, or taxes/fees that might require.[11] For instance, the Spartans were often worried about access to northern Greece through the Isthmus of Corinth, a route that could be blocked quite effectively by a hostile power. While Athens controlled the Megarid, the period 460–446, they were able to effectively block Spartan access across the Isthmus and into Attica, and it was only when Megara returned to the Spartan fold in 446 that Sparta was able to attempt an invasion of Attica.[12] Some 50 years later, in 394, the enemies of Sparta effectively harassed and damaged the Spartan army moving between Sicyon and Corinth and afterwards forced the Spartans to go by sea to Boeotia.[13] The sea provides ready and wide-ranging access, free from many of the territorial considerations that are present on land.

A distinct difference in the ancient operating environment is the lack of maritime borders, in the modern sense. While it is true that a city would be in control of its ports and harbours, there is little to suggest that they laid claim over ocean 'territory', and it is arguable that the sea was a 'commons', accessible to all, and that poleis had little regulatory reach.[14] Ephraim Lytle is mostly concerned with fishing rights and territorial seas in his work, but he points out that states did attempt to regulate the passage of ships.[15] Epigraphic evidence from Athens mentions such regulation.[16] Nevertheless, it was still easier for ships to circumvent or elude any maritime claims than it would be for any army to change its route on land, if such a thing was even possible in the given circumstances.

Environmental conditions

There are several environmental factors of importance to vessels at sea, especially tides and tidal streams, as well as currents. These factors affect long-distance sailing and local operations such as amphibious landings and battles, especially battles in

---

11 Horden and Purcell (2000): 377.
12 de Ste. Croix (1972): 190.
13 de Ste. Croix (1972): 192–3.
14 Lytle (2010): 1–2; 9–24. Others have a different view, arguing for some regulation of local fisheries. See Bresson (2016): 181–4.
15 Lytle (2010): 13.
16 IG I^3 61.18–20; IG I^3 63; IG I^3 116.3.

proximity to land, as was the case with many naval battles of the period. An example from the Peloponnesian War involves the Athenians capitalising on superior local knowledge of environmental conditions to defeat a Peloponnesian force at the entrance to the Corinthian Gulf. In 429, the Athenian Admiral Phormio used his knowledge of the local winds to wait for the moment when a change in wind conditions disrupted his enemy's formation and left them vulnerable to attack.[17] In his description of the battle of Salamis, Plutarch says that the Athenian commander Themistocles determined the best time of day for the battle, when the wind and sea ran directly from the Gulf into the strait. The heavier, taller Persian ships were said to have then been affected greatly by this wind and swell, causing them to present broadside to the Greek forces and vulnerable to ramming attacks.[18] What Plutarch is describing is the Persian ships being hit by what is known as a 'following sea', causing them to 'broach', that is, the sea from behind the ships meant that there was not enough wash across the rudders/steering oars of the Persian ships to maintain steerage, and it caused them to settle beam on to the predominant wind and sea. Meanwhile, the Greeks had no such problems as they were facing into the sea and were able to maintain steerage. Thus, knowledge of local sailing conditions – wind and sea – allowed for one side to use these conditions to their tactical advantage in battle.

The rate of evaporation in the Mediterranean basin is approximately three times the rate of inflow, derived principally from the major rivers.[19] Dynamic equilibrium is reached by strong inflow from the Atlantic Ocean through the Strait of Gibraltar, and to a lesser extent in the east from the Black Sea into the Aegean through the Dardanelles.[20] As a result of this, the predominant currents flow counter-clockwise in the Mediterranean, Adriatic, and the Aegean Seas. Due to the Coriolis force,[21] the main flow from the Strait of Gibraltar runs east along the African coast and then into the eastern basin until it is turned north by the Levantine coast, where it joins the inflow from the Black Sea and circles around counter-clockwise in the Aegean. Part of the Atlantic inflow is turned north near

---

17 See below section.
18 Plut. *Them.* 14.2.
19 Principally: Nile, Po, Rhone, and Ebro. McGrail (2001): 90; NP 136: *Ocean Passages of the World* (2004): 88.
20 The Hellespont in ancient times. I use the two names interchangeably, but will always refer to the Hellespont when citing ancient references. The rivers flowing into the Black Sea more than compensate for evaporation. McGrail (2001): 90; NP 136: *Ocean Passages of the World* (2004): 88.
21 Blondel et al. (2010): 8.

Malta and circles back towards Gibraltar counter-clockwise.[22] On average the current strength is one knot or less, contingent on local geographic influences, such as straits and channels and the depth of water. One knot is a mild force and would have minimal immediate impact on vessels underway by sail or under oars but would of course have a greater impact over long-distance journeys. However stronger forces such as those experienced in confined channels and narrows could have a much more appreciable effect, both positive and negative, on ships sailing in those waters. This was especially relevant for one of the main sailing routes, from the Aegean into the Black sea and vice versa, through the Bosporus, which has tricky currents to navigate.

The Mediterranean is almost entirely a tideless sea, with only a few regions that experience a tidal range greater than 1 m and with most of the Aegean experiencing a range of between 0.3 and 0.8 m: compare this with many other parts of the world, for instance northern Australia, where the tidal range can be more than 10 m in certain areas.[23] Thus, like the predominant currents, the effect of tidal streams on sailing conditions is minimal, with a few exceptions. For example, the strait between the mainland of Greece and Euboea experiences currents of five knots and even up to eight knots.[24] Diodorus notes this phenomenon when discussing a causeway built in 410, which narrowed it to such an extent that only a single ship could pass through.[25] A current of three to four knots would significantly increase the difficulty in rowing against such a stream, and eight knots would be all but impossible for a ship not fitted with propulsive machinery. However, these are tidal streams and thus are present only during incoming and outgoing tides and so navigable during slack water, as well as subject to variation depending on whether it is a period of spring or neap tides.[26] These environmental conditions are the sort well-known to locals and to mariners who frequent the area. Generally, currents in the Mediterranean would have presented only a moderate help or hindrance to mariners, both in terms of normal navigation and in instances of battle.[27]

---

22 McGrail (2001): 91–2; NP 136: *Ocean Passages of the World* (2004): 88.
23 McGrail (2001): 92.
24 My observations of the narrows recorded currents ranging from 2 to as much as 6 knots (25–27 January 2016). This may have been exacerbated in recent times with modern works, but the existing channel is close to Diodorus' assessment of being wide enough for only one ship.
25 Diod. 13.47.5.
26 Springs being the highest and neaps the lowest variation.
27 Broodbank (2013): 74.

Weather

Climate is a critical factor in seafaring and maritime operations. The Mediterranean is considered transitional between a cold temperate and a dry tropical climate.[28] Just as with geographical conditions, changes in the climatic conditions of the Mediterranean since the late Neolithic have been relatively minor and of minimal significance to the impact of seafaring conditions. It is not therefore unreasonable to use modern data on environmental conditions to determine general sailing conditions experienced by Classical Greek mariners.[29] Of significance are factors such as wind, current, tide, and visibility conditions. The writings of ancient authors seem to confirm present-day observations of climatic conditions, and we can draw on both classical data and modern knowledge and observations.[30] These will aid in establishing the parameters within which maritime forces could operate during the Classical period.

The primary weather factor of significance is the wind,[31] and especially so in the age of the galleys and sailing vessels.[32] It was not as prohibitive a factor as later in the age of sail: galleys can be rowed against the wind if need be, albeit with slower progress. Nevertheless, the wind had a defining, though not deterministic, impact on sailing in the Classical period. Wind in the northern areas of the basin is predominately from the north, as determined by seasonal temperature differences

---

28 Blondel et al. (2010): 12.
29 McGrail (2001): 89. Not all would agree with this however. James Beresford (2012: 63–8) argues that modern scholars should be wary of superimposing modern climactic data onto the ancient world, and that the period 850–200 BC saw different climactic conditions to today. He argues it would have experienced cooler and wetter conditions, hampering celestial navigation because of poorer visibility. Nevertheless, he generally uses modern meteorological data to inform his own work. The best examination of comparing modern and ancient winds remains William M. Murray's (1987) article: 139–67.
30 This is the line taken by McGrail (2001: 88–9) in his book.. This is reasonable position, backed up by ancient sources as well as modern scientific data. I accept this position, with the addition of environmental data I collected in Greece during fieldwork in January–February of 2016. These observations were taken with due consideration to the weather observations most pertinent to naval operations from my experience as an Officer of the Watch in the Royal Australian Navy (RAN), following standard format and subsequently reported to the Australian Bureau of Meteorology for reporting and forecasting.
31 Wind is referred to by the direction in which it blows *from*, not to: a northerly wind blows from the north. Wind speed is either measured directly with knots or by reference to the Beaufort scale of Force 0–12, with 0 describing no wind and 12 describing winds of over 65 knots.
32 The term 'galley' is used to refer to ships propelled primarily by oars. Sails were used during passages when wind conditions allowed. Oars were used when sails could not be utilised, contrary or no wind, and when going into battle.

between the land mass and the sea.³³ In the summer these northerly winds were highly predictable and thus reliable – the annual, *Etesian*, wind – which provided good weather in the Aegean Sea and the Cyclades.³⁴ It was this wind that Demosthenes bemoaned for hindering Athenian warships trying to sail north to confront Philip II in the latter half of the fourth century. The wind made it much slower for the Athenians to sail north, especially since there was no Athenian force ready at short notice. Philip may not have had a strong navy, but he knew how to use the weather to his advantage in order to make it more difficult for Athenian sea power to counter his advances.³⁵ This helps demonstrate that such knowledge and calculations with regard to maritime considerations had an impact at the strategic level.

In addition to these seasonal winds, coastal winds, land and sea breezes, are prevalent in the Mediterranean, especially in the summer and can have an impact on vessels from 5 nm up to 20 nm from the shore.³⁶ Especially important is the fact that there is much intraregional variation in winds throughout the Aegean, especially among the islands. Some locations, such as Chios, record lower risks of encountering strong and gale force winds in wintertime than in other places during the summer. Melos averages four times the level of strong and gale force winds of Iraklion in Crete,³⁷ though they are separated by a mere 85 nm. Aristotle in his *Meteorologica* describes in detail the different winds and offered the first explicit example of the twelve-point wind rose,³⁸ used throughout antiquity and in later history, though it is probable that his is merely the first *explicit* explanation of the system and that it was used by mariners for some time before him.³⁹ A more practical (from a navigational perspective) eight-point rose was developed in the Hellenistic period.⁴⁰ Unsurprisingly, the ancient Greeks and mariners in particular would have been interested in the wind and developed a deep knowledge of both seasonal and local wind patterns.

---

33 Blondel et al. (2010): 13.
34 McGrail (2001): 93; Blondel et al. (2010): 14.
35 Dem. 4.31.
36 McGrail (2001): 95. These coastal breezes are the result of a temperature inversion between the land and the sea. A sea breeze occurs in the morning when the land quickly warms up and wind flows from the sea to the land. A land breeze is where the land cools down quickly and wind flows from the land out to sea. A land breeze predominates in the late afternoon and into sunset. A sea breeze predominates in the early hours of the morning until mid-forenoon. The effects of a sea breeze are stronger than those of a land breeze. For a more recent work on this, see Gal et al. (2021).
37 Beresford (2012): 68–9.
38 Arist. *Met.* 363a–4a.
39 As Beresford (2012: 177) reasonably concludes; also, Murray (1987): 139–67.
40 Beresford (2012): 177–8.

A topic of great contention is the idea that ships rarely if ever sailed during the winter. Winds in winter, November to March, are still predominately northerly but with a greater chance of southerlies. Of particular note is the fact that winter sees weather that is subject to rapid change, making it far less predictable.[41] Winds during winter are likely to reach Force 7 or above on 6–9 days of the month in the Aegean and East Ionian Sea,[42] hazardous wind conditions for vessels at sea. Nevertheless, the case for ships being shut during winter has been extremely overstated and rests on shaky evidence and will be discussed in detail below.

Another critical weather consideration was visibility, for navigational purposes as well as for tracking the movement of shipping both in and outside of battle. Like the wind, visibility conditions varied with the season. An important fact, often overlooked, is how much of the surrounding land can be seen from a vessel at sea in the Mediterranean and especially in the Aegean and Adriatic, where a vessel would *never* be out of sight of land in normal visibility conditions. The islands of the Aegean can be seen at quite a distance, both from the sea and from the mainland. The Athenian fort at Cape Sounion would have provided an excellent vantage point to the west and south/southeast. The island of Melos, some 58 nm distant, is visible from Sounion on a good day.[43] This is a fact probably not lost on the Athenians voting for the expedition to subdue Melos after the Peace of Nicias. Athenians stationed at Sounion no doubt would have seen Melos in the distance and perhaps brooded on its non-commitment to the war, an important point when voting in the assembly.[44] Additionally, the temple of Poseidon would have made an excellent landmark for ships sailing around the cape, a prominent navigational mark visible for many miles.[45] The prevalence of navigational markers and aids in the ancient world is relatively unknown, but there are strong hints that they were used. In the *Odyssey* the Greeks are said to have built a tomb for Achilles so large that it would be seen by men over the sea: not a deliberate navigational mark but clearly a monument that would be useful to mari-

---

41 NP 136: *Ocean Passages of the World* (2004): 88.
42 NP 136: *Ocean Passages of the World* (2004): 88.
43 Melos was clearly visible during my visit 9/01/2016, but not visible on a subsequent visit 30/1/2016. These visits occurred at roughly the same time of day (1700 and 1630 local time, respectively). This highlights the impact of different visibility conditions. Also visible were the islands of Ceos, Cythnos, Seriphos, and Siphnos as well as the Peloponnese.
44 Thucydides only says that Sounion was 'fortified' (Σούνιον τειχίσαντες) after the Sicilian disaster (8.4). It is likely they only felt the need to fortify the position with walls once the Spartans had fortified Decelea and maintained a permanent presence in Attica.
45 When I sailed past the temple was clearly visible by naked eye approximately 6 nm off the coast. It is reasonable to assume that the fully constructed temple, with a roof and brighter in colour, would have been even more prominent.

ners.[46] Similarly, Pausanias says that the spearpoint and crest of the statue of Athena *Promachos* on the Acropolis were visible to sailors rounding Cape Sounion.[47] Later monumental structures, such as the Pharos of Alexandria in Egypt, demonstrate the clear desire to build even larger and more prominent navigational aids.

For vessels on the sea, optical distance to the sea horizon is calculated by a simple formula: 2.08 √height (metres), where *height* is the distance above the surface of the observer.[48] Therefore, an observer on the deck of a trireme (2.5 m deck height + 1.5 m eye height) would have a visible horizon of 4.16 nm. An observer up the mast might have a visible horizon of 7 nm.[49] This is for conditions of normal visibility, and phenomena such as super-refraction increase the visible horizon.[50] This is of course a distance to the horizon, and so ships and other objects on the sea can be seen at greater distances due to their added height above the horizon, meaning an enemy warships could be sighted at greater distances.

Navigation

Navigation is the art and science of taking a vessel from one place to another safely. It is aptly called an art and a science,[51] even with modern technology, for

---

[46] Hom. *Od.* 24.80–5.
[47] Paus. 1.28.2. In his meticulous reconstruction of the statue, Gorham Phillips Stevens concluded that a 25-foot-tall statue would have it rising 158.54 m above sea level, visible for 7–10 km at sea towards Sounion on a clear day. From experience, such an object as a bronze statue would on a bright day be noticeable to the naked eye and a distance of 7–10 km is perfectly feasible. The statue of Athena *Promachos* would thus be a useful navigational mark under the right circumstance. Whether or not this was deliberate on the part of the builders is another matter, and one on which the sources are silent. See Stevens (1936): 470, 494–9.
[48] BR 45 vol. 1 (Admiralty Manual of Navigation), Section 15–7 'Radar Theory and application'. Alternatively, 2.07 √height (metres): Bowditch, *The American Practical Navigator* (1995): 340. This is the formula for the optical horizon as opposed to the geometric horizon. Obviously, the radar horizon is not applicable in this case.
[49] For a 10 m mast + 1.5 m height of eye.
[50] Super-refraction occurs when a visible light (or radio wave) is bent downwards around the Earth's surface in a duct. Super-refraction is often present over the sea due to Hydrolapse (a decrease in humidity with height), especially in the Mediterranean during the summer months: at least a 20% chance, or 1 in every 5 days. See BR 45 vol. 1 (Admiralty Manual of Navigation), Section 15–7 'Radar Theory and application'.
[51] The point made at the very beginning of *The American Practical Navigator*, colloquially known as *Bowditch* after its original author, Nathaniel Bowditch.

technology cannot compensate for experience in navigationally difficult situations.[52] The evidence for navigational techniques and practices is patchy at best and comes predominantly from indirect sources and references. Nevertheless, much can be gleaned from these sources, and a picture can be formed of how Classical sailors navigated around the Mediterranean and beyond. There are two different scenarios requiring two different skill sets for navigating in the ancient world, which may be termed 'coastal' and 'ocean' navigation. These are not precise definitions but serve to make a distinction between navigating with reference to the shore and out of sight of land.

Pilotage can be considered a subset of coastal navigation, in so much as it occurs in sight of land. It refers to navigating in confined waters such as a harbour or channel and should not be conflated with coastal navigation, whereby a ship sails along a coast several miles offshore, a trap some scholars have fallen into.[53] Pilotage waters are dangerous areas where the primary concern of the navigator is avoiding dangers such as shoals, rocks, and indeed other ships, an art that relies on a high degree of experience and local knowledge. Local knowledge is of great importance, even in the modern age with charts and electronic navigation systems: modern vessels still require pilots when entering ports or transiting dangerous waters such as the Suez Canal and the Great Barrier Reef in Australia.[54] So too did the Greeks rely heavily on local knowledge. Polybius, in

---

[52] This section draws heavily from my own training and practical experience as a Maritime Warfare Officer in the Royal Australian Navy (RAN). The primary role of an MWO aboard a ship is as the Officer of the Watch, charged with the safe navigation of the ship and answerable only to the Commanding, Executive and Navigating officers. Obviously, navigation techniques and technology have changed drastically over the intervening 2,500 years, but the basics of navigation and the sea itself are unchanged, and military training accounts for worst case scenarios, foremost of which is the removal of modern technology to a level comparable to the ancient world.

[53] Beresford (2012): 175. Coastal navigation and pilotage rely on the same skill set, but with a different focus and different dangers and issues to contend with.

[54] These pilots provide advice to the ship's bridge crew and control the local tugs; they do not usually steer the ship. Many modern works translate the ancient Greek word κυβερνήτης as 'pilot', which can be a misnomer as the *kybernetes* seems to have steered the ship rather than navigated it. This is not to say that they were not trained in navigation, but that they were not pilots in the sense of specialised navigators for a particular area such as a port. Beresford (pg. 186) falls into this trap when he quotes Herodotus as listing 'pilots' as one of the seven occupational classes in Egypt (Hdt. 2.164). Herodotus uses the word *kybernetes* and seems to be referring to steersmen of vessels in general, not pilots in the sense of experts of local waters, although those who travelled the same waters would have developed an expertise. For this reason, *kybernetes* will be translated as 'helmsman' throughout this work. For more on the role of *kybernetes* in the Athenian navy, see Jordan (1972): 138–43.

describing the dangerous waters of Maiotis, says that large ships require a pilot to navigate the area.⁵⁵ As mentioned earlier, in 429 the Athenian Admiral Phormio, confronting a superior force of enemy vessels, waited for the usual morning wind to blow up and disturb the enemy formation, which it promptly did and allowed him to attack the disordered enemy.⁵⁶ In a subsequent naval engagement, Peloponnesian vessels ran aground, as Thucydides says, through their ignorance of the local waters.⁵⁷ Such local knowledge could be critical to the safety of a ship, including in battle, as demonstrated in relatively confined waters off the coast of Naupactus in two separate engagements there under Phormio.

Ships sailing in coastal waters other than pilotage waters could use several different aids to navigation. The land itself would provide the most obvious source of information, not just prominent features such as mountains and landmarks but also the contours of the coast itself: capes, bays, inlets, small islets, and such. Additionally, human features such as towns and settlements would have provided well-known reference points. James Beresford is correct in saying that the visible coast has never been superseded as an aid to navigation.⁵⁸ It is here that Greek navigation differs from the modern in the conception of maritime space itself. For several hundred years mariners have been able to use nautical charts to aid in their navigation. As far as is known, the Classical Greeks did not have such an aid but perhaps could have used a *periplous*, a written guide to particular sailing routes and waters, although it is possible these documents were aimed at non-specialists and that mariners relied instead on their own professional knowledge.⁵⁹ In any case, without reference to charts and a compass with which to determine their position, ancient sailors would have relied on a 'dy-

---

55 Pol. 4.40.8. Silting being the main navigation hazard. Polybius here uses the word καθηγεμών which I have translated as pilot and reinforces the point above that a *kybernetes* was primarily the steersman and cannot be assumed to have been an expert navigator in all the waters they travelled.
56 Thuc. 2.84.
57 Thuc. 2.91.4.
58 Beresford (2012: 183) though again erroneously conflates pilotage with coastal navigation. Only with the advent of GPS and satellite navigation has reference to the visible coastline waned in importance as a navigational aid. Nevertheless, modern navies at least teach and practice coastal navigation, and any good modern mariner would be versed in the skills as well – electronics break, especially in the rough and remote conditions which can be experienced at sea.
59 This is the view taken by Beresford (2012: 1), which has merit. Graham Shiply (2020: 11–15) sees *Psuedo-Skylax's* Periplous as a work of geography, with an academic agenda. So few *periploi* remain that it is hard to judge them within the context of other works and as their own genre of writing. In my opinion, the details contained within provide insufficient data for a mariner navigating their way from one place to another. There is simply not enough concrete navigational information.

namic reference to the surrounding environment'.[60] Kowalski, Claramunt, and Zucker describe well how the Greeks sailors would have viewed the sea and maritime space without reference to charts: 'a space of itinerary descriptions rather than a space described'.[61] Nautical charts depict the world in a very specific way, a bird's eye view. What they do not do is present geography in a way in that is actually experienced by a mariner on the deck of a ship.[62] It can be hard to appreciate how much more familiar Greek sailors would have been with the environment, something which can distort the views and opinions of modern authors who retrospectively dismiss the abilities of Greek sailors due to their own divorcement from the maritime environment.[63] Ancient mariners and navigators were clearly able to visualise maritime space and geography in such a way that allowed them to accurately sail coastal waters without modern equipment such as the compass or nautical charts.

The final form of navigation required by sailors is ocean navigation, out of sight of land – a rarer but nevertheless necessary skill for the ancient Greeks and one practiced from very early on. The first point to note is that this kind of navigation may be required when theoretically in sight of land, but where visibility conditions such as rain or heavy cloud obscure the land and coastal navigation features. The wind can be an aid to navigation in this case, since, as discussed above, seasonal and local wind patterns were often predictable and well-known by sailors, going as far back as Homer in his description of Odysseus in his wanderings.[64] With wind comes swell, and this too can be used as an aid to navigation, providing clues as to the presence of land in the refraction of swell patterns.[65] Other clues to the presence of land include cloud formation over land and the loom generated by the increased reflection of light over land, as well as observations of marine life such as birds, whales, and schools of fish. These are methods that have been used throughout the globe by navigators, especially in the Oceania region, where sailors were consistently able to find their way to small islands over extraordinary distan-

---

60 Kowalski et al. (2007): 48.
61 Kowalski et al. (2007): 49.
62 Thompson (2019): 95.
63 This not to say modern scholars are fundamentally incapable of writing about sailing in the ancient world, but to note that technology has divorced many people in the modern world from such things as close environmental knowledge.
64 Hom. *Od.* 12.285–90; 14.458–60.
65 Beresford (2012): 178. Swell differs from sea state in that the sea state is directly caused by the local wind, whereas swell is generated far off by distant wind – swell off the coast of Lemnos could be caused by winds down in the southern Aegean, for instance.

ces.⁶⁶ This is not to say that the Greek *must* have used the same techniques as those in Oceania but to illustrate the point that there are many different techniques available for long-distance navigation across open ocean that do not require any advanced technology, and that it is dangerous to assume a limited navigational capacity on the part of Classical Greek sailors because of their 'primitive' technological capabilities.

In addition to terrestrial methods, celestial bodies can be used as navigational aids, especially the sun and the stars. Odysseus in Homer's *Odyssey* uses the Bear (Ursa Major) to navigate away from Calypso's island.⁶⁷ He knows that by keeping particular stars in a certain relative quarter to the ship, this will allow him to sail in a certain direction – thus by keeping the Bear, and hence the North Pole, on his port beam, Odysseus would be assured of sailing due east.⁶⁸ Further, Homer makes it clear that he and others knew that this was one of the star groups that, in Mediterranean latitudes, did not sink below the horizon: 'alone has no part in the baths of the Ocean'.⁶⁹ Tiphys, the helmsman of the *Argo*, was said to have been an expert in determining a course by sun or star.⁷⁰ Stars were especially useful for sailing on an east–west axis, and it is possible to use circumpolar and zenith stars to navigate this way, possibly explaining myths that connected the geography of Sicily and mainland Greece.⁷¹ The ancient Greeks were keen observers of the environment and celestial bodies, and there were many different navigational aids at their disposal for crossing stretches of open sea.

Lack of technology has often been used as an excuse for minimising the abilities of the past. In 1956 a scholar published a work on Polynesian sailing, arguing that the absence of technology such as the compass and sextant and the inability to keep precise location details, in the form of latitude and longitude, essentially meant there was no evidence to support Polynesians voyaging any great distance except by sheer accident.⁷² This point of view derived from the sceptical turn in

---

66 See McGrail (2001): 311–45; and Paine (2013): 17–22. These navigational techniques were passed down orally from mariner to mariner, in all likelihood similar to how it was done in the Greek world. The magnetic compass and reliable charts are recent developments in the relative timespan of human seagoing activities.
67 Hom. *Od.* 5.270–7.
68 McGrail (2001): 101.
69 Hom. *Od.* 5.275.
70 Ap. Rhod. *Argon.* 108.
71 Tomislav Bilić makes a good case for this using the myth of Alpheus and Arethusa and the connection between the western Peloponnese and Sicily. The connection is explained via latitude sailing between the two places using celestial observations. See Bilić (2009): 116–32.
72 Sharp (1956), *Ancient Voyagers in the Pacific*.

scholarship, away from the more romantic school of viewing the past.[73] This same sceptical bend seems to have infected the scholarship on Greek seafaring ability too. We know that the Polynesians were masterful navigators who settled the remotest extents of the Pacific without chart, compass, or timepiece, in small yet hardy vessels considered 'primitive' to Western scholars. These scholars were often far too ready to dismiss Polynesian navigation ability because they themselves could not recreate the same systems of thinking.[74] While Classical scholarship has finally caught up to the more refined and less limited extent of Greek seafaring, many scholars of modern strategy and naval history have been quick to place extreme limits on the extent of Greek seafaring, explicitly or by omission.[75]

Sailing season

Finally laid to rest was one of the most contentious issues regarding maritime operations in the ancient world, the idea of a distinct sailing season with the remainder of the year witnessing a 'closed sea'. The assumption of a highly periodic sailing season has tainted much of the scholarship for maritime activities in the ancient world, and has remained almost entirely unchallenged until recently.[76] This not only minimises the importance of naval operations but also reinforces the 'minimalist' view of the ancient economy.[77] Additionally, there a host of new, and not so new, archaeological evidence that contradicts the idea of a closed sea.

The usual evidence presented to support the idea of a closed sea is quite slim: two sources of questionable veracity on the topic. The first is Hesiod and his *Works and Days*, which advises a paltry 50 days of the year as suitable for sailing – but only if Poseidon or Zeus is not opposed to it.[78] At best this could tentatively be used as evidence for the Archaic period when he was writing, but even that is a doubtful prospect. By his own admission Hesiod had little to no experience of ships or the sea and had only ever sailed from Aulis to Euboea, a short journey of a mere nautical mile or two.[79] Further, this limited experience is far removed from the Classical

---

73 Thompson (2019): 312.
74 For a fantastic insight into the history of Polynesian history, see Thompson (2019), *Sea People*.
75 See note 18 above. In many cases, the ancient Greek world is ignored entirely when discussing sea power or maritime strategy.
76 Beresford (2012): 1.
77 As seen in Finley, whose minimalist model influenced Chester Starr and his examination of sea power. Beresford (2012): 2.
78 Hes. *Op.* 663–5.
79 Hes. *Op.* 649–51. This is a body of water which was so narrow that as Beresford (2012: 10) points out it, it was spanned by a bridge less than 300 years later.

period where shipbuilding and seafaring were far more advanced.[80] More importantly, Hesiod's testimony is contradicted by virtually every Classical source which describes maritime operations throughout the year, as well as archaeological evidence.

The second source often used is Vegetius, writing much later,[81] who had a more realistic appraisal of sailing conditions, considering only mid-November to mid-March as a *mare clausum*.[82] The first and most obvious problem with Vegetius as a source is that he is a Roman author writing some 700 years after the Greek Classical period. It would be unwise to transplant the views of a Late Roman author into the minds of Classical Greeks. Importantly, it seems likely that his sailing season was tailored to suit Roman warships and not all seagoing vessels.[83] Secondly, this sailing calendar does not take into account the significant diversity in the climactic conditions around the Mediterranean region.[84] As mentioned above, winds, currents, and other weather conditions are not universal around the Mediterranean and seasonal variation does not lend weight to the idea of a universally applicable sailing calendar.

In arguing for a highly periodic sailing season, it is unwise to use as evidence two works of literature from different societies and separated by 1,000 years given that technological, economic, political, and military developments would have impacted on seafaring strategies.[85] Classical authors and archaeological evidence directly contradict the advice of the archaic poet Hesiod and the Roman military writer Vegetius, and the idea of a *mare clausum* should be dismissed as an illusion created by these works.

Other written sources paint a very different picture of winter sailing and make it clear that the sea was not closed by the advice of ancient poets. In a speech of Demosthenes, the speaker explicitly states that sailing from Rhodes to Egypt was uninterrupted.[86] In another maritime case, the contract for a voyage to the Black Sea and return to Athens lists different interest rates depending on when the ship left the Black Sea for its return voyage. It sets an interest rate of 22.5% if the vessels departed before the rise of Arcturus, around mid-September, and a rate of 30% for after this time.[87] The increase in interest rate reflects the increase in risk for sailing

---

80 Beresford (2012): 12.
81 Anywhere from 383 to 450 CE. Allmand (2011): 1.
82 *Res. Mil.* 4.39.
83 Beresford (2012): 15.
84 Beresford (2012): 16.
85 Beresford (2012): 13.
86 Dem. 56.30.
87 Dem. 35.10.

during the latter part of the year, but most importantly demonstrates that financiers were willing to accept the higher risk of sailing at this time rather than not financing a journey at all. Despite the increase in risk due to weather, they still expected to make a return on their investment. Perhaps the most compelling piece of evidence, relatively newly found, is the so-called Elephantine Palimpsest, which records a series of customs duties in the Egyptian city. It has been dated to either 475 or 454,[88] and it records the dates of foreign vessels which arrived and departed from the city, including Greek vessels. It documents Greek vessels arriving at the port every month except January, with arrival and departure dates in February and December – months when the sea was supposedly 'closed'.[89] That no ships are recorded during January may reflect no ships entering or leaving, or it may be that the traffic was so light that they could not justify the operation of the customs house during this reduced activity period.[90] In any case, the document clearly records Greek merchant vessels sailing into and out of Egypt during the winter months, including December and February, and doing so in the mid- or even early fifth century. Further, the cargoes reveal something important. The imports were of a mixed variety, and all the ships took onboard a single cargo of natron (mineral soda), used in textile production among other things: cargoes not of critical value like grain but routine, meaning these were not voyages of an extraordinary need.[91] This paints a picture of routine rather than extraordinary trade during the winter months, a more complex economic environment than scholars have previously argued.

Reinforcing the written evidence that contradicts a closed sea is the vast array of archaeological evidence, including experimental archaeology and ship reconstruction. Shipwreck evidence has grown substantially over the years as underwater archaeological technology and techniques have improved. The number of recorded shipwrecks has increased dramatically even from the 1970s, and many of the wrecks can be dated to the Classical period.[92] A recent find in the Fourni islands has vastly increased the number of wrecks known in the Aegean, from all time periods, including the Archaic and Classical, and demonstrate the diversity of goods traded and the places they were traded.[93]

---

[88] Tammuz (2005): 151; Beresford (2012): 17.
[89] Tammuz (2005): 151–2. The table which Tammuz has reconstructed lists the arrival and departure dates from the Aramaic and converted them to modern equivalent dates.
[90] Tammuz (2005): 151–2.
[91] Horden and Purcell (2000): 149; Beresford (2012): 21.
[92] See the tables in Horden and Purcell (2000): 368 and 371.
[93] For details, see Campbell and Koutsouflakis (2021): 279–98.

Experimental archaeology has helped demonstrate the capabilities of ancient seagoing vessels and revealed them to be far sturdier and weather-proof than has been previously assumed. The reconstructed merchant vessel *Kyrenia II*, based on a Hellenistic wreck found off the coast of Cyprus, was able to safely sail in weather that included Force 9–10 wind conditions (45–50 knots) and reached speeds in excess of 12 knots, a speed most scholars would have thought ancient ships incapable of reaching.[94] These ship reconstructions have helped demonstrate that ancient sailing vessels were not nearly as fragile as has been thought and they were far better able to weather storms.[95] A warship such as a trireme would not have weathered such conditions, with a shallower draft and quite long and narrow hull.[96] Nevertheless, archaeological finds demonstrate a wide proliferation of trading vessels in the ancient world, with a huge diversity of cargoes from many different areas of the Mediterranean, and experimental archaeology has demonstrated the great capabilities of ancient seagoing vessels.

An issue that must be raised is the idea of coastal versus 'open sea' sailing, a topic that is much confused in the scholarship. It is mostly a matter of perspective, clouded by a failure to realise that ships sailing around the Mediterranean and especially the Aegean need not stray far from land in any case, and that 'open sea' in the Aegean is a subjective and misleading term. For instance, it is possible to sail from Rhodes to the eastern coast of Attica without venturing further than 13–15 nautical miles from land.[97] The islands of the Cyclades, with large and prominent terrain features, would have ensured visibility of land throughout the journey in all but the worst of visibility conditions. Asserting that vessels would not have ventured the 'open sea' during winter because they would have preferred the proximity of shelter afforded by the near coast makes little sense. At a pessimistic speed of 2½ knots, a vessel 15 nm from shore would have no more than a 6-h journey to reach land. No doubt sailors weighed the risk of sailing during the winter by knowing how far they had to stray from land for a particular crossing, and as highlighted above the risk in winter was statistically greater, but that does not mean there was no good weather during winter. This is

---

94 For further discussion, see Beresford (2012): 120–2.
95 Beresford (2012: 107–72) devotes a long chapter to this, which explores in depth the sturdiness of ship construction in the ancient world. Far less is known about the construction and seakeeping abilities of warships from the period.
96 This hull shape would have rendered it far more susceptible to issues such as 'hogging' and 'sagging'.
97 This roughly follows a route north from Rhodes to the Fourni Islands, site of the newly found shipwrecks mentioned above, and from there across to Mykonos and hence through the Cyclades to Attica.

obvious from the Greeks themselves, discussing the 'halcyon days' where calm weather supposedly prevailed for 14 days in the middle of winter,[98] as well as from simple modern observation which demonstrates clear and good sailing weather during winter. Observations taken aboard the reconstructed vessel *Ma'agan Mikhael II* bear this out, with the authors of a study on sailing conditions thanking the crew of the vessel 'for their assistance in dozens of hours of measurements and for sailing together from Israel to Cyprus and back during the winter, just to prove a point'.[99]

During fieldwork in Greece, I took a ferry from the Piraeus to the island of Thera (Santorini) in early February 2016. Weather for the duration of the trip was exceptionally good. My notes record the following weather observations at local time 1230 in position off the port of Paros: Wind – West at 5–10 knots; sea state – 1; swell – west at 0.3 m; cloud cover – 1/8; visibility – 10+ nm (Figure 2). This is good sailing weather, with the main issue being the light wind encountered in some areas. The sea was as far from dangerous as it is possible to be. Such weather conditions held for 3 days before deteriorating and ending in a storm on the fifth day, abating slightly on the sixth when I departed. This example neatly highlights the above point: weather was perfect for sailing for a run of days before deteriorating, giving sailors the opportunity to sail as required and seeking shelter once the weather became too dangerous. This is how mariners practice their trade: not by the say so of texts but by observation and experience and driven by necessity. They would not pass up good sailing weather just because it fell during a particular time of year. Sailing the Mediterranean and especially the Aegean need not have involved straying far from land, even in areas subjectively labelled 'open sea', and as such ships need not have been far from safety if the weather turned. Ultimately, ships in the ancient world were sunk due to poor navigation, weather, or a combination of both. Ships sink in the modern world because of these factors. It is a universal truth that sailing the seas at any time in any place is inherently risky.

The implication for naval operations during winter is that they were not entirely curtailed as often argued. Warships would have operated on a shorter leash, more closely tied to the land. They would have probably operated in smaller numbers and operated more conservatively, keeping within the reach of sheltered harbours or landing spots. The case study above involved 3 full days of

---

[98] Arist. *Hist. an.* 542b. These days of calm weather were said to occur 7 days before and 7 days after the Winter Solstice. The phenomenon is named after a bird and its attendant myth, found in Ovid *Metamorphoses* 11.270–748, and must have been grounded in some reality. See Chronopoulou and Mavrakis (2014): 66–9.
[99] Gal et. al. (2021): 14.

good weather, sufficient to make a journey across the Aegean.¹⁰⁰ Thus, naval operations in winter would have included greater risk mitigation, such as operating in smaller numbers and on well-known routes where they could be assured of shelter if the weather deteriorated. There is no reason for naval operations to have ceased entirely in winter.

Figure 2: Winter sailing in the vicinity of Paros.¹⁰¹

The idea that the sea was 'closed' in ancient Greece is of importance not just for naval operations but for maritime trade and the economy. The argument that weather curtailed maritime trade has been used by scholars to minimise the importance of international trade and develop a minimalist model of the ancient economy.¹⁰² One of the single-best pieces of evidence against this view is the

---

100 Noting the example of the Athenian warship sailing from Athens to Lesbos in a 24-h period, a distance of 184 nm. Noting it is at the extreme limit of a warship sailing distance, one might still estimate that in 3 days a warship could cover 300 nm.
101 Author's collection. 1 February 2016.
102 The most influential of these works is M.I. Finley's *The Ancient Economy* (1973).

above-mentioned Elephantine Palimpsest, which describes a port trading in a single valuable commodity.[103] The opportunity for olive oil to be traded as a major commodity was only made possible by maritime transportation, and similarly with wine.[104] The island of Thasos was a great wine-producing centre, and clearly this was only possible because of maritime transportation. Space precludes a thorough re-evaluation of the ancient Greek economy; however, work by Josiah Ober, building upon the excellent work of Alain Bresson, goes a long way towards correcting the scholarship.[105] In *The Rise and Fall of Classical Greece* Ober uses comprehensive demographic data to highlight some simple but important facts about the nature of the economy. Firstly, unless Classical Greece was substantially more productive in its agriculture than nineteenth-century Greece, between 1/4 and 1/3 of the population of classical Greece, 0.7–1.2 million people, would have relied on imported grain.[106] As Ober says, the Greek world can no longer be entirely defined by subsistence agriculture or local exchange: imported food had to be paid for by commodity exports, manufactured goods or the extraction of rents.[107] Ober argues against the premise that ancient Greece was defined by subsistence agriculture rather than possessed of a sophisticated and diversified economy in which many people lived above bare subsistence and where trade in commodities and luxury goods were of great significance.[108] With this view of the ancient Greek economy, the prevalence of maritime trade becomes obvious, a trade that was not nearly as small as has been argued.

Sailing in the ancient world, as it has been in every age, was a risky business no matter the time of year: the sea is an inherently dangerous and unforgiving environment. However, the idea that the Greeks, so highly dependent on the sea, would not venture to sail in certain parts of the year is unsustainable. There were certainly times of the year where the statistical risk was higher and maritime activities dropped off, but it is untenable to say that maritime activity was suspended altogether. Necessity, whether in war or in obtaining vital food supplies, would drive ancient mariners to risk the sea at all times of the year.

---

[103] Horden and Purcell (2000): 148–9.
[104] Horden and Purcell (2000): 212–3; 217.
[105] Alain Bresson, *The Making of the Ancient Greek Economy* (2016).
[106] Ober (2015): 86. This is based on Ober's population figures, which if one were to take as optimistic and cut in half would still require imported grain for 350,000–600,000 people.
[107] Ober (2015): 86.
[108] Ober (2015): 88.

Natural resources

As discussed in the Introduction, one of the core uses of the sea is as a resource. As far as the Greek world is concerned, this was primarily marine life for consumption, although the sea and sea water also played a role in Greek religious practice and this consideration should not be discounted. Fishing was an important activity throughout the Mediterranean and provided a portion of people's protein intake. It is an activity which does not have great visibility in the records, but this should not lead scholars to discount it. It was and still is not a glamorous activity, but one of profound importance which can have very unexpected and dire consequences. In the modern world, even with modern farming techniques and food abundance, fishing quarrels have led to indirect and direct conflict – the 'Cod Wars' of the 1960–1970s,[109] the drastic increase in piracy off the coast of Somalia,[110] and continued conflict between half a dozen different nations in the South and East China Seas.[111] Some have even argued that the Greeks had a regulatory regime in place to control fishing grounds and fishing rights, a claim that has been robustly countered by Ephraim Lytle.[112] At the same time, a polis' cadre of fishermen could contribute in other ways to maritime endeavours. This could range from local environmental and navigational knowledge through to representing a body of sailors who might be pressed into service in an emergency. Fish-

---

109 A dispute between the UK and Iceland over the fertile cod fishing grounds of the north Atlantic. Not a trivial dispute: people were injured and killed and there were strategic ramifications to the conflict, especially regarding NATO. For a recent re-appraisal of the conflict, see Steinsson (2016): 256–75. As recently as August 2018 UK and French fishermen clashed at sea over a scallop fishery. https://www.theguardian.com/uk-news/2018/aug/28/french-and-british-fishermen-clash-in-scallop-war-skirmish.
110 Locals forced out of the fishing business by foreign fishing vessels, mainly sailing from Asia and Europe, led to many Somalis taking up arms and using their fishing vessels to engage in piracy, first against the foreign fishing vessels which had taken away their livelihood and then against international shipping, forcing a reaction from NATO, Australia, the USA, and even China to protect the vital shipping routes the pirates preyed upon. This Illegal, unreported and unregulated (IUU) fishing is of great significance to the modern world and can cause many different problems; demonstrative of the fact that the natural resources of the seas are and have been of great significance throughout history, even in the modern age.
111 China, Taiwan, the Philippines, Japan, Malaysia, and Vietnam all stake claims to various islands, atolls, and reefs in the region, often for the oil and gas resources thought to be present but also the important fishing grounds there. Indeed, the conflict is manifesting itself through clashes between fishing vessels of the different countries, and China has been known to arm its fishing vessels.
112 Lytle (2012).

ing and fisheries disputes can have major and far-reaching consequences and should not be passed over.

The Mediterranean contains a rich variety of sea life, including many species exploitable by humans. These include fish from sardines and anchovies up to mackerel and tuna, as well as other species such as squid, octopus, and eel – the 'fish-filled sea' of Homer.[113] All of these would have required vastly different methods of fishing to exploit, from both the shore and by boat. Ancient sources concerned with fishing are rare, as with most issues dealing with daily life in the ancient world and beneath the concern of upper-class authors.[114] The only dedicated ancient work dealing with fishing is Oppian's *Halieutika* from the second century CE, a Greek poem in hexameter verse. It therefore seems more reliable as a general source rather than as evidence for specific and technical detail,[115] fitting into the same category as farming manuals by the likes of Varro, with the added caveat that Oppian was clearly not a sea fisherman.[116] Indeed, unlike these works on agriculture, economic aspects of fishing are left out in Oppian's work, with no mention of prices, costs, efficiencies, or how fishermen were organised.[117] Bekker-Nielsen points out that the information Oppian uses is almost certainly out of date, and parts of it relied on Aristotle, thus making it dangerous to use as a source for fishing in the second century CE;[118] however, these problems increase its utility as a source for Classical-era fishing. Elsewhere in Greek texts the activities of fishermen are mentioned, sometimes in quite an important manner. One of Pindar's *Odes* speaks of the sweetness of different payment for different work, whether to the shepherd, ploughman, fowler and 'one whom the seas nourishes' since everyone strives to keep hunger at bay.[119] The implication is that all of these jobs, including fishing, are capable of keeping off starvation, thus profitable enough to live off. Later works, especially comedy, make endless reference to fish-

---

113 Hom. *Il.* 9.4; also, the 'fish-filled ways': *Od.* 3.177.
114 Bekker-Nielsen (2006): 83.
115 For instance, the vocabulary used by Oppian illustrates the many types of nets used by ancient fishermen, who names but a few of the innumerable types used (3.79–84). For a brief examination of the net types, see Bekker-Nielsen (2006): 91.
116 Dating aided by the fact that the work is dedicated to the emperor Marcus Aurelius. At line 3 the poet address 'Antonine', usually taken to be Marcus Aurelius. See the introduction to the Loeb edition – Mair (1928) xx; Bekker-Nielsen (2006): 83.
117 Bekker-Nielsen (2006): 83.
118 Bekker-Nielsen (2006): 84.
119 Pind. *Isthm.* 1.45–50.

ing and seafood, in the context of rich and poor alike.[120] The fruits of the sea are a topic which comes up throughout ancient works.

Little modern work has been done on fishing in the ancient world until quite recently. The few works which did exist were inadequate and arguably fall into the same category as other 'primitivist' works, assuming a Greek world that far less able and sophisticated than was the case. One work in particular uses nineteenth- and twentieth-century fishery statistics from the Mediterranean and does not give many details on the data used.[121] Indeed, one of the most serious mistakes is assuming that the biological environment of the Mediterranean has remained unchanged over the intervening 2,500 years. Ecosystems change over time, and in the case of a marine ecosystem this change affects the abundance of fish and therefore the catches made,[122] and as recent works on the Mediterranean point out, human factors such as pollution and overfishing have had major and even dire impacts on fish stocks.[123] For example, eels and sturgeon stocks have been severely depleted, with sturgeon all but wiped out from the Mediterranean due to overexploitation of their eggs for caviar. Thankfully, much work has been done in recent years to refute the primitivist view of fishing in the ancient Greek world, though fishing as an important economic activity is still often ignored or minimised.[124]

Fishing could be a greatly productive activity, especially when treated properly as a specialist industry rather than as a vague activity conducted uniformly across the ancient world. An oft-used example neatly illustrates this principle. Pausanias relates in his account of Delphi a bronze bull dedicated by the Corcyraeans as an offering for particularly good haul of tuna caught by the city.[125] Such a dedication demonstrates how valuable fish were. There are other indications that the fish trade was widespread during the period and had an important place in the ancient economy. Excavations in Corinth revealed a large building clearly engaged in overseas trade, fish in particular. The 'Punic Amphora Building' con-

---

120 Comedy is the main genre where the topic of fish comes up a lot, and there are many fragments of works that give tantalising clues about the topic, not least in the names of some of these works. For instance, Antiphanes' *The Fisherman* (fr. 26) and *The Fair Voyage* (fr. 98). For a very detailed and comprehensive survey, see Wilkins (2000), especially pp. 293–304.
121 T.W. Gallant, *A Fisherman's Tale* (1985). Jacobsen calls the data Gallant uses 'weak and incoherent' and points out that better data was readily available. Jacobsen (2006): 97.
122 Jacobsen (2006): 97.
123 Blondel (2010): 91–4.
124 Both Tønnes Bekker-Nielsen (2006): 83–95 and especially Anne Lif Lund Jacobsen (2006): 97–104 do an admirable job of deconstructing and refuting Gallant's analysis. For a good exploration of the impact of Gallant's work on the scholarship, see Mylona (2008): 8–11.
125 Paus. 10.9.3–4.

tained many transport amphorae from around the Mediterranean region, including Spain, Sicily, Chios, and possibly even Massalia and North Africa.[126] The early use of the structure is dated to the second quarter of the fifth century, and although it was mixed use residential and commercial to begin with, it seems as if the building was then entirely given over to commercial activities and in particular the import of large quantities of fish packed in amphorae.[127] The Black Sea region was considered rich in fish, and a law court speech of Demosthenes mentions a cargo of salt fish from the region, and Polybius' survey of the region mentions the export of preserved fish in great abundance.[128] The archaeological evidence for imports of Black Sea fish to Greece is fragmentary but suggestive of some form of trade, though perhaps not as large scale as some have imagined but also not as negligible as some would have it.[129]

Certainly, authors of the time, writing in various genres, spoke of fish and seafood products in many different contexts and in such a way as to make it clear that these products were an all-pervasive factor in the daily lives of rich and poor alike. As Horden and Purcell point out, such windfalls as the Corcyra one serve to demonstrate the most important role of fishing in the Classical world, as a source of income – a resource more valuable as a commodity than as a mere source of protein. Fish were a cash crop, and cash crops can be considered a 'subsistence' strategy itself.[130] Fishing was an important industry in Greece and contributed to the economy, both in in terms of short and long-distance trade and consumption.[131]

Conclusion

Just as with trade, fishing in the ancient world has been minimised by too many scholars, skewing the view of the ancient economy in favour of a minimalist model, a model out of tune with reality. This model relies on maritime trade and other maritime activities like fishing being of minimal importance and of a primitive nature, neither of which is the case. Seaborne trade was far more prolific

---

126 Williams (1979): 117.
127 Williams (1979): 111.
128 Dem. 35.31; Polyb. 4.38.4.
129 This is the position of John Lund and Vincent Gabrielsen, whose view appears somewhat pessimistic, though they readily acknowledge that the archaeological evidence is scant and very few solid conclusions can be drawn about the nature of Black Sea fish imports into Classical and Hellenistic Greece. Lund and Gabrielsen (2006): 161–9.
130 Horden and Purcell (2000): 194–5.
131 For a recent, excellent examination of the role of fishing in the Ancient Greek economy, see Bresson (2016): 175–87.

than many academics have argued. The notion of a 'closed sea' has been wildly overstated and trade by sea was conducted throughout the year, with high and low seasons as naturally befitted sailing conditions. A better reading of the ancient sources combined with archaeological evidence demonstrates this and enables us to reach beyond the now untenable position that the ancient Greek economy was small, unsophisticated, and based entirely on agrarian concerns.[132] This is aided by the proper placement of fishing and other sea-based economic activities into the wider whole of the Greek world. Aside from being a useful source of food, fish and fish products were a commodity to be gathered and traded for profit out of proportion to its mere nutritional value. Fishing was an important economic activity, which could also make it a target for pirates and for navies in wartime. The interruption of fishing could thus cause economic loss, including loss of income and less food in the agora. Moreover, in acknowledging the prevalence of fishing it becomes clear that poleis had a larger number of mariners to call upon, in peacetime and war. Fishermen could provide valuable knowledge of local waters, including navigational knowledge and information about shipping in the area, for example. All these different maritime considerations were important to the Greeks, and as will be seen later influenced maritime strategic calculations.

Maritime activity was far more prolific than has previously been acknowledged. This includes trade activity and fishing as well as naval operations during winter. Winter curtailed seaborne traffic, especially warships, which did have inferior seakeeping characteristics to merchant vessels. Nevertheless, curtailed operations do not mean *no* operations and thus sea power was not as temporally limited as many scholars have argued. This should relax the conceptual boundaries on what was and was not possible in the realm of ancient Greek maritime operations, in peace and in war.

---

[132] Criticism of previous scholars should be tempered by the knowledge that many archaeological discoveries have come to light since they have written. Perhaps scholars such as Finley would have written differently about the ancient economy had they know about such finds as the Fourni islands shipwrecks and the Elephantine customs account papyrus. In Finley's time there were around 450 recorded shipwrecks; by the 1990s there were close to 1,300 (Horden and Purcell 2000: 368). Fourni Islands: Campbell and Koutsouflakis (2021): 279–98.

Chapter Two
Wooden walls: ships and naval organisation

Aside from geography and environment, human factors were critical in governing maritime operations. At the core of this was the organisation of naval forces, proceeding from private to state ownership of ships beginning sometime in the last quarter of the sixth century, generally speaking. Ships were the primary asset in maritime operations, both warships and merchant vessels, and their capabilities and limitations are critical considerations. Ships required many skilled personnel to operate, and shortages of rowers and sailors could have a negative impact on naval operations. Infrastructure was of great importance, from ship-sheds and port facilitates through to such constructions as the Corinthian built *diolkos*, a paved track that stretched from the Gulf of Corinth to the Saronic Gulf, sited near the present location of the modern Corinth Canal. This chapter will highlight the material and personnel issues that an ancient Greek polis had to contend with to operate a navy. This in turn will illustrate how complex, and expensive, these issues became when scaling up a polis' sea power.

Naval organisation

Even more so than for armies, a resilient system of organisation is required for naval operations. This is especially true when conducting extended operations overseas, as both the Athenians and Spartans did during the Peloponnesian War. This is not only in terms of personnel but also of the ships and associated equipment. Evidence for the sixth century and the two decades before the Persian Wars is slim, yet the growth of sea power can be observed in many Archaic-era Greek poleis. As Borimir Jordan points out, it is very unlikely the Athenians became master seamen and naval warfare tacticians with a large fleet during a few years of the 480s: there must have been a robust naval organisation in place long before the Persians attacked in 480.[1] More recent works, especially by Hans van Wees, have illustrated the fact that naval developments stretches back further than have generally been acknowledged and that states took a more active role in naval organisation during the last half of the sixth century.[2]

---

[1] All at the behest of a single politician, Themistocles – even more unlikely. Jordan (1975): 6.
[2] He strongly and convincingly makes the case in a 2010 book chapter, '"Those Who Sail Are to Receive a Wage": Naval Warfare and Finance in Archaic Eretria', and more recently in his book, *Ships and Silver, Taxes and Tribute. A Fiscal History of Archaic Athens* (2013).

An inscription uncovered in 1912 illustrates naval organisation in the Euboean polis of Eretria, dated to approximately 550–525:

> Those who sail are to receive a wage if they go beyond the Petalai or Kenaion. Everyone must contribute. Those who are in the country. . . . Anyone who took . . . will not be open to dispute.[3]

Despite the inscription having been discovered over 100 years ago, as Van Wees points out, it is rarely ever mentioned in modern scholarship, and if mentioned at all, it is usually dismissed as obscure.[4] Van Wees thinks this inscription has not gained much traction in the literature because it flies in the face of orthodoxy that naval organisation in Greece was a private and not a public affair before 500.[5] While it is a neat fix to see the rise of Athenian sea power and the advent of the trireme as the starting point of state-funded and built navies,[6] such a sudden shift in naval organisation seems unlikely.

There are other pieces of evidence that point towards naval organisation in the sixth century, including for Sparta. It is worth noting that the Spartans had a specific military position of 'Admiral' (*nauarchos*). Thucydides only ever uses the word *nauarchos* to describe a Spartan commander, never for the Athenians, who had the office of *strategos*, a military leader by land and sea.[7] Aeschylus uses *nauarchos* in his play *Persians*, indicating a usage as far back as the Persian Wars.[8] Aristotle in *Politics* heavily criticises this office, insomuch as it was so powerful as to be like a third kingship.[9] The position did cause angst for the Spartans near the end of the Peloponnesian War, when Lysander, having already undertaken the office once, was forced into the position of 'Vice-Admiral' since no one could hold the office of *nauarchos* more than once.[10] Xenophon says that Lysander was really in charge despite not holding the official office, but the existence of a one-term limit to naval

---

3 IG XII.9 1273.1274, lines 10–16. Translation Van Wees, following Francis Cairns' 1991 restoration of the text. Van Wees (2010): 205–8.
4 Van Wees (2010): 206. Especially note 2.
5 Van Wees (2010): 210.
6 For instance, Lambert (2018): 49–50.
7 In thirteen instances throughout his work: 2.66.2, 2.80.2, 3.16.3, 3.26.1, 4.11.2, 8.6.5, 8.20.1, 8.23.1, 8.24.6, 8.26.1, 8.29.2, 8.50.2, 8.99.1.
8 Aesch. *Per.* 363.Accepting the play was written c. 472. Regardless of whether or not Aeschylus actually fought at Salamis, more likely than not considering the manpower mobilised by Athens, it would have been a term familiar to his audience who had fought at Salamis under the supreme command of the Spartan Eurybiades.
9 Arist. *Pol.* 1271a, 41–2.
10 'Vice-Admiral'. On the disquiet in losing a successful Admiral, see Xen. *Hell.* 1.6.2–6; On Lysander taking up the position of Vice-Admiral: 2.1.7.

command perhaps hints at an appreciation that naval command had very different characteristics to command of armies. All of this helps demonstrate that naval organisation in Sparta was codified back as far as the Persian Wars, if not earlier. While such organisation does not necessarily mean Sparta was a strong sea power – witness their lacklustre performance at sea during the first half of the Peloponnesian War – it is indicative of a command structure with a clear demarcation between military operations on land and at sea. Indeed, as Aristotle's contention in *Politics* and Lysander's conduct indicate, by the late fifth century the office of *nauarchos* needed to be rigidly controlled because of its power.

The best evidence of naval organisation is from Athens, and here a large and comprehensive system is found, stretching back through the sixth century, and much of it was governed or at least overseen by the state. This goes back to the Archaic Athenian organisational unit known as the *naukrariai* and the officials in charge of these units, the *naukraroi*, mentioned in the *Athenaion Politeia*.[11] Van Wees sees these *naukraroi* as officials who combined financial and military functions, on both a local and national level.[12] This is the organisation that Borimir Jordan reckons must have been in place long before the Persian Wars. Van Wees puts forward a reasonable and practical explanation for such an organisation, especially in highlighting the naval operations which were conducted by Athens in the period before the Persian wars.[13] Further, others have used coinage to demonstrate evidence for increased expense in Athens during the late sixth century and tied to this the need to pay sailors of a state-owned trireme fleet.[14]

Naval organisation in Athens during the fifth and fourth centuries was complex, and there are excellent works on this topic.[15] All organs of the Athenian government were involved in naval administration, including the *ekklesia* and the *boule*.[16] This ranged from high-level strategic decisions about fleet movements down to specific technical matters. For instance, an inscription refers to the *boule* making decrees concerning the structural braces used for ship construction.[17] Importantly, it was not just a high degree of technical knowledge that helped characterise the democracy's naval expertise but also the high level of participation.

---

[11] *Ath. Pol.* 8.3.
[12] Van Wees (2015): 44–61.
[13] Van Wees (2015): 57–60.
[14] Aperghis (2013): 1–24.
[15] Borimir Jordan has examined in detail the Athenian Navy in the classical period, including the organisation and administration ashore. Jordan (1975): 21–116; see also Morrison et al. (2000): 107–26.
[16] Jordan (1975): 21–30. See also Rhodes (1972): 113–22; 153–8.
[17] IG II² 1628, lines 231–33; Jordan (1975): 29.

With 6,000 people needed for a quorum in the *ekklesia* in the fourth century, 500 sitting on the *boule*, up to 2,000 needed as jurors in the law courts, and around 700 annual magistracies, most citizens in Athens would have had direct experience in decision-making on both naval and more general maritime matters.[18] This participation in government covers all manner of maritime issues, from the strategic positioning of naval assets, naval administration including personnel and equipment, through to maritime trade cases in the law courts. In many ways, Athenians were involved not just in maritime operations themselves but also in maritime and naval administration and organisational issues. The Athenians were not just good rowers and sailors but also found themselves steeped in operational and strategic matters.

A final issue of organisation concerns logistics, for no naval or maritime campaign could be undertaken without a solid logistics plan. This is a very opaque topic, for the ancient authors seem little concerned with the subject. The best evidence comes from Thucydides and the Sicilian expedition. It was such a large operation, as this required a huge amount of support, both local and from mainland Italy and Greece. The Athenian *strategos* Nicias realised this, and in a speech to the Athenians he attempted to discourage them from what he saw as a folly by saying that the expedition would require a substantial naval and land force, able to operate away from home for an extended period.[19] It is one of the few examples where logistics units are mentioned, albeit briefly. An advance force of vessels, including the allied vessels, was assembled at Corcyra, and this included grain transports.[20] Thucydides goes on to say that the expedition was furnished with troops and ships to be ready for a long or a short expedition.[21] Thucydides lists the forces sent across, of which the logistics train consisted of a horse transport and thirty merchant vessels carrying grain as well as various tradesmen, and finally boats and merchant vessels that followed of their own volition for the purposes of trade.[22] In a similar example, the Carthaginians, preparing a large invasion force to go to Sicily, assembled a fleet of 1000 cargo ships, according to Diodorus.[23] The number is probably exaggerated, but it is important that Diodorus does mention cargo ships as part of the invasion force. These examples give a glimpse at what might be required for a large amphibious force sent on an over-

---

18 See Hansen (1991): 313, esp. notes 198–204. On the rotation of personnel through the different forms of participation, pp. 313–14.
19 Thuc. 6.21.
20 Thuc. 6.30.1.
21 Thuc. 6.31.3.
22 Thuc. 6.43; 6.44.1.
23 Diod. 13.80.5.

seas expedition. Clearly, ancient Greek naval forces had some mechanism in place for the sustainment of their fleets, though of course this might involve no more than plundering the nearby territory, a method also utilised by land forces. Nevertheless, ships could carry far more supplies than a land force could with a baggage train.

While all these examples are based on Athens, a hegemonic sea power, we can extrapolate for smaller poleis. Any polis with maritime interests and a small navy must have had some level of basic naval organisation similar, albeit on a much smaller scale, to Athens'. Navies required the same core set of personnel, sailing equipment, and infrastructure, regardless of size. The logistics forces that a polis could muster would have been a key factor in the reach and sustainment of maritime forces operating away from home territory. Without the ability to keep a maritime force resupplied, a polis would be severely restricted in the scale of expeditionary operations. In a similar vein, poor naval organisation would have led to poorly equipped and crewed naval forces. This is not necessarily a matter of scale but of competency. Smaller poleis may have been quite effective if backed by a rigorous system of crewing and equipping warships, and major poleis may have suffered from a lack of proper naval organisation. The level of sophistication of a polis' naval organisation may help explain why some were more successful than others.

Ships and ship design

There were many different types and sizes of vessels used by the ancient Greeks in terms of both civilian ships and warships. The various uses and different operating environments ensured that ship types varied, and although classes of ships such as the trireme were generally of the same size and construction, this does not indicate a universal design for each class of ship. No intact warships have been found archaeologically, unsurprising since the wooden warships of the period would not have sunk to the bottom of the ocean as in later times. This is an important fact to note, as it tells us that when ships are described as 'sunk' in the ancient sources, they are likely describing ships that have become severely disabled or broken up, perhaps remaining neutrally buoyant but for all intents and purposes sunk. They might sink below the surface and subsequently break up but would not really have sunk to the bottom of the seafloor. Ships lost in ancient naval battles likely would have been in various states of seaworthiness. Some warship rams have been found on the seabed, which are invaluable as evidence for what was essentially the primary 'weapon' of the trireme, and recent efforts have been made to digitally reconstruct ship dimensions from later Punic warship rams.[24] However, the primary evidence for the dimensions of triremes comes from the remains of shipsheds, which help indicate the size of the triremes housed within. Much existing scholarship is concerned with ship design and construction, and there is still debate on many of the key issues, especially regarding the trireme. This section is not intended to debate the merits of the different arguments but merely to help establish the general capabilities and limitations of ancient sailing vessels and highlight the potential impact upon maritime operations.

Warship design evolved slowly over the centuries, though older designs of ships could still be found in later fleets. The pentecontor appears to have been the main warship of the sixth century, a 50-oared vessel that was designed for boarding and ramming attacks on enemy warships.[25] However, Herodotus says that the Phocaeans used pentecontors for trade instead of 'round ships', that is, traditional merchant vessels.[26] It seems that pentecontors were quite versatile vessels,[27] capable of a range of maritime operations, including as a warship in battle and for the transport of both personnel and cargo. As a smaller vessel with a smaller crew, it would also have been a cheaper warship to build and crew – important factors for smaller poleis needing some form of naval capability.

The primary warship of the Classical period was the trireme. Initially, combat tactics revolved around boarding actions on other warships, supported by archers. However, by the Persian Wars, more experienced and trained crews were employing ramming attacks against other warships. According to Thucydides, those using primarily boarding tactics during the Peloponnesian War, such as the battle of Sybota that he describes, were fighting in a more archaic manner than the sophistication of ramming attacks. Athens was not free from such 'archaic' combat at sea, and there is good reason to believe that in Athens, ramming tactics were a more democratic way of warfare. Firstly, the emphasis on ramming meant that it was the sailors and rowers, not the hoplite-class, that won the most prestige in naval battles. Secondly, boarding actions were costlier in terms of casualties suffered, and this could be politically unacceptable to the Athenian demos. This can be seen in the reaction to the loss of life after Arginousai in 406,

---

24 A notable example is the Athlit ram, from a Hellenistic-era ship found near Haifa, Israel, in 1980. Oron (2006): 63–76. There is also a wonderful example of half a bronze ram, dated to the classical period, in the Piraeus Archaeological Museum. Numerous rams were found at the site of the battle of the Aegates islands (241 BCE). See Royal and Tusa (eds.) (2020), chapter 4 by Royal and Tusa. On 3D reconstruction from an Aegates ram: Polakowski (2016).
25 For more on the development of the ram in naval vessels, see Mark (2008): 253–72.
26 Hdt. 1.163.2.
27 For more on pentecontors, see Casson (1971): 53–65; Morrison et al. (2000): 25–41.

built upon the precedent of Cimon's boarding tactics at Eurymedon in 467, which also saw the Athenians suffer more casualties than was expected.[28]

Triremes were also occasionally used as transport ships, even transporting horses as attested by Thucydides.[29] The specific characteristics of a trireme are not known for certain and based heavily on a reconstructed ship, the *Olympias*, supposed to represent an Athenian trireme.[30] This is an important distinction to make, as it is unlikely that triremes, or any other warship for that matter, were all of one standard design. Just as modern naval nomenclature talks of 'destroyers', 'frigates', and 'patrol boats', but the size, armament, crew size/makeup, and other details of these ships can vary substantially, so too is it likely that triremes differed in detail from shipbuilder to shipbuilder. An ancient Greek trireme, while certainly standard in many core features, should be thought of as a class of ship rather than as one specific design with one set of physical characteristics. The *Olympias* underwent much testing and several underway trials, demonstrating the potential of the design.[31] However, not all scholars agree that the *Olympias* accurately represents an ancient trireme.[32] Regardless of how representative of a trireme the *Olympias* is, some basic characteristics of the ship can be highlighted from both ancient sources and modern reconstruction and trials. The ship was fitted with a ram and was propelled by oarsmen in battle to ram and disable enemy ships, though less trained crews might attempt to come alongside an enemy vessel and take it by boarding. The full complement of a trireme appears to have been approximately 200 personnel, comprising 170 rowers, 15 sailors, and 15 marines.[33] The maximum speed appears to have been about 10 knots for short durations, with a potential cruising speed of between 7 and 8 knots by sail or under oar.[34]

---

[28] Thuc. 149.1. For a good discussion of this, see Strauss (2000): 315–26.
[29] The first instance of triremes used as horse transports in 430, according to his account. 2.56.2.
[30] The *Olympias* was launched a Hellenic Navy ship in June 1987. For details on the history of the reconstruction, see Morrison, Coates and Rankov (2000): xvii–xxviii.
[31] See reports in Morrison and Coates (eds.) (1989), Shaw (ed.) (1993), and Morrison et al. (2000).
[32] The most vehement critic is Alec Tilley, who argues that triremes never had three levels of rowers. Tilley (2004). However, objections to the *Olympias* design are older. For a very interesting and little-known work on the topic, see Nellopoulos (1999). Published posthumously by his son, Nellopoulos criticised the *Olympias* in ways very similar to, but predating, Tilley. Both sides of the argument make convincing points about the design of the ship, and it is probable that no side is entirely correct.
[33] These are approximate numbers, for an Athenian trireme. For a more detailed discussion on crew complement, see Jordan (1975): 153–268; Morrison et al. (2000): 107–18. For more on *epibatai* and social status, see Herzogenrath-Amelung (2017): 45–64.
[34] Morrison et al. (2000): 102–6; Rankov (ed.) (2012): 145–60.

Range is a more contentious issue and would have depended on weather conditions and the training of the ship's rowers. The most famous example of a long-distance dash is that of the Athenian trireme sent from the Piraeus to Mytilene in order to reverse a previous decision made by the assembly, a distance of 184 nm covered in approximately 24 h.[35] It is obviously a stand-out example of what a trireme and well-trained crew could accomplish and should not be taken as the maximum range for all warships of the time but as an indicator of potential sailing time if the need was great enough. In another example, Xenophon contends that the route from Byzantium to Heraclea on the Black Sea was 'a long day's voyage for a trireme under oars', approximately 130 nm.[36] Xenophon is speaking generally and not of a specific example like Thucydides, which may indicate that 130 nm is a more realistic figure for a maximum daily range of a trireme.

Sometime from the mid- to late fourth century, larger and more powerful ships than triremes were built, commonly referred to by number: 'four', 'five', and even larger in the Hellenistic period, often referred to generally as 'polyremes'. The meaning of the numbers is unknown, though scholars agree that it cannot denote the number of decks and must refer to multiple rowers per oar.[37] There is much speculation on all aspects of their design: dimensions, number of levels, and oar system, but no real picture of exactly how 'fours' and 'fives' (and greater) operated.[38] The most important things to note about these warships is that they were larger and thus represented an even greater investment in resources than triremes, in terms of both materials and equipment and personnel. They required a larger crew and were physically bigger ships to build and maintain. It is also likely that these bigger ships had better seakeeping characteristics than the smaller triremes and thus could survive more inclement weather. Their use represents a significant escalation in the scale of maritime and naval operations conducted in the late fourth century and beyond.

---

35 184 nm is given by Morrison et al. (2000: 104) in their calculations, a measurement I concur with in plotting the most expedient course from the Peiraieus to Mytilene (using chart BA 180). This in turn gives an average speed of 7.6 knots.
36 Xen. *Anab.* 6.4.2. Which depending on how long of a rest break (if any) was taken and depending on how long a 'long day' was, amounted to an average speed of between 7 and 8.5 knots according to Morrison et al. (2000): 103.
37 Casson (1971): 97–103.
38 Many of the arguments rely on pictorial evidence for very specific details and is extremely subjective. Different scholars and indeed seventeenth-century artists have seen the Lenormant relief as representing a two or a three-level ship. Morrison and Coates (1996): 185–7; Tilley (2004): 35–8. It is hard not to see the phenomenon of 'confirmation bias' in arguments over these artistic representations, especially by those who insist the Lenormant relief (and other pieces) clearly show a three-level ship that *must* represent a trireme. Morrison and Coates (1996): 267–71.

Different types of warships could be found in a polis' fleet, not just the predominant model of the time. Even when superseded by larger or more sophisticated types, older and smaller warship designs still had their uses as either combatants or auxiliary vessels. When listing the naval order of battle for Artemision, Herodotus has the Ceans and the Opountion Locrians contributing pentecontors to the fleet.[39] In Sicily, a Carthaginian fleet attacked by the forces of Syracuse consisted of a mixed force of pentecontors, triremes, and merchant vessels.[40] The Athenian fleet of the late fourth century was of mixed type, with the Assembly in 323 said to have ordered the construction of 40 triremes and 200 'fours', and 'fives' were added around the same time.[41] Athenian naval lists also detail a mixed fleet, before the Assembly's ambitious build programme.[42] During Athenian operations near Amphipolis in the 360s, Demosthenes mentions a disloyal mercenary taking some of their light vessels, the 30-oared triacontor.[43] Vessels such as triacontors, pentecontors, or triremes could fulfil a number of auxiliary roles inside and outside of direct combat. They could potentially be used to finish off disabled enemy vessels, rescue friendly sailors in the water, be used as dispatch vessels, and for general scouting.

Merchant vessels of the ancient world varied wildly in size and construction, ranging from small coastal freighters up to large cargo vessels designed for long-distance trade and carrying bulk cargo such as grain. As mentioned above, they were commonly referred to as 'round ships', as opposed to 'long ships' – warships. Inscriptions indicate that their cargo-carrying capability varied substantially, ranging from 20 up to 165 tons in the Classical period.[44] In a law court speech by Demosthenes, the cargo ship in question was contracted to load 3,000 jars of wine.[45] Little is known how many people could be transported in merchant vessels. It seems likely that people who needed to travel by sea went aboard merchant vessels carrying cargo and passengers.[46] In a law court speech of Antiphon, the defendant mentions the fact that he and other passengers were travelling from Lesbos to Thasos on a ship with no deck and were forced by bad weather to

---

[39] Hdt. 8.1.2.
[40] Diod. 14.73.2.
[41] Diod. 18.10.2. Though there is some debate over the reading of the manuscript; some scholars have the numbers reversed to read 200 triremes and 40 'fours'. Morrison et al. (2000): 48; on fives, see Murray (2012): 261.
[42] IG II² 1627.24, 1629.801–11; Morrison et al. (2000): 48.
[43] Dem. 23.149.
[44] Neatly summarised by Casson (1971: 183–4) in an appendix.
[45] Dem. 35.10.
[46] Casson (1974: 66) says as much but gives no reference.

switch to a vessel that did have a deck.⁴⁷ Firstly, it indicates that there were several paying passengers, and secondly it appears to have been a fairly straightforward process to swap boats to something more suitable. It also demonstrates the differences in trading vessels being used around the Aegean. Clearly, the original intent was to cross from Lesbos to Thasos in an un-decked ship, and it was only inclement weather that forced them to swap. It seems likely that many of the vessels used for trade and ferrying passengers, in particular local trade, would have been very small vessels and crewed by a very small number. The same is true of fishing vessels, which would have ranged in size from small two-man vessels up to much larger boats used for larger and more migratory fish such as tuna. It is fair to say that different areas would have favoured types and constructions of vessels designed and built to local conditions.

Personnel

Personnel considerations are a critical factor in maritime operations, not only in terms of the available pool of manpower,⁴⁸ but also in terms of training and ability. A trireme on average carried 200 crew, and so a fleet of triremes represented a substantial investment in personnel. Thucydides says the largest Athenian fleet deployment of the Peloponnesian War, in 428, saw the Athenians with 250 triremes at sea: this would represent 50,000 personnel if triremes were fully crewed.⁴⁹ Not only did they have to be paid and kept fed and healthy, they also represented a large pool of manpower which could not be used in other military roles such as hoplites or light-armed troops. Sailors and rowers required a great deal of training and practice in a very particular skillset.

Just as with soldiers, experienced and well-trained sailors and rowers could find work across the Mediterranean, selling their talents to the highest bidder. Lacking a body of experienced rowers could severely hamstring a polis' naval power and increasingly became a problem in the fourth century. A law court case of Demosthenes/Apollodoros very aptly demonstrates the personnel problems associated with keeping a trireme at sea.⁵⁰ The speech is of great importance for all

---

47 Antiphon, *On the Murder of Herodes*, 22.
48 Women of the time being excluded from Greek military operations. They were however, greatly affected by male relations' absence, as told by the speaker in a law court speech by Demosthenes, who relates the story of his wife and mother besieged by creditors and illnesses in his absence. [Dem]. 50.60–2 (see below).
49 Thuc. 3.17.
50 Oration 50. On the issue of authorship, see Bers (2003): 19–20.

aspects of the office of trierarchy. It concerns Apollodorus (the speaker) suing Polycles for taking over from Apollodorus the duties of trierarch when he should have, causing the speaker much financial and personal hardship. The first note about personnel was the seeming difficulty in finding enough skilled rowers and sailors. The speaker says that the deme members who showed up for service as *nautai* were incompetent, forcing him to hire his own *nautai* as well as hiring the best seamen he could.[51] He speaks of desertion caused by lack of pay or by simply pulling into the Piraeus; the second eventuality forced on him when he took an ambassador back home and forced him to hire replacements for the deserters.[52] He loses more sailors in the Hellespont, where suffering from a lack of pay they are lured away to ships from Thasos and Maroneia.[53] This is interesting not just because of the desertion but also because of the fact that ships from Thasos and Maroneia could afford to poach sailors away from an Athenian fleet. Further, he says that the deserters had great confidence in their rowing ability and so could chase after the highest wage.[54] The speaker goes so far as to accuse the *strategos* in charge, Timomachos, of deliberately keeping Apollodorus on as trierarch because his replacement Polycles would have done a bad job and Timomachus needed Apollodorus' well-crewed and efficient ship for his services.[55] This speech highlights the core difficulties in manning a trireme and keeping it operationally effective on campaign in the Aegean. It gives an insight into the importance of skilled rowers and seaman, who like experienced soldiers could sell out their talents to the highest bidder.

An often-overlooked feature of naval service is the social impact of overseas service. [Demosthenes] 50 is also useful in this respect, detailing some of the social issues involved in overseas military service. When the speaker mentions de-

---

51 Dem 50.7. There is debate over the different terms used, *nautai,* and *hyperesia*. *Nautai* seems to refer to the rowers and the *hyperesia* appear to have been the skilled seamen – the helmsman, boatswain, rowing master, piper, carpenter, and other roles required for the sailing and running of the ship, outside of rowing. Included in this complement seems to be the *epibatai,* the hoplites and archers who can be termed 'marines' in modern parlance. See Morrison (1984): 48–59; Gabrielsen (1994): 106; Morrison et al. (2000): 107–26; Van Wees (2014): 210–1. For a different view of the meaning, which argues for a difference in social status as the defining difference between *nautai* and *hyperesia*, see Jordan (1975): 210–68. Jordan, following L.J.D. Richardson (1943), points out that the etymology of *hyperesia* strongly suggest rowing, connected as it is to the word ἐρέτης. My thanks to Dr Peter Londey for illustrating this linguistic point to me in an early revision of this work.
52 Dem. 50.11–12.
53 Dem. 50.14.
54 Dem. 50.16.
55 Dem. 50.43–52.

sertions when ships return to their home port of the Piraeus, he says that many refused to re-embark unless given extra money to cover household expenses.[56] This is highlighted further by the speaker's own personal difficulties, certainly raised and perhaps exaggerated to elicit sympathy from the jury,[57] but nonetheless a set of circumstances that must not have been uncommon for men serving on overseas campaigns for years at a time. His mother was extremely sick and died on the sixth day after his return, having suffered difficulties in her property and unable to give him as much inheritance as she wanted.[58] His wife was sick for much of his time away, his children only small, much of his money tied up in his current trierarchy and faced with agricultural difficulties with his land producing nothing for harvest that year.[59] Interestingly, these worries were apparently not all heaped upon him on his return, for while he was away he received news from travellers as well as actual correspondence from home.[60] It seems as if regular news and even correspondence could and did reach people on campaign and is perhaps indicative of a solid and basically reliable level of information exchange throughout the Aegean at the level of, essentially, mail services.

Lastly, [Demosthenes] 50 demonstrates how well travelled many Greeks in the Classical period could be thanks to maritime activities. The speaker and his 200 or so crew members visited many different places in the course of their service. They visited the Hellespont, including Hieron, Sestos, Maroneia, Thasos, Styrmon River, and Tenedos. It was the kind of shared experience that could be mentioned in comedy and joked about. In Aristophanes' *Wasps*, the chorus leader reminisces and jokes about sharing guard duty in Byzantium, and again later on campaign in Naxos.[61] There is no specific mention of their service as either sailors or soldiers, though the former is suggested in a later passage of the chorus. What this passage demonstrates is the typical nature of service in Athens: on campaign overseas as part of an expeditionary force, not arrayed in a phalanx on the fields of Attica. Even though this passage comes from a comedy, a notoriously difficult source to use for historical purposes, the nature of the passages makes them credible. They are the reminiscences of the old men of the chorus, not central to the

---

56 Dem. 50.11.
57 A common courtroom tactic, though such a high-profile speaker must have had enough of a public profile that much of his private life was not so private. There would be a limit to how many details he could lie about or exaggerate. The circumstances he describes were probably verifiable to the jurors, especially the poor harvest and drought that he describes.
58 Dem. 50.60.
59 Dem. 50.61.
60 Dem. 50.62.
61 Ar. *Vesp.* 235–6; 354–5.

plot and thus not in need of comic exaggeration. Indeed, it is a far cry from the usual trope of having the old men represent the 'Marathon-men' (*marathonamachoi*) that haunt the comedies. They are describing military operations known to many and probably not far from the audiences' own experiences. This is of course an example from Athens, but many poleis conducted overseas campaigning, and the experiences as described by this chorus are perhaps not so far from the experience of many Greeks on military service during the Classical period.

Infrastructure

Infrastructure is a key enabler of maritime operations, both military and non-military. Merchant and fishing vessels require safe harbours and basic port facilities to conduct their business. This includes facilities for loading and unloading cargo as well as the availability of storage facilities for some goods. As seen in the example of the Elephantine Palimpsest, government infrastructure such as customs houses was required. Warships require regular maintenance and protection from the elements when not in use, as well as storage facilities for the massive amount of gear – oars, sails, and other fittings – required to operate them. Additionally, these facilities often required some form of fortification or protection, from both external and also sometimes internal threats.

The shipsheds of the Piraeus are perhaps the most impressive of all naval infrastructure projects in Greece, as befitted the supreme sea power of the day. Between the three harbours, Zea, Kantharos, and Mounychia, by 323/2 Athens could house 372 ships.[62] Additionally, the harbours themselves were protected zones, with fortification walls and towers protecting them and even a form of access control, with chains positioned to block off the harbour mouth as required.[63] Further, the Long Walls from Athens down to the Piraeus should be considered essential maritime infrastructure, providing unimpeded access to the sea for both civil and military purposes. Further afield, the two harbours of Syracuse in Sicily could hold many ships by the beginning of the fourth century, with Diodorus saying the tyrant Dionysius I constructed 160 new and costly sheds, most of which

---

[62] 196 in Zea, the main naval port, 94 in Kantharos, and 82 in the smallest harbour, Mounychia, also primarily a naval port. Archaeological remains have been found in Zea and Mounychia, but none for Kantharos. These are attested to in epigraphic evidence (along with the others): IG II² 1627.398–405; 1628.552–9; 1629.1030–6; 1631.252–6 for the years 330/29, 326/5, 325/4, and 323/2, respectively. Blackman and Rankov (2013): 437, 476–85. A great deal of work has also been done by the Danish Institute in Athens under Dr Bjørn Lovén.
[63] Blackman and Rankov (2013): 435–7.

could hold two ships, and he also repaired the existing 150 sheds.[64] Such a large building project represents a significant investment in maritime infrastructure and was a clear statement of intent by a city which considered itself a premier sea power.

It was not just in Athens and the other major sea power cities that shipsheds could be found, and the prevalence of such infrastructure indicates the importance of navies around the Greek world. Remains have been found of four shipsheds at Sicilian Naxos, a city of medium size, indicating possession of a small fleet.[65] The number of shipsheds does not necessarily reflect the total number of warships operated by the state. Ships might be off on operations or training, alongside or at anchor elsewhere near the city, with the sheds being used for maintenance or longer-term storage. It is not unreasonable to assume Naxos might have possessed 8–12 warships in total, though only having four sheds. Only larger and richer poleis, like Athens, may have built enough sheds for all their ships. In any case, for such a medium-sized city this represents a significant investment in resources and indicates the importance of such infrastructure. Function dictated the size of the sheds, but the large size of the buildings, not unreasonably called 'monumental architecture' by the archaeologists, dwarfs other buildings: they were ten times the size of a typical temple in the city.[66] This illustrates how naval infrastructure in even a moderate city of limited naval power was considered important, and it highlights the prominence of the maritime realm in that city.

The paved track that connected the Corinthian Gulf with the Saronic – the *diolkos* – is perhaps the largest and most impressive piece of maritime infrastructure in Greece, a significant asset of potential strategic value. That it was used to transport ships across the isthmus is attested in Thucydides, where in 428 the Spartans and allies made preparations to haul ships from the Corinthian Gulf across the isthmus in order to go to the aid of Mytilene, and again in 412 to aid Chios.[67] The *diolkos* was still in use two centuries later, when Demetrios and Phi-

---

[64] Diod. 14.42.5. For more on the shipsheds at Syrakousai, see Gerding (2013): 535–41.
[65] It seems to have had a rather large territory, listed as 200–500 square km (size 4) in *Inventory of Archaic and Classical Poleis*. Hansen and Nielsen (2004): 218–20. The city itself was of a medium size, as described by the archaeologists who worked in the shipsheds. See Lentini, Blackman, and Pakkanen (2008): 301.
[66] Lentini, Blackman, and Pakkanen (2008): 354. A temple being as wide as a single slipway (out of four) but only 1/3 the length. Lentini, Blackman, and Pakkanen (2008): 354.
[67] Thuc. 3.15.1; 8.7. That the ships were not actually hauled across the isthmus was because of the slowness to react by Sparta's allies and interference from an Athenian naval operation. In neither case is Thucydides saying that ships being dragged across the isthmus are remarkable feat: he is detailing a military operation.

lip V of Macedon used it to transport warships.⁶⁸ Unexpectedly, the *diolkos* is mentioned in a comedy of Aristophanes, where Cleisthenes says of another: 'That's some isthmus you've got there, man. You shuttle your cock back and forth more than the Corinthians!'.⁶⁹ This certainly suggests frequent movement across the isthmus via the *diolkos* and would seem to indicate commercial traffic as well as military.⁷⁰ Indeed, most scholars think that the *diolkos* was primarily used for commercial traffic, particularly cargo rather than actual merchant ships.⁷¹ The Corinthians' primary intention in building the *diolkos* is unknown and probably unknowable, but it can be said with certainty that it represented a significant investment in resources and was a resource of strategic importance, allowing for the passage of goods as well as warships.

Finance and wealth

Navies were a very capital-intensive investment, not just in initial outlay, but in upkeep. This includes the ships, attendant infrastructure, and personnel. The ability to properly finance a fleet was one of, if not the, most important factor in determining a polis' naval power. In Athens the burden of funding the fleet was shared between state and individuals. Athenian state finance in large part relied on the Delian League to provide funds for its fifth-century sea power. Sparta, as well as Athens and Thebes at different point in the fourth century, relied heavily on Persia for naval funding.

Like most issues of detail in the maritime and naval realm, the best evidence of fleet finance comes from Athens, although problems of financing the Spartan fleet are well illustrated in Xenophon as well.⁷² The first major expenditure was on the ships themselves, both construction and upkeep. Ships seem to have been built as part of a specific programme, as well as during an annual replacement programme.⁷³ It does not seem likely that there was anything like a standard cost for a trireme, and so much of the cost depended on the availability of the shipbuilding

---

68 Polyb. 4.19.7–9; 5.101.
69 *Thesm.* 647–8.
70 Salmon (1984): 137.
71 Salmon (1984: 136–9) and MacDonald (1986: 191–5) both argue that commercial uses were the primary purpose of the *diolkos*, though not discounting its enduring potential for military use.
72 For instance, Teleutias in 388 addressing his crews on the issue of money and supplies, specifically, the lack thereof. Xen *Hell.* 5.1.14.
73 Gabrielsen (1994): 131–6.

material, in particular, timber.[74] Ships could of course be acquired in battle or captured along with a city or other similar military campaign,[75] but would in most cases require maintenance to restore the ship to fighting quality. Still, this was almost certainly cheaper than a new build, albeit an unreliable way of bolstering ship numbers. Additionally, there was much equipment needed for the outfitting of a trireme, including oars, oar sleeves, masts, sails, and rigging, to name a few.[76] Equipment was also an issue, not just 'expendable' items that wear and tear would mean they needed to be replaced, but also easily portable gear that could, and certainly in Athens, was misappropriated on a regular basis.[77] All of this equipment required a variety of different goods, from flax and papyrus for ropes and sails, through to leather for the oar sleeves, wood, and iron for much of the other fittings. These are the sorts of goods Athens required for the navy but does not produce in Attica, hence the control of trade being of the utmost importance.[78]

The most enduring financial burden for a navy was personnel. Not just in finding and training enough, but also in paying them. With a nominal crew complement of approximately 200 per trireme and pay of between 3 obols and 1 drachma per day, this represents a significant monetary outlay.[79] As the Apollodorus speech above indicated, rowers could expect good pay while away on campaign, and such campaigns could last for months. The imperative to pay crews was perhaps the primary driving factor behind *strategoi* on campaign collecting money from allies and non-allies in the area of operations. As will be seen later, the collection of this money on campaign caused much angst amongst allied and neutral powers alike. Of note too is the fact that pay must have been roughly standardised across the Greek world, otherwise the risk of underpaying would see trained rowers defect in even greater numbers, as seen in Apollodorus' speech on his crewing issues. In this way the burden of financing a fleet on campaign had not just operational ramifications but potentially strategic ones as well.

This brings us to the second part of the money equation: wealth. Beyond the everyday concerns of funding the fleet – building, maintenance, and paying crews – there was the underlying issue of a polis requiring enough wealth to

---

74 Gabrielsen (1994): 139–42. This certainly true of shipbuilding in later ages, especially Gabrielsen's point about the importance of the state's relationship with suppliers of critical building material.
75 For example, Lysander's capture of the Athenian ships at Aigispotamoi. Xen. *Hell.* 2.1.28.
76 For more detail, see Morrison et al. (2000): 161–78.
77 Gabrielsen (1994): 146–69. See especially pp. 153–7 on misappropriation.
78 As outlined by the 'Old Oligarch', 2.11–12.
79 On the financial aspects, see Gabrielsen (1994): 105–25; and for Archaic-era Athenian finances: Van Wees (2015): 63–75.

maintain a fleet. This is at the core of Pericles' advice to the Athenians at the outbreak of the war. In this famous speech, after his preamble he first addresses the issue of wealth and the ability to pay for war. He reminds the Athenians that the Spartans are essentially an agrarian society, too devoted to the land to amass any monetary reserves, and that any absence from their land, say on a military campaign, imposes a direct cost in time and effort lost.[80] This in fact echoes the warning given earlier by the Spartan king Archidamus, where he tells the Spartans that they have a far greater deficiency in both their treasury and their private wealth.[81] Both of these speeches make Thucydides' point that what counts in the upcoming war is money.[82] Navies required constant expense after the initial outlay of building the ships and required infrastructure. Ships needed to be maintained and repaired, and much of the gear carried, from ropes to sails to oars, all would wear and require replacement at regular points. Ships clearly had a service life, perhaps of 8–12 years depending upon how often they were sailed out or engaged in battle, and so old ships needed to be fully replaced in order to maintain a ready and effective fleet. Then there is the personnel aspect, for it was not just that Athenian sailors were paid, it was the fact that they regularly sailed out for operations or training. It was the training and experience of the Athenian fleet that set it apart from other navies, and this required a constant expense which in turn required a constant income, in Athens' case from the Delian League.

Importantly, it was not just the amassing of this wealth that allowed Athens to maintain its supremacy at sea and, by extension, the very maritime empire that funded its sea power. As Lisa Kallet-Marx has argued, it was the Athenian willingness to spend this money that mattered most.[83] This constant expenditure kept the Athenian fleet maintained, well-crewed, and, most importantly, out at sea on operations around the Mediterranean. A constant stream of income and a huge reserve of ready cash would have been little use had Athens not spent money to maintain and operate the fleet on a regular basis. This is why Sparta's sea power was so short-lived, because they did not have the institutional arrangements to amass large swathes of money, save the period where Persian financial backing had granted them a fleet and a temporary Aegean empire. Importantly, this highlights the need for cash reserves. Without ready cash reserves, anything that saw an interruption to a polis' income stream would have an immediately detrimental impact on the ability to keep a fleet maintained and crewed. Without

---

80 Thuc. 1.141.3–4.
81 Thuc. 1.80.4.
82 Kallet-Marx (1993): 94.
83 Kallet-Marx (1993): 6.

that naval power to extract money from allies or enemies, this would further hamper income collection and protection, leading to a death spiral. Cash reserves, like those Athens was able to maintain for a large part of the Peloponnesian War, gave a buffer. The inability of Athens to finance a large fleet in the fourth century, comparable to the fleets of the fifth century, is directly traceable to a lack of money, money that had earlier been extracted from a strong maritime empire enforced by a strong fleet, built over time as money was reinvested into the navy. This highlights the virtuous circle of money empowering a fleet which in turn allowed for the extraction of more money through trade or direct tribute, enforced by sea power.

Conclusion

All these practical considerations demonstrate that navies were not a small investment. Great amounts of material and money were required for even a small force of warships. The construction, outfitting, maintenance, and crewing of a warship represented a significant investment for any polis. The mere fact that a polis would invest large amounts of effort and money into constructing shipsheds demonstrates an intent to maintain a fleet of warships to a high standard, even if that might be four triremes. As will be seen in the chapters that examine maritime operations, the size of a navy was not indicative of its effectiveness. Effective sea power boiled down to more than mere numbers, and the efficacy of a polis' maritime operations relied upon material factors such as equipment, trained crews, logistics, and cash reserves. In the context of strategy and its core elements of means-ways-ends, the practical considerations discussed in this chapter represent the 'means' aspect of how a polis might utilise sea power as part of its wider strategy.

Chapter Three
The ship of state: Greek maritime consciousness

As important as practical considerations are – men, ships, and money – there is also the issue of how a polis/state/country thinks about the sea and maritime matters. This is seen in many other well-known sea powers throughout history. Rome would eventually call the Mediterranean 'our sea' (*mare nostrum*). In Venice there was the annual maritime procession whereby the Doge was ceremonially wed to the sea. Great Britain had a long Maritime tradition that was portrayed in many ways, from poems/songs such as 'Rule Britannia' through to monuments, like Trafalgar Square and Nelson's column. In the lead-up to the First World War and the naval race between Britain and Germany, there was 'Dreadnought Fever' where certain politicians, the press, and the pubic clamoured for an increase to the Royal Navy's build program of new Dreadnoughts, demanding, 'we want eight, and we won't wait'.[1] In recent times, the People's Republic of China has increasingly looked to the sea and its maritime interests, resurrecting the memory of their great admiral Zeng He and his expeditions around the Pacific and Indian Oceans. It is not enough to have money, ships, and sufficient crews: there has to be an idea and a popular will behind a Navy.

How much the Greeks thought about the sea and maritime considerations can, in part, be illustrated by the way they discussed such matters and to what extent they developed what might be termed a 'maritime consciousness'. Whether depicted on stage, in myth, or even on display in artistic representation and architecture, this maritime consciousness can help illuminate the extent to which the maritime realm was conceptualised in the Greek world. Myths, epics, tragedies, and comedies are useful in examining this consciousness. This is often seen in the stories themselves, many of which are dominated by nautical themes, from long sea voyages through to overseas expeditions. It can also be seen in the language used, where nautical metaphors and imagery abound. In exploring the stories of the Greeks, one can see how important the sea was to both their practical but also to their conceptual world. This chapter will focus on the idea of a 'maritime consciousness' in Greece by exploring stories, be they in myth, in epic, or on stage. It will be a rather cursory examination of the topic, but hopefully a salient reminder that the sea was of great important to the Greeks, going beyond just trade and warfare.

---

[1] Massie (2007): 616.

Myth and epic

Myths were important to the Greeks, and it is necessary to explore some of the ways in which maritime topics and themes appeared in these stories, and how this might have helped shape a maritime consciousness. The maritime realm and maritime deities feature prominently in Greek creation myths. According to Hesiod's *Theogony*, the sea is one of the primeval elements that shaped the world.[2] More broadly, the sea connected all parts of the world through a vast hydrological network. From the outer Ocean all the world's rivers flowed inward, through the lands and then into the sea, and eventually outward again into the Ocean.[3] Hesiod lists all the important rivers, ending his short catalogue by naming the most important of them all as the Styx, though there are countless rivers, too numerous to name.[4] As Marie-Claire Beaulieu points out, this hydrological network connected all parts of the world, 'from the invisible world of the gods and the dead beyond the Ocean, to the underworld, to the surface of the earth'.[5] In this view of the world, rivers and the sea may be distinct but are not viewed as entirely separate as in the modern Western world. Of great importance to those who used the sea, Hesiod also describes the birth of the winds. Interestingly, bad winds that wreck ships and sailors are born from the terrible beast Typhoeos, as opposed to the good winds, Notos, Boreas, and Zephyros. Although he mentions winds destroying things upon the earth as well, the primary context in which Hesiod describes the winds is with regard to sailors and seagoing activities.[6] The sea and the winds which affected the seas were important features of Greek cosmology and which helped interconnect the Greek and the wider world.

Many of the deities associated with the sea are powerful and just, especially the 'old men of the sea' – Nereus, Phorcys, and Proteus – to whom can also be added the goddess Thetis.[7] All are knowledgeable and provide advice and aid to mortals. For instance, Proteus is twice described as 'truthful/unerring' and knows the depths of all the seas.[8] Heracles gains knowledge from Neleus of the way to the island of the Hesperides.[9] Alternatively, he is given Helios' cup from Neleus in

---

2 Hes. *Theog.* 131–2; Beaulieu (2016): 1.
3 Beaulieu (2016): 30.
4 Hes. *Theog.* 337–70.
5 Beaulieu (2016): 30.
6 Hes. *Theog.* 869–80; 878–80.
7 Beaulieu (2016): 36–7.
8 Hom. *Od.* 4.349, 401; 4.385–6.
9 Apollod. 2.114.

order to sail over Ocean to reach the Hesperides.[10] This follows the Titan Oceanus, who is also seen as a force for good in both actions and counsel.[11] In Aeschylus' *Prometheus Bound*, Oceanus gives counsel to Prometheus as well as trying to convince Zeus to free Prometheus.[12] Of the Olympians, not only Poseidon but Aphrodite also has a strong connection to the sea, being born from foam arising out of it and being associated with the islands of Cythera and Cyprus.[13] Most people, including scholars, tend to view Aphrodite as a deity concerned with love and related matters. Yet, Aphrodite had a strong connection to the sea from which she was born and had several epithets related to the sea.[14] Further, there are abundant finds of votive offerings made to her by seafarers on her birthplace island of Cyprus.[15]

The sea was a space inhabited or visited by all manner of divine creatures, and seawater itself was important to the Greeks and the gods. Seawater is considered pure and incorruptible.[16] This is how Aeschylus describes it in *The Persians* (578), and Euripides has Iphigeneia say that 'the sea washes away all human evils'.[17] Seawater was particularly useful when dealing with the pollution of death, and purification by seawater in the case of houses polluted by death was legally mandated in Ceos during the fifth century.[18] Moreover, ambrosia was brought to Zeus by doves from Oceanus.[19] The association between ambrosia and Oceanus endured from the time of Homer through to Hyginus, who lists the personified Ambrosia as one of the daughters of Oceanus.[20] Like the sea, Ocean is pure, and its purity is used by the gods and all the celestial bodies for bathing, except for the Bear, a constellation we encountered in the last chapter as useful for navigation precisely because it did not 'bathe in the ocean'.[21]

---

10 Stesich. fr. 184a. Beaulieu (2016): 36–8.
11 Beaulieu (2016): 38–9.
12 Aesc. *PV*. 284–396.
13 Hes. *Theog.* 192–200.
14 Larson (2007): 123.
15 I am grateful to Dr Amelia Brown of the University of Queensland for this information, provided in private correspondence as part of her Australian Research Council (ARC), Discovery Early Career Research Award for her project: 'Like frogs around a pond: Maritime Religion and Seafaring Gods of Ancient Greek Culture'.
16 Beaulieu (2016): 33.
17 Eur. *IT*. 1193.
18 IG XII 5.593. It seems as if salt could be added to fresh water if needed. See also Parker (1983): 226–7.
19 Hom. *Od.* 12.63.
20 Hyg. *Fab.* 182, 192. Beaulieu (2016): 36.
21 Beaulieu (2016): 34.

Dolphins have an interesting place in the Greek world from at least the Minoan and Mycenaean periods onwards. Early authors described dolphins as swift and wild, and indeed Achilles during his rampage against the Trojans is likened to a dolphin corralling terror-struck fish.[22] Classical authors thought highly of dolphins, which were seen as enjoying music and entertainment, experienced human-like emotions, and sympathised with and aided men. This included rescuing sailors and taking an interest in burial rights, not just for other dolphins but for humans as well, most famously the somewhat thalassophobic poet Hesiod.[23] Perhaps most interestingly, Plutarch argues that dolphins were the only animal that engaged in friendship with man for no advantage.[24] It is not unreasonable then to see dolphins as representing man's counterpart in the sea.[25]

Sea voyages are prominent in myth, featuring in the lives and deeds of heroes such as Heracles, Theseus, Jason, and of course Odysseus. The sea plays an active role in the lives of Greek heroes and their mythic journeys.[26] These sea voyages are often linked with Greek colonisation and the rapid expansion of geographic knowledge. A good example of this is the case of the 'Clashing Rocks', which feature in the Argo's journey. In early forms of the *Argonautica* story, the Argo encountered the Clashing Rocks on the return journey. The *Odyssey* says that the only ship to have passed through the rocks was the Argo, when sailing from Aietes.[27] The later authors Pindar and Apollonius Rhodes have the Argo sailing through the rocks on the outward journey, and most importantly, the rocks ceased their clashing once the ship has passed through, unlike in the earlier version of the story.[28] Later accounts required the Clashing Rocks to be tamed as they became more firmly located in the Bosporus,[29] a passage regularly sailed through by ships in the time of Pindar. Herein a myth appears to rationalise the world as the Greeks gained better geographic knowledge and experience of the Black Sea.

The *Odyssey* is *the* maritime adventure of the ancient Greek world. No book dealing with maritime issues can afford to ignore the *Odyssey*, but discussion

---

22 Hom. *Il.* 21.22–6.
23 Beaulieu (2016): 119–20, esp. notes 6–8, 11–14.
24 Plut. *Mor.* 984c,d.
25 Beaulieu (2016): 119–44. She has three case studies: Arion, Hesiod, and Melicertes. The chapter also looks at the important role of dolphins in colonisation and in the most important of Greek institutions, Delphi.
26 For a good examination of sea voyages by Perseus, Theseus, and Jason, see Beaulieu (2016): 59–89.
27 Hom. Od. 12.70. West (2005): 40.
28 Pind. *Pyth.* 210–11; Ap. Rhod. *Argon.* 604–6; Hom. *Od.* 12.62–5.
29 West (2005): 41.

here will be necessarily brief. Perhaps one of the most intriguing elements of the story is that of the Phaiacians, master sailors and merchants. The Phaiacians can be seen as playing the role of 'gateway to the ethnographic imagination of the world of the *Odyssey*'.[30] Firstly, they form a polarised opposition to the other great seafarers and traders of the time, the Phoenicians.[31] In stark contrast to the Phoenicians and other notable maritime traders, the Phaiacians are extremely hostile to outsiders, differing greatly in character with the somewhat cosmopolitan nature of other trading hubs like Phoenicia and Athens. The *Odyssey* has deep roots in the maritime realm, and the simple fact is that there are two great Homeric epics, and half of them are concerned with sea journeys. This alone should say a lot about how the maritime realm permeated Greek society from earliest times.

The sea and maritime endeavours are not prominent when first considering Heracles and his deeds, yet he had an important relationship with the sea. Heracles utilised the sea several times for his journeys, including his stint as one of Jason's Argonauts. A quick survey of his exploits includes his expedition against the Amazons, where he sails into the Black Sea, which he names *Euxeinos* ('hospitable'); sailing from Crete to retrieve the cattle of Geryon; setting up his Pillars in Gadeira; and sacking Troy.[32] Going beyond the mortal realm, Heracles sailed across Ocean in the cup of Helios, a popular scene depicted in art.[33] Heracles is the most recognisable and popular Greek hero, and it is important to note that the sea is an important feature in his deeds, allowing the hero to traverse the length and breadth of the Mediterranean and beyond.

Myth has an important aetiological function with regard to ships and sailing. The *Argo* was considered either the first ship or the first sea-going ship, Diodorus saying that before the *Argo* men put to sea in rafts or small boats.[34] Diodorus says that no small number of prominent youths were ready to take part in the journey,[35] and the crew of the *Argo* were exceptional, demigods in their own right who went on to great things, not just Heracles, but the Dioscuri (Castor and Pol-

---

[30] Dougherty (2001): 103.
[31] Dougherty (2001): 103. She examines this topic of overseas trade in a previous chapter (pp. 38–60).
[32] Diod. Sic. 4.16.1 18; Diod. Sic. 4.17.1–3; 18 ships according to Diodorus (Diod. Sic. 4.32.2) or 6 ships according to Homer (Hom. *Il.* 5.638–42), an alternate number acknowledged by Diodorus: Diod. Sic. 4.32.3–4.
[33] Obtained from either the 'old man of the sea' Nereus or from Helios himself. Stesich. Fr. 184a; Pherekydes *FGrH* F18a. For more on this episode, see Beaulieu (2016): 47–53. On art, Beaulieu (2016): 49, n. 145.
[34] Eur. *Andr.* 865; Diod. Sic. 4.41.1.
[35] Diod. Sic. 4.41.1–2.

lux), Orpheus, and Euphamus, whom the rulers of the city of Cyrene claimed as their ancestor to stake a claim to Jason's story.[36] Clearly, this was a momentous occasion and budding heroes/demigods approached the expedition and long sea voyage not with fear but eagerness. Myth is also used to explain the origin of sails in rationalising accounts of Daedalus and Icarus. Palaiphatos in his fourth century *On Unbelievable Tales* noted the impossibility of the pair actually flying through the air and says that they escaped by boat with a favourable wind which gave the appearance of them 'flying'.[37] Pausanias in his account says that Daedalus invented sails for his escape ship, previously unknown to sailors, in order to out-run the oared fleet of Minos.[38]

Perhaps the most important aetiological story is that of the Pillars of Heracles. Often seen as boundary markers, including by some ancient authors, they are also said to have been monuments to Heracles' achievement in making the Mediterranean Sea safe for mariners. Diodorus tells two quite contradictory stories about the Pillars, both of which illustrate Heracles' key role in maritime endeavours. Either Heracles narrowed the entrance to the Mediterranean Sea and thus prevented monsters from entering, or he cut a channel through what was land and thereby opened the Mediterranean to the Atlantic Ocean.[39] The first explanation seems to pick up on Euripides, who in his tragedy *Heracles* has the chorus sing that Heracles' adventures to the farthest recesses of the sea had made it safe sailing for men.[40] This first explanation is obvious in its benefit to mankind, but the second one also indicates a positive aspect to Heracles' journey and deeds, merely in a different light. This second explanation has Heracles opening up the sea to travel, a contentious issue in modern scholarship,[41] though it is hard to accept Diodorus as presenting this story in anything other than a positive light – he is of course praising the deeds of the great hero Heracles. Regardless of which story was more widely believed, they return to the idea of Greek geographic knowledge expanding as waves of Greek colonisers and traders expanded out to the furthest reaches of the Mediterranean.

---

36 Pindar's *Fourth Pythian*.
37 Palaiphatos, On Unbelievable Tales, 12.
38 Paus. 9.11.4.
39 Diod. Sic. 4.18.4–5.
40 Eur. *HF* 400–2.
41 Some interpreting the Pillars as a barrier, and in some cases postulating it as a rationalising account of the Greeks being cut out from this end of the Mediterranean because of the Carthaginians. It is of course possible that there is a simpler explanation: that by cutting a channel through the land monsters could be driven *out* of the Mediterranean.

Myth is not only important in the grand, panhellenic sense, but also on a more local level, and this is where much can be gleaned of the maritime consciousness of Greek cities. Despite losing in the contest for patronage of Athens, the sea-god Poseidon was still very important to the city. Poseidon was prominent in many other Greek cities as well. In Troezen, Theseus was allegedly born a son of Poseidon, the city's chief deity and god of choice for their coinage.[42] Pausanias describes the importance of Poseidon to the Achaean towns of Helice and Aigai, who worshiped 'Heliconian Poseidon', referenced twice in Homer, and still worshipped in Pausanias' day.[43] As mentioned above, Pindar's *Fourth Pythian* connects the ruling family in Cyrene to the expedition of the Argonauts and references the colonisation.[44] The rule of Cyrene is thus divinely mandated by Medea and the Delphic oracle,[45] and Cyrene then possesses a charter myth connected to a famous sea voyage.

Cult worship could also unite different poleis across a wide geographic area. One of Poseidon's most notable sanctuaries was on the island of Calaureia just off the coast of Troezen, a city noted above for its strong connection to Poseidon. More than being the place where the politician and orator Demosthenes met his end in 322,[46] the sanctuary hosted an amphictiony. Little is known about the amphictiony, other than a brief mention by Strabo, who names the seven members: Hermione, Epidaurus, Aegina, Athens, Prasieis, Nauplieis, and Minyan Orchomenos.[47] The dating is also problematic, most likely the end of the eighth or first half of the seventh century.[48] Of particular relevance as concerns the notion of a panhellenic maritime consciousness, it is quite obvious looking at the members of the amphictiony that they are all located on or very near to the sea. It was a community of mariners from around the Saronic Gulf, a religious network defined by its maritime nature.[49] Related to this sanctuary is the island of Delos and its rise as a prominent cult centre. In Pausanias' story of the sanctuary at Calaureia, he tells of how it was originally sacred to Apollo, and Delos to Poseidon, and that the two gods essentially swapped islands.[50] Though there appears to have been no formal amphictiony on Delos comparable to the one at Calaureia, it was nevertheless an important cult site for the Aegean islands and arguably a 'religious centre not of a purely Ionian

---

42 Plut. *Thes.* 6.1.
43 Hom. *Il.* 2.569–77, 8.198.207; Paus. 7.24.5–7, 7.25.12.
44 Pind. *Pyth.* 4.64–9.
45 Beaulieu (2016): 80–1.
46 And himself came to be worshipped there. Paus. 2.33.3, 35.5. Constantakopoulou (2007): 29.
47 Strabo 8.6.14. There is debate about which Orchomenos this is: the one in Boeotia or in Arcadia. For a summary of the discussion, see Constantakopoulou (2007): 31–2.
48 Constantakopoulou (2007): 32–6.
49 Constantakopoulou (2007): 37.
50 Paus. 2.32.2.

world, but predominately of a *nesiotic* world'.⁵¹ These are two excellent examples of how the maritime realm, through myth, reinforced networks around the Greek world and helped foment and maintain a maritime consciousness.

Dionysus is a deity not normally associated with the sea or maritime concerns, yet there are strong links, especially in Athens. The god's capture by pirates is a well-known story, told in the *Homeric Hymn to Dionysus*. Dionysus is introduced as standing next to the sea, where he is then taken by Tyrrhenian pirates.⁵² The helmsman alone recognises Dionysus as a god, naming several and concluding he must be a resident of Olympus, whom they must release lest he raise a storm against the ship.⁵³ The story ends with the pirates diving overboard and transforming into dolphins.⁵⁴ This is not necessarily the end for the pirates though, as their transformation into dolphins may represent a transformation into worshippers of Dionysus.⁵⁵

This is not as odd as it first appears, for dolphins have a close connection with Dionysus and revelry, and in particular the symposium. There are numerous examples of wine vessels adorned with dolphins as partaking of wine and revelry, accompanying Dionysus and/or symposiasts, including on pottery depicting land scenes where dolphins still appear.⁵⁶ Added to this is the metaphor of a symposium as a ship at sea. This is most vividly depicted in a passage of Timaeus, who relates a story in which a group of symposiasts in Acragas, Sicily, became so drunk as to believe that they were in fact aboard a ship in a storm and as a result became panicked, throwing furniture 'overboard' in order to lighten 'the ship', as well as some of them hiding under 'rowing benches'. Afterwards the house became known as the 'Trireme' because of this curious incident.⁵⁷ Two items of Attic black-figure pottery dated to the third quarter of the sixth century found on Thera also show a connection between drinking and the sea. One, a *krater*, has four ships painted alongside the inside rim sailing on a sea, with the added effect that when the *krater*

---

51 Nesiotic: of islands. Constantakopoulou (2007): 58; for discussion on the site's activity and its place as a religious network, Constantakopoulou (2007): 38–58.
52 Hom. Hym. Dion. 1–9.
53 Hom. Hym. Dion. 17–24.
54 Hom. Hym. Dion.51–3. See also Apollodorus *Library*, 3.337.
55 Beaulieu (2016): 172–3. Beaulieu (2016: 145–66) also devotes an entire chapter to diving into the sea and metamorphosis.
56 Beaulieu (2016): 173–7, esp. notes 26–36 for further details and descriptions of the pottery. The ANU Classics museum holds in its collection an Attic black figure *skyphos* from the third quarter of the sixth century which depicts eight leaping dolphins on either side of the cup. ANU Classic Museum, Item 76.10.
57 FGrH 566 F 149; Ath. 2.37b-d.

was filled they would appear to be floating on a sea of wine. Similarly, a rather large band cup has six ships with individually detailed helmsmen sailing alongside the inside rim (See Figure 3). In the centre of the cup is a scene of Poseidon fighting the giant Polybotes. Euripides in *Alcestis* has Heracles tell a servant to drink and be happy and uses a metaphor involving the drinker and the sweep of oars in the cup moving him from one anchorage to another.[58] Finally, much like the pirates who captured him, Dionysus is at one time forced to dive into the sea. In the *Iliad*, Diomedes relates the story of how Lycurgus harassed and threatened Dionysus and forced him to dive into the sea, where he is embraced by Thetis rather than turned into a dolphin,[59] giving Dionysus an early literary connection to the sea.

Figure 3: Theran band cup.[60]

Stories of Dionysus and the sea were also important on a local level. The town of Brasiae in Laconia had a story that Cadmus had put Semele and Dionysus into a chest and cast it into the sea, to eventually wash ashore in their territory.[61] In Athens the Dionysia was a great festival with a strong connection to sailing, especially in the fact that it coincided with the abating of winter weather conditions at sea and an increase in overseas trade. More than just the timing, there were other elements connecting the festival to the sea. There are pottery examples that portray Dionysus and Satyrs riding wagons fitted out like ships, and it is likely that ship-like wagons were used during the parade in the Dionysia, just as they

---

58 Eur. *Alc.* 798. A metaphor which could be said to be 'rowing for Dionysus': Beaulieu (2016): 181. For more on drinking/rowing and cups, see Davies (1978): 72–90.
59 Hom. *Il.* 6.130–37.
60 Held in the Archaeological Museum of Thera, author's photograph.
61 Paus. 3.24.3–4.

were used during the Panathenaic festival.[62] These disparate stories, practices, and visual motifs about Dionysus and the sea at the very least demonstrate that the sea could be found in the lives of those with no obvious connections to the maritime realm, including gods. It is in these less well-known and local stories that we glimpse the all-pervasive nature of the maritime realm in Greek life.

Tragedy

The sea features commonly in tragedy, both in theme and in language. Of importance is the fact that a tragedy was a performance watched by many and was not just for the literate or privileged: it had a wide audience. The main drawback is obvious in that these are primarily Athenian tragedies for an Athenian audience, although *The Persians* was produced in Syracuse.[63] That such a naval-themed play would be staged in the city of Sicily's greatest sea power is noteworthy. An examination of the tragedies helps to expose a maritime consciousness deeply ingrained within Athens and Athenian society, and the audience of Athenian tragedy expanded with time, and the genre was no doubt influential in shaping wider views of particular mythic stories. Plutarch in his *Life of Theseus* had some choice words on the effects of 'Athenian chauvinism' in the case of Minos, whom he saw as much maligned by the Athenians, saying:

> It is undoubtedly dangerous to incur the wrath of a city which has a tradition of speech and song. Minos always ended up spoken ill of, abused even, in Attic theatres, with no help coming to him from Hesiod, who called him 'most royal', or Homer, who designated him 'trusted friend of Zeus'. The tragedians overruled them and showered down insults from the stage, making him a violent, cruel character.[64]

This is important in examining the multiplicity of mythic stories in ancient Greece,[65] but also in its acknowledgement that Athenian tragedy seems to have had more influence on wider Greece than may be imagined.

The ways in which the sea and maritime concerns are portrayed in tragedies range from the overt to the subtle. The most obvious is Aeschylus' *Persians*, dealing with the battle of Salamis. The interpretation of the play is contentious. The

---

62 See Csapo (2012): 37–9; and Csapo 2013 and 2015 lectures, including to the Friends of the Australian Archaeological Institute in Athens (AAIA), presented in Canberra 2015 and based off his Houseman Lecture at UCL, 20 February 2013. Wachsmann (2012): 237–66.
63 There are of course exceptions. See Garvie (2009): liii–lvii; See also Smith (2017): 7–53.
64 Plut. *Thes.* 16.3. Translation: Hawes (2014): 162.
65 Tragedies often acting as a foil to Plutarch's preferred rationalisations. See Hawes (2014): 162–3.

two opposing sides were viewing the play as either traditionally 'tragic' or alternatively as akin to triumphalist victory propaganda. The first view seems more reasonable, as it is a tragedy that fits the conventions of others. That the play is concerned with foreigners is not far removed from other Athenian tragedies, where the action takes place in locations other than Athens – think of the Oedipus story, set in Thebes, or the many Trojan War stories set far away. The Persians in Aeschylus' play might be an Athenian projection, but it is not so different from the Thebes of Athenian tragedy, for instance: a creation of the Athenian stage. While there is admonishment of the foolishness of Xerxes in the play, it comes not from the Greeks but from other Persians, and indeed not a single Greek is mentioned by name in the play, hardly in keeping with the view that the play is glorifying the Greek victory. This is not to say that *Persians* does not allude to Athenian victory – the obvious counterpart to Persian defeat – or that it does not seek to remind the Athenians that they defeated the most feared power of the time but to illustrate that the play cannot be reduced to a single interpretation and that tragedies in general were not so simple in their message and morality.[66] Interestingly, many in the audience, not to mention the playwright Aeschylus himself, would have had a direct experience of the battle, as combatants or as civilians whose future rested on the outcome, a mere 8 years before the play was staged.[67] This context is of great importance when examining what is said in the play, especially regarding Athens' maritime character.

The play puts precedence on Salamis as the victory that destroyed the Persians, all but overlooking the battle of Plataea. The messenger's speech opens with the lament that Persia, harbour of great wealth, has been destroyed in a single blow.[68] The chorus later says that the 'sea-washed isle of Ajax holds the power of Persia'.[69] The disaster is such that Persian defeat at sea is the doom of the land army, when the queen tells the ghost of Darius that 'The naval force was ruined, and that doomed the land army to destruction'. Darius' response is even more telling, for he asks if the army was destroyed by the spear, clearly thinking the army has been physically destroyed by war.[70] Without naval support the army could not triumph, and defeat at sea has thus caused the defeat of the entire expedition. Indeed, at the end of the play the chorus laments, cataloguing all the vast empire and wealth controlled by Darius, giving a brief geographic survey of all the lands and islands over which Persia held sway and finishes by saying that it

---

66 For a detailed discussion, see Garvie (2009): xvi-xxxii and Kyriakou (2011): 17–35.
67 Kyriakou (2011): 17.
68 Literally a harbour: λιμήν. Aesc. *Per*. 250–2.
69 Aesc. *Per*. 596–7.
70 Aesc. *Per*. 729. Garvie (2009): 289.

all was in jeopardy because of mighty blows struck at sea.[71] The prominence of the maritime world is heavily emphasised throughout the play. This could reflect Athens' maritime character at the time of the battle, or the play itself could be a solidification of this view of Athens. In either case, Athens' place in the Persian Wars takes on a distinctly maritime characteristic from early on.

The language of tragedy often evokes the sea and ships, especially in the form of metaphor. Perhaps the most well-known is that of the 'ship of state', which has an epic antecedent in Pindar, who closes *Pythian 10* with the phrase 'the diligent steering of states' in referring to a city's ruling lineage.[72] The steering metaphor is also expanded upon and used to refer to the steering of one's spirit in Bacchylides' *Ode 17*.[73] Pindar and Bacchylides are both early examples of this metaphor usage, picked up by the tragedians, and help demonstrate a view of the world in which the maritime related to the mundane. The steering of the ship of state is evocatively invoked by Eteocles in the second line of Aeschylus' *Seven Against Thebes*, where he talks of steering the city from the stern. Aeschylus' *Seven* is rife with other nautical imagery, and the land-locked city of Thebes is portrayed as a ship beset by waves and storms in the form of the Argive army.[74] Sophocles in *Antigone* makes constant use of nautical metaphor, especially in terms of Creon and steering the ship of state, by Creon himself and by Tiresias when referring to Creon's rule.[75] Nautical language and metaphor were thus rife in tragedy and provide useful insight into how the maritime world and maritime considerations played on the minds of the Greeks in a popular medium.[76] Nautical imagery was powerfully evocative and eminently relatable to the Greeks. Even tragedies set in land-locked cities and concerned with sieges and their aftermath could be related in terms of the sea and sailing. While no doubt such metaphor is used almost ad nauseum by today's politicians, it is useful to remember the origins of such language, at a time when the users of it were far more connected to the inspiration for it.

---

71 Aesc. *Per.* 852–906. For a comprehensive commentary on this episode, see Garvie (2009): 325–36.
72 Pind. *Pyth.* 10.73. Beaulieu (2016): 69.
73 Bacchyl. 21–23.
74 For further discussion, see Kirkwood (1969): esp. 19–22; Pritchard (1999): 171.
75 Soph. *Ant.* 188–90, 994.
76 For a more thorough survey of the topic, see Pritchard (1999): 163–95. For a survey of political imagery: Brock (2013).

Comedy

Much as with tragedy, comedy can be used to explore how the maritime world pervaded contemporary Athenian life, though perhaps more than tragedy a uniquely Athenian context. The comedies of Aristophanes in particular are of great utility, especially when considering how highly reflective of Athenian life they are.[77] The comedies reflect many different aspects, ranging from everyday life to issues related directly to contemporary events, most notably the Peloponnesian War. The language of the plays includes a rich variety of nautical imagery,[78] and maritime issues and nautical references are found throughout Old Comedy.

There are many overt references to contemporary events in Athens which characterise the city as a sea power. In response to the question of their origins, two Athenians in *Birds* respond, 'from where the fine triremes come from'.[79] Aristophanes' first extant play, *Akharnians*, deals with the Peloponnesian War and the issue of Athenian war strategy, especially Pericles' maritime approach. Dicaiopolis bemoans the money spent on Thracian mercenaries and says that the rowers 'who save the city' would be unhappy to hear of the expense.[80] When offered a 5-year peace, Dicaiopolis says that it smells of 'pitch and warship construction', and later on in the discussion of the Megarian decree and causes of the war, the Athenian response and preparations are described in terms of sending out 300 ships and other naval preparations.[81] The number of 300 ships must have been comic exaggeration, but what it illustrates is that the default Athenian response is to send out ships.[82] Further, when the chorus goes on praising the poet

---

[77] The issue of using Old Comedy as evidence for popular Athenian culture in the fifth century has been a topic of debate, most notably with G.E.M. de Ste. Croix's contention that Aristophanes' views represented that of the elite ('The political outlook of Aristophanes': 1972: 355–76). Influential for many years, this view no longer seems tenable, and scholars such as Keith Sidwell and David Pritchard view comedy as being of great value for providing insight into popular Athenian culture. See Sidwell (2009); Pritchard (2012): 14–51.

[78] Space again precludes a thorough examination, but a few examples to illustrate the point: ship of state metaphor *Assemblywomen* 109; *Wasps* 29 (with nautical pun afterwards); a helmet and its ear-holes as 'oarports' *Peace* 1232, 1234; 'rowing two boats with one oar' *Assemblywomen* 1091; 'back-water' or 'reverse oars' *Wasps* 399, *Birds* 648; a character's name in the play *Women at the Thesmophoria*, Nausimache, 'victory at sea', 804; a character like a warship in dangerous waters, and other sailing metaphors, *Akharnians* 95–7.

[79] Ar. *Av.* 107.

[80] Ar. *Ach.* 162–3.

[81] Ar. *Ach.* 190, 535–56.

[82] MacDowell sees suitable comic expression in this passage but nothing that is inconsistent with Thucydides' account of the issue. MacDowell (1995): 66.

of the play, they say that the Persian king, when deciding which side to support, asks whom the poet has abused, but firstly which side has more ships.[83] Finally, when the chorus leader complains about how he and the other old men of the city have been treated, he says that their treatment is unworthy of the sea-battles they have fought.[84]

Aristophanes was an astute observer of naval and maritime affairs and was able to discuss sea power with an audience in ways that resonated. He clearly understood the critical link between wealth and sea power and how they functioned in a feedback loop – wealth enabling sea power which in turn allowed for more wealth. The Cleon of *Knights* is always asking for swift ships to collect revenue.[85] The chorus of *Wasps* are explicit in their opinion of what made Athens great and rich: their generation, whose skill and power at sea elicited fear in Athens' enemies, defeated the Medes and was responsible for the riches flowing to Athens for the younger generations to steal.[86] It is the same wealth that also enabled Athenian sea power. Chremylos asks the god Wealth the rhetorical question of whether or not it was he who filled the triremes, and the Spartan Lampito tells the Athenian Lysistrata that Athens would not give up the war so long as they had triremes and money in their treasury.[87] Athenian reach was strong thanks to its sea power, with a character in *Birds* saying that they could not live anywhere near the sea, for they would wake up one day to see the Athenian dispatch trireme *Salaminia* waiting to summon them.[88]

It was not enough that Aristophanes recognised and discussed sea power and its enablers and uses, for he gave explicit advice as to Athens' best course of action in the war. In *Peace* he has Hermes tell the Athenians that if they truly want to bring Peace forward, they should move towards the sea.[89] In *Frogs* Aristophanes has the most hallowed of Athenian playwrights, Aeschylus, give the Athenian polis strategic advice to not worry about the Spartan occupation of Decelea but to consider Spartan territory their own, their ships as wealth, and wealth as poverty.[90] He is telling the Athenians that their fleet *is* their wealth and their power, providing the ability to strike the Spartans in their own territory more

---

[83] Ar. *Ach.* 649.
[84] Ar. *Ach.* 677–8.
[85] Ar. Eq. 1070–1. It is followed in the next line by a pun/joke on foxes and triremes being swift, further illustrating the use of maritime language throughout Aristophanes.
[86] Ar. *Vesp.* 1091–100.
[87] Ar. *Plut.* 172; *Lys.* 173–4.
[88] Ar. *Av.* 145–7.
[89] Ar. *Pac.* 506–7.
[90] Ar. *Ran.* 1463–5.

than the Spartans can theirs, and that money not spent was essentially useless and thus akin to poverty. He is in essence echoing Periclean war strategy at the beginning of the war.[91] Aristophanes not only appreciated the maritime realm but explicitly gave the Athenians advice that they should embrace their sea power.

Finally, there is the curious example of Theophrastus' *Characters*, a work that is hard to place in any specific genre, although possibly qualifying as in the comic realm.[92] Much like the comic plays, maritime aspects are often incidental to the main story being told, which means that these aspects are grounded in reality and not just an exaggeration to make a point. The setting of *Characters* is anything but timeless or idealising and is unmistakeably the last few decades of the fourth century BCE in Athens with the customs, institutions, and prejudices that formed the backdrop of the characters in the work.[93] The maritime aspects of the work cover both peace and war, the important and the mundane. The 'boorish man' goes to the market to buy preserved fish, and the 'shameless man' also goes to the market for fresh or preserved fish, a subtle reference but clear in highlighting the different kinds of fish sold in Athens.[94] Overseas trade is an everpresent concern, both in terms of trade goods and Athenians engaged in trade. The 'Idle-chatterer' discusses the sea-lanes being open, and one of the other characters lists numerous different trade goods, including 'Sicilian pigeons, and dice made from gazelle horns, and oil flasks from Thourioi of the rounded sort, and walking sticks from Sparta of the twisted sort'.[95] Interestingly, he talks of this character engaged in the transhipment of goods from around Greece and the Aegean: 'but for foreigners he buys letters of commission for Byzantium, and Laconian dogs for Cyzicus, and Hymettos honey for Rhodes, and as he does so he tells everybody in town about it'.[96] The man with petty ambition ensures he has an Ethiopian attendant and a Maltese dog.[97] The 'fraudulent' man stands on the breakwater and brags to strangers about how much money he has invested in shipping and talks of how he turned down an offer to export timber duty-free

---

91 MacDowell's conclusion, hard to argue with. MacDowell (1995): 296. For more on Pericles' war strategy, see Chapter Seven.
92 There is no example of virtue in the work, which follows Theophrastus' mentor Aristotle's thought that comedy depicted people who were not to be taken seriously. *Poet.* 1149a32. Rusten (2003): 21. For an excellent recent work on *Characters*, see Pertsinidis (2018).
93 Rusten (2003): 9. On the dating of the work to circa 319 BC, see Boegehold (1959): 15–19; Rusten (2003): 10–11.
94 Theophr. *Char.* 4.15, 6.9.
95 Theophr. *Char.* 3.3, 5.9. Translation Rusten (2003).
96 Theophr. *Char.* 5.8. Translation Rusten (2003).
97 Theophr. *Char.* 21.4, 9.

from Macedonia.[98] Travel is also evident in the different characters, with the man of 'bad taste' delaying people who are about to set sail.[99]

War and naval matters get an airing in the different characters as well. The 'rumour-monger' discusses people who have won battles by land and sea.[100] The 'ungenerous' man is so because he takes the bedding of his helmsman while he serves as trierarch, and he declines to discuss all of the warships that he has paid for, while the 'authoritarian' man complains about the burden of the trierarchy.[101] Finally, there is the coward who when at sea is frightened by cliffs, thinking them to be pirate ships. He even goes so far as to take off his clothes, so that he is better prepared to swim, and begs to be put ashore.[102] This is telling in several respects. It suggests that those frightened of sailing could be considered cowardly, and that swimming was something most Greeks could do. The passage merely says he takes off his shirt and hands it to his slave with the assumption that this will make it easier to swim. It is worth noting that the nature of this work suggests perhaps comic over-exaggeration. Piracy was probably a legitimate concern, but not as much as the character portrayed would suggest; he is after all a cowardly character and the fear he displays is then by definition unwarranted and unreasonable: suitable for mockery. It is a fascinating insight into what one Athenian thought the city would find humorous about themselves.

History and philosophy

It was not just on stage or in the stories of myth that the sea and maritime issues pervaded the consciousness of the Greeks. Politicians, philosophers, and historians also had much to say on the subject in their speeches and writings. Just as the dramatic and mythic works show a culture steeped in maritime tradition, so too do the works of historians and politicians reveal the everyday workings of sea power in Greek thought and action. The great chronicler Thucydides entwines so much of his thinking and analysis within his narrative, and so his views on sea power will appear in later chapters along with the other historians.

---

98 Theophr. *Char.* 23.2, 4.
99 Theophr. *Char.* 20.3.
100 Theophr. *Char.* 8.11.
101 Theophr. *Char.* 22.5, 23.6, 26.6.
102 Theophr. *Char.* 25.2.

Herodotus, Xenophon, and Diodorus

Herodotus is interested in the seas themselves and in describing different maritime areas to his audience. He describes the Caspian Sea, firstly giving a geography lesson on how it is a self-contained sea and does not connect to the Mediterranean. He mentions that the Mediterranean is connected to the Erythraian (Red) and Atlantic Seas and that in fact these all constitute a single sea.[103] He then goes back to the Caspian Sea and gives the sailing times for crossing it, both north-south and east-west at the widest point.[104] He briefly describes the dimensions of Erythraian Sea and makes specific mention of the fact that the level of the sea rises and falls every day.[105] This contrasts with the virtually tideless Mediterranean, and the fact that he leaves this unspoken indicates that the reader will grasp this difference between them. He also gives details on the dimension of the Pontus, Bosporus, Propontis, and Hellespont,[106] a region of increasing importance to the Greeks and especially the Athenians as the fifth century progressed. Of great importance, Herodotus has much to say about sea power and how it affected the great conflict of his time, the Persian Wars, which we will encounter in the next two chapters.

Xenophon is not often credited with possessing great interest in the sea or sea power; however, it does play a part in his narratives, and he does pay close attention to the impact of sea power in his histories and in his other works. A surprising amount of detail can be revealed from Xenophon's works other than his history, including the *Oeconomicus*. Although it is a work concerned with household management and agriculture, ships and the sea appear throughout.[107] In discussing the proper ordering of a household, he uses a trireme as an example: a frightening sight to enemies and a pleasant one to allies because of its swiftness, a swiftness made possible because the men do not get in each other's way since they are so well-ordered.[108] Continuing with the ship theme, the speaker says that the best arrangement of equipment he ever saw was a Phoenician merchant ship, and he proceeds to describe how well-ordered the ship was and lecture his wife on the

---
103 Hdt. 1.202.4 He refers to the Mediterranean as 'the one which is navigated by the Hellenes'. It is worth noting that to the Greeks the Erythraian Sea included what we today consider the Red Sea and the entire Indian Ocean.
104 Hdt. 1.203.1. 15 and 8 days, respectively, in a sailing ship with oars.
105 Hdt. 2.11.1–2.
106 Hdt. 4.85–6.
107 Some would argue that it is not in fact a simple work on the topic but a philosophical dialogue. Gabriel Danzig sees it as almost an apology of Socrates' and Xenophon's way of life, saying 'In a sense, then, the *Oeconomicus* is both Xenophon's parting words about Socrates, and Socrates' parting words about Xenophon'. Danzig (2003): 57–76.
108 Xen. *Oec.* 8.8.

subject.¹⁰⁹ The merits of order are once again discussed with reference to a trireme, where the speaker illustrates the point that a well-ordered crew not only sails to its destination faster but also does not suffer poor morale.¹¹⁰ That Xenophon uses such nautical imagery shows that his audience, non-Athenians, non-philosophers, and perhaps even women,¹¹¹ readily related with such imagery. It is a small, subtle, and yet vital glimpse of a society, not just Athenian, that could relate on an everyday level with maritime issues.

Xenophon's *Poroi* ('On revenues', or, 'ways and means') has much to say on maritime matters, particularly with regard to maritime trade and the economy. Xenophon calls the seas around the Attic coast no less productive than the land – an important point about the productivity of the sea in feeding Athens, and even more salient coming from an upper-class figure such as Xenophon.¹¹² Like Thucydides and the Old Oligarch before him, Xenophon compares Athens to an island, saying that although Athens is not surrounded by sea it enjoys the benefits of being like an island.¹¹³ However, as Philippe Gauthier astutely points out in his commentary, Xenophon is referring only to the commercial benefits of being like an island, not the military ones as discussed by previous ancient authors.¹¹⁴ Clearly, the 'Athens as an island' metaphor could be used both in a commercial and a military context, well into the fourth century.¹¹⁵ Xenophon deals heavily with issues of commerce and maritime trade in particular. He discusses Athens' fine shipping facilities, the importance of magistrates not delaying the sailings of ships, and the importance of peace for the city's prosperity, especially with relation to the growth of maritime trade.¹¹⁶ Perhaps most interesting of all is his, seemingly original, suggestion that Athens take a cue from its state-owned warship fleet and invest in a state-owned merchant ship fleet.¹¹⁷ It is a controversial

---

109 Xen. *Oec.* 8.11–23.
110 Xen. *Oec.* 21.3.
111 Pomeroy is reasonable in seeing the audience as international in character, considering the career of Xenophon and the nature of the work on a universal topic (estate management). On women as an audience, the wife of the speaker Ischomachos appears to have been literate (9.10), and Pomeroy (1994: 9–10) does not seem to be making too much of a leap in suggesting women may have read a treatise on estate management.
112 Xen. *Poroi.* 1.3. The abbreviation for this work in the *Oxford Classical Dictionary* is the Latin 'Vect.' but I prefer the original Greek.
113 Xen. *Poroi.* 1.7.
114 Gauthier (1976): 51, i.e. Thuc. 1.143.5; Old Oligarch 2.15.
115 If one dates the *Poroi* to 355/4 as Gauthier (1976: 1) does.
116 Xen *Poroi.* 3.2, 3.3, 5.1–5, 5.12.
117 Xen. *Poroi.* 3.14; Gauthier (1976): 107.

idea, in modern scholarship at least,[118] but the idea certainly had merit, especially for a state as dependent on overseas trade as Athens. This would have entailed an entirely new enterprise but perhaps could have used a model like the trierarchy for funding and crewing of such a fleet. At the same time, this may have taken resources away from the all-important trierarchy, and no doubt the prospect of leading a state-sanctioned, and potentially lucrative, trading mission would have caused more problems than it fixed. Nevertheless, in his *Poroi*, Xenophon demonstrates a keen interest in the sea and in maritime affairs.

Perhaps Xenophon's most famous work, the *Anabasis*, has an important point to make about the Greek army and the sea. To the Greek army the sea was seen as safety. The goal of the retreating army was to reach the sea, encapsulated by the most famous of cries when they finally arrive there: 'the sea, the sea!' Xenophon provides his audience with an evocative scene, with the generals and other leaders embracing and weeping at the very sight of the sea.[119] They were so comfortable with their situation that they dismissed their guide and lavished him with gifts.[120] So confident were the Greeks in their safety that it was enough to merely reach the sea. Finally, when confronted by a local group, the Macronians, the Greek reassured them that they meant no harm to them but only wanted to get to the sea.[121] To the Greeks the sea represented safety and the promise of returning home. Of note is that the Ten Thousand was a mixed force of Greeks. They were not just Athenians and islanders but Greeks from a variety of poleis, including Sparta. Here is a glimpse of a maritime consciousness that extended beyond Athens and the other well-known maritime poleis and pervaded a mixed force of soldiers.

Finally, a note on the later historian Diodorus Siculus. Diodorus as a source once provoked strong, usually negative, opinions amongst classical scholars, although this view has thankfully changed in recent years.[122] As far as his history is concerned with respect to naval and maritime matters, he is an important source, especially for events in Sicily during the fifth and fourth centuries when Syracuse and Carthage were engaged in constant warfare, often at sea. Importantly, that Ephorus was one of Diodorus' main sources is of great benefit. The harsh critic of historians, Polybius wrote that Ephorus possessed sound knowledge of naval war-

---

118 'Naïve' in the words of Cawkwell (1963): 64; unnecessary and impractical in the view of G.E.M. de Ste. Croix (1972): 393–6. See also Gauthier (1976): 107–8.
119 Xen. *Anab.* 4.7.25.
120 Xen. *Anab.* 4.7.27.
121 Xen. *Anab.* 4.8.6–7.
122 For a survey of these criticisms, and a hearty rebuttal, see Green (2006): 1–47.

fare and was a useful source for it.¹²³ This helps give Diodorus added weight as a historian of maritime affairs during the period.

Dissenting voices

Aside from the unknown author known as the 'Old Oligarch' (see Chapter Six), there were others who did not view sea power in a positive light. These views are important in highlighting the extent to which sea power was taken for granted in Athens by those who opposed its prominence. Perhaps the most obvious and vehement example of those who did not favour sea power is Plato. Indeed, Plato created an entire myth – that of 'Atlantis' – in order to make his point, not to mention inspire an entire line of pseudo-mythological examinations that inspired everyone from Nazis to treasure hunters.[124] Let there be no mistake – Atlantis is nothing more than an imaginative fiction created by Plato to extol the evils of sea power and the superiority of the landed aristocracy and showcase the superior form of city as envisioned by his most famous work, *The Republic*. Much like Plato's famous cave, Atlantis can be found only in the minds of those who hear the story.

Plato uses two dialogues to create his Atlantis myth, *Timaeus* and *Critias*. It is done by presenting two mythic ideals of Athens. The first is 'Atlantis', the historical Athens of the fifth century, a city that controls a maritime empire in the form of the Delian League, and at the time of writing seemingly on the rise again with the Second Athenian League in the fourth century. The second ideal presented is the titular Athens of the two dialogues, bearing more than just a coincidental resemblance to Plato's ideal polis of the *Republic*.

The primary storyteller in both dialogues is Critias, in which the titular dialogue contains the most detailed account of the Atlantis myth. As leader of the Thirty Tyrants in Athens, Critias' opposition to democracy, and by extension the navy, makes it clear that he will not be speaking in its favour. According to Plutarch, Critias and the Thirty went so far as to have the bema of the Pnyx, which faced the sea, reoriented to face inland – such were the steps they would take to distance themselves from the sea and all things maritime.[125] The choice of speaker in this dialogue is thus of critical importance.

---

123 Polyb. 12.25 f. Though he considered Ephorus a poor source for land battles, going so far as to say he provoked laughter on the matter. Poly. 12.25 f.
124 For a more thorough exploration of the myth, including into modern times, see Vidal-Naquet (2007).
125 Plut. *Them.* 19.6. Though of course this meant that the audience would be facing the sea.

Athens in Plato's story represents his ideal state of the *Republic*.[126] 'Athens' is guarded by a military class who lived apart, the 'guardians' of the ideal state who required freedom from other tasks and lived apart in a separate camp.[127] The guardians of Athens are armed with spear and shield, gifts from the Goddess, presumably Athena.[128] The land of his Athens, unlike the one in which he actually lives, surpasses all other lands in the excellence of its soil. It is a land rich in trees and pasturage as well as fresh water in springs and fountains.[129] Finally, they have no need for gold or silver, much like in the *Republic*, where the only gold and silver is that of the divine, ever in their souls.[130] Plato is however aware of the fact that the sea is tempting and powerful, hence his siting of the ideal polis at least 80 *stades* away from the sea.[131] Indeed, the occupants of the *Republic* would not even deign to eat seafood – the heroes of Homer may have campaigned next to the Hellespont but did not stoop to the level of eating fish, according to him at least.[132] However, these guardians of Plato's protect not only Athens but all of Greece.[133] Indeed, it is Athens, standing alone and abandoned by all others, that defeats Atlantis and sets free those living within the boundary of the pillars of Heracles.[134] For Plato it was of course the battle of Marathon that stood out as Athens' finest moment, when Athens and its farmer-hoplites defeated a great foreign enemy and saved Greece. Marathon and Plataea bookend the salvation of Greece, while the naval battles of Artemision and Salamis made the Greeks worse.[135]

By contrast, the Atlantis of the myth represents Athens of the fifth century at the height of the Delian League – the actual historical city of this tale. The land was taken as an allotment by Poseidon when the gods were dividing the earth, but not as a result of strife – a direct contradiction to Plato's own earlier story – and neatly excising the story that the sea god Poseidon was once ever in a posi-

---

126 The city of the *Republic* is 'brought to life' in the Timaeus and Critias in the words of Nicole Loraux (2006): 370.
127 Plat. *Ti.* 24b; *Crit.* 110c; *Resp.* 374e, 415d,e.
128 Plat. *Ti.* 24b.
129 Plat. *Ti.* 110e, 111c-d.
130 Plat. *Crit.* 112c; *Resp.* 416e. See also *Laws* (*Leg.* 801b) where no wealth of silver and gold should exist within the state.
131 Pl. *Laws* 704a. Momigliano (1944): 5.
132 *Resp.* 372; 404c. The speaker mentions Homer but no specific passage. This privileging of cereals and meat over fish is prevalent in literature, especially comedy. See Wilkins (2000) and Wilkins (2006): 21–30.
133 Plat. *Crit.* 112d.
134 Plat. *Ti.* 25c.
135 Plat. *Leg.* 707c.

tion to compete for the status of patron deity of Athens.[136] This is to go even further than those in Athens who disliked sea power and merely highlighted the victory of Athena over Poseidon.[137] Plato reaches the stage of casting Poseidon out of Athens and Athenian history altogether.

Atlantis is also a rich city, but in a decadent sense. It has a hot and a cold spring, and the land produces food in plenty.[138] It is a city that possesses wealth so vast it has never been seen before or after that time, and these riches include many imports from overseas.[139] It has an Acropolis but with a temple sacred to Poseidon and ornately adorned with gold, silver, and 'orichalcum'.[140] The most obvious allusion to Athens follows, where he describes the shipyards full of triremes.[141] Considering this Atlantis existed 8,000 years before Plato tells the story, these clearly could not have been triremes, and Plato is using the famous symbol of Athenian power as a not-so subtle signal. Atlantis has a strongly walled outer harbour that is filled with ships and merchants from all over, causing clamour day and night.[142] Finally, it is said to have enough men to man 1,200 ships.[143]

That the Athens and Atlantis of Plato's myth represent two different forms of Athens – one historical and one idealised – is not a revelation.[144] In examining the myth, it shows the extent to which Plato and other opponents of sea power had to go in order to combat a well-entrenched fact of life in Athens: it had been for a century, and remained in his day, a strong sea power. So deeply ingrained is the maritime character of Athens that Plato felt that he must change the historical and mythological past. It is for this reason that the myth of Atlantis comes via the most hallowed of Athenian lawgivers and wise men: Solon.[145] In this, 'Plato's Solon wished to turn the myth of Atlantis into poetry that would rival the heroic and didactic of Homer and Hesiod'.[146] The authority of Solon, as cited by Plato's Critias, is of critical importance to the authenticity and authority of his story.[147] So too must he cite Homer in the *Laws* in order to highlight how ships induce

---

[136] Plat. *Crit.* 113c; *Menex.* 237c-d.
[137] For instance, as the old kings of Athens supposedly did. Plut. *Them.* 19.3; Frost (1980): 177.
[138] *Plat. Crit.* 113e.
[139] Plat. *Crit.* 114d.
[140] Plat. *Crit.* 114d. Orichalcum being an alloy of copper and zinc and a valuable metal at this time.
[141] Plat. *Crit.* 117d.
[142] Plat. *Crit.* 117e.
[143] Plat. *Crit.* 119b.
[144] Vidal-Naquet (1964): 420–44; Morgan (1998): 114.
[145] Pl. *Ti.* 20e–21d; *Criti.* 108d.
[146] Morgan (1998): 109.
[147] Morgan (1998): 112.

men to cowardice in giving them a means to escape danger.[148] Plato must invoke the authority of Athens' lawgiver *par excellence* and the greatest poet of the age in order to begin the fight against a history and a reality which was deeply maritime in character. The great irony of all this is that Plato in his musings in the dialogue *Phaedo* gives us the evocative image of the Greeks living around the Mediterranean 'like ants or frogs around a pond'.[149] In the end not even Plato could escape the maritime geography that shaped his world.

Plato's student Aristotle had more mature and practical views on sea power, though he was no fan of the 'naval mob'. Aristotle saw sea power as not only useful for a state but also necessary for one seeking power and influence.[150] His city would be well-placed with due consideration to the land and the country.[151] A state with access to the sea was much better off defensively: land power was fine but stronger when combined with sea power. He even encouraged the state to use the sea for commerce, importing commodities lacked by the state and exporting excess goods.[152] Finally, he considered naval force necessary for a polis to engage properly in international affairs and to gain any hegemony.[153]

Aristotle did however have his teacher's disdain for mixing with foreigners and traders and for those whose profession related to the sea. Too much contact with foreigners and people raised under different systems was harmful to the state.[154] He would mitigate against this by ensuring a healthy distance between the city and its port and the proper regulation of citizens' contact with the port.[155] He saw no need for his navy to be manned by citizens, and the hoplite infantry would go aboard as marines in command of the vessels and crews,[156] assuming their 'natural' place above the naval mob. So while he had the typical aristocratic disdain for maritime matters and those lowly people who were associated with the sea, he nevertheless saw the utility of sea power, not just as a defensive and offensive military force, but also for maritime trade and communications.

Finally there is Isocrates, rival of Plato, but who also took a dim view of sea power and was deeply critical of both Athens' and Sparta's maritime adventures.

---

148 Pl. *Laws* 706 d–7a. The passage he quotes from Homer refers to Odysseus admonishing Agamemnon for suggesting they bring up their ships and retreat in the face of the attacking Trojans. *Il.* 14.96–102.
149 Plat. *Phae.* 109b.
150 Ober (1978): 124, n. 32.
151 Arist. *Pol.* 7.5.2.
152 Arist. *Pol.* 7.5.3.
153 Arist. *Pol.* 7.5.7.
154 Arist. *Pol.* 7.5.3.
155 Arist. *Pol.* 7.5.5.
156 Arist. *Pol.* 7.5.7.

However, Isocrates' criticisms of sea power fundamentally differ from those of Plato. As discussed, Plato saw sea power and maritime matters as fundamentally corrupting of the state. Isocrates appears to have disliked sea power because of its effectiveness: so powerful as to corrupt those who wielded it.

Isocrates fully acknowledges how sea power had been a decisive factor in Greek history. He tells of Athens' glorious history, when they justly held the rule of the sea,[157] thus implying that rule of the sea could be a just and worthy thing. He credits Athens with saving Greece three times, not only from the Persians at Marathon and Salamis but also from the Spartans at sea at Cnidos in 394. Indeed, he echoes Herodotus by saying no one is so prejudiced against Athens as to deny the fact that they saved Greece through their instrumental role in victory at Salamis.[158] Beyond just military triumph over an invader, Athenian sea power led to the Piraeus being established as a market at the centre of Greece, where things which were difficult to find in other cities could be found with ease.[159] This sentiment is a familiar one, spoken by Pericles in Thucydides' funeral oration where the great politician speaks of the greatness of Athens where goods flow from all over the world, and is repeated in the work of the 'Old Oligarch'.[160] He even laments the absence of the merchants, foreigners, and metics – or at least the revenue they generated – who were absent from the city because of the Social War. This is a far cry from the noisome port of Athens/Atlantis in Plato's myth.

Nevertheless, the use of sea power bothered Isocrates greatly, and in his mind it appeared to be a corrupting force. He has a litany of complaints, and pines for the 'good old days' when citizens fought as hoplites and the fleet was rowed by others, when Athenians could find work in the fleet and not the law courts, and when citizens did not expect payment merely for showing up to military parades.[161] More than just criticising the maritime empire of Athens, he is also deeply critical of Sparta's maritime adventures. The potency of sea power was especially high when combined with supremacy by land, as in the case with Sparta. To Isocrates it seems as if the problem with sea power was not that it was inherently corrupting but that it was too powerful: so powerful that it corrupted. He could say that Athens justly held the rule of the sea, and so it was not a bad thing in itself, but it was how Athens, and then Sparta afterwards, used this power which Isocrates saw as an evil. The opening of his *Areopagiticus* makes it clear that this is his line of thinking. He begins with the rhetorical question of

---

157 Isoc. *Paneg.* 20.
158 Isoc. *Paneg.* 98.
159 Isoc. *Paneg.* 42.
160 See Chapter Six.
161 Isoc. 8.48; 7.54; 7.82. See also Ober (1978): 129.

why he thinks it is necessary to speak of the security of Athens as if there is a danger. There clearly cannot be a danger since Athens possessed more than 200 triremes, enjoyed peace in its territory and ruled the sea, with many allies ready to lend aid and others paying contributions and following orders.[162] The problem as Isocrates sees it is that Athens' soul is in danger by the wealth and power possessed by the city thanks to its maritime empire, for wealth and power produce and are accompanied by foolishness and lack of restraint.[163]

The Spartans too suffered from this, rising from their humble beginnings and becoming arrogant once they gained control of land and sea, an arrogance which saw them lose supremacy of both.[164] He returns to this again in his letter to Philip II of Macedonia, where he takes the well-trodden path of blaming Alcibiades for evils done,[165] and again in *On The Peace*, where he states that the beginning of Sparta's troubles was when they acquired rule of the seas.[166] After discussing the corruption and troubles that befell Athens and Sparta, he asks his audience:

> How can you praise this empire when it has such grievous results? Or how can you not loath and reject something that induces both cities to commit and compels them to suffer so many terrible wrongs?[167]

Sea power was the key enabler of this empire, which led to the fall of both Athens and Sparta, not only a fall from power but a fall from grace as the states themselves were corrupted by the evil they did, not just the evil they suffered. Even the short-term ascendency of Thebes demonstrated this, for having just defeated the Spartans at Leuctra they embarked upon all manner of exploits, including sending triremes to Byzantium with the intent of becoming rulers over land and sea.[168] This demonstrates the Pan-Hellenic nature of the potential and actual corruption.

Sea power in Isocrates' eyes is a powerful force indeed. It is not inherently corrupting but allows for an accumulation of power and wealth that leads to a corruption of the state. Unlike Plato's ideal state, Isocrates' still leaves room for sea power, but as a defensive force protecting Athens and the other Greeks from Persia as they did in the Persian Wars. Otherwise sea power becomes, quite literally in his eyes, tyrannical. He admonishes his audience for listening to him with

---

162 Isoc. 7.1–2.
163 Isoc. 7.4. He brings in the city's soul (*psyche*) a little later in his speech: 7.14.
164 Isoc. 7.7. Momigliano (1944): 4.
165 Isoc. 5.60–1.
166 Isoc. 8.101.
167 Isoc. 8.105. Translated by T.L. Papillon.
168 Isoc. 5.53. See Chapter Ten on the short-lived Theban navy.

tolerance on the subject of tyranny but with intolerance when he speaks about the rule of the sea, despite the fact that the rule of the sea that the Athenians consider the 'greatest good' does not differ from one-man rule.[169] Just as a tyrant had too much power to do good or ill, sea power had too much potential to corrupt. It is the sort of power that led to incidents such as the destruction of Melos in the Peloponnesian War. Indeed, notable students of Isocrates, Theopompos and Ephorus, had differing views of sea power: the former scornful and the latter supportive of it.[170] From this it appears that Isocrates' views on sea power were complex and changeable, as well as being pervasive in the works of later authors.

These dissenting views are important for two reasons. The most obvious is in exploring an alternative, albeit minority, point of view of sea power and maritime matters in Athens. Moreover, they show how deeply ingrained the maritime world was in Athens by highlighting the opposition to it. Plato especially is fighting a losing battle against reality, the reality of an unequivocally maritime Athens. In examining the opponents of sea power like Plato and Isocrates much can be revealed about the character of maritime Athens and to a lesser extent, wider Greece.

Conclusions

This is by no means a comprehensive survey of the sea in Greek myth and culture, a topic deserving of its own work. Rather this chapter has aimed at providing a brief survey while illustrating the fundamental point that the sea and maritime themes and language pervaded the Greek and especially the Athenian consciousness. It shows a level of interest and knowledge of maritime affairs that is greater than just a passing interest or shallow understanding. This is especially true of Athens, where a large portion of the citizen population would have been making regular military and political decisions concerning sea power. This is not to say that these decision makers were all experts in the application of sea power, though some certainly would have had much experience, but to argue that their exposure to the maritime world was significant and that it is proper to think of many if not most of the Greeks as having possessed a maritime consciousness to some degree, small or large.

---

169 Isoc. 8.114–5. See Papillon (2004):160, n. 61.
170 Momigliano (1944): 4.

Chapter Four
The birth of navies – sixth-century Greece

Not strictly the 'Classical period', the sixth century BCE nevertheless saw the birth of the first Greek navies. Navy here is used in the sense of a maritime combatant force controlled by and in some part, if not entirely, financed by the state. Contemporary sources are scanty for this time, though there is some evidence. Importantly, the Greeks of the fifth century and later reached back to this age, and further, when looking for the antecedents of their own sea power. The idea of a thalassocracy – a 'rule by the sea' or perhaps more easily, a 'sea power' – finds its origins in this time. Many of the poleis that feature in this period – Corinth, Aegina, Corcyra, for instance – are discussed in more detail in the final chapter, where I explore the idea of a 'non-hegemonic' sea power. What follows in this chapter is context for the period that follows, the rapid rise of sea power in the fifth century.

We have already seen how the sea and maritime-naval endeavours featured prominently in the great Greek myths. Of these many myths there is of course that of the Cretan King Minos and the Labyrinth of the Minotaur, conquered by the great hero Theseus. However, there is far more to the story than this, and in fact the rule of King Minos is often referred to by later Greeks as the first thalassocracy. As the paradigmatic Athenian hero,[1] Theseus was more than just handy with navigating mazes and slaying beasts and had a close connection to the sea. The stories of Theseus began to take on a more than mythic telling by the Athenians. Theseus supposedly defeated Minos' general Taurus in a naval battle.[2] Although the sea often features prominently in heroic tales, naval battles do not, and so this instance adds a sense of retrospective historicity to this version of the story. It soon became apparent that Theseus is not just a slayer of the Minotaur but in fact a true naval hero. An alternative account related by Plutarch comes from Cleidemos,[3] whose story revolves around naval matters. He says that there was a general Hellenic decree that no 'trireme' could sail out of port with a crew larger than five men, Jason and his Argonauts being the only exception since they were clearing the sea of pirates.[4] That Plutarch does use the word 'trireme' in this passage, which clearly cannot be correct for the time he is discussing, is most likely indicative of just how prominent the trireme was in popular narratives. It

---

1 Hawes (2014): 153.
2 Plut. *Thes.* 19.2.
3 Which Plutarch acknowledges as 'rather peculiar and eccentric' – 19.4; Hawes (2014): 163.
4 Plut. *Thes.* 19.4.

was the quintessential Greek warship of its day, much like 'ship of the line' and 'battleship' became synonymous with big warships in later times, even when describing warships of different sizes and capability. Minos defies the decree by chasing Daedalus to Sicily with his warships, and after Minos' death, his son Deucalion threatens Athens for the return of Daedalus, which causes Theseus to build a fleet in secret and confront and ultimately defeat Deucalion.[5] Indeed, not just Theseus but also his crew members were lauded in Athens after their time. The festival of the Kybernesia was celebrated in honour of Theseus' steersmen Nausithos and Phaiax, who had hero-shrines built for them by Theseus in Phaleron.[6]

Of course, Theseus also rounded out his hero profile and undertook a famous land journey to Athens from Troezen, and as Greta Hawes says of the journey, 'The footprints of Heracles are everywhere'.[7] In this we can see how Theseus' transformation into an Athenian hero required that he gain stronger connections to the sea to reflect an Athenian society increasingly looking towards the sea for its future. Further, we start seeing the idea that a naval battle could have a profound effect on the course of Greek history, at least as far as the Athenians reckoned. It is no doubt a reflection of the time, when myths were becoming more codified, and at the same time as naval battles were becoming more prominent than they had been in the archaic period and earlier.

Herodotus appears as the first writer to explore thalassocracy as a distinct idea in Greek history, an idea later broadened by Thucydides.[8] Both Herodotus and Thucydides catalogue mythic and historical figures who were the first 'thalassocrats'. According to Herodotus, it was Polycrates, tyrant of the island of Samos, who was the first Greek to attempt to rule the sea. He passes over the legendary King Minos and others before who, he suggests, belong to mythical times.[9] This contrasts with the normally less credulous Thucydides, who lists Minos as the first Thalassocrat in history.[10] This is unsurprising given that Thucydides is constantly emphasising the importance of sea power throughout history, and by placing Minos as the first ruler of the sea, he is able to extend the concept of thalassocracy to predate the all-

---

5 Plut. *Thes.* 19.4–6.
6 Plut. *Thes.* 17.6.
7 Hawes (2014): 160.
8 Momigliano (1944): 1.
9 Hdt. 3.122.2.
10 Thuc. 1.4. Though as Simon Hornblower (1997: 20) points out in his historical commentary, Thucydides uses the word 'hearsay', which Hornblower sees as more sceptical, or more precise than Herodotus.

important Trojan War.[11] The existence of a Minoan Thalassocracy is debatable,[12] but regardless of its historical veracity, many ancient Greek authors, including Herodotus and Thucydides, gave it credence.

At this point something needs to be said about the curious case of the 'thalassocracy lists'. Writers working much later than Herodotus and Thucydides went on to develop long lists of thalassocracies, with Eusebius' list, taken from now lost books of Diodorus, listing a continuous line of thalassocracies from the eighth down to the sixth centuries.[13] It includes Caria on the list, puzzling many scholars,[14] as well as Sparta for the sixth century.[15] It places Sparta as the dominant sea power for the short period 517–515, superseding Polycrates' Samos and in turn superseded by Naxos.[16] Some scholars have been willing to accept a fifth-century origin for the Eusebius list, passed down through Diodorus. It is however a contentious area, and Momigliano was willing to accept it as possible, but without any proof in his time.[17] Later scholars have remained unconvinced, seeing it as a 'scissors and paste work', likely an attempt to fill in the gap of thalassocracies between Minos and Athens.[18] Eusebius' thalassocracy list is an interesting work, less important for what it tells us about maritime history in the eighth to sixth centuries but quite revealing of the importance of sea power as the Greeks saw it in their own history and the enduring interest in how it shaped a possible 'universal history' of Greece.

Back on more steady ground, Herodotus' narrative at many points shows he has a grasp of sea power and how it influenced the history he writes about. In discussing the Ionians in 546, he says that the islanders were safe from the predations of Persia because the Persians were not seafarers and had not yet con-

---

11 Cf. Hornblower (1997): 3.
12 See *The Minoan Thalassocracy. Myth and Reality. Proceedings of the Third International Symposium at the Swedish Institute in Athens, 31 May–5 June, 1982*. Robin Hägg and Nanno Marinatos (eds.).
13 Many are, rightfully, sceptical of the lists. Van Wees calls the lists 'late, impossibly schematic and unreliable in their chronology': Van Wees (2010): 217. For a thorough examination of the list, see Jeffery (1976): 252. And especially: L. Myres (1906): 84–130. For a more recent discussion, see Constantakopoulou (2007): 90–9.
14 See Burn (1927): 165–77; Ball (1977): 317–22.
15 Anthony Papalas is ready to lend credence to the idea of Spartan sea power in the sixth century. Papalas (1999): 10. I am more sceptical, and while it is probable that Sparta had some form of sea power, given later history it is extremely doubtful that Sparta was ever a 'thalassocracy'. I would conjecture that Sparta's inclusion is a product of the author feeling the need to include powerful Sparta in a list detailing hegemonic poleis.
16 Myres, 1906: 99–101.
17 Momigliano, 1944: 1.
18 Jeffery (1976): 252–3.

quered the Phoenicians.[19] He does not mention why the Persians having not conquered the Phoenicians are important in this context, but it appears obvious that it was because the Phoenicians were the great sea power of the eastern Mediterranean and thus Persia's sea power was of little consequence until they subsumed Phoenicia.

It is easy to forget that many of the early conflicts in the Greek world involved the projection of power over the sea. Whether or not it was Peisistratus who was responsible, the Athenians had influence and perhaps power over the River Strymon and the islands of Naxos and Delos from around 546 onwards.[20] Herodotus' history of the late sixth century Aegean is littered with examples of Greek poleis attacking others from the sea. Polycrates of Samos used his fleet to attack and conquer many different islands and mainland cities. He is said to have possessed a fleet of 100 warships and 1,000 archers, using them to great effect to capture many mainland cities and islands, including Lesbos, whose forces were themselves absent on an overseas campaign helping the Milesians.[21] Polycrates was even able to send a force of 40 warships and troops to help the Persian Cambyses in his Egyptian campaign. Polycrates apparently chose people he most suspected of being liable to revolt and sent them on the campaign. Herodotus gives differing accounts of their fate. Falling into the generalised ship nomenclature discussed earlier, he also says the ships sent were 'triremes', despite him saying earlier that Polycrates' fleet consisted of 100 pentecontors. In one version, the exiles engage Polycrates' fleet in a naval battle upon their return to the island.[22]

After this the Spartans and Corinthians launched a joint campaign against the Samians for past wrongs inflicted by them. The Spartans went to war over the supposed theft of a bowl, bound from Sparta to Croesus in the Anatolian city of Sardis as thanks for the alliance between the two states.[23] This is illuminating because it shows that Sparta had overseas interests and alliances across the Aegean in the sixth century, requiring a maritime link. Further, the Corinthians had a grievance with the Samians for their help in aiding an enemy of Corinth, their

---

19 Hdt. 1.143.1.
20 Hdt. 1.64.
21 Hdt. 3.39.
22 Hdt. 3.44–45.
23 Herodotus (1.70) gives two accounts of what may have happened with the bowl. In the first instance, the Samians capture the ship carrying the bowl, and in the second the Samians arrive after Croesus' defeat and sell the bowl on Samos and then on their return to Sparta claim it was stolen. In both cases, Samos bears the blame, and the Spartans use this as a pretext for war some 20 years later. Hdt. 3.47.1–2.

own colony of Corcyra.²⁴ The Spartans attacked and besieged Samos for 40 days, winning a battle but unable to take the city. According to Herodotus, this was the first time the Spartans had ever led an army into Asia.²⁵ Herodotus does not mention naval actions, which considering that Polycrates possessed a large and powerful fleet is puzzling. It would seem to indicate that the combined Spartan and Corinthian fleet was a powerful one, allowing them to land on Samos unhindered. The traditionally powerful Corinthian navy might have been their key contribution to this combined force, with the Spartans providing the land forces. Regardless of dubious motives, this example neatly illustrates not only the political connections across the Aegean in the sixth century but also the ability of various powers to project power overseas with maritime forces.

Greek naval operations in the second half of the sixth century onwards appeared to be increasingly aimed at engaging the enemy fleet in battle. The Phocaeans, having lost their island to the Persians and settling in one of their colonies in Corsica, were forced to fight a naval battle with the Etruscans and Carthaginians, who had grown tired of their attacks. Taking place sometime around 540, the Phocaeans engaged the enemy at sea and won a 'Cadmean Victory' off the coast of Corsica near Alalie but were forced to flee.²⁶ The battle appears to have been a set piece, both sides sailing out with the intention of destroying the main fleet of the other. The fact that the Phocaean fleet lost two-thirds of its strength was obviously enough to render a tactical victory into strategic defeat, and they could not remain secure in their position and were forced to move on. Similarly, in 519 a group of Samians who settled on Crete at Cydonia were attacked and defeated in a naval battle by a combined force of Aeginetans and Cretans. The Aeginetans attacked because of earlier Samian raiding, and the prows of the defeated Samian ships were dedicated to the sanctuary of Athena in Aegina.²⁷ That the Aeginetans were able to form a coalition with the Cretans and attack the Samians on Crete shows a high degree of cooperation and ability on part of the small, but clearly powerful, island of Aegina. The Cretans almost certainly provided local logistics support, and this example is indicative of complex naval operations being conducted across the Aegean decades before the rise of Athenian sea power. Indeed, this example demonstrates that Aegina possessed a very capable fleet, able to conduct operations far from home and prevail in battle against another capable naval force.

---

24 The story is told by Herodotus at 3.48–9. It is perhaps episodes like this which, if accurate, would cause later authors to add Sparta to a Thalassocracy list.
25 Hdt. 3.54–6.
26 Hdt. 1.166.
27 Hdt. 3.59.

Thucydides

Sea power is a defining factor in Thucydides' history, not just of the Peloponnesian War, but Greek history as a whole. As noted above, he places the kingship and thalassocracy of Minos in the historical realm and establishes him, rather than the much later Polycrates, as the first Greek thalassocrat. Thucydides' emphasis on Minos as the first ruler of the sea goes beyond mere military considerations. He says that cities were usually built away from the sea due to the predations of pirates but that Minos and his sea power cleared the sea lanes and made communication by sea easier. This security led to prosperity, enabling cities to acquire wealth and walls and to become more powerful and eventually grow by subjugating smaller cities.[28] Here we have an explicit expression of opinion that sea power and the security it provided for the Aegean were directly connected to wealth and prosperity, and the acquisition of even greater power – not only connected, but responsible for this geopolitical phenomenon of hegemony. It also shows how the concept of sea power had advanced in the minds of the Greeks since Herodotus' work.

The question of piracy in the ancient world is a vexed one that includes excruciating dives into language, semantics, legal issues, and a host of questions not easy to answer. This is true of piracy in any age to be frank. It is only in the last four decades that piracy has taken on a specific, and very narrow, legal definition. International law, such as Article 101 of The United Nations Convention on the Law of the Sea 1982 (UNCLOS), very strictly and narrowly defines piracy.[29] Prior to this 'pirate' was often a pejorative term used to describe any maritime activity a state deemed as unsavoury. No such legal definition was conceived of or used in the ancient world. Language is not helpful, for the Greeks used words that can all be translated as either having to do with robbery or attack either on land or by sea. The only helpful guide is context, and whether or not an ancient author is describing this raiding/attacking being carried out by state-forces or by what we might describe as 'non-state actors' – bandits or pirates. The label of 'pirate' or 'brigand/bandit' seems to have often been used in a purely pejorative

---
28 Thuc. 1.7; 1.8.2–4.
29 Of note is the strict delineation of international maritime borders in the modern international legal system. This includes concepts such as Territorial Sea, Contiguous Zone and Economic Exclusive Zone. To this add the idea of vessel registration: where a vessel is 'flagged'. With these terms, piracy in the modern world is conducted by stateless vessels outside the Territorial Sea of a state. Inside this boundary it is considered armed robbery, not piracy. UNCLOS even considers when a naval vessel has mutinied and when it can be considered a pirate vessel. See UNCLOS, Articles 101–7. Other international bodies, such as the International Maritime Bureau (IMB), have a different, and broader, definition of what constitutes piracy. For more on the history of the legal definition of piracy, see Campbell (2010): 19–32.

sense, as it has been used in later times, with the great Athenian statesman Demosthenes at one point calling Philip of Macedon a 'pirate'.[30]

Piracy in Thucydides' *archaeology* section appears to be a mix of what we might think of as traditional piracy as well as state-sanctioned raiding. However, tangential to the issue of piracy is the important point that Thucydides says it was the increase in communication by sea that caused and allowed people to turn to raiding.[31] In Thucydides' world, the opening of maritime communications allowed for the very development of the Greek world, both in terms of increased trade and hegemonic ambitions, Minos as a case in point. Thucydides describes these raiders as making the practice their main source of livelihood, but most importantly he says that at the time there was nothing inherently bad about what they were doing, and even something a bit glorious in the eyes of the old poets.[32] This raiding was so prevalent that, as mentioned above, many cities were built away from the sea, regardless of whether they were situated on an island or the mainland, and all coastal populations seafaring or not, and even other raiders, were potential targets.[33] Thucydides does say that the raiding was organised by the most powerful men in order to serve their own greed, but also to help the needy.[34] This complicates matters, for it makes this raiding seem like it was organised by individuals and small groups, rather than higher authorities, government or organised rule, and that personal gain was the prime motivation. This seems a lot like piracy as we might define it. The scale of activities and how widespread it was, however, are counter arguments to this view of it as some form of 'institutional piracy'. It seems more like a legitimate way of making a living than an aberration, at least in that time. This takes the topic into debates around political organisation and economy for a period where such topics are extremely difficult to be sure about. The main takeaway from this is that the maritime world was opening across the Mediterranean, for trade and for warfare, both state-sanctioned and individualised (piracy), and for powerful rulers, like Minos, to gain wider hegemony through sea power.

Moving away from piracy and King Minos, the first glimpse of Thucydides' famous *realpolitik* follows in his discussion of the Trojan War, when he says that Agamemnon was able to launch the Trojan expedition not because of the oath of

---

30 Or a brigand; Demosthenes merely uses the generic word 'leistikos' which can be translated either way. Dem. 10.34.
31 Thuc. 1.5.1.
32 Thuc. 1.5.1–2.
33 Thuc. 1.7.
34 Thuc. 1.5.1.

Tyndareus, but because of his superiority in strength.[35] This was a superiority over the other Greeks enabled by his navy, which must have been superior to all others given that Mycenae itself was, as Thucydides says, a land power.[36] After the Trojan War and ensuing turmoil, the Greeks grew in power and desired more wealth, and 'Greece fitted out fleets and clung more to the sea'.[37] Corinth becomes the first city to build the warship that would dominate the Classical period, the trireme, and again wealth is connected to a navy, which helps supress the aforementioned rampant piracy which in turn promoted the growth of more wealth.[38] This is Thucydides highlighting what he thought to be the most important things in war: financial and maritime resources.[39] This can be seen as a wider trend, with several other poleis gaining prominence through a growth in their sea power. As we saw in Chapter Two, the small polis of Eretria in the late sixth century appears to have had a well-defined system for naval campaigning, suggestive of more than merely defensive use of its warships. As we will see in the next chapter, the islands of Aegina, Chios, and the Corinthian colony of Corcyra had navies by the beginning of fifth century and the outbreak of the Persian Wars. Such naval power does not spring out of nowhere, so clearly the seeds had been sown in the sixth century for this growth.

While none of these budding navies were as large as Athens' would be at the height of the Delian League, Thucydides did not see this as any kind of issue. He says of the early Greek navies that despite their smallness, they were a great power for those who acquired them, both in terms of revenue and power gained over others.[40] Moreover, wars by land amongst the Greeks were basically non-existent, save for the usual border conflicts.[41] Here we see Thucydides speaking on a strategic level, weighing the worth of sea and land power and expressing his opinion that it was sea power which predominately led to wealth and thus greater power. It is critical to note that he describes these navies as being of great strength and power *despite* their smallness. If doubt is ever cast on the efficacy of ancient Greek navies, it is important to remember that the contemporary general and historian Thucydides judged navies, no matter how small, to have been of extreme importance to his world and the shaping of its history.

---

35 Thuc. 1.9.1. Hornblower (1997: 31) sees Thucydides as not denying the oath motive as relevant, but merely as the public pretext and not the 'true cause'.
36 Thuc. 1.9.3–4.
37 Thuc. 1.13.1.
38 Thuc. 1.13.2–5.
39 de Romilly (2012): 157.
40 Thuc. 1.15.1.
41 Thuc. 1.15.2.

Of navies and sea power in the sixth century, we have but tantalizing glimpses of what was happening around Greece. Myths related to Minos and his thalassocracy hint at a world in which navies were becoming a reality and a powerful force to be reckoned with, even if the myths were solidified in the context of the fifth century. By the mid sixth century Polycrates of Samos provides us with a more historical picture of thalassocracy, and afterwards, the blooming of naval and sea power in other Greek polies such as Phocaea, Corinth, Corcyra, Aegina, and Chios. While little is known about the conduct of maritime operations in this period, we get clues as to what might have been happening across the seas. First and foremost, the stories of Minos and Agamemnon show them projecting power across the Aegean with their warships. The famous 'Catalogue of Ships' in the *Iliad* describes the Greek force that attacked Troy not in terms of phalanxes or soldiers but primarily by the number of ships each city sent on the great expedition. The naval battle at Alalia in c. 540 and the battle between the Samians and a combined force of Aeginetans and Cretans in 519 both demonstrate that by the late sixth-century navies were used in fleet-on-fleet actions and that battle at sea could be decisive.[42] The piracy that was apparently rife throughout this time, whether it be traditional piracy or state-sanctioned raiding, was supposedly combated by the growth of state navies. As the seas opened for trade and colonisation, clearly piracy was seen as bad for business, and so we see stories of Minos and Corinth actively supressing piracy in order to protect their seaborne wealth. By the opening of the fifth century navies were being used across the Aegean as instruments of state power, and the scene was set for a century of endemic warfare across the seas.

---

42 Hdt. 1.166; Hdt. 3.59.3.

Chapter Five
Divine Salamis: the Persian Wars

If the sea power of the sixth century is a whisper of its potential, then the fifth century is an explosion of this potential released, with the great conflict between the Greeks and Persians and the primacy of sea power. The Aegean Sea would prove no obstacle to the projection of power across the Greek and Persian worlds and it would set the scene for the first historical Greek empire, the Athenian controlled Delian League. It would all start with a naval-fuelled rebellion in the eastern Aegean.

The Ionian rebellion

In around 500, the deputy ruler of the city of Miletus, Aristagoras, joined with a group of exiles from the island of Naxos and hatched a plan using Persian support to take over the rule of Naxos and the surrounding islands, including Paros and eventually Andros and Euboea.[1] They approached the Persian governor of Sardis, Artaphrenes, who agrees to the plan except that instead of the 100 triremes proposed by Aristagoras, he prepared 200 for the attack.[2] With the assent of the Persian King Darius, the combined fleet launched for a secret attack on Naxos. However, while the fleet was laid up in Chios, a quarrel broke out between Aristagoras and the Persian general Megabates, which led the latter to send a message to Naxos to warn of the impending attack.[3] Forewarned, the Naxians were able to hold off the assault, and fearing for his position within the Persian empire, Aristagoras plans for a revolt and is then pushed to do so by a message from Histiaios, the tyrant of Miletus, who had been detained at the Persian court.[4] In the debate that followed at Miletus in 499 on whether they should revolt from Persia, the dissenting voice of Hecataios says that in order to be successful they must gain control of the seas. Moreover, they needed money to do this and so they must seize the wealth dedicated by Croesus at the sanctuary of Branchidai to be able to afford this sea control.[5] This suggestion was not heeded, and instead they sent to Sparta for aid, who promptly refused to help.

---

1 Hdt. 5.30–1.
2 Hdt. 5.31.
3 Hdt. 5.33.
4 Hdt.5.35.
5 Hdt. 5.36.2; 5.36.3.

Following the rejection of aid from Sparta, the Ionians then went to Athens, who agreed to help.[6] The decision by Athens to support the Ionian rebellion in 500/499 with 20 ships had far-reaching consequences. Herodotus is quite explicit in his analysis of the long-term consequences, calling these ships the beginning of evils for both the Greeks and the Persians. This is of course Herodotus applying his analysis in hindsight, if not also being dramatic, but he is not far wrong.[7] The primary goal of this force was to help the Ionians militarily in their campaigns, not provide mere diplomatic reassurance, though the latter was a side effect and signalled to the Persians as much as the Greeks where the Athenians stood in this matter. Twenty ships were a significant contribution, especially before Athens had significantly bolstered its navy under Themistocles after the silver strike at Laurion.

The war between the Ionians and the Persians in the 490s saw two large naval battles, off Cyprus and Lade. In 497 a Persian assault on the city of Salamis in Cyprus drew the Ionians into aiding the Cypriots.[8] The Greeks were victorious at sea but the Cypriots were defeated on land, causing the Ionians to abandon the island.[9] Three years later the Ionians decided the best way to defend Miletus against the Persians was to assemble as large a fleet as possible and confront them at sea off the island of Lade, just off the coast. Abandoned by the Samians and Lesbians, the remaining Ionian forces, comprised largely of ships from Chios, fought on but were defeated, allowing the Persians to besiege Miletus by sea as well as land.[10] In both cases the need for sea control was great. Success at sea in Cyprus was necessary to prevent the Persians from cutting off the island, but with defeat on land and the death of the king of Salamis the Ionians were fighting for a lost cause. Victory at sea had been a necessary but not a sufficient condition for the war effort. At Lade, the fate of the campaign against Miletus rested with the fleets. Persian victory allowed them to invest the city by land and sea, whereas a defeat would have allowed the Ionians to reinforce the city against the Persian siege and to conduct operations against other parts of the Persian Empire, potentially drawing off forces from the siege of Miletus. Notwithstanding the defection of the Samian and Lesbian forces at Lade, both operations demonstrate a willingness and ability to assemble large fleets of warships from many different island poleis and put them into battle for a decisive effort.

---

6 Hdt. 5.97.
7 Hdt. 5.97, 99, 103, 105.
8 Hdt. 5.108.
9 Hdt. 5.110–15.
10 Hdt. 6.6–15.

An interesting episode in the wake of the failed Ionian revolt returns us to the vexed question of piracy. A certain Dionysius of Phocaea, upon determining that the Ionian revolt was doomed, decided not to return to his homeland. Instead, he seized three enemy ships and sailed to Phoenicia, where he sank some merchant vessels and collected a large sum of money. From there he sailed to Sicily and set himself up as a 'pirate', though he made a point of never attacking Greeks, only Carthaginians and 'Tyrrhenians'.[11] Herodotus assigns no motive to the selection of targets and the exemption of Greeks, perhaps out of morality not to harm fellow Greeks, or perhaps he considered it prudent not to do so and invite retaliation by the Sicilian and other Greeks. The episode shows what might drive someone to piracy: a loss of a homeland and exile. It highlights the enablers of piracy, namely, nautical skills and money. It is also worth noting that he had a force of three ships to conduct his activity, implying organisation and at least a moderate if not an advanced degree of command and control. Finally, it shows the opportunism of the venture, targeting both Carthaginians and Italians, a general predation except for Greek targets.

Adding to the above example, in approximately 494 the recently exiled Milesian tyrant Histiaios manned eight warships and sailed to Byzantium where he seized ships sailing out of the Pontus, excepting those that were willing to follow him.[12] Herodotus does not use language related to piracy/raiding but merely says he 'seized' the ships.[13] This seems to be a straightforward case of piracy. Histiaios is no longer the ruler of Miletus or any other city, seemingly 'stateless'. He was given support by Mytilene in the form of ships, yet these ships were not used by him to fight Miletus but in the service of seizing ships from the Pontus. He did manage to draw quite a bit of support from Lesbos and did gather a formidable force yet was still forced by food shortage to land at Atarneos on the mainland and attempt to harvest grain.[14] This seems to indicate that whatever support he was getting from Lesbos, it was not so great that he did not have to worry about basic logistics, a problem he solved by further raiding. In this sense, he is not acting much like an exile or a 'rebel', but opportunistically attacking shipping and raiding coastal settlements. An interesting theory suggests that although Histiaios was effectively acting as a pirate (*leistes*), perhaps he was not labelled as such because of his high status.[15] A comparison with Dionysius above does not indicate any stark difference, other than Histiaios being of higher status. Perhaps raiding

---

11 The only time Herodotus uses the word 'leistes'. Hdt. 617.
12 Hdt. 6.5.3.
13 Rather than the verb associated with piracy raiding, he merely uses one for seizing.
14 For the full story of his activities, see Hdt. 6.25–30.
15 Scott (2005): 87. See also pp. 71–2.

was a means to an end for Histiaios on the road back to power, whereas Dionysius made raiding his life. The case of Histiaios is arguably one demonstrative of piracy, though there is enough ambiguity to argue that his activities may not have been viewed as such by all his fellow Greeks, including the historian Herodotus. It is also a clear illustration of the supply difficulties that were encountered by even a small fleet, especially in the absence of state support.

Meanwhile, maritime rivalries continued in Greek waters. The Saronic Gulf was an important area for trade routes coming south out of Corinth, as well as from the island polis of Aegina and Athens. Aegina possessed a strong navy and was in an ideal position to threaten Corinthian interests in the gulf. This rivalry manifested in the years before the second phase of the Persian War when Corinth aided Athens in the latter's attack on Aegina in 490. Aegina could muster 70 warships, but the Athenians could only manage 50, and so the Corinthians 'loaned' the Athenians 20 ships. They were rented to the Athenians for the suspiciously low price of five drachmae per ship, since, according to Herodotus, in accordance with the law they could not be given for free.[16] The extra ships tipped the balance, and the Athenians prevailed in battle. Aegina remained an influential sea power after this loss, as their performance in the battle of Salamis would demonstrate. Nevertheless, this defeat at the hands of Athens set the stage for further conflict and gave the Athenian politician Themistocles a palatable pretext for his warship building programme.

The (Persian) empire strikes back

While Athens and Aegina quarrelled, the Persian King Darius planned to exact his revenge on Athens for their support of the Ionians. This campaign ended with the attack on Attica at the beach of Marathon. The sea power equation was extremely lopsided in this campaign, with the Persians bringing such an overwhelming number of ships that the Athenians chose to meet them on the beach rather than at sea. The Athenians, aided by a hoplite contingent from the nearby city of Plataea, defeated the Persian forces. They then marched back to Athens in time to prevent the Persian fleet from landing there and attacking the undefended city.[17] While this was clearly an Athenian victory, the fact was they had done nothing to degrade the sea power of the Persians, who had already proven they could cross the Aegean with impunity. With their sea power left intact, the

---

[16] Hdt. 6.89, 92.
[17] For the full story: Hdt. 6.95–117.

Persians would try again, and it would not be a mere punitive expedition, but a full-scale invasion.

Sea power was critical to the Persian invasion of Greece in 480, both in terms of the Persian offensive and for the defending Greek forces. In the Persian discussion over the proposed invasion of Greece, Xerxes' uncle Artabanos cautioned the king, warning that if the Persians were to lose a naval battle the Greeks may well sail to the Hellespont and destroy the bridge there, a calamity for the Persian forces.[18] This fear was almost realised after the loss at Salamis when Xerxes was forced to despatch warships to the Hellespont to guard the bridge.[19] As it happened, the bridge across the Hellespont was destroyed by a storm, and the Persian army was ferried across by boats anyway.[20] Fear of a destroyed bridge seems irrational considering this, and the real fear was probably the presence of a Greek fleet that could block attempts at crossing the Hellespont by boat. However, Herodotus' narrative of these events remains somewhat unsatisfying, and we are left to guess. What it does demonstrate is a fear held by the Persians that a superior Greek fleet would put their land forces in danger.

Herodotus is clearer when discussing other naval operations of the war. He states that the aim of the King's expedition was not just to punish Athens but to conquer all of Greece.[21] Crucially, the Greeks who had not submitted to Persia were in great fear because there were not enough ships to confront the invader.[22] The pre-eminence he places in ships for the defence of Greece sets the reader up for his next statement. He says he will put forward a controversial opinion and then makes his most important declaration about Greek victory in the war.[23] He declares that it was Athens which contributed most to the defence of Greece. He baldly states that if Athens had not opposed Persia, no other Greek power would have opposed Persia at sea.[24] Had that happened, the Persians would have been able to use their fleet to outflank the wall at the isthmus of Corinth and would have been able to conquer the states of the Peloponnese or otherwise convince them to medize – either way, the Greeks would have been defeated.[25] Thus, before he even narrates the invasion itself, Herodotus makes his judgement on why

---

18 Hdt. 7.10β.2.
19 Hdt. 8.97.1, 8.107.
20 Hdt. 8.117.1.
21 Hdt. 7.138.1.
22 Hdt. 7.138.2.
23 Controversial and flying in the face of Greek popular opinion outside of Athens. Hale (2009): 135.
24 Hdt. 7.139.2.
25 Hdt. 7.139.3–4.

the Greeks were able to resist Persia. He even has a non-Athenian, a certain Chileos of Tegea, explicitly say that the wall at the isthmus was all but useless without the Athenian fleet, which in turn forced the Spartans to march north to Plataea.[26]

A critical role for naval fleets is providing cover to land forces, preventing an enemy fleet from interfering with friendly land forces by outflanking them or disrupting supply lines. One of the earliest and most well-known examples of a covering force is that at the battle of Artemision, a naval engagement fought to cover the land forces fighting at Thermopylae. It is often overlooked as a separate operation and folded into the more heroised action at Thermopylae. The Persian army, covered by their fleet, was the main threat to the Greeks, and hence the decision to send a ground force north to oppose them. Since the fleet's job was to cover the land forces, the position of the land forces had to be chosen first. Choosing a defensive point inland might not require a covering force, or a naval force positioned differently depending on the geographic situation. Having chosen Thermopylae as the defensive position by land, Artemision was chosen as the fleet base. From here the ships could defend the strait and protect the seaward flank of the army. Further, they could keep watch for a Persian move to the south end of Euboea, an attempt which did indeed eventuate, although it led to the destruction of the Persian ships by a storm while they were sailing along the lee shore of Euboea.[27] The fate of one force was directly tied to the other and the Greeks had a boat ready with both the fleet and with the army at Thermopylae in order to convey news to the other force should things go badly for one of them, as happened to the land force.[28] Although already contemplating withdrawal after their third engagement with the Persians, it was news of Leonidas' defeat that caused the fleet to retire from the area altogether.[29] The fleet had done its job, covering the land force by preventing the Persian naval force from turning the army's flank until the latter's destruction.

Once the land army had been destroyed, the fleet was in a vulnerable position as Persian land forces could move down the coast and deny them landing spots, though the ability to land on Euboea mitigated that risk. More importantly,

---

26 Hdt. 9.9.2.
27 All 200 Persian ships apparently wrecked. Hdt. 8.7, 13.
28 Hdt. 8.21.
29 Hdt. 8.21.2. At 8.18 Herodotus says that the Greeks were deliberating over a retreat to the interior waters of Greece. This implies that the Greek fleet was contemplating moving position further towards Thermopylae and to more confined waters, rather than retreating entirely from their covering position. Such a move would have been entirely tactical in nature, though the tone of Herodotus does imply some urgency. Bowie (2007): 109.

the fleet's job was done and there was nothing to be gained by staying in the area. The successful withdrawal of the fleet without undue risk or loss ensured that there was a sufficiently large and powerful Greek naval force able to confront the Persians later at Salamis.[30] More than this, there are other facets of the battle off Artemision which had a strategic impact. There was the increase in skill and confidence the Greek fleet gained operating in battle together, invaluable experience for Salamis and a point made by Plutarch.[31] Further, he quotes Pindar in saying that the Athenians at Artemission helped lay 'the bright foundation of freedom' for the Greeks.[32] The number of Persian ships supposedly lost to storms because they took the dangerous course of sailing on the weather side of Euboea in a desperate flanking move was a huge blow to the Persian fleet. More than just providing cover to the maritime flank of the land forces at Thermopylae, what the Greeks learned and experienced in these battles contributed to the success of the Salamis campaign and can be considered of strategic significance. The Greek fleet's continued existence as a 'fleet-in-being' in a strategic sense acted as a covering force protecting the isthmus of Corinth. It was of paramount importance that the Greeks always had a fleet sufficient to counter that of the Persians and so deny them strategic mobility. The Greek fleet did their bit at sea, and it was the defeat of the land army that caused them to withdraw, having gained valuable experience, not suffering many casualties, and while causing many on the Persians. By these metrics, the strategic situation for the Greeks at sea did not deteriorate, whereas the loss of Persian ships had an unfavourable impact on their strategic situation at sea. It was an important series of actions in the campaign at sea leading up to the Battle of Salamis.

Having failed to block the Persian forces by land, the Athenians faced the awful prospect of Persian invasion. They made the remarkable decision to evacuate the city, with much of their goods and livestock being moved offshore to the island of Salamis and most of the population moved to Aegina and Troezen. This evacuation was a massive undertaking, and the Greek fleet, not just the Athenians, played a vital role. After leaving Artemision, the Greek fleet put into Salamis at the request of the Athenians to help with the evacuation.[33] Referring directly to women and children, the evacuation described by Herodotus was of Attica's 'non-combatants'. The narrative of Diodorus, though brief, makes clear

---

30 Strauss (2004): 32–7; Hale (2009): 43–54.
31 Plut. *Them.* 8.1.
32 Plut. *Them.* 8.2. Pindar. Fr. 77. It is quoted four other times by Plutarch, including in his essay *On the glory of the Athenians* (350A) and *On the Malice of Herodotus* (867C). Frost (1980): 108–9; Marr (1998): 90.
33 Hdt. 8.40.1.

reference to boats being used to evacuate women, children, and useful goods to Salamis.[34] Plutarch too has Athens being evacuated by sea, albeit in a more emotional and evocative passage.[35] Images of warships evacuating military and civilian populations in the modern era are quite common, from Dunkirk in 1940 to the evocative images of the fall of Saigon and helicopters being pushed off the deck of US Navy carriers. It is not the kind of maritime operation we immediately think of when considering the ancient world, but by all accounts, the evacuation of Attica in the face of the Persian advance was a remarkable achievement. Not just for the physical feat of evacuating so many people and their goods, including livestock, but because of the strategic impact on the course of the Persian Wars. Knowing that their family and at least some of their most valuable property were safe, it motivated Athenians to continue the fight against Persia. This factor is seemingly always overlooked in discussion about the battles that came after the evacuation.[36] Even more salient is the fact that the Athenians were considering their options long before the battle at Salamis, and the inscription known as the 'Themistocles Decree' indicates that the evacuation of Attica had begun before the battle of Artemision.[37] In this we see the Athenian strategy at play from the beginning of the Persian invasion. The ability to evacuate the entire population of Attica was the key enabler of continued Athenian resistance, as well as a leverage point, allowing them to make sure that the combined Greek fleet fought at Salamis. Without the Athenian fleet, the other Greeks would have no chance against the Persians, and so the most benign use of triremes as mere transports helped ensure the decisive confrontation at sea with Persia.

As the most famous naval battle of the ancient world, Salamis in 480 was a critical turning point in the Persian invasion. Much has been written about the battle itself, so this examination will be brief, concentrating only on how Salamis fit strategically within the Persian Wars as a whole.[38] The Greek coalition assembled at Salamis is fascinating in and of itself. It contained warships from all over mainland Greece and many of the islands, and even a tiny contingent from Croton, in southern Italy. They were all led, not by an Athenian, but again as at Arte-

---

34 Diod. 11.13.3.
35 Plut. *Them.* 10.4. See also Graninger (2010): 308–17.
36 The evacuation itself is mentioned or discussed, but rarely the strategic ramifications. For instance, see Lazenby (1993): 153–5; Strauss (2004): 72–89; and Hale (2009): 56–60. The closest appears to be Victor Davis Hanson, who says that the presence of a large population of Athenians on Salamis allowed Themistocles to pressure the other Greeks in to fighting there to protect them: Hanson (2001): 40–3.
37 In August 480. Strauss (2004): 75.
38 For the best work on the battle of Salamis and the surrounding events, see Strauss (2004). For other works dealing with the battle itself, see Lazenby (1993): 151–97; Hale (2009): 55–74.

mision by the Spartan Eurybiades. Herodotus rattles off the names of poleis, throwing in anecdotes about the lineage of these different Greek cities, in a section reminiscent of the Catalogue of Ships in Homer's *Iliad*.[39] Importantly, with a few exceptions noted by Herodotus, these different poleis all sent triremes to fight at Salamis. The vast majority were not sending smaller ships like penteconters, but the supreme warship of that age. Even those who sent penteconters were contributing, and perhaps this tells us that the ship was still favoured over triremes in certain places. There is an interesting point in one of the navies that did not show up, that of Corcyra. Despite mustering 60 ships to aid the Greeks at Salamis, they never made it past the Peloponnese, blaming contrary weather but according to Herodotus because they did not believe that the Greeks would prevail against the Persians. In contrast, the nearby polis of Leucas sent three ships to Salamis and they made it to the battle. Perhaps the ships from Leucas departed earlier and missed the bad weather – along with the other ships sailing from the west like Croton and Ambracia – or perhaps the Corcyraean navy, despite its size, was not as effective as the other poleis' and lacked the same investment in time and effort, which might account for their later poor performances in battle during the Peloponnesian war. Finally, perhaps Herodotus is correct and the Corcyraeans were conducting a diplomatic operation with their navy, sending a fleet to appear as if they wanted to help the Greeks, but without any intention of fighting. A fleet of 60 triremes is a large force, so they could claim large-scale mobilisation rather than token effort and were only stymied by the weather. Thus, we can see an attempt to win political influence with their navy, without having to risk them in battle.

The Greeks had solid defences across the Isthmus at Corinth that could protect against a Persian land advance, but if the Persians were able to gain sea control, their fleet could easily outflank the isthmian defences. Such a move would no doubt fracture the tentative Greek alliance as the different poleis looked to their own defences, or their own capitulation. In this sense the objective of the Greeks was to contest the seas, not win control of them. So long as the Persians did not have the freedom of manoeuvre to land troops on the Peloponnese the Greek defences at the isthmus could be held. Longer term, this might exhaust the Persians and force them to go home. Some Greeks recognised this, but the majority wanted to confront the Persian fleet near the isthmus, not Attica where they could potentially be surrounded and cut off.[40] According to Herodotus this was also clear to some on the Persian side. Artemisia is said to have counselled re-

---

39 No doubt what he was going for. Hdt. 8.41–8.
40 Hdt. 8.49.

straint and let Greek infighting and lack of supplies at Salamis drive them to disperse, a fear expressed earlier in the narrative by the Athenian Mnesiphilos.[41]

These are both discussions about the **'operational level'**: how the campaign should be conducted. Plutarch tells the story of the aristocratic Athenian statesman Cimon before the battle of Salamis, who led his knights up to the Acropolis and dedicated his horse's bridle, and then marched down to the sea saying that at that moment Athens needed people to fight at sea.[42] It is a good story, which if true demonstrated that the division between sea and land power proponents was not so deep and that even the most aristocratic of Athenians knew when it was time for warships to decide matters.[43] Whether this happened or not, the story did seem to have a long life, and may have been considered true enough by the Athenians to have warranted re-telling as an example of unity in the face of adversity and the pervasiveness of Athenian naval pursuits. Clearly both sides realised the need to fight at sea: the Persians to destroy the Greek fleet and allow them the freedom to manoeuvre around the Peloponnese, and the Greeks to block and Persian moves by sea, in a similar albeit grander manner than they had done at Artemision. The Greek decision to fight at Salamis was recognition that they were in a good strategic position to offer battle on terms favourable to them.

The battle itself was a decisive victory for the Greeks. Funnelling the numerically superior Persian forces into the narrows of the Salamis Strait meant these numbers counted for little and the Greeks prevailed. Interestingly, after the battle it was decided that the Aeginetans had been the 'best of the Greeks'.[44] To be considered the best amongst the 21 other Greek poleis that fought at Salamis, including Corinth and Athens, is a powerful statement on how effective a fighting force the Aeginetan navy must have been. It is possible the Peloponnesians banded together to vote the Aeginetans best of the Greeks as a way of checking Athenian arrogance, in light of their self-promotion. Nevertheless, Aegina had already provided 18 triremes at the battle of Artemision and they sent 30 of their 'best' triremes to Salamis, while also maintaining a force of warships to guard their own

---

41 Hdt. 8.68, 8.57.
42 Plut. *Cim.* 5.2–3.
43 J. F. Lazenby (1993: 154–5) suspects the story is possibly a family tradition told down the ages, demonstrating the selflessness and moral courage shown by the Athenians as they evacuated their homes before the invading Persians. Barry Strauss (2004: 78–9) does not appear to have any problems with the veracity of the story and includes it in his narrative of the Salamis campaign, a credit to the aristocratic Cimon acknowledging Themistocles' maritime strategy and putting country before politics.
44 Hdt. 8.93.1.

coast.⁴⁵ This seems to have been an entirely prudent move, preserving some forces to guard the island, not all that far from the Persian threat. This is not terribly surprising; Aegina is listed in the 'Thalassocracy list' for the years 490–480 and is the last polis named before the obvious ascendancy of Athens in the wake of the Persian Wars.⁴⁶ Athens provided the most ships at Salamis, and Aegina supposedly provided the most effective ships, and so we see an interesting dynamic at play regarding the state of different naval forces in Greece at the time.

The destruction and rout of the Persian naval forces allowed the Greeks to establish uncontested control of the seas around the Greek mainland. The victory diminished but did not erase the threat to Greece, with the large Persian army of Mardonios still a powerful force to contend with. The upshot was that without the support of the fleet the Persian land army left in Greece was necessarily restricted in size to that which could be supported by the locals and a long overland supply chain. This put it at a size that the combined Greek army could be confident in defeating, thus the confrontation and eventual Greek victory at the battle of Plataea. Victory for the Greeks at Salamis was a necessary, but not a sufficient, condition of victory against the Persians in the defence of Greece. Herodotus was not the only one to see the battle of Salamis as of supreme importance, and the judgements of modern scholars on the battle are almost uniformly correct in identifying Salamis as a turning point in favour of the Greeks,⁴⁷ a conclusion that is hard to dispute. The battle is an example of two battle-fleets positioned to compete for control of the sea by pitched battle, a rare but at times necessary operation. The outcome would have strategic ramifications for the war, no matter who was to be victorious.

Occurring on the same day as the Greek victory on land at Plataea, the land battle that expelled the Persian forces from mainland Greece, the battle of Mycale in 479 illustrates how powerful the Greek fleet must have been after its victory at Salamis. It is also an excellent example of a naval force being perceived as so powerful that an enemy would cede sea control without a fight. The Persians felt too weak to fight the Greeks at sea and so beached their ships instead.⁴⁸ Nevertheless, the Greeks attacked, and Herodotus is explicit in what was considered at

---

45 Hdt. 8.1.2, 8.46.
46 See Myres (1906): 95–6.
47 Though apparently not always the point of view, with Hignett pointing out that many German scholars did not see Salamis as a battle of any consequence to the war: Hignett (1963): 264, esp. n. 2 and 3. Burn (1962: 471) comes to the sensible conclusion that it saved Greece from long occupation but did not put an end to the Persian threat. Lazenby's (1993: 197) conclusion is also noteworthy and hard to surpass.
48 Hdt. 9.97.

stake by both sides: not only control over the islands but also control of the strategically critical chokepoint of the Hellespont.[49] The Greeks sought a decisive battle at sea but were denied by the Persians out of fear of Greek warships. A powerful and proven naval force could, through mere existence, have an impact on the strategic calculations of an enemy. In the example of Mycale, it caused the Persians to offer battle on land, but to no avail. The Persians were defeated and lost their ships in the aftermath of the battle, leaving the Greeks with full control of the sea.[50] This allowed the Greek forces to sail to the Hellespont unimpeded to destroy the bridges and when they found these already destroyed, they were able to blockade Sestos, where a large group of Persians and their allies were holed up.[51] This demonstrated the reach of Greek sea power. At the same time, it provides a glimpse of the freedom of movement the Persian fleet would have gained had they been victorious at Salamis. A wall on the isthmus of Corinth would have meant little to a Persian fleet able to range the seas around the Peloponnese with impunity.

Although the Persian threat to the Greek mainland had been effectively countered with the Greek victories at Plataea and Mycale in 479, the Greek continued to fight the Persians overseas. Traditionally the Persian Wars are said to have ended with these two battles, but it is also possible to see the final battle of the Persian Wars as the one at Eurymedon River in the late 460s.[52] The Persian naval force attempted to dodge battle with the Athenian fleet under the command of the Athenian Cimon, who Plutarch says was prepared to force the issue if the Persians were reluctant.[53] The Persians were apparently awaiting the arrival of 80 Phoenician ships, indicating that despite the Persian force being of superior number,[54] they were not confident of victory without the Phoenicians and again indicating how powerful the Athenian navy was perceived to be. The battle progressed from sea to land, with 200 ships captured by the Athenians and the Persians subsequently also defeated during the fighting on land.[55] In Plutarch's account Cimon goes even fur-

---

49 Hdt. 9.101.3.
50 Hdt. 9.106.1.
51 Hdt. 9.114–15.
52 Dated to either 469 or 466. See Meiggs (1972): 81–2.
53 Plut. *Cim.* 12.5.
54 Plut. *Cim.* 12.4. Plutarch gives two numbers for the Persian ships, 600 and the more credible 350 according to Ephoros. 12.5.
55 Both Thucydides and Plutarch give the number of captured ships as 200, though Thucydides says that it was the entire Phoenician fleet that was captured: Thuc. 1.100.1; Plut. *Kim.* 12.6–13.2. Diodorus gives a different account, where the naval battle is fought off Cyprus and the Persians fight hard, are defeated, and the Athenians capture over 100 ships: Diod. 11.60.6–7. After this the Persians are defeated in a land battle at Eurymedon River: 11.61.

ther, sailing out to interdict the 80 Phoenician ships on their way to reinforce the Persians, destroying or capturing them all.[56] The victory is hailed by both Diodorus and Plutarch as a major triumph, not just for Cimon and the Athenians but also as a great feat in the history of Greece. Diodorus says that to his day there had not been an occurrence of a military force fighting and winning such important actions by both sea and by land.[57] Plutarch is even more dramatic, saying that with two battles in a single day he had surpassed Salamis with a land battle and Plataea with a sea battle.[58] Of note, there is no indication of either side carrying independent ground forces aboard their ships, and so the fighting on land mentioned by Diodorus and Plutarch probably refers to the marines being carried by the fleets. In this case it shows that marines carried by Greek warships could be incredibly effective in battle on land as well as at sea. When we talk of Greek warships projecting power ashore, this helps explain how that could be achieved even without embarked land forces. What Eurymedon River demonstrates is a Greek force projecting power across the Aegean, superior by sea and land, both necessary to triumph in the littoral environment of the Aegean. Sea power alone would have been insufficient at both Mycale and Eurymedon, but likewise the land army would have been nowhere without the naval force to protect them as they campaigned against a still strong Persian fleet.

Herodotus and other Greeks had a clear idea of what enabled the Greeks to eventually prevail: Athenian sea power. Salamis would live large in the minds of the Greeks and especially the Athenians, who never tired of reminding others what they had done to save Greece. It even lived on through the architecture of Athens. Samantha Martin-Mcauliffe and John Papadopoulos argue that during the reconstruction of the Acropolis after the Persian invasion, the Athenians deliberately changed the orientation of the entrance, the Propylaea, so that upon leaving the Acropolis one was presented with a direct view of Salamis. In doing this they were 'framing victory' and reminding visitors that the wonder of Athena's sanctuary on the Acropolis was all derived from victory at Salamis which not only freed the Athenians but enriched them through the Delian League.[59]

When discussing the Persian Wars, Thucydides gives equal precedence to land and sea battles, saying that the war was decided by two sea and two land

---

56 Plut. *Cim.* 13.3–4.
57 Diod. 11.61.7.
58 Plut. *Cim.* 13.3.
59 Martin-Mcauliffe and Papadopoulos (2012): 332–61.

battles.⁶⁰ He does not say which battles were the critical ones,⁶¹ but the important thing to note is that the fighting by land and sea is given equal status. Sea power was the deciding factor in the Persian Wars. The Ionian Revolt was a series of maritime campaigns and which was decided at sea by superior Persian sea power. It was this that allowed the Persians to invade Attica in 490 at Marathon, unimpeded. Finally, it was the defeat of this sea power by the Greeks that allowed them to triumph in the defence of mainland Greece and to take the fight to Persia, freeing the Ionian Islands and the Hellespont from Persian hegemony. But perhaps the most defining outcome was the ascendancy of Athens. Themistocles' wooden walls would soon spread throughout the Aegean and give rise to the Delian League and subsequently the Athenian Empire, an empire of the seas.

---

60 Thuc. 1.23.1.
61 Gomme (1945: 151) presumes Thucydides is talking of Artemision and Salamis, Thermopylae and Plataea, though possibly Mycale instead of Artemision. Hornblower (1997: 62) understands it as Salamis and either Artemision or Mycale, and Thermopylae and Plataea by land, dismissing Marathon as a possibility. Thucydides either presumes the reader will know which exact battles he means or will be able to make a judgement call about it. This also indicates that Thucydides considers the Persian War to have ended in 479, but of course he was attempting to minimise the wars that came before his narrative of the Peloponnesian War and so this should not be a surprise.

Chapter Six
Rulers of the sea: Athens and the Delian League

When the dust settled from the Persian Wars a new balance of power had emerged in the Aegean. Athens found itself in possession of a large, battle-proven navy, superior to any other naval force in the region. How it reconciled itself with this newfound sea power was to shape the remaining seven decades of the fifth century in the Aegean and beyond. Our main source for the period known as the *pentekontaetia*, the '50-year period' between the Persian Wars and the Peloponnesian War, is Thucydides. Unfortunately, he brushes over the period in only a brief examination with little detail. Nevertheless, from Thucydides, Diodorus, and others we can piece together important details of the rise of Athens as a sea power. This includes the work *The Constitution of the Athenians* by the unknown author known as the 'Old Oligarch'.[1] In this pamphlet the author details the character of Athens as an imperial power in control of the seas. Throughout we see maritime concerns at the forefront of the various antagonisms leading up to the Peloponnesian War.

Walls of wood and stone

Having seen the power that could be wielded with navies, another development aided the efficacy of a polis' maritime power. An island or coastal state could reap enormous benefit from building city walls. While this seems like a rather mundane development, this combination of a navy and walls became incredibly powerful. Siege warfare at the time was extremely basic, essentially requiring the besieging force to starve out the enemy city or have someone inside open the gates. It was not until the middle of the fourth century that developments in siege technology led to more direct attacks on walled cities, albeit nothing of the effectiveness of later siege warfare. This meant a well-supplied walled city could hold out for a long time under siege. Where this became even more potent was when it was combined with a navy that could allow for the continued supply of the city through a port, and in the case of an island potentially cut off any would-be attackers, who themselves would have been reliant on a maritime supply connection. In the case of Athens during the Peloponnesian War, we will see how this

---
[1] For a copy of the text with analysis see Marr and Rhodes (2008).

https://doi.org/10.1515/9783111342931-007

combination not only allowed them to weather serious attacks on Attica but also shaped their entire war strategy.

An early glimpse at this new development comes from Herodotus. The island of Thasos, off the coast of northern Greece, had supposedly been settled by the great seafarers, the Phoenicians.[2] They controlled very productive gold mines, both on the island and on the mainland. Herodotus says that the Thasians used the great wealth derived from its mines to build warships and to enclose the city in a stronger wall.[3] In 491 the Thasians assented to a request by the Persian King Darius to tear down the walls and give over their ships.[4] Clearly, the Persians, stung by the recent Ionian revolt, were wary of cities possessing a navy not under their control and it is clear in this example that they also feared the idea of a city having strong revenue, a fleet, and an enclosed city. This is the first instance where we see this revenue-fleet-wall combination being presented as a polis' defensive strategy.

In the aftermath of the Persian defeat in 479, Athens made the decision to rebuild the city's walls. This caused anxiety in Sparta, though it was Sparta's allies that allegedly goaded the Spartans into confronting Athens, fearing the Athenian navy and the valour which they had displayed against Persia.[5] This is the first time in his work that Thucydides makes a link between sea power and walls, left unspoken in this instance. It is also noteworthy that he says it was Sparta's allies who were most concerned: allies who were nearer to the coast than Sparta and therefore more vulnerable to Athenian warships. The explicit linking of walls and sea power comes soon after when he tells of Themistocles' efforts to fortify the Piraeus. Thucydides sees Themistocles as the one who spurred Athens into becoming a sea power and as such laid the foundations of the Athenian Empire.[6] As important as this development was, it was the construction of the Long and Phaleric Walls that truly turned Athens into a maritime-fuelled fortress. Having enclosed the city and the port at the Piraeus, in 457 they constructed the Long Walls between the two, and a wall from the city down to enclose the older harbour and beaching site at Phaleron Bay, ensuring complete walled access from city to sea.[7] This in effect turned Athens into an island, a metaphor that would be used by the Athenians themselves to describe their strategic position.

---

2 On the likelihood of this and arguments around the matter, see Scott (2005): 207–9.
3 Hdt. 6.46–7.
4 Hdt. 6.48.1.
5 Thuc. 1.90.1.
6 Thuc. 1.93.3–7.
7 Thuc. 1.107.1, 1.108.3. Full dimensions of the walls: 2.13.7.

We saw in Chapter Four Thucydides' *archaeology* chapters, where he discusses sea power throughout history. More than just a preface to his own history, these chapters are integral to understanding Thucydides' thoughts on the factors that controlled his world. It forms the basis of Thucydides' construction of a model of power, taken first from the two great moments in history before his time, the thalassocracies of Crete and Mycenae,[8] and further influenced by the Athens of his time. It is here that Jacqueline de Romilly has the most incisive insight into 'the mind of Thucydides'. For her the Athenian system represents the model of power on which all the Greek world sits:

> A *fleet* allows *commerce*. Commerce brings *revenue*. Revenue creates a *treasury*. The treasury, for its part, is tied to *stability*, which leads to the existence of *walls*. And these three terms, fleet-treasury-walls, make it possible for a state to *group* numerous other states under its domination, and to acquire a *force*.[9]

As she says, Thucydides never gives such an explicit analysis in his work, but the text itself is what establishes the basis for a systematically realistic interpretation of history.[10] Josiah Ober follows this judgement, referring to (Athens') 'perfection of a technology of power', in the form of a 'material' triad of money, walls and ships.[11] Athens epitomises this supreme model of power in Thucydides' age. From this we can see Thucydides describing sea power as strategy. This is apparent when he discusses Athens' actions in the aftermath of the Persian Wars. Of particular note is the fact that Thucydides was himself a naval commander during the Peloponnesian War and was involved in the campaign around Amphipolis in 424/3.[12] This is important when considering what he has to tell us about naval matters and strategy during the war.

Plutarch also credits Themistocles with the Athenian turn towards sea power as strategy, the one who 'fastened the city to the Piraeus and the land to the sea'.[13] However, where Thucydides relates bare facts, Plutarch adds colour to this maritime turn, even if the stories are rather dubious. He reports that the old kings of Athens had discouraged Athens from leading a maritime life, as proven by the story of the triumph of Athena's gift of an olive tree over Poseidon's spring, rightly considered 'an absurd anachronism'. After all, the contest between the two deities was considered fitting enough to make up the theme of the western

---

[8] de Romilly (2012): 165. Her work was originally published in French as *Histoire et raison chez Thucydide*, in 1967.
[9] Emphasis in original. de Romilly (2012): 157.
[10] de Romilly (2012): 157.
[11] Ober (2006): 146.
[12] Thuc. 4.104–8; On his exile: 5.26.5–6.
[13] Plut. *Them.* 19.2–3.

pediment of the Parthenon, built at the height of Athens' maritime imperialism in the 440s.[14] However, what this story does say is that later historians overemphasised the radical nature of the turn to sea power by Athens in the age of Themistocles.[15] Plutarch over-characterises the divide between sea and land power proponents in Athens during the fifth century.[16] Regardless of the veracity of these various stories, what Plutarch is trying to convey is the high level of maritime consciousness thought to have been present in Athens during the fifth century.

The 'Old Oligarch'

One of the most prominent and important works dealing with Athenian sea power is that of the *Constitution of the Athenians* by the unknown author 'the Old Oligarch'.[17] There is debate as to the dating of this work, either a fifth-century anti-democracy/anti-naval tract, or a fourth-century rhetorical work on the dangers of navalism and using Delian League Athens as a prop. I favour a fifth-century dating for the work, a reflection of the anti-navy crowd in Athens in the early years preceding the Peloponnesian War.[18] It is important to note that it is a work of the Athenian anti-navy crowd, and although it describes very well the details of Athens' maritime character, it is not done so in favourable terms.

From the beginning of the work the author is clear about who it is that holds power in Athens: the navy. The steersman, boatswains, officers (literally, 'leaders of fifty men'), lookouts and shipwrights made the city powerful.[19] The author returns to Athenian citizens' familiarity with the sea, where he says that both they and their slaves have learned to row without noticing it, an inevitable result for

---

14 Plut. *Them.* 19.3. As Frost points out in his work: Frost (1980): 120–1; also, Marr (1998): 177.
15 Hans van Wees' (2015) recent book elaborates on the growth of Athenian finance in the sixth century and the almost certain existence of a state-run navy in Athens before Themistocles' reforms.
16 Frost (1980): 122; Marr (1998): 178. See also Chapter Three and the story of Critias and the reorientation of the bema of the *Pnyx*.
17 I prefer referring to this unknown author as the 'Old Oligarch' rather than as 'pseudo-Xenophon'.
18 On the dating debate, see Hornblower (2000), who dates it to the fourth century. Momigliano (1944): 2, especially n. 2; de Ste. Croix (1972): 308–9; Osborne (2004): 8–9, who all give a fifth-century date. A discussion and comprehensive list of scholars and their proposed dating of the work is found in: Marr and Rhodes (2008): 3–6; 31–2.
19 Old Oligarch 1.2.

people who often had to travel by sea.[20] As he then says, this experience came from sailing boats, cargo vessels, and triremes, a broad experience of sailing. He shows that the Athenians are very experienced seamen, experience gained in peacetime and translatable when required for service in warships. The Old Oligarch makes quite clear the maritime nature of a large part of the Athenian population.

A large section of this treatise is devoted to the character of Athens' empire, more specifically how maritime power was used to control it. It is quite revealing of Athenian strategy in the fifth century. The first point he makes is about Athenian hoplites and that although they may not be a match for their enemies, they are still stronger than their tribute paying allies, and that was sufficient.[21] It is a strong indication that the Athenians did not intend to use their land forces to directly confront a 'peer-competitor' in pitched battle,[22] making it clear that Athenian strategy was a maritime strategy. Their land army only needed to be stronger than any of the allied states. Even then, they could use this inferior force in a superior way. As the author says, the Athenian navy could land a superior force of troops wherever they wished:

> Since it is possible for the rulers of the sea to sometimes do as land powers do, to ravage the land of the stronger; for it is possible to sail about wherever there is no enemy or wherever they are few, and to embark to sail away as the enemy approaches[23]

During the Peloponnesian War this was demonstrated by Athenian raids on the Peloponnese. Further, Athens exploited geography to its strategic advantage. Land powers could easily band together whereas islands were geographically separated by the sea. This sea was controlled by the Athenians, who if failing to prevent the islanders from coming together in the first place could still cut them off from outside supply and starve them out.[24] The threat levelled against Melos during the Peloponnesian War was made with the implicit understanding that Athens' navy could cut off and invade the small island without outside interference. As for the mainland cities, Athens ruled over them by fear.[25] This was not because of a superior land army alone but through a combination of Athens being able to control the flow of imports and exports and the superior mobility granted to Athens on ac-

---

20 Old Oligarch 1.19.
21 Old Oligarch 2.1.
22 Marr and Rhodes (2008): 100.
23 Old Oligarch 2.4.
24 Old Oligarch 2.2.
25 Old Oligarch 2.3.

count of a strong navy.²⁶ Control over imports and exports was a consistent feature of Athenian rhetoric and action, as demonstrated here and in Thucydides, where he too talks of non-maritime powers being cut off from trade by Athenian sea power:

> All of us who have already had dealings with the Athenians require no warning to be on their guard against them. The poleis more inland and away from the main routes should understand that if they do not support coastal powers, the result will be to injure the transit of their produce for export and the reception in exchange of their imports from the sea; and they must not be careless judges of what is now said, as if it had nothing to do with them, but must expect that the sacrifice of the coastal powers will one day be followed by the extension of the danger to the interior, and must recognise that their own interests are deeply involved in this discussion.²⁷

Such was the power that Athens was seen to hold over coastal states, that if left unchecked would see inland poleis under the sway of Athenian markets, and though removed from the sea, subject to Athenian sea power nonetheless.

The Old Oligarch goes into detail about the economic advantages of sea power in general and how it affected Athens in particular. Firstly, he notes that in times of famine, land powers could be badly affected whereas sea powers could bear it 'easily', since bad conditions did not affect the whole earth and therefore it was possible for 'the rulers of the sea' to import what they needed.²⁸ Athens was a cosmopolitan place where, because of their sea power, they had mixed with many different people from around the world. It was a place where every kind of luxury could be found, from Sicily, Italy, Cyprus, Egypt, Lydia, Pontus, the Peloponnese, or anywhere else: all could be found in Athens.²⁹ It even extended to the cross-pollination of language, diet, and dress, a mixture from Greeks and non-Greeks.³⁰ Critically, Athens could control the flow of trade, especially timber, iron, copper and flax needed for shipbuilding, and the Old Oligarch twice in two lines asks what a city rich in such goods alone could do without the permission of the rulers of the sea – Athens.³¹ The Athenians could prevent these goods from being transported and despite the fact that the land of Attica produced none of these goods, Athenians nevertheless possessed all of them because of the sea.³² The Old Oligarch thus details the social, economic, and even military issues and

---

26 Old Oligarch 2.3–5.
27 Thuc. 1.120.2.
28 Old Oligarch 2.6.
29 Old Oligarch 2.7.
30 Old Oligarch 2.8.
31 Old Oligarch. 2.11.
32 Old Oligarch 2.12. A somewhat exaggerated claim. Marr and Rhodes (2008): 119.

advantages that sea power bestowed on Athens. Many Athenians would have disputed the benefits or good of the social aspects – mixing with foreigners especially – but it no doubt helped Athens become and maintain its position as the most influential Polis in the second half of the fifth century and into the fourth.

Even the language used throughout the work highlights the maritime nature of Athens' power. Athenians sailed out to bring vexatious judicial charges against citizens within the allied states, who were compelled to 'sail' back to Athens: the default way of doing business by sea.[33] This refers to a law which made it mandatory for all capital crimes throughout the Delian league to be tried at Athens, as well as grain contracts requiring the carriers to return to Athens first. This was another form of control, based on sea power. All of this was the natural result of their being rulers of the sea, and the *Constitution of the Athenians* is replete with variations of the term 'rulers of the sea' when referring to the Athenians.[34] As the work makes clear, it is sea power and the control of the maritime domain that allowed Athens to rule over its allies, be it through litigation, control of imports and exports, or the implicit understanding that the Athenian navy could deliver a sufficiently powerful force of hoplites wherever needed, with better mobility than other military forces were capable of.

The most telling and blatant expression of Athens' position as a maritime power is at passage 2.14–16 where the Old Oligarch compares Athens to an island. The author lays out the different strategic advantages if Athens had been an island. This includes the internal security benefits, namely freedom from the fear that oligarchs would open the gates of the city to an enemy, one of the few guaranteed ways for a besieging force to enter a city. As Marr and Rhodes point out, the section is seemingly a digression but could be seen in light of the popular notion at the time that Athens would be better off if it were an island.[35] It is directly comparable to Pericles' speech in Thucydides where the 'Athens as an island' topic is broached.[36] Marr and Rhodes reasonably conclude that the Old Oligarch is not necessarily quoting Pericles directly or taking it from Thucydides but echoing a common sentiment in Athens at the time.[37] This helps explain the symbolism of the City and Long walls of Athens, not just protecting the city and port of Athens but during wartime cutting it off from the rest of mainland Greece.

The Old Oligarch's *Constitution* not only highlights the maritime nature of Athens as a city but also several important aspects of Athenian strategy. The Athe-

---

33 Old Oligarch 1.14, 1.16.
34 Old Oligarch 2.2, 2.3, 2.4, 2.5, 2.6, 2.7.
35 Marr and Rhodes (2008): 121.
36 Thuc. 1.143.5.
37 Marr and Rhodes (2008): 121.

nians had a realistic appraisal of the capabilities of their land army and what they would use it for. Against continental powers they could raid from the sea almost with impunity. Over islands, especially small islands, the army would be superior and thus able to subdue these poleis with outright military force if required. Athens used geography to their advantage, carving out an empire of islands and coastal cities, all vulnerable to their superior naval and land forces, either through military action or in the position of being directly threatened or starved into submission through blockade. All of this demonstrates a conscious and well-developed maritime strategy on the part of Athens in the fifth century.

The *pentekontaetia*

Diodorus reports the rise of Athenian sea power in the post-Persian War era in similar terms as does Thucydides, with the additional comment that Themistocles did not see the Spartans as having an aptitude at sea.[38] Critically, Diodorus and no other author reports that Themistocles persuaded the *demos* to approve a continuous building program of 20 triremes a year.[39] This would have assured a steady supply of new warships for the fleet, not necessarily to grow the size of the fleet by 20 triremes a year but to ensure new warships could replace old ones from service and thus keep the fleet in good operating order. If Athens maintained a fleet of 200 triremes, then replacing 20 a year would ensure that no trireme was older than 10 years. Diodorus relates another previously unknown episode, albeit one confusing in nature. In the aftermath of the Spartan general Pausanias' missteps in Asia following the Persian invasion, Diodorus has the Spartans debating war over regaining leadership over the sea.[40] Diodorus seems to be discussing leadership and command, in the sense of military command over forces, using the world 'hegemony' rather than 'rule'. However, he then implies that Spartan rule would be incomplete without one of the two leaderships, presumably meaning the land and sea.[41] Further, the debate in the *Gerousia* indicated that the Spartans were willing to go to war over regaining hegemony, and that the Athenians were building extra triremes in anticipation of a confronta-

---

38 Diod. 11.39.2, 11.41.2–3, 11.41.5.
39 Diod. 11.43.3.
40 Diod. 11.50.1. Diodorus dates the incident to 475, but others are rightfully sceptical, dating it to earlier: 478 or 477. See Meiggs (1972): 40; Green (2006): 111. Some authors think it may be an invented story: Lendon (2007): 264.
41 Diod. 11.50.4.

tion.⁴² This is deeply confusing considering that Spartan sea power at this time was in no way capable of defeating Athenian sea power. This is either Diodorus misreading the military strategic situation at the time or it is an issue of language usage for the different concepts of 'leadership' and 'rule'. In any case, Diodorus does recognise that in remaining unchallenged at sea, Athens was then able to expand its power.

Elsewhere Diodorus uses language to describe cities of the time in terms of their sea power. Interestingly, the Tyrrhenians are at one point called rulers of the sea, as are the Athenians in 464.⁴³ The Tyrrhenian example leaves little to analyse, but certainly his assessment of Athens as rulers of the sea in 464 is an accurate strategic appraisal. In 460 the Athenians and allies had sent a fleet of 200 ships to Cyprus when they received an invitation from Egypt to aid them in their revolt against Persia.⁴⁴ Thucydides gives us little to work with as far as motivations or even details of the campaign. It is probable that Athens saw this as a chance to further damage Persia and win friends in Egypt, a great source of grain, a consideration always on Athens' mind.⁴⁵ Seeing as this came around the same time as Athens began work on the Long Walls connecting Athens to the Piraeus, this fits nicely into their strategy of turning Athens into an island supplied from overseas grain. It is also possible to see this campaign as a continuation of the war against Persia, though perhaps more by proxy and circumstance rather than a deliberate Athenian campaign. As noted in the previous chapter, I have marked the battle of Eurymedon River as the end of the 'Persian War', but ongoing Greek campaigns such as the ones in Cyprus and Egypt could argue for a later dating of the end of the war. Alternatively, it is possible to see 479 as the end of the Persian War and the conflict that comes after as something new. Hard and fast delineations rarely work when trying to separate different 'wars' in the ancient context. In any case, after a long campaign the Egyptians and Delian League forces were defeated by the Persians, losing many ships in the process, although almost certainly not the full 200 ships that had initially been sent there.⁴⁶ Continued Athenian campaigning soon after suggests that this defeat did not cripple, or even seriously damage, Athens' sea power.

Athens continued to strengthen its maritime influence by subduing that of its rivals. While still campaigning in Egypt, in approximately 458, after a naval battle and a siege the Athenians subdued Aegina and apart from paying tribute to

---

42 Diod. 11.50.2, 11.50.8.
43 Diod. 11.51.1, 11.70.5.
44 Thuc. 1.104.
45 This is the conclusion reached by Russell Meiggs (1972): 95.
46 Thuc. 1.105; 1.109–110; Meiggs (1972): 104–5.

Athens, they were forced to surrender their ships and destroy their walls.[47] Here again we see the fleet and walls combo in play. Without walls or a fleet, the island was at the mercy of the Athenian fleet and Aeginetan sea power ceased to be a threat to Athens, though the island would be used to great success as a base of operations by the Spartans to attack Athens in the fourth century.[48] Lying so close to critical Athenian sea lanes, the threat of Aeginetan sea power was too much for Athens to ignore. At the same time as this, fighting over control of Boeotia saw the Spartans defeat Athens at Tanagra, followed 62 days later by an Athenian victory at Oenophyta over the Boeotians, the Spartans having returned home.[49] This first battle may have proved the superiority of Sparta on land, but that superiority counted for little if they were not present to help their allies and so strategically speaking, the Spartan efforts were for nought. Indeed, a year or two after Athenian victory at Oenophyta, they conducted a maritime campaign around the Peloponnese, burning the Spartan naval facilities at Gytheum, taking the Corinthian city of Chalcis at the entrance to the Corinthian Gulf, and sailing to the end of the Gulf to Sicyon, where they defeated the Sicyons in battle.[50] So we see that despite the victory of Spartan hoplites at Tanagra, it was Athenian sea power that dictated the tempo of operations in the years that followed, gaining far more than they had lost at Tanagra. Here too we see a textbook example of how sea power consists of more than just warships, and to be truly effective must be able to employ land forces. Athens could project power around the entirety of the Peloponnese, with warships providing cover to ground forces, the latter of which were able to not only raid the coast but defeat another land force in battle.

A second Athenian attack on Cyprus came sometime around 451/450, led by the statesman Cimon, naturally featured sea power as a core element.[51] Thucydides gives no more than the basic facts of the campaign, saying only that the Athenian fought and won by both land and sea.[52] Diodorus gives more detail, and importantly he places greater emphasis on the role sea power played. He begins by saying that Cimon reached Cyprus and established sea control over the area.[53] Diodorus reinforces the point, saying again that Cimon was ruler over the sea

---

47 Thuc. 1.105.2–5, 108.4–5.
48 See Chapter Nine.
49 Thuc. 1.107–8.
50 Thuc. 1.108.5; Meiggs (1972): 100.
51 Sometime around 451/450. Meiggs dates the opening of the campaign to 451, Green to 450. Meiggs (1972): 124–6; Green (2006): 179.
52 Thuc. 1.112.
53 Diod. 12.3.3.

and this allowed him to begin subduing the cities of Cyprus.[54] Cimon targeted the city of Salamis, which Diodorus says would put him in control of the island and deal a blow to the Persians, who would be unable to relieve the city.[55] This account of Diodorus makes it clear that sea power was the defining factor in the fight over Cyprus and is far more explicit about it than Thucydides and Plutarch,[56] both of whom give the impression that it was sea power that won the day but are not as explicit as Diodorus, who constantly uses strong language in his narrative.

An early detailed example of a blockade is the Athenian operation against Samos in 441/0. The island had revolted against the recently Athenian-installed democracy, causing the Athenians to send out an expedition of 60 ships. Sixteen ships were detailed as scouts to watch for the Phoenician fleet, as well as taking orders to Lesbos and Chios for reinforcements.[57] The remaining 44 ships were under the command of Pericles and near the island of Tragia, 13 nautical miles south of Samos, they intercepted 70 Samian vessels sailing from Miletos. This example is useful in highlighting the idea of battles being fought 'near' land. Thucydides says that the battle took place 'off Tragia'. The route from Miletus to Samos would not need to pass any closer than eight nautical miles to Tragia: it is not directly on the way. In all likelihood, the Athenian fleet was stationed near the island and so it was merely the closest terrestrial reference point for the battle. It is quite probable that this naval battle did not take place any closer than 4–8 nautical miles from land. The Samian fleet included 20 transport ships and so had only a slim numerical superiority, but they were defeated by the Athenians. Reinforced by 40 more Athenian and 25 Chian and Lesbian vessels, the Athenian-led forces laid siege to the city by land, building three walls to circumvallate the city while simultaneously blockading the harbour.[58] That this was a proper blockade by sea is clear by examining the next incident. After Pericles took 60 ships to search for and engage a potential Phoenician relief fleet, the Samians made a surprise attack against the Athenian forces and were victorious in a sea battle. This made them masters of their own seas for two weeks and allowed supplies to flow into the city. Pericles' return caused the Samians to once again be blockaded.[59]

---

54 Diod. 12.4.1.
55 Diod. 12.4.2.
56 Thuc. 1.112; Plut. *Cim.* 18.5. There are however issues over the chronology of the death of Cimon and other finer points of the narrative in Diodorus. See Meiggs (1972): 124–6; Green (2006): 179–81.
57 Thuc. 1.116.1.
58 Thuc. 1.116.
59 Thuc. 1.116.3–117.1–2.

This siege demonstrates the complexity of besieging and blockading an island and the different naval operations required, with the same naval forces engaged in different tasks at short notice. Athenian naval forces first had to send out scouts to keep watch for the enemy fleet, as well as gather allied reinforcements. The remainder of the Athenian vessels engaged in a fleet action, interdicting the enemy fleet and transport ships. Once these operations were completed, they then laid siege to the city and commenced a blockade. Although we are given no details, it seems likely that by blockade, it was meant the Athenians were primarily focused on the port, not the entire island. It would have been all but impossible for the Athenians, or any other naval force, to control the entire coastline. It would have been enough to blockade the port and any major landing spots on the island. This required a further sortie by the main fleet and caused the Athenians to lose sea control around Samos. The siege and blockade lasted for nine months and is a great example of the complexities required of naval forces when besieging and blockading a hostile island. This is an important consideration when examining the Peloponnesian War and later conflicts between Athens and the islands, where such operations were frequent.

Athens and the Delian League

> He [Pericles] displayed their power to the barbarian tribes living around and to their kings and lords the magnitude of their power and the confidence and impunity with which they sailed where they wished, having made all of the sea subject to their control.[60]

The Plutarch passage above details an Athenian expedition to the Black Sea conducted by Pericles in approximately 438–432.[61] It is a textbook example of the use of a naval force for diplomatic purposes – 'gunboat diplomacy' in more infamous terms. The Athenian fleet's presence off the coast of the Aegean islands and the Black Sea region demonstrated Athens' potential power to friend and foe alike, without encroaching on any territory or engaging in any hostile act. Athens demonstrated her dominance at sea to allies as well as to other neutral or potentially hostile powers throughout the Mediterranean. Pericles' show of force in the Black Sea was aimed at Greeks and foreigners alike, including powers with which they

---

60 Plut. *Per.* 20.1.
61 Stadter (1989): 216. His arguments are solid. First is the point that after the loss of the Egyptian campaign, Euxine grain would have grown in importance to Athens. Secondly, according to Diodorus (12.31.1) a new king took power in the Cimmerian Bosporus region in 438/37; perhaps one of the 'kings' Plutarch is referring to.

were at peace. As Plutarch understands, it is also more than just the sailing around of a large body of warships: the real point of the exercise was in demonstrating Athenian sea control. The ships displayed naval and military power in a region distant from Athens and with the clear implication that Athens could project this power anywhere and at any time – the power, confidence, and impunity of sailing where they wished, 'having made all of the sea subject to their control'. It is also quite possible that this cruise by Pericles helped establish Athenian relations with the various cities of the Black Sea, many of which would later appear on the Athenian Tribute Lists. The list of 425/4 offers a tantalising glimpse at some of the areas Pericles may have visited, and indeed the Black Sea region seems to have featured prominently in Athenian thinking towards the end of the century.[62] From this it seems as if Pericles' cruise was very successful as a demonstration of Athenian power and reach, all thanks to their strong sea power.

In addition to the above power projection cruise, Plutarch says that Pericles did many things to please the people of Athens, including 'sending out sixty triremes each and every year, in which many of the citizens were sailing for eight months being paid'.[63] Aside from being a manner in which the 'naval mob' were kept happy, it acted as an annual demonstration of Athenian sea power to the outside world in both having a well-practiced navy and especially the act of having a substantial force of warships sailing about for a large portion of the year. The training benefit of such a cruise should not be underestimated. This cruise is precisely this sort of naval practice that Thucydides has Pericles laud in his opening speech at the beginning of the war, when he says that the Spartans will not easily pick up skill at sea, for it is a skill that must be practiced constantly and leaves no room for other endeavours.[64] The skill in seamanship that Thucydides talks about is not just the skill of rowing well but clearly refers to the whole range of skills and the practice needed to operate a *fleet*, not just a ship. Some scholars believe that 60 is too large a number, pointing out that it would have incurred too great an annual cost, but regardless of numbers it remains an example of the frequent use of Athens' navy for diplomatic purposes.[65] Russell Meiggs

---

[62] For example, Euripides' *Medea* and *Iphigenia in Tauris*. See Gallo (2013): 159–61. Add to this the fact that the Black Sea region was increasingly becoming a critical area for the supply of grain to Athens.
[63] Plut. *Per.* 11.4.
[64] Thuc. 1.142.6–9.
[65] Meiggs (1972): 206; Eddy (1968): 142–55. Though Plutarch's language implies that it was sixty ships under pay for the entire eight-month period, it seems more reasonable to think that a portion of the sixty ships were sent out at times throughout an eight-month period. This would ensure a healthy training rotation of ships and crews whilst maintaining a presence throughout the

suggests that the main function of the fleet in peacetime was as a police force, with the threefold duty of showing the flag, instilling confidence in the hearts of their friends and suppressing piracy.[66] Although correctly identifying the roles, he mistakenly identifies the first two as constabulary operations when they are in fact diplomatic ones – the two most prominent and important diplomatic roles undertaken by navies. The ultimate goal of such posturing was diplomatic, to establish in the minds of friend and foe alike the Athenian capacity and will to control the seas.

The Delian League was initially a defensive organisation that existed for the defence of Greece against Persia. The primary means of defence was through maritime power, centred on a strong naval capability. Meiggs is explicit in his analysis: 'the foundation of Athenian power was her fleet.'[67] From the beginning of the League's formation it was decided which states would contribute money or ships.[68] Thucydides lists the two things most important to the League's power – money and ships – with the understanding that money would help further enable the League's sea power. Importantly, Thucydides relates how the allies eventually became sick of campaigning and so arranged to pay their tribute in money rather than ships, simultaneously strengthening Athenian sea power and weakening that of the allies.[69] By the outbreak of the Peloponnesian War, only Chios, Lesbos, and Corcyra were providing ships to the alliance, and the rest contributed money and soldiers. Plutarch is explicit in his description of how this imbalance worked, telling of how the allies stayed at home to become farmers and merchants and causing them to eventually fear those who were continually sailing under arms, reduced to the status of subjects rather than allies.[70] Plutarch's narrative has Cimon, as an agent of Athens, deliberately encouraging this course of action and thus establishing it as Athenian policy. This strengthening of Athenian sea power at the expense of the allies led to the situation whereby a force of Athenian triremes could get its point across without resorting to force, with members of the Delian League knowing 'that Athenian triremes might appear at any moment . . . '.[71] With the erosion of their navies, it was Athenian sea power that guaranteed security of Delain League members from Persia or other hostile powers. This is the duality of Athenian sea power and the Delian League – the power to either protect allies or

---

Aegean at a lower cost than having all sixty out at once, though this perhaps might have occurred for certain periods of time.
66 Meiggs (1979): 206.
67 Meiggs (1979): 205.
68 Thuc. 1.96.1.
69 Thuc. 1.99.1–3.
70 Plut. *Cim.* 11.2–3.
71 Meiggs (1972): 205.

withdraw that protection, and the ability to interfere directly in an ally's business.[72] This demonstrates Thucydides' belief that Athens' subjects were in part responsible for their own subjugation, given that they agreed to pay for their defence rather than make it their own business and thus handed Athens the power needed for hegemony over the League. In these two core ways, the Athenian fleet was wielded as a powerful diplomatic tool.

Athenian control over allies extended beyond the use and threatened use of military force directly against recalcitrant or rebellious allies. Athenian sea power allowed Athens to control her allies in other ways. As discussed, the Old Oligarch neatly laid out ways in which Athens controlled the allies' trade, both imports and exports. As the Old Oligarch implies, Athens is controlling not only generally valuable commodities but commodities essential for a city attempting to build or maintain a maritime force. There are incidences of Athenians specifically regulating the import of grain into allied cities. In one decree, dated to perhaps 429/8, the Athenians granted the city of Methone the right to import a quantity of grain from Byzantium, giving notice to the Athenian Hellespont guards.[73] This shows that Athens controlled the imports of an allied city, and did so in an indirect manner. They did not need a garrison or officials in Methone to control the grain imports but could rely on their officials controlling the strategically important choke point in the Hellespont. In controlling this vital sea route, the Athenians could regulate the Black Sea trade and especially the important grain trade. The revolt of Lesbos in 428 happened earlier than planned, and part of the preparations involved importing grain from the Pontus, something made impossible once the Athenians learned of the revolt and closed this route to the Lesbians.[74] In all these different ways Athens was able to establish more than just military control over allies through a range of different policies, all with a particular maritime aspect. Athens is effectively utilising the economic side of sea power.

Conclusion

The end of the Persian Wars opened a new front for the various Greek poleis to consolidate power. The efficacy of sea power was obvious, but it would be Athens above all who capitalised most on this development. They developed a concerted maritime strategy, utilising the trinity of wealth, ships, and walls to establish the

---

72 Thuc. 1.99. As de Romilly notes. de Romilly (1979): 311.
73 Meiggs and Lewis (1969): 176–80; Meiggs (1972): 206.
74 Thuc. 3.2.1–3. Meiggs (1972): 206.

Delian League, which gradually morphed into the Athenian Empire. On the eve of the Peloponnesian War Athens was the unsurpassed master of the seas around Greece and into the Aegean and the Hellespont. The question remained, however, how effective this Athenian sea power would be in the face of a peer competitor. The Greek world was about to find out how effective Athens' wooden walls would be against the heirs of Thermopylae, and the outcome would determine the course of the next five decades in Greece.

Chapter Seven
The great war: the Peloponnesian war from Corcyra to Sicily

Thucydides wrote his history of the Peloponnesian War because he believed it was a greater war than any before in the Greek world: bigger than the Persian Wars and bigger even than the mythical Trojan War. It was a war that ranged from Sicily in the west up to the Black Sea in the east, across the lands and the seas of most of the Greek world. Perhaps the most interesting observation is that little warfare outside of raiding occurred in the lands of the two main protagonists, Athens and Sparta. Sure, the Spartans raided the lands of Attica for a few seasons, but this was quite ineffective and ceased after Athenian victory at Pylos. As we shall see in the next chapter, even the permanent Spartan occupation of Attica at Decelea had a minimal impact on Athens' military ability to fight on, though no doubt it took a psychological toll. The Peloponnesian War was a maritime war, fought on and across the seas. Sea power defined the war: Athenian in the first half and Spartan in the second half. Sparta might have been the supreme land power in 431, but it was only when they embraced a maritime approach, funded by Persia, that they were able to overcome Athens. The war was not the quintessential land versus sea power dichotomy that it is so often portrayed.[1] Sea power – which included the ability to project power ashore with land forces – was what decided the great war of Thucydides' time.

Crisis in Corcyra

One of the crises that triggered the Peloponnesian War was conflict in 435 between Corinth and its former colony of Corcyra over Corcyraean interests in its own colony of Epidamnus, located on the Adriatic coast of Illyria. Escalating rivalry between the two cities became a full-blown conflict. Corcyra was considered a strong naval power, with 120 triremes in their fleet, considered threatening enough that the Corinthian force sent to relieve Epidamnus went by land for fear of the Corcyraean fleet.[2] After refusing arbitration, the Corinthians declared war and sent a fleet of 75 warships and 2,000 hoplites to relieve Epidamnus. Refusing to heed Corcyraean warnings they engaged 80 ships of Corcyra and were de-

---

1 For a few recent examples, see Parry (2014): 276; Rovner (2019); and Messina (2019).
2 Thuc. 1.25.4, 1.26.1–2.

feated. Interestingly, Thucydides notes that 40 of Corcyra's ships were engaged in the siege of Epidamnus, hence the 80 in the naval battle.³ The Corcyraean fleet was thus fully engaged in operations and was apparently strong enough to defeat the navy of Corinth. More than that, after their victory, the fleet of Corcyra campaigned against several poleis that had supported Corinth, Thucydides saying that Corcyra had sea control in those waters.⁴ This spurred Corinth into a major building programme of warships and recruitment.⁵ The maritime rivalry between the two powers was heading towards a second showdown.

To that point non-aligned, Corcyra decided to approach Athens about joining their alliance. Despite Corinthian protestations and threats, Athens decided to conclude a defensive treaty with Corcyra in 433. Both Thucydides and Plutarch say that Athens needed to aid Corcyra lest their naval power go over to Athens' rival Corinth.⁶ Athens sent 10 ships to aid Corcyra and what is especially noteworthy is the inclusion of three *strategoi* to command the contingent, a high level of command for such a small number of ships. For comparison, a later raid on the Peloponnese during the first year of the war, involving 100 ships, had the same number of *strategoi*.⁷ The three commanders sent to Corcyra were under strict instructions not to provoke Corinth or do anything that would lead to a violation of the treaty Athens had with them but to prevent an incursion into Corcyraean territory. The ships were under the overall command of Lacedaemonius, the son of Pericles' rival Cimon, and Plutarch sees this, combined with the fact that he gave him 'only' 10 ships, as an insult.⁸ However, this does not bear scrutiny, as Plutarch entirely omits any mention of the two other *strategoi* and the strict instructions that were given to them.⁹ Athens sent out a tightly controlled force of ships to aid an ally, Corcyra, while simultaneously making a show of force and a demonstration of Athenian resolve in the face of Corinthian aggression. Donald Kagan put it best when he described this manoeuvre as less a military than a diplomatic one.¹⁰ Any contention that the Athenian orders were unrealistic misses the point that it was a diplomatic rather than a military use of sea power and the situation was already balanced on a knife edge.¹¹ It was the presence of Athenian

---

3 Thuc. 1.29.
4 Thuc. 1.30.2.
5 Thuc. 1.31.
6 Thuc. 1.44; Plut. *Per.* 29.1–2. With the caveat that Plutarch is likely just following Thucydides.
7 Thuc. 1.45, 2.23, respectively.
8 Thucydides is silent on this matter. Plut. *Per.* 29.2–3; Hornblower (1997): 88.
9 Diotimos and Proteas were the other two generals. Thuc. 1.45.
10 Kagan (1969): 244–5.
11 Hornblower (1997): 90.

ships to begin with as opposed to their number that was the entire point, and the fact that they were commanded by three *strategoi* shows the delicate nature of the task. From the outset of tensions, Athens was careful to employ naval force as a diplomatic rather than as a purely military tool. Nevertheless, Athenian intervention was required to save Corcyra from defeat, thus giving the Peloponnesian League a justification for war.

War at sea

At the outbreak of the Peloponnesian War, Thucydides says that the three naval powers of note in Greece were Athens, Corinth, and Corcyra.[12] Athens began the war with what was regarded as the pre-eminent naval force in the eastern Mediterranean, bolstered by the recent alliance with Corcyra and their large fleet and favourable strategic position. This did not mean that their enemies failed to contest Athenian sea control. It was only through subsequent battles that the Athenian navy reinforced its reputation and solidified its strategic position. The Corinthians attempted to convince the Spartans that one large-scale naval battle resulting in the destruction of a large part of the Athenian navy would spell their doom.[13] This was a theoretically sound strategy to defeat Athens but without effective ways or means by which they might accomplish this end state, it was an unworkable strategy. It was perhaps the hope of the Corinthians that they would accumulate enough money from various sources, Delphi or Olympia for example, and attract enough rowers to man a fleet capable of fighting Athens at sea. Persia eventually provided enough funding to the enemies of Athens for this to eventuate, and Thucydides here is foreshadowing how the Athenians are eventually defeated two decades later. At the outbreak of the war, the enemies of Athens had the right strategy without the means: by 405 they had the correct strategy and the means to make it work. However, at the outbreak of war in 431, the Spartans and their allies were in no position to fight, let alone win, a decisive naval battle against Athens or indeed at any point before the Peace of Nicias. It would only be with the destruction of the Athenian fleet in the Great Harbour of Syracuse during the Sicilian expedition that the balance of naval power would be altered in favour of the Peloponnesian League. The original Corinthian strategy of decisive battle was eventually proven sound and, in concert with other maritime operations, eventually led Sparta to victory. But this was still two decades in the future.

---

12 Thuc. 1.36.3.
13 Thuc. 1.121.4.

This line of thinking on decisive battle has a striking parallel in the early twentieth century and the First World War. It is reminiscent of German naval strategy under Admiral Tirpitz of the 'risk fleet': the idea that the inferior German High Seas Fleet could catch a portion of the Royal Navy's Grand Fleet and defeat it, thus altering the balance of naval power in favour of Germany with one grand battle.[14] Corinthian thinking, at least as projected by Thucydides, was that defeating a large Athenian naval contingent would bring the Peloponnesian side closer to parity with the Athenian fleet, thus negating the greatest advantage of the Athenians. As we saw, the Athenians in 480 were able to erode the Persian fleet's fighting ability at Artemision, admittedly with the help of two storms, and soon after at Salamis were able to defeat the Persians at sea, making Plataea possible and finally eliminating the Persian threat to the Greek mainland. The proposed Corinthian course of action was an explicit expression of decisive naval battle as a conscious strategy. Taken with the Persian War example, they show that over a 2,000-year period the appeal of 'Mahanian' battle at sea to determine the outcome of a war remained an appealing strategy.[15] The Corinthians correctly assessed the fleet as Athens' centre of gravity and it is hard to escape another comparison with the First World War, where it was said of the British Admiral Sir John Jellicoe that he was 'the only man on either side who could lose the war in an afternoon'. This is referring to the potential for him to lose a naval battle and thus cede control of the sea to the Germans, leaving Britain completely defenceless against the German High Seas Fleet, susceptible to attack and blockade.[16] Likewise, the destruction of Athenian sea power could put them in a similar position. No doubt recognising this themselves, the Athenians made quick progress strengthening their strategic position in Greece and establishing maritime supremacy wherever possible.

---

14 This was the essence of the strategy *after* war had broken out. Tirpitz's 'doctrine of risk' (*Risikogedanke*) originally envisaged a German navy that would eventually be strong enough to deter the Royal Navy altogether from war. The outbreak of war in 1914 was earlier than Tirpitz expected the German fleet to achieve this, 1915 being his earliest estimate, and thus the goal for German naval strategy during the war became concerned with whittling down the Royal Navy until parity was achieved. For Tirpitz's 'doctrine of risk', see Halpern (1994): 2–5.

15 Referring to Alfred Thayer Mahan's idea that the destruction of the enemy battlefleet was the decisive effect at sea and therefore, the wider war. Other decisive naval battles which came after, such as Actium, Lepanto, Trafalgar, and Tsushima (amongst others) had an influence on German naval strategy. The Peloponnesian War seems to provide the first extant explicit expression of decisive battle as a legitimate naval strategy, no doubt taking as an example the Persian War before it.

16 Gordon (1996): 21.

The strategy of Pericles and his successors

Athenian strategy under Pericles has been the source of much debate and misconception.[17] It was a maritime strategy, and it was a defensive strategy, which is not to say it did not envision offensive actions. Athens as a metaphorical 'island' guaranteed its landward defence through the city and Long walls and assured its supply lines by sea. By evacuating the lands of Attica during Spartan invasion, or rather, only those areas under threat and not the entirety of Attica, the Athenians would not be drawn into an unfair hoplite battle with the dreaded Spartan phalanx. Secure behind their walls, Athens could then strike at Sparta and Spartan allies using manoeuvre from the sea. Pericles' strategy was an evolution of the strategy developed by those who came before him, back to Themistocles and the Persian Wars. The evacuation of the city in 480 had allowed the Athenians to commit everything to their navy. This attitude is summed up in a story by Herodotus. Before the battle of Salamis, a Corinthian delegate attacked Themistocles' counsel and dismissed him since Athens had been evacuated and thus, he did not even have a city to his name. Themistocles replied that not only did he have a city, but he had one even greater than the Corinthians so long as the Athenians had 250 ships fully manned.[18] It was a story that could be drawn upon in Athens for at least a century and a half afterwards, and even in Rome in the second century AD. In his speech *On the Crown*, Demosthenes invoked the spirit of the Athenians before Salamis and noted their willingness to abandon their land and make their triremes their homes.[19] Appian wrote that during the civil war Pompey gave a speech to his army after they abandoned Rome and reminded them that the Athenians had abandoned their city, knowing that a city consisted not of buildings but of its people.[20] Clearly Pompey and the runaway Senate were in a far different circumstance, yet they too thought it was enough to have an army and importantly, a navy with which to fight. This is the attitude that Pericles had drilled into the population of Athens by the outbreak of war with Sparta.

Pericles' first speech has a clear elucidation of the way in which war was fought and the role of sea power in the impending conflict. He derides Sparta's ability to provide funding for a war, saying they lack public and private funds and are without experience of fighting long wars across sea.[21] The first point is

---

17 A topic I have discussed previously, see Nash (2018).
18 Hdt. 8.61.
19 Dem. 18.204.
20 App. 2.50. Noting that Appian was writing in the second century AD but discussing events of the first century BC.
21 Thuc. 1.141.3.

perhaps exaggerated,[22] but the second is closer to the mark and the implication is that Sparta would need to conduct long wars across seas in the impending conflict, a sound analysis since the basis of Athenian power was located almost entirely overseas. He returns to the issue of money which will hinder the Spartans in the war, especially since 'the opportunities of war do not wait';[23] a sentiment echoed more famously by Cicero in the now common military aphorism, 'the sinews of war, infinite money'.[24] This is a comment on the character of war as Pericles/Thucydides saw it, not just with respect to the requirement for money, but also that war was not some slow-paced endeavour, but one which required quick and decisive action to make use of opportunities as they arose. He believes sea power provides the speed of action necessary for modern wars, something which of course required large amounts of capital. He goes as far as to say that Athenian naval skill was of more use on land than Spartan military skill would be at sea. Once again wealth and sea power are the two poles upon which supreme power rest.[25] This forms a virtuous circle, where sea power produces wealth which further enables sea power that helps create the conditions necessary for wealth, and so on.

In the final part of his speech Pericles outlines his strategy for the impending war. His strategy is centred on sea power, which he assesses as more capable than Sparta's land power. The Athenians could sail out and attack the Peloponnese and the ensuing damage would be greater than the result of Sparta ravaging even all of Attica, for the Athenians had territory outside the reach of Sparta, namely the islands.[26] As Pericles himself says, such is the rule granted by control of the sea, the core message of Thucydides' *archaeology*.[27] He then makes one of his most famous statements, where he compares Athens to an island and bids the Athenians to think of their city in such a manner.[28] Thucydides, through Pericles, is laying down the character of the war which is to follow, a war in which maritime considerations would be at the forefront of the war effort. More explicitly, when Thucydides eulogises Pericles and assesses his role in the war, he deems that Pericles had set the Athenians up for victory, including in telling them to at-

---

22 As Hornblower (1997: 228) points out it was a common fiction that there were no individually wealthy Spartans.
23 Thuc. 1.142.1.
24 Cic. *Phil.* 5.5.
25 Thuc. 1.142.5. An observation not lost on Momigliano (1944: 3) writing as far back as 1944.
26 Thuc. 1.143.4.
27 Hornblower (1997): 229.
28 Thuc. 1.143.5.

tend to the navy, and it was in not following his advice that Athens lost the war.²⁹ It is an important passage of Thucydides' work for the light it throws on his own political views.³⁰

To analyse Athenian war strategy in the Archidamian War, we can – cautiously – separate the strategic level of war from the operational level.³¹ This is a somewhat fraught endeavour, as the lines between these two levels of war are blurry.³² Nevertheless, they are useful constructs that aid us in our analysis of how the war was fought. In simple terms, the operational level of war can be defined as campaigning, which consists of a series of operations or battles that fit into the larger strategy. To reiterate, strategy is about 'maintaining a balance between ends, ways, and means; about identifying objectives; and about the resources and methods available for meeting such objectives.'³³ Pericles' strategy can thus be summarised as such. Athens was protected from land attack by her powerful walls and an army that, while perhaps not as powerful as say Sparta's, was still an effective fighting force against virtually all other Greek poleis. Athens possessed a powerful navy that was capable of power projection across the Aegean and into the Black Sea, their area of primary strategic interest. This area consisted of an empire that provided an immense, continuing, source of capital with which to fund the aforementioned navy, and support Athens materially. Athenian policy under Pericles aimed at maintenance of the *status quo ante bellum*. The campaigns which Athens launched against the Peloponnese in the Archidamian War is the operational level of war: these campaigns are the precise *ways* in which Athens used its *means* – sea power – for the desired *ends* – a favourable settlement to the war that preserved the fleet and the Athenian empire in the Aegean. The strategy of Pericles did not, as some would claim, fail.³⁴ The successors of Pericles maintained this power projection strategy. What did change was that they pursued it more vigorously, more aggressively on an *operational* level. Pericles' strategy was one of maritime power projection as a means of coercing

---

29 Thuc. 2.65.
30 As Hornblower (1997: 340) says, he is also correct in pointing out that Thucydides was wrong in saying there was a radical difference between the policy of Pericles and those of his successors.
31 This section is based on a previous analysis of mine, published in 2018, *Sea Power in the Peloponnesian War*. Further research and analysis has not changed my mind in that time.
32 Many scholars and military practitioners see the idea of 'Operational Art' as having consumed or confused the relationship between strategy and tactics. For a greater discussion on this, see Kelly and Brennan (2009); Strachan (2013): 210–34.
33 Freedman (2013): xi.
34 Kagan (1994): 41 and (2009): 85. Kagan's views on Pericles and his strategy have not changed since his four-volume series on the Peloponnesian War of 1969, 1974, 1981, and 1987.

Sparta into peace. In this, it was a strategy that ultimately succeeded in 421 with the Peace of Nicias.[35] Thucydides may have thought that this peace was an imperfect one, and really just an 'interlude' in the war, but here we should avoid the seduction of Thucydides' carefully crafted narrative. Rather, we should take heed of the advice of Nicole Loraux, who advised that we should not treat Thucydides as a colleague but rather as a source of history.[36] Periclean strategy worked for Athens. It was only when this strategy was abandoned in favour of more aggressive expansion that things went badly for Athens.

The opening of the war saw both Sparta and Athens initiate their war plans. Sparta invaded Attica in the hope of drawing out and defeating the Athenian hoplites, while Athens gathered its allies and prepared 100 ships for a raid on the Peloponnese.[37] Most scholarship likes to summarise the first year of the war as the Spartans doing widespread damage and the Athenians expending considerable time and money for little gain, with the Spartans inflicting more damage than they received in turn.[38] This is a poor assessment of the events of that first year, both overestimating the damage done by Sparta and grossly simplifying and underestimating the damage done by Athens. There is little doubt that the Athenians were greatly upset by the Spartan invasion of Attica and the despoiling of their land: Thucydides says so, and the significance of this should not be discounted.[39] However, the invasion and ravaging of Attica had already been presaged by Pericles and it made the Athenians more angry and resolute rather than despondent, and it certainly demonstrated to the Spartans that their ravaging strategy would not induce the Athenians into any rash actions or quick capitulation. The idea that the Athenian population would be so despondent at the destruction and ravaging of their land that it would cause them to capitulate by engaging in a hopeless land battle is reminiscent of the underlying assumption in the early twentieth century that the use of strategic bombing in war could bring a nation to its knees. As the wholesale destruction of German and Japanese cities at the hands of Allied conventional bombers, and the constant stream of V-1 and V-2 rockets bombarding England showed, this was flawed logic.[40] J.E. Lendon pro-

---

35 John Hale (2009: 184) calls the Peace of Nicias a triumph for Athens that would have gratified Pericles. Platias and Koliopoulos call the peace favourable to Athens, ruined only by the Sicilian expedition (2010): 56.
36 Loraux (2011). Advice proponents of the 'Thucydides Trap' should heed.
37 Thuc. 2.18–21; Thuc. 2.17.4.
38 Kagan (2009): 80. Westlake (1945): 81; Lazenby (2004): 253.
39 Thuc. 2.21–22.
40 Though of course this was not the sole aim of the Allies' strategic bombing campaign – merely one school of thought on the British side. It should also be remembered that it was Hitler who first decided to use bombers on the population centres of England, following the notorious exam-

poses that the actions of the first six years of the war were aimed at damaging the honour of the other, striking moral blows more than physical ones.[41] The fears expressed by Spartan allies during the rebuilding of the Athenian walls do not seem to be concerned with damage to honour, but their livelihoods and property. Lendon does concede that Athenian actions included offensive operations rather than purely defensive ones.

It also assumes a negligible effort by Athens to defend Attica, which is not the case. As small as it might have been, there was an effort by Athens to defend Attica with cavalry, both boosting morale and limiting the damage that could be done by the cavalry-deficient Spartan army.[42] The effects of Spartan efforts during the first years of the war have been exaggerated by many scholars, perhaps because the traditional nature of Spartan land invasion appears more effective in comparison with the more unorthodox Athenian maritime strategy and because of the measurement of damage in material terms, rather than in more intangible strategic results.

On the issue of the Spartan invasions and the overstatement of their effectiveness, instances of agricultural ravaging during this period appear to have been greatly exaggerated in their material effects. In his ground-breaking work *Warfare and Agriculture in Classical Greece*, Victor Davis Hanson convincingly argued that the systematic destruction of crops and ravaging of land is extremely difficult. Grape and olive vines are extremely hardy and difficult to destroy, requiring many hours to do so. Further, grain is only vulnerable to fire and other widespread destruction during a narrow window of time. Of particular importance is a passage in the *Hellenica Oxyrhynchia*, in which the unknown author describes Attica before the Spartan fortification of Decelea as the most lavishly equipped part of Greece, having suffered only slight damage from the Spartans in previous attacks.[43] Thucydides too describes the fortification of Decelea as one of the prime causes of Athenian ruin, in stark contrast to the invasions of the Archidamian War.[44] Hanson calculates that the Spartans spent a mere 150 days in Attica during the entire Archidamian War, hardly enough time to 'ravage' the

---

ple of the German Condor Legion and its bombings against civilian targets during the Spanish Civil War.
41 See Lendon (2005): 107–283. It is an interesting proposal, but one I do not find entirely convincing.
42 Thuc. 2.22.2. See also Spence (1990): 91–109.
43 *Hell. Oxy.* (London Fragments) (trans. P.R. McKechnie and S.J. Kern: 1988): 17.4–5; Hanson (1998): 237.
44 Thuc. 7.27.3–5.

countryside, especially while under threat from Athenian cavalry.[45] Not everyone is convinced by Hanson's argument, arguing that the example of the ravaging of Attica is not representative of the economic impact of ravaging in Classical Greece because Athens alone could bear such hardship. If anything, this argument reinforces the effectiveness of Athenian sea power during the war.[46] As late as the writings of Polyainos it was said that the first Athenian attack on Laconia did more damage to the Spartans than was done by the Spartans to Attica.[47] The idea of Sparta having laid waste to Attica looks like hyperbole and the effectiveness of Spartan strategy vastly overstated. Sparta's original strategy was ultimately a failure.[48] As we will see, even a permanent Spartan presence in Attica would not be enough to bring Athens to its knees.

In contrast, the accomplishments of Athens during the first year of the war were strategically significant. The Athenians, along with a contingent of 50 ships from Corcyra and other allies, conducted their own ravaging of enemy territory. This raiding included an attack on the city of Methone in the helot homeland of Messenia. This represented an attack on an area where the Spartans felt particularly vulnerable. Although they did not take the city, it clearly worried the Spartans, whose greatest fear was of a helot revolt. Concurrent with this operation, thirty Athenian ships raided further north into eastern Locris, taking hostages, and defeating the Locrians who assembled there to resist them. Finally, the Athenians secured the islands of Aegina and Cephalonia, the latter taken without a fight.[49] Occupation of the former island ensured the security of the Saronic Gulf and control of the latter helped secure a base off the west coast of the Peloponnese and Acarnania.

By the end of the first year of the war, the Athenians had done as much material damage to the Spartans as the Spartans had to the Athenians. Diodorus' account gives the impression that it was the Peloponnesians that suffered most from the raiding of the first year, 'terrified' by the Athenians 'ravaging many places of the coastline'.[50] Plutarch says that not only did Athenian raids on the Peloponnese cause more damage than the Spartan ones on Attica but that if it had not

---

45 Hanson (1998): 147.
46 See Thorne (2001): 225–53.
47 Polyain. 1.36.1.
48 As Kagan finally admits at the end of his survey of the Archidamian War. Kagan (1974): 333. However, Lazenby (2004: 253) comes to the strange conclusion that Sparta still did more damage to Athens than Athens did to Sparta with this strategy, a conclusion with no solid foundation.
49 Thuc. 2.25.1; 2.26; 2.27; 2.30.2.
50 Diod Sic. 12.42.7–8. B.X. de Wet (1969: 103–19) is one of the few authors who also concludes that Athens did more material damage. It is also an early, yet overlooked, example of a scholar arguing for a strong offensive element to Athenian war strategy.

been for the plague outbreak in Athens, the Spartans would have given up entirely.[51] This is no doubt Plutarch's well known penchant for exaggeration, but it does at least fit with the view that Athens did considerable damage to Spartan interests. What is far more important, and absent from analyses of these events, is the fact that Athens had accomplished far more in solidifying and improving its strategic position in Greece, as well as proving the capability and reach of its sea power. By taking the islands of Aegina and Cephalonia the Athenians were even better placed to secure their own sea routes, disrupt those of the enemy, and launch attacks against the Peloponnesian seaboard.

The offshore Greek islands were important strategic locations for both sides, for different reasons. The islands were potential bases for the Athenians to control sea lanes, deny them to the enemy, and to launch attacks against the Peloponnesian coast. Naturally, denying their use by the Athenians was a goal of the Peloponnesians. The Ambraciots convinced the Spartans that the conquest of Acarnania would lead to the islands of Zakynthos and Cephalonia falling, which would make Athenian cruises around the Peloponnese much more difficult.[52] More important was the possession or control of Corcyra. This island poleis not only possessed a strong navy but the island itself was situated on the best sailing route from Greece to Italy, while also being poised in a position to threaten the entrance to the Gulf of Corinth. Athenian and Spartan interference in Corcyraean affairs were not aimed at conquest but at establishing a friendly government that could secure the island for their interests, first and foremost of which was control of the critical sea lanes around the island. An Athenian attack on the island of Cythera in 424 had a twofold purpose. First, the island was a landing place for merchant ships sailing from Libya and Egypt. Second, the island was in a position from which Laconia could be secured from attacks by 'privateers', which also made it an excellent position for the Athenians to set up a base and raid the Peloponnese.[53] As a bonus, the Athenians were also able to exact a tribute of four *talents* from Cythera. Again, it is important to emphasise that this is not a departure from Athens' original strategy,[54] but a change in operational approach. This was part of Athens' campaign to use sea power offensively, attacking the Peloponnese and wearing down Sparta while simultaneously strengthening its strategic position by further encircling the Peloponnese with potential bases of operation.

Pericles' strategy at the opening of the Peloponnesian War had two parts. The first part was to utilise maritime forces for the projection of power against targets

---

51 Plut. *Per*. 34.2.
52 Thuc. 2.80.1.
53 4.53.3; Plut. *Nik*. 6.4.
54 Thuc. 4.57.4; As Kagan (1974: 261) thought it was.

in and around the Peloponnese. This required land forces. These land forces needed to be covered from attacks by the Peloponnesian fleet, the second part of the operation. This is what Athenian sea control allowed: free reign to move naval and land forces as required, without concern that the Spartan fleet could interfere in these operations. Athenian sea control was so complete that rather than try and combat these amphibious operations with a maritime force, the Spartans took the unusual step of raising a mobile land force of archers and cavalry.[55] The Athenian navy was such a powerful force that the Spartans did not attempt to contest Athenian sea control. The mere presence of the Athenian navy offshore was enough to deter the Spartans from interfering. In this way the fleet could provide cover to land forces, both during raids and during more prolonged operations, such as blockades. Many of the blockades of the war saw maritime forces acting in a dual role.[56] Not only was the city blockaded and supply lines cut-off, but outside attempts to relieve the city by attacking the besieging land force were prevented. Whether a short-term raid or prolonged siege, the provision of cover to a land force by the navy was vital in allowing the land force to achieve its objective without interference from the sea.

The ultimate success of Periclean strategy was the overwhelming Athenian victory at Pylos and the capture of Spartan forces on the island of Sphacteria in 425. Once again we must look at Thucydides' narrative with a critical eye, as he heralded this success as nothing more than a stroke of good luck. Although luck was certainly part of Athenian success, it was really the fruition of Athenian maritime strategy. Luck is a convenient explanation for Thucydides, whose distaste for the populist politician-strategos Cleon is well known. Rather than credit Cleon with a well-earned victory, Thucydides opted to ascribe the victory to good fortune as opposed to good leadership by a person he despised. The leader of the operation, Demosthenes, conducted the campaign in line with Periclean strategy.[57] Although it is true that Pericles had mentioned establishing fortifications in the Peloponnese but had never carried it out, Pericles' death early in the war means it would be premature to assume it was just a vague and empty threat and not part of his campaign plan.[58] Even the 'Old Oligarch' spoke of how the availability of headlands and offshore islands around Greece gave the 'rulers of the sea' many opportunities to establish bases from which to harm those on the main-

---

55 Thuc. 4.55.2.
56 For instances of blockade during the war, and at other times, see Appendix 1.
57 This is of course not the Demosthenes of the great fame during the much later war with Macedon.
58 Thuc. 1.142.4.

land.⁵⁹ Demosthenes' decision to fortify Pylos was an operation designed to increase pressure on Sparta through raids and attacks on its territory, using the sea as a 'manoeuvre space'. Two modern scholars quite correctly interpret the Pylos campaign as the logical corollary of Periclean strategy.⁶⁰ Although Thucydides writes that it was due to a storm that the Athenians ended up at Pylos, he also says that it was the location which Demosthenes landed to 'do what was wanted there' and to fortify the position, as that was the object of the voyage in the first place. Thus, it was not a random deserted headland as Thucydides has the two Athenians generals sneeringly say in his narrative but was territory in the heart of Messenia amongst the helot population that posed a constant threat to Sparta.⁶¹ The original Athenian plan as described by Pericles is unchanged, merely more aggressively pursued at the *operational* level.

Unsurprisingly, an Athenian fortification and garrison at Pylos quickly drew the attention of Sparta. King Agis and the Peloponnesians that were at the time ravaging Attica heard the news and immediately packed up and marched back. Once they had returned to Sparta they called together allies from around the Peloponnese.⁶² The Spartans attacked the Athenian garrison on Pylos but made the fateful, and inexplicable, decision to land a force of hoplites on the island of Sphacteria. This was apparently done in order to prevent any relieving force of Athenians from establishing a base nearby.⁶³ The Spartans had also sent a naval force, but this was quickly challenged by the Athenians. Victorious in this naval battle, the Athenians this trapped the force of Spartan hoplites occupying Sphacteria. This situation was deemed so dire that the Spartan commanders resolved to immediately ask Athens for a truce. So serious did the Spartans feel the situation was that as part of the truce negotiations they temporarily surrendered to the Athenians all their warships in Laconia, sixty in total.⁶⁴ In doing so it shows that the Spartans were willing to destroy their remaining naval power in order to retain a small contingent of hoplites. This seems to indicate that the Spartans lacked confidence in naval matters and valued their hoplites over their ships. It also clearly demonstrates the Athenian's capability in conducting amphibious operations. Athenian land and naval forces could be used in close concert not just to

---

59 Old Oligarch 2.13–14. Cautious of the danger that this passage is taking Pylos/Sphacteria as its primary example, leading to a circular argument.
60 Platias and Koliopoulos (2010), p. 49.
61 Thuc. 4.3.1–3.
62 Thuc. 4.6, 4.8.1–2.
63 Thuc. 4.8.3–8. For more details on the conduct of the Pylos campaign, see Lazenby (2004), pp. 67–79.
64 Thuc. 4.15–16.

raid territory but to deal a serious military blow to Sparta that had a strategic effect on the course of the war.

The full magnitude of Athenian victory at Pylos is evident in Spartan actions after the capture of their hoplites on Sphacteria. Thucydides calls the surrender of the approximately 120 Spartiates the most surprising thing to happen in the war.[65] The surrender of Spartan hoplites in such a number was unheard of, and certainly diminished the vaunted reputation of Spartan hoplites, heirs to the '300' of Thermopylae. The most immediate effect was the Athenian threat to execute the prisoners if the Spartans invaded Attica.[66] This ended the direct threat to Athenian territory and freed it up for full use and assuaged the residents who had been forced to abandon their land. The Spartans sent envoys to Athens to recover both the prisoners and the territory at Pylos, for they were seriously alarmed by the Messenian raids being conducted from Pylos into Laconia, stoking the age-old fear of widespread helot rebellion.[67] Importantly, victory at Pylos did not stop Athenian naval operations for the year. They raided Crommyon in Corinthian territory and established a fortified base at Methana from where they could raid into the territory of Troezen.[68] In the northwest, the Athenians based in Naupactus made an expedition against the Corinthian city of Anactorion, taking it and settling people from Acarnania there.[69] This meant that the entire northern shore of the Corinthian Gulf from Naupactus to Ambracia, with the minor exception of Molycreion, was hostile to Corinth and the Peloponnesians. These widespread amphibious operations demonstrate a powerful Athenian maritime capability that saw their enemies unable to develop an effective defence. This was a maritime strategy at work.

Thucydides gives a blunt assessment of the above events and their effects on Sparta. The Spartans were forced to split their forces and station them throughout the most threatened areas of the Peloponnese. They even took the unusual, and probably ineffective, step of raising a force of cavalry and archers to act as a mobile reserve. This had the effect of ensuring Sparta would have to think very carefully about concentrating any forces for an offensive, lest they leave an area unprotected and vulnerable to attack, including helot revolt. Thucydides describes the Spartans as on the defensive, fearing internal revolution, afraid of another disaster like Pylos/Sphacteria, and lacking all confidence in themselves.[70] The cause of this fear was constant Athenian raiding from the sea, unimpeded,

---

65 Thuc. 4.40.1. Hornblower (1997: 194) calls this a typical rhetorical superlative.
66 Thuc. 4.41.1.
67 Thuc. 4.41.1–3; Diod. 12.63.5.
68 Thuc. 4.45.
69 Thuc. 4.49. Salmon (1984): 318.
70 Thuc. 4.55.1–4.

along the Peloponnesian seaboard.[71] To paraphrase British Admiral Jackie Fisher discussing the roles of the British Army and Royal Navy, the Athenian army was being used as a projectile fired by the Athenian navy.[72] This strategy of maritime power projection was made possible by a strong Athenian navy, able to land a force of troops in hostile territory, protect them from enemy naval intervention, and bring them off again safely or keep them supplied and protected so that they could cause even greater damage in an ongoing campaign.

War in the east and west

In parallel with Pericles' strategy there were numerous other important maritime operations underway across the Aegean. The free use of the seas was an important factor in the war, especially for Athens, reliant on maritime trade and a widely dispersed support base in the form of the Delian League. It is not a surprise then that the Peloponnesians attempted to target this trade, with their own forces and using *leistai* – 'raiders' or even 'privateers'. Just as piracy is a tricky concept to define in the ancient world, so is that of 'privateering', a concept that has always had a somewhat tenuous nature. In the age of sail, private citizens could be issued with Letters of Marque, papers that employed them by their state to attack the shipping of that state's enemies.[73] It was often used in cases where naval resources were stretched thin, such as the United States during the War of Independence, who often turned to privateers since they had only a small navy to call upon. Many of those employed as privateers might be of dubious character and loyalty and were often considered pirates by those they attacked and were not always protected by their Letter of Marque. So far as is known, there was no ancient equivalent to a Letter of Marque and independent maritime forces, who otherwise might normally engage in actual piracy, were employed by states in much the same way as mercenaries on land.

In the first year of the Peloponnesian War, Athens fortified the island of Atalante off the Opountian coast to prevent *leistai* from sailing out of Opous and the rest of eastern Locris and attacking the important island of Euboea.[74] It was only with the outbreak of war that Athens found the need to fortify this position, suggesting that piracy was not an enduring regional issue of concern to Athens before this point. Thus, we might assume they were concerned with a new threat,

---

71 Thuc. 4.56.
72 Or A.K. Wilson: the attribution is disputed. Halpern (1994): 22.
73 On privateering and commerce raiding, see Elleman and Paine (eds.) (2013), esp. pp. 1–8.
74 Thuc. 2.32.

probably Peloponnesian-hired raiders. The position of Locris near Euboea, an important island for Athenian support, made it a good base of operations, and the fact that the Spartan navy was relatively weak meant that the Spartans were unlikely to be able to establish their own base there, hence the need to gain the support of *leistai*.

In the second year of the Peloponnesian War, the Athenians sent ships to Naupactus under Phormio (see below) and six ships under Melesandros to Caria and Lycia on the Anatolian coast.[75] Melesandros' task was twofold, to collect tribute and to prevent 'the Peloponnesian raiders' from attacking merchantmen.[76] Thucydides names Phaselis and Phoenicia as ports for these merchantmen. This seems to indicate an early Athenian trade connection with these places, and Phaselis is noteworthy considering that a Phaselian appears as the defendant in a trade dispute in the Athenian law courts some 75 years after this operation.[77] Phaselis is on the Athenian Tribute lists for the period and although Melesandros was certainly collecting tribute from there, it is made clear that the Athenians were also there to protect the city's trade. Lacking naval reach, Sparta engaged the services of 'privateers' to attack Athenian interests in the eastern Aegean, forcing Athens to ensure the protection of one of its tributary cities. As Hornblower points out, the options open to Sparta for attacking Athenian shipping were limited, and thus the employment of *leistai* was a useful option.[78] Other passages indicate that the Spartans were indeed working closely with *leistai* during the war. In 427 Nicias made an attack against the island of Minoa off the coast of Megara, to enable a closer blockade and to prevent both Peloponnesian triremes and *leistai* from sailing out from the island.[79] Clearly, both sides saw the importance of shipping and of contesting the sea lanes, and with a smaller navy the use of 'privateers' was an appealing option for Sparta.

The Athenians quickly moved against the sea lanes of Sparta's allies and especially those of Corinth. They gained control of the seas in the Saronic Gulf, causing the entrance to the Corinthian Gulf to become even more of a strategically vital waterway for the Corinthians. Having launched operations against the Peloponnese in 431 and 430, the Athenians dispatched 20 ships under the command of Phormio, who established himself at Naupactus near the entrance to the Corin-

---

75 Thuc. 2.69.1.
76 Thuc. 2.69.1–2.
77 Demosthenes 35 *Against Lakritos*, dated to perhaps 355 or 351. See MacDowell (2004): 130–3.
78 Hornblower (1991): 355. Antony Keen (1993: 153–7) concurs with this assessment but does not believe that this was the primary mission of Melesandros.
79 Thuc. 3.51.2.

thian Gulf during that winter.[80] Their role was to keep watch against ships sailing into or out of the gulf. This not only highlights another example of a naval force operating during winter, but it also demonstrates that there was other maritime traffic, military and/or civilian, operating during winter. Phormio's operations in 430/29 began as trade interdiction but progressed swiftly into the interdiction of enemy warships and transports. His squadron quickly had an impact on Corinthian operations. Phormio with 20 ships attacked the 47 Corinthian ships which were fitted out primarily as troop transports rather than rigged for battle, relying on their superior numbers as a deterrent to attack.[81] Rather than keep the enemy ships bottled up, Phormio clearly wished to engage in battle and disable as many as possible, for he is said to have watched the ships sail along the coast and wished to engage them in the 'open sea', as in, once they were through the narrowest part of the gulf and closer to Patrai.[82] The successful Athenian attack disabled many ships and captured 12. A second battle followed, and, after an initial setback, the vastly outnumbered Athenians managed to prevail, with the remaining Peloponnesian ships sailing back into the Gulf to Corinth.[83] Reinforced with 20 more ships soon after, the Athenian contingent ensured the maintenance of sea control in the area around Naupactus and over the important sea lane. This sea control restricted the ability of Corinth to move troops and supplies through this area.

An incident following these operations highlights an important point about strategy: it is not conducted in a vacuum. Events arise during war that require action outside what might be foreseen or planned for. Phormio's squadron of ships operating out of Naupactus, having defeated the Peloponnesians, called for aid in preparation for a second battle.[84] Athens responded by sending 20 ships, however, they were first directed to sail against the Cretan city of Cydonia to aid the Athenian *proxenos* Nicias.[85] This diversion of ships to Crete and the failure to immediately reinforce Phormio has been dismissed by some as 'typical of Athenian complacency', or is often overlooked.[86] The issue here is not Athenian complacency or a lack of focus or strategy in play but that this was a time sensitive

---

[80] Thuc. 2.69.1. The Corinthian Gulf is called the Crisaian Gulf by Thucydides.
[81] Thuc. 2.83.1–3.
[82] Thuc. 2.83.2.
[83] Thuc. 2.84, 2.90–2.
[84] Thuc. 2.85.4.
[85] Thuc. 2.85.6. A Cretan of the city of Gortys, not to be confused with the Athenian politician of the same name.
[86] Lazenby (2004): 46; it receives scant mention in Hornblower's (1991: 367–8) commentary.

matter, to be acted upon by Athens immediately.[87] Clearly, the Athenians felt that sending aid to a Cretan *proxenos* was important. According to Thucydides, the hope of the Cydonian Nicias was to help reduce Cydonia but also to intimidate the neighbouring city of Polichna.[88] In this sense, the Athenian fleet was to conduct a military operation directly against one city with the concurrent goal of intimidating an adjacent city through this display of power projection. It was also a move that helped reassure an Athenian *proxenos* and maintain a friendly power in the island, an island that could be used as a base to harass up into the Aegean by a hostile power. Further, The Athenians must have had great confidence in Phormio's ability to continue to hold the entrance of the Corinthian Gulf, a faith that was well-placed.

Elsewhere, the Athenians faced dangerous insurrection by members of the Delian Leage. The revolt of Mytilene on Lesbos in 428 was a major episode in the early years of the war and an event that could have had serious ramifications for Athens if successful. The Athenians initially blockaded Mytilene by sea, with the land siege only put in place before the onset of winter.[89] The blockade was clearly effective, for Thucydides and Diodorus say that Mytilenean food supplies began to fail.[90] The Spartan response was lacklustre, and they failed entirely to relieve the Mytileneans. The Spartan admiral Alcidas refused to even attempt a relief effort or any other operation against the Athenians in the east. Thucydides is critical of Alcidas and the Spartans, in particular their sloth and inaction. The relief fleet of 40 Peloponnesian ships proceeded in a 'leisurely' manner from the Peloponnese to Icaros.[91] After rejecting the proposal for an attack on the Athenian forces at Mytilene,[92] Alcidas rejected the proposal to establish a base in the east from where he could induce Ionian cities to revolt from Athens. Thucydides sees this as a reasonable proposal, saying that the Ionians would welcome it and such a move would not only deprive Athens of revenue but also incur additional costs in requiring them to blockade the Ionian cities and possibly convince the Persian governor Pissuthnes to join the war, to Athens' detriment.[93] Alcidas was not interested in any of these proposals, and because he had failed to relieve Mytilene was

---

87 As Kagan (1974: 112) grasps in his analysis.
88 Thuc. 2.85.5.
89 Thuc. 3.6, 3.18.
90 Thuc. 3.27.1; Diod. 12.55.7.
91 Thuc. 3.29.1.
92 The proposer of this move, and Elean by the name of Teutaplos, suggested that a night attack would see them successful against the Athenians – Thuc. 3.30.3.
93 Thuc. 3.31.1.

eager to return to the Peloponnese as soon as possible.[94] Some scholars have tried to defend Alcidas' conduct,[95] and though it is true that an attack on the Athenians at Mytilene was a high-risk operation, to sail back to the Peloponnese having done nothing more than kill some prisoners collected along the way was not just a wasted opportunity but also an action that as the Ionians pointed out, was not endearing them to the Spartan cause.[96] Alcidas' squadron accomplished nothing more than a demonstration that the Spartans had no intention of carrying out the war where it would hurt Athens the most. Pro-Athenian Ionians could rest easy knowing that they were safe from the Spartans, and anti-Athenian factions saw that the Spartans arrived too late to help the Mytileneans and were unwilling to help anyone else. The fault may not have been Alcidas, for he may have been under higher orders to do nothing should he arrive too late at Mytilene. In either case, it clearly demonstrates a lack of Spartan initiative on the strategic level.

Pushing the limits

As we have seen, the use of naval forces to project power from the sea was a defining element of the first half of the Archidamian War. This did at times go beyond the scope of Periclean strategy. The first Athenian expedition to Sicily in 427 does not fit with the war plan outlined by Pericles and appears to have been a move to extend Athenian power against Pericles' strict warning not to do so. The ostensible aim of the expedition was not conquest but to aid Athens' Sicilian allies. The size of the first expedition is demonstrative of diplomatic intent rather than military. It was not a full-scale invasion force like the one that followed a decade later. Like the Corcyra incident that opened the war, the initial Athenian force was relatively small but with a heavy command component: 20 ships with 2 commanders.[97] It was an operation that began slowly but gradually ramped up in intensity and eventually dragged in the major Sicilian powerhouse, Syracuse. Thucydides says from the outset that Athenian appeals to Ionian solidarity were really a cover for a desire to test the possibility of subjugating Sicily in the future.[98] This is further reinforced by the speech in which Hermocrates of Syracuse says that the divisiveness of the Sicilians was leaving them open to the menace

---

94 Thuc. 3.31.2.
95 See: Roisman (1987): 385–421.
96 Thuc. 3.32.1–2.
97 Thuc. 3.86.1. Of course, this could be a precaution in case one of them became incapacitated – as happened a few months into the expedition. Thuc. 3.90.
98 Thuc. 3.86.3–4.

and ambition of Athens.[99] Despite reinforcements, including the replacement of one general with three, and several military successes in their campaign, the disparate poleis of Sicily and southern Italy agreed on peace and the Athenians sailed home to a cold reception. Athens withdrew from Sicily having neither lost nor gained anything significant. However, the Athenian population did not see it this way and banished two and fined one of the generals, thinking that they should have conquered Sicily.[100] Thucydides calls this a false hope, saying that Athens' recent successes, almost certainly referring to the decisive victory at Pylos and Sphacteria, meant that the demos were confusing strength with their hopes. It is possibly the first signs of Athenian ambitions growing beyond the conduct of a defensive war.

However, it is important to note that the first Sicilian expedition was primarily diplomatic in nature, and Thucydides perhaps downplays the motivation of Athens in attempting to aid their Western allies. After all, the Peloponnesians had strong friends in the west too, and for Athens to ignore their allies' call for help would have weakened their position in the west, if not in the other territories where they had allies. Failure to aid their allies would have made Athens look weak, and thus the dispatch of a naval expedition to Sicily in 427 can be seen as a response to external events rather than as a radical change in Athenian strategy, if not policy. As the war dragged on it became more complex, and these instances again highlight the point that strategy is not practiced in a vacuum and external events can strain a carefully developed strategy. It also seems likely that confident in how the war was going for them, the Athenians decided to make a highly visible display of power projection farther afield in the west than was usual for them. It was a diplomatic use of sea power demonstrating Athenian intent and confidence in Sicilian waters.

The final campaign of the Archidamian War was conducted in northern Greece and relied heavily on maritime forces on the Athenian side. Spartan operations in the Chalcidice region marked a change in Sparta's strategy and revealed the effectiveness of Athenian strategy up to that point. Thucydides explicitly states that Spartan operations in the northwest Aegean were aimed at distracting Athens and relieving the pressure they were putting on the Peloponnese and Laconia especially.[101] Further and even more importantly, Thucydides says that the Spartans were happy to have an excuse to send out helots from the Peloponnese since the occupation of Pylos was thought to have increased the chances of a

---

99 Thuc. 4.60.
100 Thuc. 4.65.
101 Thuc. 4.80.1.

helot revolt.[102] It also marks the point at which Sparta abandoned all hope of confronting Athens at sea until well after the Peace of Nicias, for they decided to avoid naval operations in favour of a purely land campaign. It is also a campaign which demonstrates the limitations of naval forces, with sea power a limited factor in the outcomes of the campaigns in Thrace. Brasidas' march through Thessaly into Thrace was a bold move. It was not an easy endeavour and relied on a careful set of favourable circumstances which highlights some of the difficulties in marching overland due to the human geography. Going by sea does not require passing though the lands of any poleis, and so there is no negotiation as is required for a crossing army. Nevertheless, Brasidas and his army did make it to the Chalcidice and were able to fight Athens into a negotiated settlement.

This Chalcidice campaign was forced upon the Athenians by the awakening initiative of Sparta. The region was an important base for the Athenians operating in the north Aegean and was a good source of shipbuilding timber and other resources. Brasidas' campaign in the region was not a serious threat to the Athenian Black Sea grain supply, as some scholars have seen it.[103] To take seriously the prospect of Sparta threatening the Hellespont from Thrace in 424 is to misread the strategic situation. It is true the Hellespont could be threatened by land: it was threatened by Philip in the fourth century, but this was far outside the capabilities of Sparta in 424, and in a strategic environment that is not remotely comparable. There was no realistic way for Sparta to threaten the Hellespont from Amphipolis. Just because Brasidas started to build an unknown number of triremes does not prove an attack on the Hellespont was planned and it is to ignore the litany of defeats at sea the Spartans had continually suffered before this, especially at Pylos. Either the triremes were intended for local defence or Brasidas was wildly and hopelessly optimistic about their renewed chances at sea. It also ignores what happened later in the war, when this sea lane was eventually threatened by Sparta, using maritime forces in and around the Hellespont, not based out of distant Thrace. The battles at Pylos and Sphacteria showed that the Spartans in 425 could not even rescue a force of their own hoplites trapped a mile offshore on an island just off the coast of Messenia in their own territory. There was virtually no chance of them rebuilding a fleet, having surrendered theirs at Pylos, and then threatening the Hellespont from distant Thrace. Even if the cap-

---

102 Thuc. 4.80.2.
103 Knight (1970): 154. Brasidas' campaign did not demonstrate 'the possible vulnerability' of the 'Athenian life line to and from the grain fields of the Black Sea area' (157). There is simply no evidence for this assertion. Both Kagan and later Hornblower accept this faulty analysis of the intent of Brasidas' campaign. Kagan (1969): 186–88; Kagan (1974): 288–9, 294; Hornblower (1997): 255–6.

ture of Amphipolis did open the overland route to the Hellespont, Brasidas' force was far too small to hold onto gains in the Chalcidice and simultaneously threaten the Hellespont, especially in the face of greater Athenian mobility at sea. This would have required reinforcements, and these reinforcements would have had to go by the hazardous overland route through Thessaly, whereas the Athenians could reinforce the area by sea. The loss of Amphipolis was a blow to Athens, for the loss of timber and silver, and as Thucydides says, the fear that other allies might revolt from Athens.[104] The Spartans were not able to threaten the Hellespont, and the campaign in Thrace demonstrates that just as there was a limit to Athenian sea power and what it could accomplish, there was a limit to Sparta's land power and what it could do.

The 'Peace' of Nicias

The campaign in Chalcidice drained both Sparta and Athens, and with the deaths of their respective generals Brasidas and Cleon the will to fight on both sides dissipated. What followed, the 'Peace of Nicias', was not terribly peaceful, though Athens and Sparta did by the letter of the treaty refrain from direct engagement.[105] Free to pursue a consolidation of their empire, the Athenians revealed a darker character, enabled by their unparalleled control of the seas.

The island of Melos had remained neutral during the war, and the fact that they were an island that refused to submit seems to have especially vexed the Athenians. In 416, having used several of their warships to transport Spartan sympathisers out of Argos, the Athenians turned their attention towards Melos.[106] The famous Melian dialogue more than any other passage reveals Thucydides' thoughts on the devolving character of Athens at that time. We get an unvarnished view of Athenian confidence in their rule of the sea. The Melos affair is an excellent example of Athenian coercive diplomacy in action and the role sea power played in Athenian policy and strategy. Leaving aside questions of political philosophy, the Melos affair demonstrates how Athens could bully and subdue an island poleis of

---

104 Thuc. 4.108.1–3. Thucydides mentions the strategically important position of Amphipolis and that losing it would open the way into Thrace, but it is a big leap to read this as meaning all the way to the Hellespont, as Knight, Kagan, and others have done.
105 On Thucydides view of the peace as merely an interlude: Thuc. 5.25–6.
106 Alcibiades sailed 20 ships to Argos to remove 300 suspected Spartan sympathisers and lodge them in islands throughout the empire: Thuc. 5.84.1.

the Aegean, in this case a neutral power rather than a rebellious ally.[107] There is not much subtlety in Thucydides' account as he has the Athenians say that the Melians have no hope of outside aid since they are an island and Athens rules the sea.[108] The Melian response, that the Cretan Sea was large and thus hard for the Athenians to control, is clearly meant to demonstrate just how weak the Melian position was. No one hearing this could believe that Sparta or Sparta's allies had much hope of conducting a maritime operation against the full might of the Athenian fleet at this time. This would only be made possible later by severe Athenian losses in Sicily. The Melians argued a second point, that even if they failed in this endeavour the Spartans could still harm Athens in Attica and elsewhere on the mainland where Athens had interests, bringing up the spectre of Brasidas.[109] Again, this is a weak argument, for as the events of the Archidamian War had shown, Sparta could do but minimal damage to Athenian interests on the mainland, at great effort, but ultimately were still at the mercy of Athenian sea power.[110] There seems to be no getting away from the fact that Melos was an island, and like the other islands of the Aegean Athenian sea power allowed them to establish control over them. Whatever the reason for Athenian aggression against Melos, it was predicated on their ability to wield sea power.[111] Initially, the hope appears to have been Melian capitulation based on an overt display of power – the Athenian fleet as an instrument of coercive diplomacy. When this failed, the fleet immediately went into action, besieging and eventually taking the island, free from outside interference. This example demonstrates how the Athenians used their fleet as a diplomatic tool and how, when this approach failed, the same fleet could be put into immediate action and conduct combat operations to subdue an adversary. Natu-

---

107 While tempting to dissect questions of Athenian imperialism and the political philosophy of Thucydides, questions of 'political realism' and other such concepts lie outside the scope of this work. For a more detailed discussion, see de Romilly (1979): 273–310; Hornblower (2008): 216–56.
108 Thuc. 5.109.
109 Thuc. 5.110.
110 One could also use this passage as evidence for the construction of the dialogue post-404, with Thucydides writing the dialogue in full knowledge of how the war played out. The last decade of the war saw the bulk of fighting occur everywhere except mainland Greece and Sparta was only successful by damaging Athenian interests in the Aegean. Thus, the Melian argument looks even weaker since the reader knows that the danger posed by Sparta to Athens as argued by the Melians is far from accurate, at least at that point in time. Knowing the outcome of the war, the Melians were ultimately vindicated in their sentiment.
111 Perhaps one of the more compelling arguments being that the Athenians needed to constantly keep their island subjects fearful of them through demonstrations of power. For more on this, see de Romilly (1979): 287–9.

rally, such successful actions meant that the Athenian fleet was viewed as a dangerous foe, in the hope that the next island or polis could be subdued on threat alone.

Conclusion

The Peloponnesian War involved many different protagonists spread throughout the Mediterranean region. Most of these places were within reach of the sea, providing poleis with the opportunity to provide aid or threaten with their navy as they saw fit. In the first decade of the war, Athenian sea power was unmatched and allowed them to campaign far and wide, protecting their own interests while simultaneously wearing down Sparta and her Peloponnesian allies. Thucydides' contention that the Peace of Nicias was but an interlude in the larger war is of course his conclusion, and it should not prevent us from seeing the success of Athenian sea power strategy in the first half of the war. The overwhelming victory at Pylos and Sphacteria was the culmination of Periclean strategy. At that moment Athens had the opportunity to take a favourable peace treaty as clear victors over Sparta. Instead, the victory led to Athenian hubris and over-reach and the abandonment of Periclean strategy as the city's politicians sought more. The Spartan counterattack in the Chalcidice under Brasidas was seemingly a last gasp but an effective one, eroding Athenian power and confidence with the loss of Amphipolis. Nevertheless, the Athenians remained supreme at sea, with an intact fleet and relatively untouched empire. This would all change on the shores of Syracuse in Sicily.

Chapter Eight
The triumph of sea power: Sicily and the Ionian War

As the uneasy peace between Athens and Sparta entered its seventh year, the two sides continued what was essentially a proxy war. In 418, the Spartans had won a victory at Mantinea in the central Peloponnese, one of the few large hoplite battles during the 30 years of war. This foiled Athenian attempts at gaining more influence within the Peloponnese, especially with the large polis of Argos. It reinforced Spartan strength by land and consolidated their hold on the Peloponnese, forcing the Athenians to look further afield for more influence and power. They set their sights on the west and a more forceful return to Sicily.

The Sicilian expedition

At the behest of the Sicilian polis of Egesta, in opposition to the rival polis of Selinus, the Athenians convened an assembly to decide on an expedition to Sicily. Having voted in favour of the expedition, a second meeting was held to decide on practicalities. One of the three newly nominated *strategoi*, Nicias, gave a speech to try and dissuade the Athenians, seeing the expedition as rash and overextending Athens when they should be more directly focused on Sparta.[1] This attempt failed and a second speech trying to frighten the Athenians into abandoning the expedition only caused them to increase their commitment. Thucydides outlines the forces sent to Sicily, and the catalogue of allies involved illustrates the vast array of different places from which Athens could draw on military resources.[2] It was the high point of Athenian power, able to assemble a huge force of ships, men, and material for a campaign in Sicilian waters for an indeterminate length of time. Upon reaching the mainland Italian city of Rhegium the Athenians sent scouts to Egesta to determine if they could properly support the Athenian expedition with promised funds and when the scout ships returned and said Egesta could not, the three *strategoi* found themselves at a loss.[3] It is at this point Nicias proposed a very Periclean course of action. He suggested they sail to Selinus and

---
1 Thuc. 6.8–14.
2 For an in-depth discussion of the forces sent to Sicily and the catalogue of allies as a Homeric allusion, see Hornblower (2008): 418, 654–60.
3 Thuc. 6.46.

set matters right, either by agreement or force, and then conduct a cruise past the other Sicilian cities in an overt demonstration of Athenian power.[4] Just as with Pericles' grand power projection cruise of the Aegean circa 436, a cruise around Sicily would have demonstrated that no polis on or near the coast was safe from Athenian influence. This had been proven in the Aegean and Black Sea regions and Athens could prove it in Sicilian waters too, or so Nicias seemed to think. Even if this did not win Athens new friends and allies, it might have been enough to dissuade the Sicilian poleis from supporting Sparta in the future. It would have been an overt message that Sparta could do nothing to protect Sicily. Having been opposed to the expedition from the start, it is probable that Nicias put forward his power projection cruise as the least costly option, with the highest chance of at least some measure of success.[5] As discussed earlier, the Athenians were certainly successful in using their fleet in overt displays of power as a deterrent to adversaries.

As it happened, Nicias' plan was not favoured and the Athenians went on the attack, bringing them into opposition with the powerful polis of Syracuse. The expedition to Sicily required a long logistics chain for sustainment and reinforcement, as did Spartan efforts to keep Syracuse from falling. Unlike in the Aegean, Athenian operations in Sicily had far less support from reliable local allies. So too for the Peloponnesians, who also relied on reinforcements coming from mainland Greece. This meant that the seas between Greece and Italy-Sicily were of increasing importance, with both sides conducting naval operations to interdict reinforcements. However, the Athenians were slow in their response, and in the beginning of the campaign Nicias did not seem concerned with small numbers of Peloponnesian ships crossing over, ignoring a force of 18 vessels, which he dismissed as being out only for raiding purposes.[6] That the ships were carrying the Spartan commander Gylippos was probably unknown to Nicias, but it does seem negligent that he would not be concerned with the ships out for 'raiding' purposes, perhaps indicating that at this early stage he was not concerned about his supply line back to Greece, or indeed that the supply-line was non-existent and

---

4 Thuc. 6.47.
5 Lazenby seems to agree that of the different plans put forward by the three generals, Nicias' was arguably the best. Lazenby (2004): 139. Kagan and most other scholars agree with Thucydides that the best plan was probably Lamachus' plan to attack Syracuse directly, though Hornblower thinks that perhaps at this stage Thucydides is refraining from favouring one plan over the others. For Kagan's discussion see Kagan (1981): 212–17. See also: Hornblower (2008): 423–4.
6 Thuc. 6.104. 'Despised' the small number of ships. Hornblower makes no comment on Nicias' attitude or lack of action, but it seems as if Thucydides is characterising Nicias as somewhat arrogant and negligent in attitude. Hornblower (2008): 536.

the expedition was self-sufficient. Plutarch says that ships full of grain were arriving from cities all over Sicily, suggesting that food supplies did not need to be shipped from mainland Greece.[7] However, there was still an element of negligence, at least in the mind of Thucydides who says later that after the arrival of Gylippos and the setbacks suffered by land, Nicias began to pay more attention to the war at sea.[8] Aside from some fortification works around the Great Harbour, Nicias dispatched 20 ships to the vicinity of Locri and Rhegium to intercept Corinthian ships on their way to reinforce Syracuse.[9]

Nicias laid the blame on the Athenians back home for not preventing reinforcements from sailing over, complaining that the Peloponnesian forces mustering to sail over in the spring would elude the Athenians as they had before.[10] After dispatching 10 ships with money during the winter solstice 414/3 the Athenians then sent 20 ships to Naupactus to intercept reinforcements sailing for Sicily.[11] The Corinthians prepared a squadron of 25 ships to engage the Athenians and protect the transport ships sailing to Sicily. The Corinthians were successful, and the transport ships got through.[12] Far from being a temporary measure, the Corinthian ships appear to have been permanently stationed opposite the Athenian squadron at Naupactus to keep them distracted and unable to intercept Peloponnesian transports.[13] In Italy and Sicily, the Athenians were also unsuccessful, losing transport ships laden with stores and then failing to intercept all but one Peloponnesian transport ship near Megara in Sicily, despite having stationed 20 ships there.[14] As a result of these operations, the Peloponnesians were able to reinforce Syracuse with supplies and troops and at times interdict and destroy

---

7 *Nic.* 18.4.
8 Thuc. 7.4.4. Plutarch also paints Nicias as negligent at this stage, saying he did not set an adequate watch for Gylippos' arrival. *Nic.* 18.6. In this he seems to be following Thucydides' judgement.
9 Thuc. 7.4.7.
10 Thuc. 7.15.2. This puts the blame on the Athenians back home, though it seems at odds with the previous comment by Thucydides that Nicias was not concerned about a few ships, which he saw as out for nothing more than raiding. Hornblower is probably correct in seeing the letter as more of a speech where Thucydides is characterising him as he had before. Hornblower (2008): 568.
11 Thuc. 7.16.2–17.4; Plut. *Nic.* 20.1. Again, the Athenians sent ships out in the middle of winter, including to Sicily. It seems as if there was no squadron of ships stationed at Naupactus before these 20 are sent, for when the battle comes (7.19.5) there are only 20 Athenians ships engaged. Hornblower (2008): 571–2. This does reinforce Nicias' above complaint about Peloponnesian ships not being intercepted on their way to Sicily.
12 Thuc. 7.17.4; 19.5.
13 Thuc. 7.34.1.
14 Thuc. 7.25.1–4.

Athenian transports. This not only hindered Athenian efforts to take Syracuse but also put their plans in jeopardy as the balance of power swung in favour of the besieged Syracuse, which was acquiring supplies faster than the Athenians. Had the Athenians been able to better protect their own supplies and interdict those of the Peloponnesians, it may have tipped the odds in their favour.

The fate of the Athenian expedition to Sicily was sealed by several naval battles in the Great Harbour of Syracuse. The decision by Syracuse to construct and train a fleet was the surest strategy to enable an effective defence of the city.[15] However, according to Thucydides it was not until the Spartan commander Gylippos arrived in Syracuse that they were finally convinced of confronting Athens at sea. He convinced them that it was the only way to gain an advantage over the Athenians and that the potential rewards outweighed the risks.[16] Regardless of whether it is Gylippos or Thucydides who speaks, this was the best strategy to pursue. Despite being defeated in the ensuing naval engagement, Gylippos proved a canny leader as he took advantage of the battle to capture the Athenian forts at Plemmyrion, the promontory at the far entrance to the Great Harbour.[17] Aside from the losses in men and material, this had the much greater impact of making it difficult for all but the strongest of Athenian forces to enter the Great Harbour. This seriously jeopardised Athenian reinforcement and resupply operations, a situation that Thucydides calls the first and foremost cause of ruin of the Athenian forces.[18] In this respect the naval battle was important not as a means of defeating the Athenians directly at sea but as a diversion, which enabled Gylippos' attack by land against Plemmyrion, the consequences of which would have a major impact on the war at sea and thus the entire campaign.

Far from being discouraged by their defeat at sea, Syracuse modified their ships and tactics to confront the Athenians more effectively. They modified the prows of their vessels for head-on ramming attacks, the confined waters of the harbour making it nearly impossible for the swifter Athenian vessels to use their preferred tactics of attacking the flanks of enemy vessels, manoeuvres such as

---

15 Syracuse training a fleet: Thuc. 7.7.4.
16 Thuc. 7.21; Diod. 13.8.5.
17 Thuc. 7.22–3. Kagan sees the naval part of the action as only ever meant to be a diversion from the land attack to take Plemmyrion. Kagan (1981): 298. It seems highly improbable that Syracuse engaged in naval battle without any hope of at least a draw if not an outright victory. Had the Syracusan forces folded too quickly Gylippos' attack would not have worked. While Kagan is correct in seeing it as primarily a diversionary attack, I do not think the Syracusan forces would have engaged in battle without intending to challenge Athenian sea control in the harbour.
18 Thuc. 7.24; Lazenby (2004): 153–4.

the *diekplous* and *periplous*.[19] Such an evolution in tactics and ship modifications may have also laid the foundations for the development of heavier ships types, the '4s' and '5s'.[20] Syracuse and Athens met again in three more naval engagements,[21] the final of which saw the Athenians defeated as they tried to break out of the harbour. This was the end of Athenian naval forces in Sicily, forcing them into a hopeless retreat by land.[22] With no navy to take them off, the Athenians were forced to march through hostile territory without cavalry to screen them and with little hope of finding a way back to Greece. The battles in the Great Harbour of Syracuse may have been unorthodox but they nevertheless had a tremendous impact on the course of the entire war.[23] The Athenians never re-gained a measure of sea control around Syracuse and this was of critical importance, dragging out the siege and preventing them from conducting other operations in Sicily, which may have tipped the odds in their favour.[24] Had the Athenians been able to destroy the fleet of Syracuse their odds of success would have improved substantially. Instead, it was the destruction of their fleet in battle that led to Athenian defeat in Sicily. The failure of Athenian interdiction operations and their losses to Peloponnesian interdictions also contributed to their defeat, allowing Syracuse to receive supply and reinforcement whilst hindering their own supply line. Finally, the loss of Plemmyrion made it much harder for the Athenians to break out and withdraw by sea. Such a withdrawal would have saved at least a portion of the Athenian fleet and army, turning a total loss into something less severe. The naval operations at sea in and around Sicily during the expedition had a defining impact on the course of the war, critically weakening Athenian naval power and strengthening Sparta with a new ally equipped with a capable, and most importantly, battle-tested fleet. Further, it demonstrated to the world that the Athenians could be defeated at sea.

---

19 Thuc. 7.36; Diod. 13.10.2–3. These tactics were tested by the Corinthians off Naupactus in the battle off Erineos (above, Thuc. 7.34).
20 Murray (2012): 23–30, 69–76.
21 Thuc. 7.37–41; Thuc. 7.42; Thuc. 7.56.
22 Thuc. 7.71. Diodorus has some of the Athenians ask retreating crews if they thought they could sail back to Athens by land. Diod. 13.17.1.
23 Unorthodox with respect to the fact that they were large-scale battles conducted in the confines of a harbour and involved tactics such as block-ships and even fire-ships.
24 Lazenby (2004): 167–8.

Spartan strategy 413–404

Sparta and sea power are not often considered in the same sentence, yet it was Sparta's ability to transform itself into a sea power that allowed it to defeat Athens in the Peloponnesian War and gain ascendency in Greek affairs for a short period afterwards. This transformation into a sea power was swift, as was the decline, yet it had a critical impact on the war and a defining impact on Sparta itself.[25] Arguably, Spartan land power did not increase over the fifth or fourth centuries and, if anything, was in decline. Therefore, Sparta's brief fourth-century ascendency can be traced back to its decision to embrace a more maritime approach.

The defeat of the Athenian Sicilian expedition, according to Thucydides, left their allies willing to revolt from Athens: *too* willing in Thucydides' opinion, with the allies thinking that the Athenians would not last another year.[26] Thucydides seems to be warning the reader of Athenian resilience, and perhaps is indicating that Athens at this point still had a chance in the war if only they could endure and halt Spartan successes until a stalemate arose. The Spartans were clearly ready to capitalise on their victory, emboldened by the addition of the Syracusan navy but also taking proactive steps and ordering a shipbuilding program to bolster their naval forces.[27] This is clear acknowledgement by the Spartans that the war would be conducted across the seas and thus required the mobilisation of maritime forces. Sparta was now committing itself to a maritime war in the Aegean. In approximately 410, Diodorus says that the Spartans reckoned that for them to lose at sea constituted a setback and no more since they were still supreme by land, but defeat at sea for Athens would see them fighting not for victory, but for their very survival.[28] The point of the speech is to reinforce how highly the Spartans thought of themselves, but there is a strong element of truth in the boast. By this stage of the war the Athenians were clinging on to a fragile empire with stretched resources while Sparta's 'centre of gravity', the Peloponnese, was safe from the depredations of the Athenians.

A different Spartan attitude and approach to maritime affairs is evident after the Sicilian expedition. This phase of the war, often called 'The Ionian War', saw the bulk of combat operations occur in the east around the Aegean islands and

---

[25] This maritime transformation is neatly summarised in a chapter by Barry Strauss in a volume on maritime transformations throughout history, focused specifically on China in the twenty-first century. See Strauss (2009): 32–61.
[26] 'misplaced optimism' in the words of Hornblower: (2008): 755.
[27] Thuc. 8.2.3, 8.3.2.
[28] Diod. 13.52.6.

the Hellespont region.[29] The Spartans entered the Ionian War with a different strategy from the one with which they began the war, a strategy aimed at stripping Athens of allies. In doing so, they would attack the base of Athenian power, the allies of the islands and Anatolian littoral who kept Athens funded and fed. This strategy required naval and maritime forces that could project power across the seas to strike at the islands and other overseas holdings of Athens. The Spartans, joined by Syracuse and their strong navy, now had the means by which they could pull these subject cities away from Athens.[30] It is important to note that initially the Spartan plan was not to confront the Athenians in battle, but to launch amphibious operations that would allow the allies of Athens to revolt, much like at Amphipolis. As events in the years after the Sicilian expedition would demonstrate, the Spartans often went to great lengths to avoid a naval battle with the Athenians, even when they possessed a numerical advantage. The Athenians' best hope of victory lay in defeating Spartan naval force as well as maintaining the ability to project their own power and dissuade their allies from revolting or taking back cities that had already gone over to Sparta.

One of the first offensive actions undertaken by Sparta at the recommencement of hostilities in 414/3 was to set up a permanent fortification at Decelea in Attica. Rather than the periodic raiding of the Archidamian War, this was a permanent presence in Attica. This move not only opened a second front for the Athenians to deal with, but more importantly it forced the Athenians to transport by sea what had once been transported from Euboea overland through Decelea to Athens, further stretching Athenian maritime resources and making them even more vulnerable to Sparta.[31] This is not to say that the fortification of Decelea on its own was enough, and certainly the Spartans acknowledged the limitations of the fort (see below). It was the timing of it, coinciding with Athenian overstretch in Sicily and the subsequent degradation of their maritime power that was damaging. Merchant ships needed to transport goods from Euboea to Athens and the warships needed to protect them were no longer available to support Athenian operations elsewhere at a time when they were committed to large-scale amphibious campaigns overseas. This extension of supply lines added one more burden

---

29 413–404 BCE, commonly but misleadingly referred to as the 'Decelean War' – more appropriately the Ionian War considering that the bulk of the fighting occurred in the Ionian region. This is not to minimise the importance of the fortification at Decelea and the Spartan occupation of Attica, for this was critical to Spartan strategy. However, as Kagan (building upon Westlake) noted, Ionian war is still a misleading term and Thucydides seems to be referring to the Ionian war as part of the larger war that occurred in that region. Kagan (1987): 41, n. 57; Westlake (1979): 9.
30 Thuc. 8.2.2–3.
31 Thuc. 7.18.1–2, 7.27. Literally 'a double war'. Hornblower (2008): 573.

and one more weak point. Unlike in the Archidamian War, the Spartans did not need to maintain a large standing army in the Peloponnese, since the Athenians were not able to attack as they had under Periclean strategy. At the beginning of the war the Athenians were fighting a defensive war of *choice*: after the Sicilian expedition it was a defensive war of *necessity*. The difference lies in the Athenian ability to conduct offensive operations as a means of achieving their desired outcomes. The last decade of the war involved the Athenians conducting most offensive operations to regain losses suffered at the hands of the Spartans. The best they could hope for would have been a negotiated peace with Sparta after a long war of attrition, rather than a favourable settlement like that offered after Pylos in 425.

From the decision to build a fleet and contest Athenian control in the Aegean until the final battle at Aigispotamoi, the Spartans and their allies conducted numerous amphibious operations aimed at removing allies from the Athenians. An analysis of every operation lies outside the scope of this work.[32] Rather, it is worth examining some of the key issues in the conduct of these operations. The Spartans were deliberate in their opening actions, assessing which allies to support first, and in the case of Chios they sent a certain Phrynis to the island to report on the situation and whether it was conducive to revolt from Athens and worth Spartan support. A key factor seems to have been the fact that the Chians had no less than 60 ships, demonstrating that the Spartans had maritime and naval considerations at the forefront of their new strategy.[33] Preparations were conducted openly, including the hauling of ships across the *diolkos*, since the Athenians apparently had no fleet to speak of at sea.[34] When the Athenians grew suspicious, they asked the Chians to send ships across as surety against any disloyalty.[35] This seems to have had the purpose of weakening the naval power of Chios in case of revolt while simultaneously adding to the naval power of Athens. Nevertheless, the Peloponnesians suffered several setbacks at sea. The Spartan ships that had crossed the Isthmus of Corinth were defeated in battle and blockaded at the disused Corinthian port of Spiraeum. This was an operation that saw a combined sea and land attack on the Spartan forces, a rare but not unheard-of case of naval forces landing troops into a contested environment much like at

---

32 A database of maritime operations conducted in the period can be found at Appendix 1.
33 Thuc. 8.6. The Spartans planned on sending 40 ships in total, 10 of them Spartan, but only sent 5. This was done during winter, and it was an earthquake which caused them to send fewer ships, not the weather. There must have been some religious reason for the scaling back of the operation, a common occurrence for the pious Spartans: Hornblower (2008): 777.
34 Thuc. 8.8.4.
35 Thuc. 8.9.2–3.

Pylos.[36] The second defeat was of a squadron of 16 Peloponnesian ships returning from Sicily, which were intercepted and suffered losses at the hands of 27 waiting Athenian ships near Leucas.[37] Nevertheless, the Spartans, led by the wily Athenian traitor Alcibiades, managed to stifle news of the Spartan reversals and convinced Chios, Erythrai, and Clazomenai to revolt from Athens.[38] Alcibiades had also convinced the Spartans to send five warships with him, the presence of which surely helped influence the Chian assembly in their decision to rebel.[39] Soon after, Alcibiades and 20 ships arrived ahead of 19 Athenian ships to Miletus and induced it to revolt as well.[40] The precariousness of the Athenian situation in the east is summed up shortly after, with explicit commentary from Thucydides. The Athenian forces, having defeated the Peloponnesian forces near Miletus, contemplated taking the city when they heard of a Peloponnesian and Sicilian fleet of 55 ships approaching.[41] The Athenian commander Phrynichos is said to have had precise intelligence of this force and decided to retire and preserve his force rather than confront the enemy – a choice Thucydides praises as prudent and no disgrace, considering the danger Athens would have been in if they lost a battle.[42] Thucydides says the Athenians could not justify offensive action except out of extreme necessity.[43] This is clear recognition by the Athenians that the Peloponnesian threat required a strong naval force to counter, and a confrontation could not be risked except in dire circumstances or with careful preparation. Even then, offensive actions would be aimed at Spartan gains in the region, and the Athenians were unable to strike at core Spartan interests. This shows Spartan strategy was working well, pressuring the Athenians in many places, and forcing them to spread their fleet thin as different island and mainland-littoral cities revolted from the empire.

In 412/1 the Spartans again engaged in operations to disrupt trade along the Anatolian coast, this time sending a coalition of 12 Peloponnesian warships to Cnidos.[44] Half the ships were to secure Cnidos and half were sent to cruise around Triopion and seize merchant vessels sailing from Egypt.[45] The Athenians learned of this plan and dispatched warships from Samos, successfully intercepting and

---

36 Thuc. 8.10–11.
37 Thuc. 8.13.
38 Thuc. 8.14.
39 Thuc. 8.12, 8.14. Kagan (1987): 45.
40 Thuc. 8.17.
41 Thuc. 8.25–6.
42 Thuc. 8.27.1–3.
43 8.27.3. A difficult passage summed up well by Hornblower: (2008): 827.
44 Ten ships from Thourioi, one from Laconia and one from Syracuse, under Spartan command.
45 Thuc. 8.35.1–2.

capturing the Peloponnesian warships and almost taking Cnidos.[46] It is once again worth noting that these operations were conducted during winter. The protection of trade in eastern waters was clearly an important role for Athenian naval forces. Near the end of 410 a force of 15 Peloponnesian ships were intercepted in the Hellespont by 'the nine Athenian ships that were always keeping watch there over the merchantmen'.[47] Earlier, in 413/2, the Athenians had fortified Cape Sounion to enable grain ships to round the cape in safety.[48] This fort helped establish a naval station, which could help protect trade at either end of the Athenian supply chain, protecting the vital sea lanes that kept the city fed.

It is clear from the above operations that there were several key sea routes across the Mediterranean. Corcyra controlled the best route from Greece to Italy and Sicily, important for the grain that Sicily provided, as well as military operations. The entrance to the Corinthian Gulf was a chokepoint that Corinth constantly attempted to keep open, and Athens to shut. After the Sicilian expedition, Athens relied on Egypt and especially the Black Sea for the grain that could keep the city fed. Sea routes from Egypt north and west were targets of Athens' enemies. Of all the cargo requiring protection, grain ships were of the utmost importance to Athens in both peacetime and in war. The protection and interdiction of the grain trade, especially through the Hellespont, became a crucial issue during the last years of the Peloponnesian War. The Spartan King Agis, having fortified Decelea and cut the land route from Euboea to Athens, is said to have decried the futility of the move:

> But Agis, seeing from Decelea the many grain ships sailing into the Piraeus, said that it was of no advantage for them to shut out the Athenians from the land as they already had, if they could not hold back the grain imported by sea.[49]

The intensification of the Spartan war effort in the Hellespont region was not only aimed at taking away allies from Athens, but also disrupting the grain supply that kept Athens fighting. It was Lysander's attacks in the Hellespont and especially the capture of Lampsacos, which would draw the Athenians into battle at Aegospotami.[50] Black Sea grain was important to Athens, possibly as far back as

---

46 Thuc. 8.35.3–4.
47 Xen. Hell. 1.1.36.
48 Thuc. 8.4. The Cape provides exceptional views into the Aegean and the Saronic Gulf. The bay would have provided shelter for several warships tasked with protecting the grain ships. A more contested issue is the dating of the two rock-cut ship sheds present on the site. See Baika (2013): 525–34.
49 Xen. Hell. 1.1.35.
50 Xen. Hell. 2.17.17–21.

the late 430s as evidenced by a speech of Isocrates referring to a special relationship with the Bosporan Kingdoms.[51] As grain from other locations such as Sicily became harder to acquire, Black Sea grain became critical to Athenian survival.

The Spartans were able to use events in the east to launch small but important operations against the Athenians on the mainland. Mobilising five Sicilian and six Spartan ships, they launched a joint land and sea operation against the Athenian-backed Messenian garrison at Pylos, a thorn in the side of Sparta since 425. The Athenian relief force was turned back by bad weather at Cape Malea (a notoriously difficult cape), and the Spartans were successful in retaking Pylos.[52] This not only removed a key base for Athenian operations, but it also removed a potential bargaining tool for future negotiations.[53] The story is related by Diodorus but not Xenophon, a puzzling omission. However, Diodorus says the Athenian in command, Anytos, was accused of treason and saved himself only through bribing the jury, apparently the first case of a jury being bribed in Athenian history. It is almost certain that there were political motives behind this attack on Anytos.[54] It is odd that Anytos gave up so easily in trying to relieve the garrison at Pylos. Diodorus says that they held out for some time and one of the key factors in their surrender was a lack of food. This implies that the Spartan attack was conducted over a sufficiently long time to cause such a shortage. Even a bad storm lasting several days need not have precluded the Athenians from getting relief through in time. Anytos' conduct may not have been directly treasonous, but perhaps incompetent, or maybe the naval contingent that was mobilised was of poor quality. This would shed some light on the potentially degraded state of the Athenian fleet at the time. In any case, this may have been a small-scale amphibious operation, but it had a large impact on the war and was a demonstration of how much abler the Spartans had become at conducting maritime operations from the sea.

---

51 Satyros, who ruled from approximately 433–392. Isoc. 17.57; Garnsey (1988): 124. This was the Cimmerian Bosporus, on the eastern side of the present-day Crimean Peninsula. Kagan identifies the Black Sea as the most important 'granary' for Athens in the fifth century as well as an important source of dried fish. Kagan (1969): 179–80. Some scholars argue that the Black Sea region was an important source of Athenian grain well before the Peloponnesian War. Keen (2000): 63–73.
52 Diod. 13.64.5–7.
53 Kagan (1987): 264.
54 Kagan (1987): 264, n. 71.

As Athens lost tribute-paying allies and struggled to finance their military campaigns, an increasing burden was placed on the fleet to levy money from the remaining allies throughout the Aegean. More than this, the decision to send out generals with the warships lent weight to their operations. The Athenians sent out *strategoi* and ships to collect tribute from their allies on several occasions early in the war.[55] Importantly, the dates of these tribute collection expeditions seem to conform to Athenian reassessments of allied tribute contributions, and thus the need for some force to back up the collection.[56] This example demonstrates how diplomatic operations can fit onto a sliding scale between more benign operations during non-reassessment years with fewer ships, and more coercive operations during reassessment years, requiring more ships and accompanied by senior leadership. As the war dragged on and Athenian finances worsened, the Athenian fleet ranged further afield and in larger numbers to collect money. Thucydides, Diodorus, and Xenophon all mention incidents in 411 where Athenian ships were sent out to collect money, including Alcibiades with 21 ships levying money from Halicarnassus.[57] It is also of great significance that by the time the Athenians were sending warships to levy money they had ceased to impose a direct tribute on their allies and had moved to a system of taxing 5% of all seaborne imports and exports.[58] This means that the Athenian ships were not out collecting their regular dues, but additional funds. No doubt this double-dipping incited resentment, hence the warships.

Several years later the Athenians relied on an even more coercive use of sea power to collect money after they defeated the Peloponnesians at the battle of Cyzicus. Having established control of the Propontis, the Athenians established a 'customs-house' at the city of Chrysopolis on the Bosporus and taxed all vessels sailing from, as well as into, the Pontus.[59] The contingent left behind included 30 ships and 2 generals to watch over the Bosporus as well as to damage their enemies as the opportunity arose.[60] The use of sea power to collect money could be extremely use-

---

55 Thuc. 2.69, 3.19, 4.50, 4.75.
56 Gomme does not agree with the connection and sees the ships as merely escorts for the ships carrying the tribute. Gomme (1956): 202–3. Meiggs (1972: 533) disagrees and sees the dispatch of larger numbers of warships than normal in assessment years as a deliberate policy. The entire point is that the *strategoi* and ships were sent out during tribute reassessment years, not merely as escorts for the annual collection of tribute, lending greater weight to Meiggs' assessment of the situation.
57 Thuc. 8.108.2; Diod. 13.42.2–3. Xen. *Hell.* 1.1.8, 1.3.8.
58 In 413 BC. Thuc. 7.28.4.
59 The Greek word used is literally a 'tenths-office', meaning an office for the collection of one-tenth. Xen. *Hell.* 1.1.22. The incident is mentioned by Polybius when he describes the area. He has the Athenians taxing vessels sailing into the Pontus. Polyb. 4.44.4.
60 Xen. *Hell.* 1.1.22.

ful and effective, but it also caused a backlash that could last for decades. Having won a great victory at Cyzicus, the Athenians were buoyant and the Spartans despondent, the latter asking Athens for a peace treaty according to Diodorus, but not Xenophon.[61] The offer, reported by Diodorus as coming from the Spartan Endius, was to abandon the garrisons in each other's territory – Pylos and Decelea – and to keep all the territory they possessed at the time.[62] Donald Kagan puts forward good arguments both for and against Athens rejecting the offer of peace.[63] The most compelling reason for Athens to take the peace was the fact that they were still in a tenuous position and remained only one naval defeat away from being unable to continue the war. On the other hand, the Spartans were still in possession of vast areas of the Aegean, including such strategically significant places as Euboea, Thasos, Rhodes and Chios, amongst others, and leaving these, formerly Delian League holdings in the hands of the Spartans would have been unacceptable to the Athenians, who may have felt after their recent victory that they had the momentum to take them back by force. Of course, in hindsight it seems like a poor decision to have rejected the peace, but the Athenians clearly were not satisfied with the terms, which would have seen the stripped of their Aegean base of power. If they had any hope of regaining their empire and the fruits of that empire, they would need to take back what Sparta was holding. The Spartan offer of peace clearly reflected the fact that they thought they were in a superior strategic position, but worried enough about Athens' sea power potential to reverse the gains they had made in the Aegean.

The year 406 was pivotal in the war and the Spartan blockade of Mytilene was a key event. In contrast to Alcidas' poor showing, the Spartan commander Callicratidas extracted money, willingly, from the Milesians and Chians. He then attacked and took Methymna and supposedly sent to the Athenian Conon a message, which demonstrates how far Spartan strategy and attitudes had turned, telling the Athenian that he would 'put an end to his illicit love with the sea'.[64] As Kagan points out, the implication of the language used is that the sea rightly belongs to Sparta.[65] This is certainly bluster and a taunt towards Conon, but provides an insight into how Spartan thinking had changed over the years. It is hard

---

61 With the possibility that this comes from the narrative of the *Hellenica Oxyrhynchia*. Diod. 13.52.1–2; Kagan (1987): 248, n. 10.
62 Diod. 13.52.3.
63 Kagan (1987): 248–52.
64 Xen. *Hell.* 1.6.15.
65 Kagan (1987): 334. To translate the word simply as 'fornicating' or some other such word misses the core meaning of the word. The word is concerned with adultery, not just sex in general, and this may be a fine distinction, but it is an important one.

to imagine Alcidas or any other Spartan saying such a thing during the first 15 years of the war.

Conon managed to flee to Mytilene, but the pursuing Spartans defeated the Athenians in the city, destroying 30 Athenian ships and allowing Callicratidas to blockade the harbour and city.[66] Cut off with little prospect of obtaining food and with no word of his situation reaching the outside world, Conon managed to a message to Athens in a trireme, which successfully ran the careless Spartan blockade.[67] Conon sent two triremes, one sailing out to the 'open sea', presumably sailing directly west towards Attica and one towards the Hellespont. Xenophon describes the preparations as careful on the Athenian side whereas the Spartans had become careless, and they took their meals ashore at midday. Clearly Xenophon is highlighting how a blockade of a harbour should *not* be done. Although the Spartans caught one of the ships sailing out, the other reached Athens successfully. Clearly it was not material or technological deficiency that allowed the blockade to be run, but a deficiency in training and proper precaution. Diodorus gives a different, more confused account of this episode, although he gives extra detail on the measures taken by Conon to prevent the Peloponnesian ships from forcing the harbour entrance.[68] This included sinking small vessels filled with rocks in the shallows and anchoring larger merchant vessels in the deeper water, armed with stones. The small boats sunk in the shallow water would ensure that those waters were completely blocked off, and presumably the larger ships had stones positioned at the yardarms, to be dropped on the decks of passing enemy ships. A similar tactic was used with effect by the Athenians besieged in the harbour at Syracuse, using merchant vessels with 'dolphins' – pointed lead weights – positioned at the yardarms.[69] In both narratives however, it is the Spartan blockade and siege of Mytilene that sets up the battle of Arginousai.

The battle of Arginousai was one of the few large naval battles fought during the war and had serious ramifications at the strategic level. Conon's predicament caused the Athenians to send a relief fleet, scraping together as many ships and men as possible to relieve the ships trapped in Mytilene. The battle that ensued

---

66 Xen. *Hell.* 1.6.16–18.
67 Xen. *Hell.* 1.6.19–22.
68 Kagan does not favour Diodorus' account and all but ignores it in favour of Xenophon's. Kagan (1987): 335, n. 38. Peter Green in his commentary points out one of the key differences in the accounts: that Xenophon portrays the Spartan Callicratidas in a highly favourable light, whereas in Diodorus it is Conon who appears as the brilliant tactician. Neither account is necessarily unfavourable to the other, but merely places emphasis on the opposing leaders. Green (2010): 235–6, n. 92.
69 Thuc. 7.41.2–3.

was one of the largest naval battles of the war and indeed of Greek history to that point and saw a decisive Athenian victory.[70] In the standard narrative, Arginousai was a potential turning point for the Athenians, an opportunity to end the war on favourable terms. According to one source, the Spartans were willing to conclude a peace which included evacuating the fort at Decelea, with no comparable concession required from the Athenians.[71] However, the peace offer is somewhat suspicious, found only in the *Ath. Pol.* and it may be confusing this offer with the earlier peace offer from Sparta in 411/0 after their loss at Cyzicos.[72] Most historians seem to accept uncritically that this peace offer was made, and even when the source is acknowledged as suspect it does not seem to impact the analysis of the battle's aftermath.[73] In accepting that the peace offer was made, Platias and Koliopoulos are correct in seeing the Athenian rejection as demonstrative of unlimited strategic aims and the conservatism of Spartan strategy.[74] That the Spartans were willing to vacate the fortification of Decelea without a corresponding concession from the Athenians is significant. It is hard to agree with the idea that the Athenians were better off rejecting a peace offer. The Spartans had continually demonstrated their ability to recover from losses quickly with Persian help: far quicker than the Athenians could. The Athenians may have won the battle, but it did not lead to superiority at sea as has been suggested.[75] The Athenian fleet was clearly not in a fit state after Arginousai, with serious issues of poor training and especially poor leadership. There was good reason not to continue the war, since Athens remained but one loss away from total defeat. The Spartans were still able to contest Athenian sea control soon after the battle. This is also to view the peace treaty as nothing more than a truce and not an attempt at forming

---

70 The details of the battle and subsequent trial of the generals are beyond the scope of this current work. For more see Xen. *Hell.* 1.6.22–1.7.35; Diod. 13.97–103. Battle and trial: Kagan (1987): 335–75; Hamel (2015). On the trial: Andrewes (1974): 112–22; Asmonti (2006): 1–21. A view on Athenian casualty aversion as the core reason for the trial: Strauss (2000): 315–26.
71 *Ath. Pol.* 34.1.
72 See Rhodes (1981): 424–5.
73 Platias and Koliopoulos accept the peace offer at face value (2010: 80) as does Kagan (1987: 353) and Hanson (2005: 282). Tritle says that the Athenians may have rejected the Spartan offer, that the source (*Ath. Pol.*) might have been in error, but it does not affect his analysis of the war. (2010: 213, 221 n. 21). Other works fail to mention it entirely: Hale (2009) and Hamel (2015). Lazenby has the most to say on the issue, acknowledging that the offer of peace may be unhistorical. Nevertheless, Lazenby seems to accept that the offer was genuine, analysing the aftermath of the battle as if it existed and not considering the strategic ramifications if the offer is unhistorical. Lazenby (2004): 235–7.
74 Platias and Koliopoulos (2010): 80.
75 Lazenby (2004): 235–6.

lasting peace. If the peace offer existed then it was overconfidence or unrealistic strategic ambition that prevented the Athenians from taking it, a failure on their part to recognise just how precarious their position was, one loss away from total defeat, as would happen a year later at Aigispotamoi.

What is not taken into consideration is the likelihood of this peace offer not existing at all. It is absent from the accounts of Xenophon and Diodorus and was probably misreported by the *Ath Pol.*, either accidentally or deliberately. This changes the strategic calculations, placing the Athenians in a more desperate situation than is usually recognised. In both scenarios their situation was dire, but with a peace offer they still had a way out and therefore, a refusal demonstrates wide strategic ambition and an unwillingness to settle when they were still in possession of a strong fleet and defensible position in the Aegean. The Athenians of course could have extended an offer of peace to the Spartans. That they did not is perhaps just as indicative of political turmoil and uncertainty in Athens itself as it is of any reluctance for peace. Just as plausibly, the Athenians may have thought that such an offer would be rejected by Sparta. The trial of the Generals in Athens was hugely controversial, caused a great deal of harm, and it is not unreasonable to think peace offers were not considered because there was simply no real leadership in Athens at the time. The rabid tone, which seems to have infected the democracy at the time, did not seem to have lent itself to ideas such as offering peace, considering that not even victorious generals were immune from execution. The terrible leadership displayed by the Athenians at Aigispotamoi goes some way to demonstrating that Athens at a military-strategic level was not functioning well. Moreover, the vigorous pursuit of the war by Lysander after Arginousai would also have put pressure on the Athenians, forcing them to prioritise their responses. In a sense, the Athenians were overtaken by events.

Without the prospect of a truce or offer of peace, the Athenians were in the same precarious situation and facing a Spartan command unwilling to settle even after such a loss as theirs at Arginousai. In this scenario the Spartans were relying on their ability, with Persian money, to reconstitute their fleet quickly and to keep challenging the Athenians, almost certainly with the recognition that the Athenians were still one loss away from total defeat. The vigorous way in which the Spartans pursued the war after their loss at Arginousai demonstrates a marked shift in strategic thinking that must have occurred in Sparta, a pursuit of the war where the desired end was the destruction of the Athenian fleet. It is perhaps reason enough to disbelieve in the peace offer because the Spartans were still in a strategically superior position after the battle and offering peace with such generous conditions was not at all in keeping with their goal of victory over Athens. The Athenians could not have sustained a loss at Arginousai and were in the same strategic position after the battle. Arginousai saw Athens survive, but did little to increase their near-term chances of victory over Sparta.

Defeat at Arginousai did not prevent the Spartans from conducting further operations in the Aegean, and under the command of Lysander they were able to keep pressure on Athens. Using Persian money and under orders from Cyrus not to fight a battle at sea until the fleet was larger, Lysander built up his naval force.[76] This allowed him to attack and take the Athenian-allied city of Cedreai in Caria.[77] After this he sailed to the Hellespont and successfully took the city of Lampsacus, placing the Spartans in a position to choke the Hellespont.[78] It was this move that forced the Athenians to Aegospotami and the ensuing disaster where their fleet was caught unawares by the Spartans and annihilated. It was not really a naval battle, since the bulk of the Athenian ships were beached and the crews dispersed, with only nine Athenian ships putting to sea, which used the opportunity to escape.[79] With a concerted campaign of operations against Athenian interests in the Ionian and Hellespont regions the Spartans were able drain the Athenian base of support and eventually, at Aegospotami, draw the Athenian fleet into a battle and defeat them. The loss of their allies and their fleet was a devastating blow to the Athenians and one they could not recover from. Lysander sailed from the Hellespont to Byzantium and thus cut off Athenian ships from the Black Sea.[80] From there he sailed around the area with impunity and consolidated Spartan power in the region.[81] Lysander appears to have had privateers in his employ, dispatching the Milesian *leistes* Theopompus back to Sparta to announce the news of Sparta's victory.[82] The Spartans appear to have employed *leistai* throughout the Peloponnesian War right to the end, no doubt using Persian money to attract these raiders. Lysander was able to project Spartan power from the sea with impunity and initiate a close blockade of Athens. Within a short period of time, a combination of combat operations at and from the sea crippled Athens and led to their defeat at the hands of Spartan sea power.

The Spartans too realised the potential of using their naval forces for coercive purposes, though it took many years to approach the level of Athenian diplomatic naval operations. Aside from the Chian revolt (see above) the Spartans had learnt what the Athenians had known for a long time: the presence of warships was a

---

76 Xen *Hell.* 2.1.13–14.
77 Xen *Hell.* 2.1.15.
78 Xen *Hell.* 2.1.19.
79 See Xen. 2.1.17–30.
80 Xen *Hell.* 2.1.1–2.
81 Xen *Hell.* 2.2.3. For more on this incident, see Chapter Eight.
82 Xen. *Hell.* 2.1.30.

powerfully compelling force. After his victory at Aegospotami, Lysander dispatched a certain Eteonicos with ten triremes to 'the lands around Thrace', where he brought the settlements over to the Spartan side.[83] Considering the only naval force that could have been a threat was the Athenian one recently annihilated at Aegospotami, the Spartan ships did not need to travel in force for safety, and 10 ships seems more than required for simple treaty making, giving the force a distinctly coercive feel. This followed immediately after Lysander had sailed from the Hellespont to Lesbos, where Xenophon says, rather cryptically, that he 'ordered' the affairs of the cities there, especially Mytilene.[84] Plutarch is of little help, vaguely referring to Lysander sailing around and putting affairs into the hands of his partisans and generally wreaking havoc in the Aegean before sailing across to Attica.[85] Plutarch's account implies violence, whereas Xenophon's rather laconic account does not, though perhaps this is because it was not necessary. Lysander had 200 ships with him and such a large force in and of itself would have had a profound effect without having to resort to violence. It was a clear signal to the Greek around the Aegean that Sparta now ruled the waves.

After the defeat and loss of their navy at Aegospotami the Athenians had no way of protecting their vital sea lanes and were at the mercy of the Spartan fleet. The Athenian populace was intimately aware of this, mourning the news of the loss not just for those Athenians killed, but for themselves as well, knowing that without a fleet they were left unprotected.[86] The Spartans had the ability to interdict Athenian shipping at will and were able to affect a close blockade of the Piraeus from nearby Salamis.[87] Taken with the fortification by land at Decelea, the Athenians were surrounded and completely blockaded by land and sea. During the ensuing discussions of peace within Athens, they still could not countenance destruction of the remaining essential asset of the city, the Long Walls. They apparently imprisoned a certain Archestratos who had mentioned such a move in a council meeting.[88] Unsurprisingly the destruction of Athens' walls was a necessary condition of peace, as well as the surrender of all but 12 warships.[89] This left Athens extremely vulnerable, as demonstrated shortly after the war when Lysander and his brother Libys were able, at the behest of the Thirty Tyrants, to blockade the Athenian dem-

---

83 Xenophon is vague about which settlements or even what area of Thrace. Xen. *Hell.* 2.2.5.
84 Xen. *Hell.* 2.2.5. Neither Kagan nor Lazenby offer any commentary on this event outside of the bare facts as reported by Xenophon. Kagan (1987): 398; Lazenby (2004): 245.
85 Plut. *Lys.* 13.4–14.1.
86 For an examination of the battle itself, see Strauss (1983): 24–35; Robinson 2014: 1–16.
87 Xen. *Hell.* 2.2.9.
88 Xen. *Hell.* 2.2.15.
89 Xen. *Hell.* 2.2.20.

ocrats in the Piraeus by land and sea.⁹⁰ The ease with which Athens could be choked off from the outside world is clearly demonstrated in these two Spartan blockades. Diodorus too passes judgement, saying that at the end of the Peloponnesian War the Spartans ruled by both land and sea.⁹¹

Conclusion

Spartan success in the north-west Aegean at Amphipolis in the first half of the war presaged a bolder and more successful strategy undertaken during the Decelean-Ionian War. Brasidas had hit on the right strategy but had insufficient means to make it work outside of the Chalcidice. When the war flared up again in 415, Sparta could call upon Persian money to build a fleet and conduct amphibious operations against Athenian interests in the Aegean island and Anatolian regions. Knowing that Athens' centre of gravity was its maritime empire Sparta implemented its own effective sea power strategy.

While not minimising the importance of military operations by land, there is little doubt that the Peloponnesian War was decided at sea. At the beginning of the war Athens had a large empire to draw resources from, both materially and monetarily. This fuelled a fleet which was able to conduct expeditionary operations against Sparta and Spartan allies, wearing them down and eventually luring the Spartans into a bad position at Pylos and Sphacteria and opening the way for a peace deal. That the Athenians did not take the peace offered was a reflection of growing ambition and is indicative of how effective they thought their sea power had become. All the while the walls of Athens protected the city and the same navy, which attacked Sparta, was also able to defend Athenian trade and keep the city fed and supplied. This was all possible due to Athenian ability to gain and maintain sea control. It was the loss of this control in Sicily, which doomed the Athenian forces there. Such losses further hampered Athenian efforts to regain control of the seas in the second half of the war. Spartan strategy by this stage had shifted dramatically. To do this, the Spartans needed strong maritime forces to attack the islands and littoral poleis of the empire, a move which proved very successful. It drained Athenian resources and eroded their sea power as they were forced into constant operations. Fuelled by Persian money, the Spartans could absorb losses at sea and eventually place the Athenians in mortal danger at Arginousai and again at Aegospotami, the latter of which saw the irrevocable loss

---

90 Xen. *Hell.* 2.4.28–9.
91 Diod. 14.10.1.

of the Athenian fleet. The Peloponnesian War was not the triumph of land over sea power – a complete mischaracterisation of Sparta in the latter half of the war. The Peloponnesian War was simply the triumph of sea power. However, Sparta would soon come up against Pericles' warning from the start of the war that gaining and maintaining sea power was no easy thing. The opening decades of the fourth century would test Sparta's new maritime ability as Athens sought to reclaim the seas.

Chapter Nine
No easy thing: the fall of Spartan sea power and Athens' return

The end of the Peloponnesian War saw the rise of Sparta as a power in the wider Aegean region, thanks to its bourgeoning sea power. Athens was able to rebuild its sea power reasonably quickly, in large part to the non-naval interests such as maritime trade. However, it never reached the same strength as it had during the Peloponnesian War.[1] The other powers around the Aegean and the Mediterranean also invested in small and moderate-sized navies, to an extent that even Athens could be challenged by a coalition of like-minded island poleis. Sea power continued to play an important role in shaping the actions of different powers during the fourth century; however, sea power was more dispersed, and if there were none of the great battles at sea, as seen in the fifth century, there were still many combat operations undertaken both at and from the sea. This chapter considers the end of the Peloponnesian War as the break between the fifth and the fourth centuries, in a practical sense defining when the balance of power shifted definitively away from Athens as the main hegemonic power in the Aegean, rather than be bound by simple dates.[2]

Spartan strategy 404-370s

The final battle of the Peloponnesian War occurred (mostly) at sea and saw the Athenian fleet annihilated at Aegospotami.[3] Xenophon quite correctly points to this loss as the end of the Athenian cause.[4] This also allowed Sparta to gain an almost uncontested control of the seas for the next decade, both around mainland Greece and in the Aegean. This control was lost in the Aegean in 394 when Persian forces, partly under the command of the Athenian Conon, defeated the Spar-

---

1 For an interesting look at maritime trade in the recovery of Athens post-war, see Burke (1990): 1–13.
2 Much the same way modern scholars favour constructs such as the 'long nineteenth' and 'short twentieth centuries'.
3 After the Athenian leaders put themselves in a terrible tactical position and apparently refused the advice of the exiled Alcibiades, it was not really a conventional naval battle at sea, since many Athenian ships were caught ashore before they could be fully crewed or even launched. Xen. *Hell.* 2.1.22–8.
4 Xen. *Hell.* 2.1.29.

tan fleet at Cnidos (see below).⁵ Before this defeat, the Spartans enjoyed a short-lived hegemony in the Aegean region, effectively usurping Athens' empire and focusing on the region for the next decade. The Spartan focus on Asia Minor and the littoral areas demanded a strong maritime force, which at first glance is apparent. They had a strong position in several important coastal cities, especially in the fine port at Ephesus, as well as Smyrna, Phocaea, Cyme, and Abydos.⁶ The problems lay in their material resources and, most importantly, their strategy, which was weak and incoherent.⁷ Perhaps, the primary reason for the Spartan strategy being insufficient was the tenuous state of their fleet. The Spartans required a fleet able to provide cover and support to land forces and to contest Persian maritime attempts in the Aegean region.⁸ The Spartan fleet needed to be powerful enough to prevent Persian interference: combat operations *at* sea to sustain combat operations *from* the sea.

Another critical issue was that of funding, a constant pressure for any large sea power. The Spartan fleet that had defeated Athens was primarily funded by the Persians, who had now become their adversary. The territories in the east that Sparta controlled provided revenue and some 1,000 talents, but much of this was expended in the maintenance of this rule, and Sparta had no large cash reserves.⁹ This was a fragile financial position for sustaining a large naval force away on campaign in the east. It is a stark contrast to Athens at the beginning of the Peloponnesian War, which had both a larger revenue base and a large reserve of cash. That massive expenditure strained even the Athenian financial system, a much more robust system than the Spartan one. Much like Athens at Arginousai in 406, the Spartans were on a razor's edge and one defeat away from losing their position. It is clear that the Persians saw this, for the satrap Pharnabazos gained the support of the king, Artaxerxes, to put the Athenian exile, Conon, in charge of a fleet.¹⁰ Without a fleet, the Spartans would themselves be open to attack from the sea and unable to maintain their sea lines of communication across the Ionian littoral and back to mainland Greece.

---

5 Xen. *Hell.* 4.3.10–12.
6 Buckler (2003): 41, 45.
7 Buckler's (2003, 41) criticism is scathing, though not unwarranted. He says of the Spartans that they embarked upon the campaign in the east 'with the far-sightedness of moles'..
8 Buckler says the Spartans needed to maintain control of the Aegean and to repulse the Persian navy (Buckler, 2003, 43). Strictly speaking, these have the same objective. Repulsing the Persian fleet would be one of the effects of maintaining sea control in the Aegean.
9 Diod. 14.10.2. Buckler (2003): 42–3.
10 Diod. 14.39.1; Buckler (2003): 54–5; Asmonti (2015): 126–9.

The reign of Agesilaus began with a renewed expedition against Persia, upon learning of the Persian naval build-up. According to informants, the Phoenicians and others were building and assembling a force of some 300 triremes.[11] Lysander demanded a force to attack the Persians, or as in Xenophon's biography of Agesilaus, it is the king himself who demands such a response. Xenophon is unclear, for his *Hellenica* and his biography of Agesilaus say different things about this whole episode. Plutarch, in his biographies of the two men, has Lysander as the driving force for the expedition.[12] With the exception of Xenophon's encomium to the Spartan king, in which the intent of the work might be explanation enough for the discrepancy, Lysander appears to have been the driving force behind the Spartan expedition to Asia.[13] Having once had close relations with the Persians and having operated extensively in the region when fighting Athens, it is hardly surprising that Lysander would be the main agitator for such an expedition.[14] In either case, the Spartans launched an expeditionary operation against the Persians in Asia, spurred by the Persian naval build-up.

Based on the success of the expedition of the Ten Thousand (the conduct rather than the outcome), Lysander thought this skill and daring somehow would transfer to the Spartan navy, and believed the Greek fleet would be inherently superior.[15] This was, as Buckler says, a miscalculation, which events would soon prove to be of disastrous consequence.[16] In August 394, the Spartans engaged the fleet of the Persians, under the command of the Athenian Conon, and suffered a crushing defeat at the hands of the exiled Athenian.[17] The loss at Cnidos in 394 destroyed Spartan sea power in the Aegean and ended their ability to project

---

11 Xen. *Hell.* 3.4.1.
12 *Agesilaus* 6.1; *Lysander* 23.1–2. In Lysander's biography, Plutarch has him pushing for an expedition to Asia without any claim of a Persian build-up.
13 Surprisingly, this discrepancy is often overlooked. Hamilton, in his work on the Spartan king, does not mention the differences between Xenophon's own works. Perhaps his conclusion was the same – an *encomium* to the king would naturally give him more credit. His conclusion that Lysander was the driving force is sound, but it is an odd omission. See Hamilton (1991): 29–31, 90–4.
14 This may seem like a contradiction, but his close relationship had been with King Cyros and so he may have had no compunctions about attacking Artaxerxes.
15 Xen. *Hell.* 3.4.2.
16 Or more precisely, as he says, 'a calamitous miscalculation'. Buckler (2003): 59. Perhaps, he would have been more cautious had he known Conon was to be the commander of the Persian fleet.
17 Xen. *Hell.* 4.3.11–12; Diod. 14.83.5–84.4. For an examination of the background and lead-up to the battle, see: Asmonti (2015): 131–50.

power unhindered in the region.[18] Diodorus is quite explicit in his appraisal of the situation, saying that from that time, the Spartans lost their rule of the sea.[19] This loss had disastrous consequences, leading to a cascade of losses for Sparta, as they were unable to stop Conon's fleet, which was free to sail around to the coastal cities of the Aegean and expel the Spartan garrisons (*harmosts*), winning the poleis away from the Spartans.[20] Cos was the first to secede, and then the islands of Nisyros, Teos, and Chios, as well as the Mytilenaeans, Ephesians, and Erythraians; some of them merely expelling the Spartan garrisons and others, actively joining with Conon.[21] Conon was then able to besiege the Spartans in Abydos and win over the poleis of the Hellespont.[22]

Perhaps most damaging of all, the Spartans were left defenceless as Conon took the fleet to Greece and attacked the Peloponnese, and garrisoned the island of Cythera before proceeding to Athens and helping them rebuild the city's defences, including the vital Long Walls.[23] Xenophon has Conon tell the Persian Satrap Pharnabazos that nothing would damage the Spartan cause more than rebuilding the walls of Athens.[24] Interestingly, according to both Xenophon and Diodorus, many cities, including from Boeotia, sent craftsmen and labourers to assist the Athenians in rebuilding the wall – a universal acknowledgement that the walls of Athens were of critical importance in resisting Sparta.[25] Cities that had once called for and perhaps even aided in the destruction of Athenian walls, a mere decade earlier, helped rebuild them in the hope that, combined with the Athenian fleet,[26] Spartan power could be resisted and defeated. John Buckler does not exaggerate when he calls the restoration of the Long Walls itself a defeat for Sparta.[27] The nature of the Athenian revival is perhaps best demonstrated in the sudden rehabilitation of Themistocles' memory – a clear enough indication of the signifi-

---

18 Agesilaus marched back to Greece, rather than sailed. This happened before the battle of Cnidos, but it must have been a sign of how stretched Spartan sea power was at the time that they would not risk a quicker journey home by sea. Xen. *Hell.* 4.3.1, *Age.* 2.1; Plut. *Age.* 16.1.
19 Diod. 14.84.4.
20 Xen. *Hell.* 4.8.1–3.
21 Diod. 14.8.3.
22 Xen. *Hell.* 4.8.6.
23 Xen. *Hell.* 4.8.7–10.
24 Xen. Hell. 4.8.9.
25 Diodorus' account: 14.85.1–4. He specifically mentions 500 Thebans, whereas Xenophon says only Boeotians.
26 As noted by Tod, in Garland (1987): 40.
27 Buckler (2003): 138.

cance of Conon's restoration in the eyes of the Athenians.[28] It clearly had the desired effect, for the Spartans were greatly alarmed by the Athenian build-up of walls and ships, and sent envoys to Persia.[29] Finally, this represented not just the death of the Spartan maritime empire, but also the beginning of a new phase in relations between the Greeks and Persia that would lead to the signing of the peace of Antalcidas.[30] In these respects, Cnidos represented, not just a significant but a decisive naval battle that had long lasting ramifications for the course of the fourth-century history.

Spartan sea power was greatly diminished after their loss, but this did not prevent the Spartans from continuing their maritime operations closer to home, and for the next two decades, control of the seas around mainland Greece would remain contested. Though not large in scale, some of these operations are demonstrative of the experience built over several years. In 391, King Agesilaus attacked the walls of Corinth, while his brother Teleutias, with 12 triremes, simultaneously attacked by sea.[31] Such a combined land-sea operation is not easy to pull off and its success was a credit to the two commanders, and a good example of how armies and navies working together could be a powerful force.[32] Interestingly, Xenophon comments that the mother of Agesilaus and Teleutias could be proud because of the success on land and at sea achieved by the two brothers. Clearly, success at sea for the Spartans could be viewed as equally prestigious as success on land.

The Spartans launched a raid on the Piraeus itself in 387, a bold statement of the Spartan sea power and demonstrative of the lack of Athenian sea control in its own waters. Under the command of Teleutias, 12 warships sailed overnight and arrived off the port at dawn. Teleutias ordered them to damage and render unseaworthy any warships in the harbour, and to capture and tow off any loaded merchant vessels. In the attack, a group of Spartans landed ashore on the quayside and captured some merchants and shipowners.[33] It was the incapacitation of these Athenian warships that probably allowed the Spartans to range down the coast as far as Cape Sounion, capturing fishing and merchant vessels along the way, not only damaging Athenian trade but also funding the Spartan naval oper-

---

28 Honoured with a tomb on the Akte Peninsula of the Piraeus. See Garland (1987): 40; Hale (2009): 253–4.
29 Xen. *Hell.* 4.8.12.
30 Asmonti (2015): 153.
31 Xen. *Hell.* 4.4.19.
32 Buckler does point out that the Spartans enjoyed the element of surprise, since this was not an operation that the Spartans were really known for. Buckler (2003): 116.
33 Xen. *Hell.* 5.1.19–21.

ations for another month.³⁴ These small-scale operations were not just offensive in nature. Not long after their successful joint operation at Corinth and the port of Lechaion, the Spartan forces were defeated in a land battle. Some of the Spartans sheltered on a nearby hill and then withdrew to the coastline, where boats had been sent by the Spartans in Lechaion, who were monitoring the battle.³⁵ Thanks to the support provided by the fleet, the Spartans were able to evacuate some of their soldiers, made possible because of the Spartan sea control in the Corinthian Gulf, warding off any potential attackers by sea. No doubt, the spectre of their failure at Pylos and Sphacteria, in 425, haunted them. These examples, although small scale, demonstrate the Spartans actively using their navy to strike at their enemies and evacuate soldiers in trouble on land. This shows not only a shift in their military operations in general, but also in their mindset: a more maritime approach in their overall strategy.

Once the Athenians had rebuilt some of their former sea power, they continued to use it in much the same way as in the fifth century. In 390, Thrasybulus was elected as a *strategos* and was sent out with 40 triremes. He collected funds from the allies in Ionia and made alliances with Medocos and Seuthes, the Kings of Thrace.³⁶ Clearly, by sending 40 triremes, they were intent on making a statement, and it certainly would have helped alliance negotiations to have been backed by such a strong naval contingent. What is not clear is how coercive this cruise was. It may have been intended to reassure the allies that Athens had returned as a strong sea power, able to fight the Spartans and to defend them. However, given Athens' track record with the Delian League, it could equally have been a show of strength, a message that Athens could call for contributions, and the navy stood ready to collect. The question was if the cruise was to prove to the Thracian kings that Athens was a worthy alliance partner or an implicit threat that they would be a bad enemy to have. It seems as if the first is more likely as the Athenians were able to conclude a treaty between the warring Thracians and enrol them as allies. Together, with the good relations Athens had with Persia, this manoeuvring persuaded cities in the region to aid Athens, especially important in securing the vitally important trade route through the Hellespont.³⁷ As a flow-on effect of Thrasybulus' campaign in the area, the Thasians took advantage of the Athenian presence nearby and expelled the Spartan garrison from the is-

---

34 Xen. *Hell.* 5.1.23–4.
35 Xen. *Hell.* 4.5.17.
36 Diod. 14.94.2–3.
37 The details of the campaign and the alliances are difficult to ascertain, not least because Xenophon fails to give a thorough account. Buckler (2003): 157–9, esp. n. 28. On the alliances, see: IG II² 21–2.

land.[38] It also seems apparent that he helped win over the island of Samothrace as well, greatly strengthening the Athenian position in the northern Aegean.[39] All of this was seemingly accomplished with little to no violence. Instead, the force of 40 warships represented a show of force to friend and foe alike, a visible and tangible sign of Athens' renewed power and reach in the region.

Success in Thasos and eastern Thrace helped consolidate the Athenian position in the north. It put them into closer contact with their allies in the Chalcidice and established a strong line of influence, from there to the Hellespont.[40] Thrasybulus capitalised on this success by sailing to Byzantium, where, with local support, he replaced the oligarchy with a democracy.[41] This was undertaken with no difficulty, seeing that the Athenians had 40 warships with them.[42] It seems as if the presence of Athenian ships and any troops on board was all that was required for the change in government, and there seems to be little to no indication that the Athenians needed to engage in serious combat operations. Xenophon merely says that Thrasybulus 'changed' the government from an oligarchy to a democracy.[43] Similarly, Demosthenes says that the local supporters, Archebios and Heracleides, handed over the city to Thrasybulus, implying no direct Athenian involvement.[44] Of great aid to the Athenian treasury, Thrasybulus reinstituted the 10% tax on vessels passing through from the Pontus. Thus, with a force of 40 warships operating in a diplomatic rather than a military manner, Thrasybulus was able to greatly strengthen Athens' strategic position in the northern Aegean and the Hellespont.

The fluid nature of how sea control worked was demonstrated in the years 389–388, where several instances of blockade and barrier operations show sea control being exercised by different naval forces in different places. Campaigning in Acarnania, the Spartan King Agesilaus was forced to march an extra 20 km to cross over to the Peloponnese at Rhion, rather than at Calydon, because of the Athenian ships stationed at Oeniadai.[45] Around the same time, Athenians landed a force of hoplites, supported by ten triremes, on Aegina to stop the raids on Attica that were being launched from there.[46] The Spartans drove off the Athenian squadron and left behind 12 of their own triremes to blockade the Athenians in

---

38 Dem. 20.59.
39 Xen. *Hell.* 5.1.7. Buckler (2003): 159; Asmonti (2015): 176.
40 Diod. 14.82.3. Buckler (2003): 160.
41 Xen. *Hell.* 4.8.27; Lys. 28.5; Dem. 20.60.
42 Buckler (2003): 160.
43 Xen. *Hell.* 4.8.27.
44 Dem. 20.60.
45 Xen. *Hell.* 4.6.14.
46 Xen. *Hell.* 5.1.2.

their fort, who were not relieved for four months. The Athenians were eventually able to evacuate their troops but continued to be harassed by the Spartan ships of Gorgopas.[47] It seems that the Athenians were able to maintain sea control at the entrance to the Corinthian Gulf at the same time as the Spartans were in control of the seas in the Saronic Gulf, although the Athenians were able to contest it long enough to evacuate their troops. Clearly, Athenian priorities lay elsewhere, for at the beginning of 388, they were able to muster 32 ships and blockade a force of 25 Spartan ships in Abydos in the Hellespont.[48] This is not to say that the Athenians considered operations around Aegina unimportant, but merely less important than in the Hellespont. Sea control in the Saronic Gulf continued to be contested with the Spartans delivering the next blow by defeating a contingent of Athenian ships in a night battle fought by moonlight. The Spartan Gorgopas deliberately set up a night battle, stalking and attacking the Athenian ships on their way from Aegina to the Piraeus. Of note is Xenophon's description of the Athenian ships sailing away with the squadron commander's ship 'carrying a light, as is customary', demonstrating that night sailing was clearly routine for the Athenians.[49] The final blow was dealt by the Athenians, successfully landing a force of troops on Aegina, which ambushed and defeated a large force of Aeginetans and their Spartan advisors.[50] After this, the Athenians regained control of the sea in the area, not just through victory but also because the Spartan sailors refused to row for Eteonicos.[51] This was not the end of the matter, however, and naval operations continued in the region soon after.

The Athenian need for Black Sea grain did not diminish in the fourth century and if anything, this need grew more acute after the loss of their empire and the wide access to the goods it had provided. This reliance on one sea route was a critical vulnerability and the Spartans continued to interfere with this strategically important sea lane. In 387, the Spartan Admiral, Antalcidas, sailed out with 12 ships and intercepted a force of eight Athenian ships on their way to reinforce the main Athenian fleet. Antalcidas successfully captured all the Athenian ships, apparently without loss.[52] Antalcidas, joined by 20 ships from Syracuse, now had 80 ships under his command and was able to establish sea control in Hellespont. He was based out of Abydos and this allowed him to prevent ships sailing down

---

47 Xen. *Hell.* 5.1.5.
48 Xen. *Hell.* 5.1.6–7.
49 Xen. *Hell.* 5.1.7–9.
50 Xen *Hell.* 5.1.10–12.
51 Xen *Hell.* 5.1.13.
52 Xen *Hell.* 5.1.26–7.

from the Pontus from reaching Athens.⁵³ The loss of eight precious warships was a blow to Athens, offering a virtually unassailable position for Antalcidas at Abydos, and Xenophon says the Athenians had flashbacks to the disaster of 405/404, and so they sought a peace treaty.⁵⁴ What followed was the King's Peace, so called because it was brokered and enforced by the Persian King Artaxerxes.⁵⁵ The promise of peace did not last, and it was perhaps the Persians who gained the most from the treaty.

The King's Peace of 386 marked the height of overall Spartan power in the Classical period, but that power would be tested soon after this peace was made. This dominance can be attributed to Sparta's combined power on land and sea, even taking into account their defeat at Cnidos a decade earlier. Cnidos had destroyed Sparta's hegemonic level of sea power, but in the absence of a rival power that could seriously threaten them, Sparta remained a capable force at sea. In short, no other power in Greece had the combined weight of sea and land power as Sparta held at that time. Athens, without tribute-paying allies and the attendant money it provided, was still trying to rebuild its fleet, and the other main power in Greece, Thebes, was isolated from the outside world and surrounded by hostile poleis.⁵⁶ Sparta's potent combination of land and sea power was one that, as Isocrates would later comment on, was extremely effective. Sparta used the peace to strengthen its strategic position in Greece, taking great interest in northwest and northeast Greece and Thrace.⁵⁷ The Spartans secured their position further afield from Laconia and the Spartan heartland, a strategy arising out of campaigns in the previous decades, and enabled by their maritime endeavours. Although sea power enabled this expansion, the continued erosion of this power in Sparta was evident in the years after the King's peace. This is not to say the Spartans abandoned the maritime realm, but they were faced with a resurgent Athens, strengthened by a renewed Aegean maritime league. Moreover, they no doubt faced the same problem as Athens, and the one Thebes would have soon enough: a lack of funding.

Xenophon describes the Spartans in 379 as being in a favourable position, having defeated the Thebans and other Boeotians, humbled the Argives, brought the Corinthians into the fold, having left Athens isolated with no allies, and with

---

53 Xen. *Hell.* 5.1.28.
54 Xen. *Hell.* 5.1.29; Buckler (2003): 169.
55 Xen. *Hell.* 5.1.30–6; for an analysis of the treaty, see: Buckler (2003): 169–80.
56 Buckler (2003): 187. It is less the lack of sea power than it is a lack of connections to the outside world, enabled by the maritime realm, which was a limiting factor.
57 For a summary of these events, see: Buckler (2003): 195–204.

Sparta's own rebellious allies suitably chastised.[58] Once again, allies are identified as the centre of gravity of the Athenian power. However, Xenophon hints that not all was as it seemed, for he says that the rule of Sparta only *seemed* good and secure. Three years later, Xenophon has the allies berating Sparta for their timidity, saying they could fit out more ships than Athens and thus starve them into submission through blockade.[59] As if this was not proof enough of Sparta's neglect of its navy, the sixty triremes they outfitted were twice defeated in battle by the Athenians.[60] Xenophon also describes in detail a naval operation under the Athenian Iphicrates, going into his training regime and sailing procedures, and praising him for his efforts.[61] In 373, having been defeated by the Corcyraeans and under threat by the imminent arrival of an Athenian fleet, a Spartan force under the Vice Admiral Hypermenes decided to retreat from the island.[62] He used his transport vessels to load the captured slaves and valuables and sent them home, following soon after with his marines and the surviving soldiers from the expedition.[63] The cracks in Spartan power were beginning to appear.

Indeed, Sparta's many and blatant transgressions of the King's Peace quietly spurred Athens and other disgruntled states into negotiations. In 384, the Athenians concluded an alliance with the powerful island polis of Chios, in full accordance with the peace treaty.[64] Things proceeded quickly from 379 onwards, as other poleis sought agreements with Athens, starting with Byzantion and then including Mytilene and Methymna on Lesbos, and then Rhodes. At first, these seemed to be bilateral treaties between Athens and the respective polis, but this gradually grew into a multilateral alliance between all the relevant parties. These poleis were seemingly not directly threatened by Sparta at the time, but it may point to continued ambition by some in Sparta to regain lost Aegean holdings.[65] If so, this would point to a dangerous split in Sparta's strategic direction, for as events soon proved, they could not deal with a resurgent Athenian navy, backed by a new naval alliance, nor was their vaunted army to prove much better in their fight against Thebes, with their loss at Leuctra in 371 destroying Sparta's land power.

---

58 Xen. *Hell.* 5.3.27.
59 Xen. *Hell.* 5.4.60.
60 Xen. *Hell.* 5.4.61, 65.
61 Xen. *Hell.* 6.2.27. A useful reminder that Xenophon was clearly interested in naval operations and felt qualified to comment on the training and procedures of a naval fleet in action.
62 The Spartan leader Mnasippos, having been killed in battle.
63 Xen. *Hell.* 6.2.25–26.
64 Buckler (2003): 205.
65 For a more thorough examination of the sources, several inscriptions, see: Buckler (2003): 218–19, n. 36; Rhodes (2012): 117.

Xenophon gives a more detailed account of the operations in 376 as things heated up between the old rivals. Disgruntled at Spartan timidity, their Peloponnesian allies pushed for more action against Athens, assessing that they could put more ships to sea than Athens and thereby starve them out.[66] The Spartans agreed and fitted out 60 triremes and positioned them near Aegina, Ceos, and Andros. This caused the Athenian grain ships to shelter at Geraistos in Euboea, and the Athenian navy was forced to sail out for escort duty. A subsequent battle saw the Athenians victorious and allowed them to convoy the grain into Athens.[67] Even the landlocked Thebes was forced to send for an importation of grain from Pagasai due to a food shortage. Sending two triremes, these were intercepted and captured by three triremes under the command of the Spartan Alcetas.[68] It is a small incident, but a hint that even the Thebans had given increasing thought to maritime concerns. The Second Athenian Alliance/Confederacy was far more egalitarian than the Delian League had been, with more allied representation in decision-making and far more equitable monetary contributions, which went towards alliance and operational matters rather than the aggrandisement of Athens.[69] This would not last, but for the twenty or so years after its formation, it would be a powerful maritime and naval alliance.

Sicily and Italy

By virtue of geography, Sicily was the scene of many maritime operations throughout the fifth and the fourth centuries, not just between the rival Sicilian and mainland Greek forces, but also with the Carthaginians. The major cities of the island lay near the coast and the island itself was readily accessible by sea from mainland Italy and Greece as well as North Africa. The major power on the island, Syracuse, was at times a strong sea power. In 439, Diodorus says that the city built 100 triremes as part of a program aimed at gaining control of all Sicily.[70] That these preparations involved not only the expansion of infantry and cavalry forces but also the building of a fleet, helps demonstrate that sea power was considered a necessary component for the conquest of Sicily. Many combat operations conducted at sea were in relation to power projection operations or troop movements around the island and across to mainland Italy.

---

66 Xen. *Hell.* 5.4.60.
67 Xen. *Hell.* 5.4.61.
68 Xen. *Hell.* 5.4.56.
69 Buckler (2003): 227–30.
70 Diod. 12.30.1.

Much of the conflict that Sicily endured was during the endemic war with Carthage at the end of the fifth and into the fourth century. Interestingly, Diodorus says that initial success in Sicily led the Carthaginians to think of conquering the entire island.[71] It is striking that the Carthaginians conceived of controlling the entire island. Often thought of as fanciful or even delusional by modern scholars, this idea was a perfectly valid one when Athens turned its eyes to Sicily in the 420s.[72] Perhaps, the idea that Sicily could be controlled as a single entity was considered rational by some of the ancient Mediterranean powers of the time, or rather, those with powerful maritime interests. With its difficult interior terrain, controlling the island favoured a maritime approach, and this was clearly factored into the strategic considerations of the Athenians, Carthaginians, and the Sicilian Greeks. The major cities were all located on the coast and this is one of the defining factors of the human geography of the island. Controlling Sicily did not necessitate controlling the interior so much as having access to the sea around the island, where the main population centres were located.

In 409, the Carthaginians moved on the city of Himera. Learning of their approach, the Syracusan politician, Diocles, decided to abandon the city.[73] As part of the evacuation, half of the populace of Himera embarked by night onto triremes and sailed the approximately 100 nautical miles to Messene before the triremes continued on to protect Syracuse.[74] Although not as large a scale as the evacuation of Attica before the Persian invasion, it was an impressive feat to evacuate half the city at night and over a distance of approximately 100 nautical miles. Considering the nasty fate of those left behind in Himera – killed or taken as slaves – the evacuation of even half the population was not a trivial accomplishment.[75] It was obviously important to Diocles and the Syracusans that they did not abandon the Himeraeans, and it was their warships that allowed for the safe evacuation of part of the city's population. Diodorus does not refer to any difficulty or special arrangements for the fleet to conduct the operation, as if evacuating non-combatants was not out of the ordinary.

In 406, the Carthaginians continued their campaign and attacked the city of Acragas. However, a reversal saw them besieged in their camp, cut off from foraging, and facing a supply shortage.[76] The Carthaginian general, Himilcar, somehow learned of an impending shipment of grain to Acragas and summoned forty

---

[71] Diod. 13.80.1.
[72] Thuc. 3.86.3–4, 6.15.2; Plut. *Alc.* 17.2–3.
[73] Diod. 13.61.1–3.
[74] Diod. 13.61.4–6.
[75] Diod. 13.62.3–4.
[76] Diod. 13.88.1–2.

triremes. According to Diodorus, the Syracusans had become complacent, thinking that the Carthaginians would be too cowardly to man their triremes, especially since it was winter. What followed was a Carthaginian victory, in which they sank eight ships and captured the grain. It was such a great victory that the Campanian contingent fighting for Acragas went over to the Carthaginians for the sum of 15 talents.[77] This stunning reversal led to the Carthaginians taking Acragas, an excellent example of a relatively small naval action having a decisive strategic effect.

Faced with the Carthaginian threat, the Sicilian poleis and especially Dionysius, the tyrant of Syracuse, recognised the importance of maritime forces in Sicily. This was not just the utility of naval forces, but a recognition that their primary adversary was always going to be in possession of a naval force that would require countering. The nature of Carthage's attack on Sicily was as an expeditionary operation conducted from Africa and so they would naturally require a fleet to support their operations. In 405, Dionysius launched a counterattack against the Carthaginians. The first part of the attack involved the landing of troops against the Carthaginian camp, drawing off their forces, and allowing the Greek forces to attack the camp by land, facing less resistance.[78] Later, in 396, Dionysius led another attack on the Carthaginian forces and once again, the fleet worked in close concert with the land forces. The Syracusan ships were too quick for the Carthaginians, who were caught in the process of manning their ships, and suffered great loss.[79] Dionysius was very comfortable launching joint attacks on his enemies, using both land and sea forces in close concert. This joint manoeuvring is quite complex and indicative of how sea power had become central to Syracuse's strategic thinking.

In 396, the Carthaginians, under Himilcon, laid siege to the city of Syracuse by land and sea. Impressive as the Carthaginian naval force was, the blockade by sea was imperfect and the tyrant Dionysius and his admiral Leptines took a contingent of warships out to escort some supply ships. Seeing a grain ship sailing close by, the Syracusans, who remained in the city, manned five warships and seized the vessel.[80] The Carthaginians saw this and sailed out with 40 warships, which prompted the Syracusans to man all their remaining ships, and in the ensuing battle, the Syracusans captured the enemy flagship and destroyed 24 other vessels. Further, the victorious Syracusans sailed to the Carthaginian anchorage and challenged them to battle, which was declined.[81] These operations show a

---

77 Diod. 13.88.3–5.
78 Diod. 13.109–10.
79 Diod. 14.72.1–6.
80 Diod. 14.64.1.
81 Diod. 14.64.2–4.

navy capable of seamless transition from trade-interdiction operations immediately into a battle with an enemy fleet. This victory was important in several respects. It allowed for an immediate inflow of food and ensured that the return of Dionysius and Leptines with the bulk of the food stores would be secure. It also allowed the Syracusans to thin out the Carthaginian fleet and deal a blow to their morale. Significantly, the victory was achieved without the city's ruler, a fact that did not escape the Syracusan population, and led to a debate over the merits of Dionysius' continued reign.[82] Although Dionysius continued in his rule, it is said to have caused him fear and led him to dissolve the assembly, once again demonstrating how a naval operation could have serious strategic ramifications, including in domestic politics.[83]

Dionysius was also comfortable launching amphibious operations further afield, attacking mainland Italy. In 393, he launched a surprise attack on Rhegium with 100 triremes, attacking but failing to take the city, and then plundering the surrounding countryside, before sailing back to Sicily. A second attack on mainland Italy in 384 proved more fruitful. With 60 ships, he attacked the territory of Tyrrhenia, specifically a rich temple in the port of Pyrgi. He landed there at night and attacked the next day, taking many prisoners and collecting a huge sum of 500 talents.[84] According to Diodorus, he put this money to use, hiring mercenaries and preparing for a renewed war with Carthage. The attack also acted as a strong demonstration to both the Etruscans and the Carthaginians. It demonstrated the reach of Dionysius and his ability to project power, deep into the Tyrrhenian Sea.[85] This was a highly successful attack by a large force against a hostile shore and shows how Dionysius was able to effectively wield maritime forces to achieve a wide variety of aims, including economic and diplomatic aims.

Maritime Athens in the fourth century

We are told a lot about fourth century naval, military, and political operations in the histories of Xenophon, Diodorus, and others, but less about general maritime operations. Thankfully, there are a host of extant speeches, especially from the

---

82 Diod. 14.65–70.1–2.
83 Diod. 14.70.3.
84 Diod. 15.14.3–4. According to Polyainos, Dionysios attacked with 100 ships and he made off with 500 talents, and his soldiers and sailors collected another 1000, which he managed to retrieve half of. Polyain. 5.2.21.
85 Caven (1990): 191–2.

Athenian law courts, which help shed light on the state of the maritime world in fourth-century Greece. The main drawback is the usual caveat that the sources are from Athens and thus present an Athens-centric point of view. Nevertheless, we do get glimpses of the wider world, for the issue of maritime trade was, by its very nature, international in scope. Many of these speeches are dated to the second half of the fourth century but will be examined here rather than the next chapter as they add valuable context and background to what was happening throughout the Greek world at this time.

The Spartans may have destroyed the Athenian Fleet in 405, but the Athenian maritime consciousness endured. One of the great Athenian speechwriters was Lysias, who was in fact a *metic* – a 'resident alien' of Athens. His support of the democracy during the tumultuous post-Peloponnesian War years greatly endeared him to the Athenian population. His most famous and important speech, oration 12 *Against Eratosthenes*, presents a very particular view of Athenian history, one in which Eratosthenes, a member of the Thirty Tyrants, had helped destroy the maritime power of Athens. This speech was delivered by Lysias himself, sometime not long after the overthrow of the Thirty, perhaps around 403. The wounds of oligarchic betrayal were fresh in the minds of the Athenians, especially the men of the Piraeus – naval men – who had so vehemently defended democracy.

This speech gives us one of the most unvarnished views of the divide between the navy-hating oligarchs and the democracy-loving 'naval mob' of Athens. It also demonstrates that such a deep maritime consciousness that existed in Athens was never going to be kept down long, despite the recent defeat in the Peloponnesian War. Lysias presents the well-worn accusation that as part of the oligarchy, the Thirty had a treasonous hand in actively opposing Athenian efforts in the naval battles of Arginousai and Aegospotami, a claim that can be found centuries later in Pausanias.[86] Lysias took it further, bringing up the issue of defendants claiming what good citizens they were, representing themselves as good soldiers or even serving as trierarchs, who had taken many enemy ships or conquered hostile cities.[87] These are indeed familiar tactics in an Athenian law court, but what Lysias does is to undercut any claim Eratosthenes might have to such good character by asking the jurors to ask Eratosthenes where he had killed as many enemies as he has Athenian citizens, or taken as many ships as he surren-

---

[86] Lys. 12.36. Paus. 4.17.3–4. The charge is mentioned in the context of explaining how the Spartans were the first to bribe an enemy in warfare, first in the Messenian War and later at Aegospotami, and how this disreputable act was eventually repaid when the Persians gave money to Sparta's enemies and kick-started the Corinthian War in the early fourth century.
[87] Lys. 12.38–39.

dered, or enslaved as many cities as taken.[88] He shifts into the third person, conflating Eratosthenes with all of the oligarchs who worked for the destruction of Athenian democracy: the ships 'they themselves surrendered' and the cities 'they enslaved'. Eratosthenes and the other oligarchs destroyed Attica's defences and stripped away the Piraeus. It is a collective guilt and collective characterisation, shifted here onto the shoulders of Eratosthenes.[89]

Lysias' second accusation carried a more sinister thread, for he says that the oligarchs did not destroy the Piraeus at the behest of the Spartans, but because it would make their own authority stronger.[90] Lysias returns to this later, claiming that just as Themistocles laid the groundwork for Athenian greatness and worked for the construction of the Piraeus Walls, Eratosthenes aided his fellow oligarch, Theramenes, in bringing them down.[91] This is followed by the direct accusation that Theramenes had the walls torn down and the democracy overthrown, not at the behest of the Spartans, but of his own command.[92] This illustrates the popular opinion in Athens that oligarchs were the enemy of the navy and Athenian maritime pursuits. This goes back to Thucydides and the walls of Athens, recalling 'a party in Athens who were secretly negotiating with them [Sparta] in the hope of putting an end to democratic government and preventing the building of the Long Walls'.[93] In this, we have not just the historian Thucydides linking democracy to the Long Walls and the sea power, but also Athenians themselves reinforcing this idea in the law courts almost 100 years later. It is clear from Lysias' attacks that the Athenians were in no doubt that erosion of their sea power – including by the enemy within, the oligarchs – had led to their downfall in the war. This line continued in a subsequent speech of Lysias against the son of the mercurial Alcibiades.

Lysias, in his speech against Alcibiades, the Younger (*Oration 14*), collates all these accusations into one narrative. He first says that Alcibiades, the elder, surrendered Athenian rule of the sea to the Spartans, which in turn gave the Spartans, command of the Athenians themselves.[94] This was accomplished when, in concert with Adeimantos (the general accused by the author Pausanias), he gave

---

[88] Lys. 12.39.
[89] As Thomas M. Murphy puts it, 'a generalised character whose guilt everyone acknowledges – rather should acknowledge, if loyal to radical democracy.'; and: 'They are assimilated in a memorable composite picture of the privileged class, which many Athenians are held to blame for the recent civil war.' Murphy (1989): 45.
[90] Lys 12.40.
[91] Lys. 12.63.
[92] Lys. 12.70.
[93] Thuc. 1.107.
[94] Lys. 14.34.

over to Lysander the Athenian ships at Aegospotami.[95] Here, Lysias goes on to hold Alcibiades responsible for the death of those at Aegospotami, the enslavement of Athenians, the destruction of the walls, and the rule of the 30 tyrants – all in one sentence.[96] Passing over the contentious and, quite frankly, the outrageous claim that this was all the fault of Alcibiades, the speech draws a direct line of causation from the loss at the naval battle of Aegospotami to the fall of the Athenian empire and the subsequent rise of the Thirty. This is not only a sound conclusion from our perspective, but clearly a perfectly acceptable conclusion to draw in front of an Athenian audience. It is a curious use of naval history in a case that was actually about domestic politics and yet is technically a case against Alcibiades, the Younger, for serving in the cavalry when he was not eligible.

These speeches highlight the use of history in the Athenian law courts. A narrative emerges whereby the Spartans were merely the instrument of Athens' defeat in the Peloponnesian War. The true architects of destruction were figures such as Alcibiades and the Athenian oligarchs like Theramenes and Eratosthenes – the enemy within. The law courts were a battleground for the consolidation of Athenian history, a place where they could reconcile the narrative of defeat, linked inextricably from the naval battle and defeat at Aegospotami to the subsequent loss of the city's walls and rise of the Thirty Tyrants. Thus, Athens' fate in the Peloponnesian War was clearly and unambiguously seen as dependent on sea power and the maritime realm. It is a narrative concerned, not merely with democrat versus oligarch, but with the nature of Athenian power itself. More than this, it shows that Athens would continue its maritime pursuits and remain a sea power to the bitter end.

The fourth-century politician Demosthenes had a definite interest in naval affairs from the beginning of his career. His very first speech to the *ekklesia*, in 354/3, (*Oration 14*) dealt with maritime issues, specifically, the naval boards responsible for the outfitting of triremes. In Oration 24, he prosecuted Timocrates with a *graphe paranomon* for proposing an illegal decree.[97] Timocrates' two associates had been joint trierarchs and had captured an enemy vessel, carrying cargo

---

[95] Lys. 14.38. For an examination on Adeimantos' role in the battle of Aegospotami and the aftermath, including discussion on Pausanias' accusation, see: Kapellos (2009): 257–75.
[96] Ly. 14.39.
[97] A graphe paranomon was an 'indictment for illegality' for proposing legislation that was flawed or contradicted other legislation. It could be done before a law had passed, in which case, deliberation of the law was suspended, while the graphe paranomon case proceeded, and it could also be brought to court within 12 months of the law being passed. It came to be used as a political weapon in the courts. See Carey (2012): 4–5 and p. 22, note 12.

worth 9½ talents. They kept the money despite a court ruling that most of it belonged to the state.[98] The seemingly innocuous law that Timocrates' proposed was to give state debtors a period of nine months in which to repay their debt.[99] Demosthenes launched a vicious attack against Timocrates and this law, and after laying down the legal reasons why Timocrates should be prosecuted for his proposed law, he goes into a moral argument, telling the jury how this law imperilled the state. The state's ability to collect revenue would be severely restricted if debtors had so long to repay money owed to the state.[100] This lost revenue would hurt Athens' ability to launch naval expeditions. Not only would this restrict their ability to defend themselves and to react quickly to emergencies; more importantly, it would preclude Athens from playing her true part in the world:

> Such successes [throughout Athenian history] could only have been organized by the aid of those decrees and laws under which you levy contributions on some citizens, and require others to furnish triremes; bid some to serve in the navy, and others to perform their other duties.[101]

> If our city enacts laws for her own hindrance, laws exactly contrary to her own interests, do you think she will ever be able to play her true part in the world?[102]

Demosthenes, in this speech, is explicitly referencing the core of Athenian power – its navy. Without money, Athens could not put a fleet to sea, and without an active fleet, they would be unable to defend themselves adequately. Further, they would not be able to project their power overseas in order to protect their interests. Timocrates' proposal would upset the laws that made Athens great: first and foremost, the possession of more triremes than any other Greek power. This was bolstered by their strength in infantry, cavalry, revenue, military positions, and harbours.[103] The measure of Athens' power was in triremes, which enabled the deployment of infantry and cavalry, supported by good strategic positions and harbours. Demos-

---

98 Dem. 24.11–14.
99 Dem. 24.39–40.
100 Ian Worthington seems correct in his judgement that the amount of money that would be lost to the state would be minor. After all, Demosthenes had, only a year earlier (speech 20 *Against Leptines*), argued for the reinstatement of *ateleia*, whereby those who had done great service to Athens were exempt from paying taxes and liturgies, except for the all-important trierarchy. As Worthington points out, Demosthenes says that the revenue lost from the reinstatement of *ateleia* would be of little consequence; yet, the money owed by Timokrates' friends was even less than that of a reintroduced *ateleia*. See: Worthington (2013): 78–83; 103–05. For more on *ateleia*, see: MacDowell (2004): 127–33.
101 Dem. 24.92.
102 Dem. 24.94.
103 Dem. 24.216.

thenes understands the components of what made Athens powerful, and he implores his audience to remember this and to prosecute a politician who, far beyond proposing an illegal law, was proposing one that imperilled the state itself. That Demosthenes was seemingly unsuccessful merely shows his arguments over how much revenue would be lost were probably, and rightly, considered exaggerated by the jury.[104] His speech demonstrates an understanding of the basis of Athenian power and the role sea power played in it, presented to a general audience of Athenian citizens.

There are other law court speeches that deal with the maritime realm, from specialised maritime trading cases through to homicide trials. Demosthenes' Speech 35, *Reply to Lakritos' Special Plea*, dated 351, offers great insight into some of the trade connections around the Aegean. We are told that the cargo ship that the defendants hired could carry 3,000 jars of wine and was fitted with 20 oars.[105] The defendants allegedly put these into a place called the 'thieves harbour' to evade customs duty in the Piraeus.[106] Finally, he highlighted the obvious lie in the defendant's story that they loaded Coan wine for the return journey, saying that everyone knows wine goes *to* the Pontus from the Aegean – Peparethos, Cos, Thasos, Mende, and others – but it does not come *from* the Pontus.[107] It is a useful detail in tracking goods around the region, and it also highlights in the context of a law court speech that the Athenian audience would be familiar with such details and know that the defendant's claims were suspect, based on the knowledge of international trade goods, and their origins and destinations. Even with the caveat that these types of cases appear to have been held in specialist courts with a more specialist jury, there is still a large amount of trade knowledge assumed on the part of the jury.

Speeches, other than about maritime trade, are useful in gleaning information about the maritime world. As mentioned in Chapter Two, Antiphon's *On the Murder of Herodes* gives us insight into travel by sea in the Aegean. In a short speech in 388, prosecuting Ergocles for his conduct on a campaign of revenue raising, Lysias calls the Athenian audience to punish Ergocles to send a signal to the Athenian allies that Athens will not tolerate them being treated poorly by overzealous tribute collection.[108] Clearly, this is, playing on recent history, Athe-

---

104 That he was unsuccessful seems apparent in the appearance of Timocrates and his son supporting the opponents of Demosthenes in a later case against him in 347 (Dem.21.139). Worthington (2013): 105.
105 Dem. 35.18.
106 Dem. 35.28.
107 Dem. 35.35.
108 Lys. 28.17.

nian treatment of the Delian League in the fifth century and once again, a speech of Lysias highlighted the inextricably maritime nature of Athens' geopolitical past and present. This is a but a brief survey of the variety of insights that can be gained in examining the law court speeches, often giving us a view of the maritime realm on a practical, every-day level.

Conclusion

The defeat of Athens in the Peloponnesian War was not a lasting victory for Sparta. It did not take long for Athens to restore its democracy and, by extension, rebuild its fleet and maritime aspirations. Now on the wrong side of Persia, Sparta faced a renewed Athens, funded by the Great King. The defeat at Cnidus in 394 signalled the death of Sparta's short-lived maritime empire. Nevertheless, this did not automatically equate to Athenian supremacy, and the first half of the fourth century was characterised by a series of maritime campaigns around Greece and the Aegean, sometimes in Athens' favour, sometimes Sparta's. Most importantly of all, the first decades of the fourth century signalled that the days of one overwhelmingly powerful, hegemonic sea power were over. Athens would rebuild its fleet, growing to a size larger than ever, yet without the maritime empire to fund the necessary land and sea components required for Aegean-wide hegemony. Moreover, the other poleis of Greece had learnt their lesson from the Delian League and were not inclined to outsource their defence to Athens. This meant they retained navies of their own, in strength enough to confront Athens, if any empire-like tendencies were to arise. The lack of a maritime hegemon, like in the fifth century, only shows that by the fourth, the embrace of sea power throughout the Greek world was strong.

Chapter Ten
Aegean awakening: Thebes, war in the North, and the rise of Macedon

If the first few decades of the fourth century are rarely viewed as of great consequence in the naval realm, the last few decades of the 'Classical period' down to the death of Alexander are barely given consideration at all when discussing naval matters. Conventionally, this period is viewed as the triumph of the professional Phalanx devised by the Thebans, perfected by Philip, and then wielded by Alexander to such dramatic effect. However, maritime matters encroached on most aspects of this period. After triumphing on the field of Leuctra, Thebes cast its eye towards the sea. Philip spent years devising ways to counter Athenian sea power, and Alexander treated insurrectionist Athens with more kindness than perhaps they deserved in order to retain the services of their still powerful navy for his Levantine campaign.

The 370s saw a resurgence in maritime operations around mainland Greece and especially off the coast of the Peloponnese. Though lacking their own sea power, the Thebans appear to have appreciated its utility and in 375 requested that the Athenians attack the Peloponnese by sea to keep Spartan forces tied up and prevented from attacking Thebes. The most important strategic outcome of the resulting Athenian power projection cruise was the freedom it allowed the Thebans to march against the surrounding hostile powers in Boeotia and subdue them, free from Spartan interference.[1] That the Spartans responded to the Athenian force of 60 ships with their own fleet of 55 demonstrates that the Spartans may have let maritime matters slip but were not altogether unprepared for war at sea. The subsequent loss at sea at the battle of Alyzeia led to Sparta's weakening and willingness for peace. This was not the sum of all Sparta's naval efforts, for Xenophon comments that constant raiding from Aegina had worn down the Athenians, contributing to their desire for peace with Sparta in 375, along with other considerations, not least of which was the Persian enforcement of the Peace.[2] The nature of this raiding is unclear, other than Xenophon's use of *leistai*, implying that it was raiding of the sort pirates would engage in rather than a concerted military campaign. Nevertheless, it appears to have been a drain on the Athenians and illustrates how much of a threat a hostile Aegina could prove to Athens and Athenian interests in the Saronic Gulf.

---

1 Xen. *Hell.* 5.4.62–3.
2 Xen. *Hell.* 6.2.1.

The peace that followed was extremely short-lived and saw a renewed set of maritime campaigns in the Adriatic region. The Spartans looked to the ever-important island of Corcyra and assembled a fleet of 60 ships from several allied cities under the command of a Spartan Admiral. Aside from Sparta, ships were contributed by Corinth, Leucas, Ambracia, Elis, Zakynthos, Achaia, Epidaurus, Troezen, Hermione, and Halieis.[3] This was a neat demonstration of the wide range of cities that maintained warships and that could contribute to a maritime campaign. The fleet was dispatched with vague orders to protect Spartan interests in the region, especially interests on Corcyra. They attacked the island, 'pillaging' the countryside and besieging the city as well as blockading the port.[4] As Xenophon says, the Corcyraeans could do nothing since the Spartan fleet was superior at sea, forcing them to send for help. The Corcyraean plea for help was based on the strategic importance of their island, positioned so that forces based there could not only control the coastal sailing route from Sicily to the Peloponnese but also could attack the Corinthian Gulf and Laconia.[5] Having decided to send aid, this is exactly what the Athenians did once the Spartans had fled before them. They subdued nearby Cephallenia, consolidated their position on Corcyra, successfully intercepted a relief force of Syracusan ships sent to aid the Spartans, and prepared to launch attacks against the lands of the Spartans and their allies.[6] The Spartans had launched an initially successful operation against Corcyra but failed to exploit this success before the Athenian relief force arrived. This once again proved that Athens had regained its ability to conduct maritime power projection operations and to greater effect than the Spartans could manage.[7] Spartan land power was largely destroyed on the field of Leuctra in 371 and the Spartans rapidly lost interest in the maritime realm after this as they focused on a more hostile environment within the land environs of the Peloponnese.

---

3 Xen. *Hell.* 6.2.3.
4 Xen. *Hell.* 6.2.3–8.
5 Xen. *Hell.* 6.2.9.
6 Xen. *Hell.* 6.2.33–8.
7 However, as Buckler points out the Athenian effort reveals that there was great strain on their financial situation and demonstrated that the second Athenian-led League was not nearly as financially stable as the Delian League before it. Indeed, as Buckler says, this financial impediment to maritime operations would plague the Athenians for the rest of the century. Buckler (2003): 266.

Epaminondas and the Theban navy

One of the most puzzling incidents of the fourth century is the short-lived Theban navy. Thebes was never a great or even a moderate sea power and had seemingly little interest in maritime pursuits in the preceding centuries before Epaminondas came to the forefront of Theban affairs. Mirroring the rise of Spartan sea power in the second half of the Peloponnesian War, the rise of the Theban navy was funded by Persia in response to the threat of Athenian sea power in the Aegean. Having defeated Sparta in 371, Thebes required a navy since long-time enemies Athens and Sparta decided an alliance would be prudent in the face of a suddenly powerful Thebes. So long as Athens maintained sea control around the Peloponnese they could prevent Thebes from cutting off Sparta from outside aid. Seeing that the common peace of 366 was not ratified, the only way to take Athenian sea power out of the equation was by force.[8]

There were other spurs to Theban desire for a navy. In 368/7 when the Thebans marched into Thessaly to attack Alexander of Pherai, Alexander sent to Athens for aid, which duly sent 30 ships and 1,000 men to assist.[9] This in itself should be seen as an Athenian maritime diplomatic operation: dispatching a force of ships to aid an ally and signalling to Thebes that Athens was willing and capable of sending a relief force. The Thebans, without a navy, could do nothing to prevent this aid from being sent by sea. Neutralising the Athenian navy thus became a goal for the Thebans. At first, they tried to do this diplomatically. Sent as an envoy to the King of Persia, Pelopidas asked the King that part of a peace deal required the Athenians to 'beach their ships'.[10] It was clearly aimed at putting a halt on Athens' sea power, just as their request for Messene to be recognised as independent was aimed at neutralising Spartan land power.[11] In providing funding to Thebes for the construction of a fleet, the Persians were hoping to maintain a balance of power in Greece.[12] The threat of Spartan land power and Athenian sea power, combined with Athens' continued campaigning around Amphipolis and the Chersonese (see below) spurred the Thebans into the unknown territory of building a navy.

Not long after the Alexander incident, at the urging of Epaminondas, the Thebans instituted a ship-building program of 100 triremes. This represented a large force, and one clearly envisaged as needed to fight pitched battles against other na-

---

8 Buckler (1980): 160–1.
9 Diod. 15.71.3.
10 Xen. *Hell.* 7.1.36.
11 Heskel (1997): 127.
12 Heskel (1997): 128; Buckler (2003): 330–1.

vies.¹³ Further than the possession of a fleet for combat utility, both Diodorus and Isocrates speak of Epaminondas' desire to rule the sea.¹⁴ Later authors had a different view of Epaminondas' naval exploits. Perhaps with the comfort of hindsight, knowing that the Theban fleet appeared to have been no more than a Potemkin one, Pausanias writes that Epaminondas was frightened of the sea because of a Delphic oracle, and Plutarch says that Epaminondas feared that the Thebans would go from being steadfast hoplites to degenerate mariners.¹⁵ Boeotia is a region that is not normally associated with the sea and maritime affairs, yet we get glimpses of the sea in some stories about the region. The Boeotian town of Siphai (called Tipha by Pausanias) lying on the coast of the Corinthian gulf apparently had a strong maritime tradition. The helmsman of the *Argo*, Tiphys, is said to have come from this town.¹⁶ Additionally, Pausanias says that Siphai/Tipha claimed to have the best sailors in all of Boeotia.¹⁷ This is an interesting claim to make of a region not usually associated with maritime activities, and it is perhaps indicative of a richer maritime tradition than has been assumed. Alternatively, perhaps all that Pausanias encountered was nostalgia and some local pride of a distant past, albeit derived from a mythic story with a long life.

The rationale behind Epaminondas' naval expansion puzzles modern scholars as much as it seems to have confused the ancient authors. More can be said of what this short-lived naval force did than what it was ultimately intended for. In essence, the Theban navy appears to have acted mostly as a 'fleet-in-being'. It was a force intended to threaten Athenian sea power and potentially unite Athenian enemies against the Second Confederacy, but with seemingly little ability to conduct combat operations. This is not to say that Thebes built a fleet for prestige, or because that is just what great powers did as a matter of course – though this rationale should not be entirely ruled out – but that the Thebans hoped that possession of many warships itself was enough to make a 'navy' and thus give it a measure of sea power. As they quickly discovered however, the possession of warships does not make for sea power. Epaminondas would have been well-served by the advice of Pericles at the beginning of the Peloponnesian War when he spoke of sea power as being no easy thing to gain nor to keep.

Diodorus says that the Thebans not only voted to construct 100 triremes and attendant infrastructure but also to urge the people of Rhodes, Chios, and Byzan-

---

13 Diod. 15.78.4–79.3; Isoc. 5.53.
14 Isoc. 5.53; Diod. 15.78.4.
15 Paus. 8.11.10; Plut. *Philop.* 14.2.
16 Ap. Rhod. *Argon.* 105–6.
17 Paus. 9.32.4.

tium to assist them.[18] Curiously, Diodorus then says that Epaminondas led the fleet out to these cities and the Athenian *strategos* Laches was forced away and thus these cities went over to Thebes.[19] Strategically speaking, it is clear that Epaminondas' intention for the fleet was as a diplomatic tool.[20] The fact that the important League members of Rhodes, Chios, and Byzantium are mentioned, especially the important site of Byzantium, indicates a move to separate allies from Athens. Not just this, but these were allies whose maritime resources and sea power could aid Thebes in its rivalry with Athens, both in possessing established navies and also in the potential aid they could give the Theban navy if Thebes was indeed serious in becoming a sea power.[21] It was a very similar approach to that of Sparta at the end of the Peloponnesian War, which had proved decisively successful.

Epaminondas took the fleet to sea, sailing out of Aulis into the Aegean. The Athenians were ready, and Laches was sent to intercept the Thebans. However, as it turned out the Theban fleet was apparently powerful enough to deter Laches, who did not engage the Thebans.[22] It would appear that the Theban fleet was in some way, either numerically or materially, superior to the Athenian force, enough so that Laches felt disinclined to engage. Likewise, Epaminondas clearly felt uneasy about pushing the issue and engaging the Athenians in any sort of combat. As the architect of Thebes' new-found maritime strategy, Epaminondas led the fleet and thus it is unlikely that the fleet failed to understand the strategic intent of its deployment. Either the Athenian fleet was too large for Epaminondas to feel confident of victory, or he intended his fleet as a primarily diplomatic force. Even if it was intended as a diplomatic force with the aim of being strong enough to elicit defections from the Athenian League, the failure to engage the Athenians at any point in the cruise demonstrated that it was not in fact a credible naval force. This has been likened to the German High Seas Fleet of the First World War not wishing to risk an engagement with the Royal Navy for anything other than the chance of a clear victory, and that this was a missed opportunity for Thebes.[23] It is hard to disagree with this assessment. By refusing to engage in combat operations the Theban fleet proved to the Greek and Persian worlds that it was a hollow force, incapable of even minor military action. Iso-

---

18 Diod. 15.79.1.
19 Diod. 15.79.1.
20 Buckler (1980): 162.
21 The early stages of Thebes' maritime transformation clearly show the force intended to play a diplomatic role, but it is unclear how serious Thebes was about becoming a sea power. Buckler seems to think this was Thebes' goal. Buckler (1980): 162.
22 Diod. 15.79.1.
23 Buckler (2003): 362.

crates claims that by sending ships to Byzantium the Thebans were aiming at rule over land and sea.[24] In the case that Epaminondas' goal was to challenge Athenian sea power, avoiding battle with Laches was a poor start. The Athenian fleet remained in play as a dangerous force that could still block or reverse any gains made by the Thebans overseas. With this in mind, it seems likely that the Theban fleet was intended as a fleet-in-being, a force large enough to entice Athens' allies into defecting and thus bolstering opposition to Athenian sea control.

The efforts of Epaminondas and the naval campaign he led accomplished very little and should be considered a failure. Central to the failure of Epaminondas and the Theban fleet's diplomatic efforts is the fact that Theban sea power was unproven. The Theban fleet had conducted no military operations and so its fighting quality was unknown. There was little reason for the Chians, Rhodians, or any other power to throw their lot in with Thebes when the latter's navy was still unproven in battle.[25] The Athenians had been engaged in long maritime campaigns in the Chalcidice and the Chersonese, and certainly allies would have seen no weakness in Athenian sea power.[26] Combined with the unproven nature of the Theban fleet, the strategic calculation of the allies was sound in declining to join Thebes against Athens. This returns us to the hierarchy of maritime operations and the fact that it is the ability to conduct combat operations – both at and from the sea – which establishes a navy's ability to act as a useful diplomatic tool. It was thus a deficiency in means that caused the Theban failure at sea.

Finally, it is worth noting that we have little evidence for a Theban maritime consciousness in the classical period. By all accounts, the Thebans were rigidly continentalist in their outlook and in their strategy. By comparison, even the Spartans at the outbreak of the Peloponnesian War appear to have had a greater appreciation of sea power than the Thebans at any stage of the fifth and fourth centuries. This matters not just in resourcing and manning a fleet of warships but crucially in how to employ these ships. After all, the Persians were willing to throw vast sums of money at anyone who needed to build ships. The Spartans at least catered for naval thinking with the existence of an 'Admiral' position. The Thebans appear to have had no such office or title and no pedigree of putting fleets to sea in any number. Perhaps the other Greeks also saw this and so expected little out of the Theban navy, an impression reinforced when it failed to do anything other than sail around the Aegean, dodging any kind of serious com-

---

24 Isoc. 5.53.
25 Buckler circles around this conclusion, saying that Epaminondas needed to engage in more military action to prove the fleet in military operations and thus draw in the wavering League members. Buckler (1980): 173–4; (2003): 365.
26 Heskel (1997): 136.

bat; more prudent to just wait them out. The attempted power projection cruise was not a small action considering the various places they visited and the size of the force, but neither was it an operation of great consequence. Once it was over, no one feared or respected Theban triremes, something that could not be said of Athenian warships.

Athens, the Second Athenian League, and northern Greece

The fall of Spartan sea power coincided with the rejuvenation of Athenian sea power as the Athenians decided the time was right to rebuild their naval presence in the Aegean, especially after the reconstruction of the Long Walls. Athens could once again rely on a strategy of walls, overseas alliances, and a fleet. The strategic situation in Greece favoured such an approach, since Spartan sea power had eroded into non-existence and the dominant Greek power, Thebes, notwithstanding its short-lived flirtation with a navy, was a land power. The Theban General Epaminondas quickly realised his hopes of intercepting the Athenians marching to Mantineia in 362 would not materialise as the Athenians simply decided to go by sea to the Peloponnese and march from the coast to Mantineia, thus evading Theban interference.[27] Athenian participation in the battle of Mantineia was not trivial, and it was thanks to the mobility provided by the sea that Athens could join their allies unhindered. Athenian ambitions in the north, especially concerning the cities of Olynthos and Amphipolis, required a renewed campaign of maritime power projection operations.

In the decade between 371 and 360 Athens was embroiled in campaigns in the northern Aegean as it tried to re-establish its power and influence over the region, especially the city of Amphipolis. As we saw in the previous chapter, throughout the early-mid 370s the Athenians had established a new naval alliance in the Aegean under their leadership. Julia Heskel sees Athens engaged in two different wars in the northern Aegean, one for Amphipolis and one for the Chersonese, and while it was perhaps not so neat a distinction in the eyes of the Athenians, in practice this is a fair appraisal.[28] The Athenians never seem to have gotten over their loss of Amphipolis to the Spartans in the Peloponnesian War and in the years after constantly sought legitimacy for their claim over the city. Amphipolis was an im-

---

[27] Xen. *Hell.* 7.5.6–7. However, the Athenian cavalry did go via the isthmus of Corinth, though obviously after the Theban army had moved on: Xen. *Hell.* 7.5.15. Buckler (1980: 208) says that Epaminondas was deceived by a false report of the Athenians going by sea, but it seems as if the Athenian army did go by sea and only the cavalry went by land.
[28] Heskel (1997): 15.

portant city, possession of which would strengthen Athenian power in the northern Aegean. Firstly, it was rich in natural resources, especially silver and gold, and was also a source of timber, critical for shipbuilding. Secondly, it was in a strategically significant position that would provide the Athenians with a solid base of operations for its maritime forces across the northern Aegean, from Thrace to the Hellespont, a region quickly becoming an important centre of Greek affairs. A permanent presence in Amphipolis would also give the Athenians a strong position to threaten Thebes from both north and south.

The Athenians launched their campaign in 369, sending the *strategos* Iphicrates and a small force of ships.[29] The protracted operations in the area were centred around the siege of the city and fighting with the Chalcidian forces on land. Eventually, Iphicrates was removed from command and replaced by Timotheus, and the new general quickly realised that in order to be successful in taking Amphipolis he first needed to take away its primary base of support: Olynthos.[30] Timotheus' campaign saw the Athenians taking the coastal cities of Pydna and Potidaea, which along with Torone gave Athens control of the seaboard and isolated Olynthos.[31] Seeing that his operations were having the desired effect of drawing the Olynthians away from Amphipolis, Timotheus sent Alcimachus to the city with a small force. However, Alcimachus became engaged with a force of Thracians and accomplished little. Of note is that Alcimachus was sent by land, not by sea, and this almost certainly, as has been noted, caused his force to become bogged down through lack of supplies or other issues, perhaps a matter of negotiating passage through another polis' territory.[32] This incident helps demonstrate how stretched Athenian maritime forces must have been that Alcimachus was sent by land, especially considering that there seems to have been no significant naval threat posed by Athenian opponents and so the sea routes were open. Despite this setback the Athenians continued to push for Amphipolis and sent Callisthenes with another expeditionary force.[33] However, it seems as if the Athenians could not muster a force strong enough to successfully take the city, and the constantly changing alliances of different powers such as Macedonia made the conditions for Athenian success unfavourable.[34] In the end it was a deficiency in land forces that

---

29 Aisch. 2.27.
30 Heskel (1997): 46–7.
31 Diod. 15.81.6; Dem. 4.4; Isoc. 15.108, 112–13; Buckler (2003): 370.
32 The identity of these Thracians is contested, with Heskel assessing them to have probably been Edonians in the vicinity of Amphipolis. Heskel (1997): 48.
33 Heskel (1997): 49.
34 For an examination of the timeline and the various changes in allegiances, see: Heskel (1997): 19–52.

hindered the Athenian siege efforts. Sea power provided the Athenians with the ability to conduct a campaign in the north Aegean around Amphipolis, a notable feat in itself and one where they were seemingly in absolute control of the local seas, but they simply did not have the land forces necessary to carry out a successful campaign against Amphipolis and its supporting poleis. The campaign amply demonstrates the limits of Athenian land and sea power at this point in time.

While the Athenians were conducting their campaign to take Amphipolis, they were also conducting a campaign in the Chersonese. This campaign was far more complex, intertwined as it was with the Persian satraps' revolt, and it is poorly documented.[35] The campaign began with the Persian satrap of Phrygia, Ariobarzanes, sending a messenger, Philiscus of Abydos, to Athens to tell them that the Persians would recognise Athens' right to the Chersonese along with a large sum of money.[36] Money was of course key, for such a campaign would require a maritime expeditionary force. The first major operation was an attack on the island of Samos. In 366 under the command of Timotheus the Athenians sent 30 triremes and 7,000–8,000 troops, with strict instructions to avoid breaking the King's Peace.[37] It was a complicated situation, with the Athenians wanting to help Ariobarzanes, who had given them money for their fleet with the expectation of aid, but not wanting to invoke the ire of the Persian King, who it appears was about to engage in a war with the renegade satrap Ariobarzanes.[38] The siege was successful after 10 months, and the Athenians dubiously installed a cleruchy.[39] This was a big gain for Athens, helping to establish themselves on a strategically important island in the eastern Aegean. After this, Timotheus was bogged down in the continued attempt to take Amphipolis, as well as operations against Philiscus in Cyzicus and other places in the Hellespont, especially Proconnesus.[40]

This series of events represented a direct threat to the Athenian grain supply, with ships being forced into Byzantium, Chalcidice, and Cyzicus and causing the assembly to send out ships 'to provide aid to everywhere'.[41] Especially as their grain supply became threatened, the Athenians were forced into campaigns across the Chersonese and into the Hellespont. Athenian ambitions appear to have been

---

35 Much of what is known comes from speeches, especially Demosthenes. For an examination of the chronology, see Heskel (1997): 53–122.
36 Heskel (1997): 125. The Athenians reacted in typical fashion by giving both the envoy Philiscus and the satrap Ariobarzanes, whom he represented, Athenian citizenship. Dem. 23.141.
37 Isoc. 15.111, who says he had 8,000 troops. Polyainos says 7,000: Polyain. 3.10.9.
38 For a discussion, see Heskel (1997): 132–5.
39 Isoc. 15.111; Dem. 15.9; Diod. 18.18.9. It was a dubious move as it could most certainly be seen as breaking the King's Peace term of autonomy for the island. See Heskel (1997): 136.
40 Heskel (1997) 140, 144–5.
41 βοηθεῖν ἑκασταχοῖ: [Dem] 50.6.

too great, and they continued to suffer setbacks, taking and then losing Sestos and all the while funnelling resources into the fruitless siege of Amphipolis.[42] Having rebuilt their sea power, the Athenians were able to conduct a multitude of different and often simultaneous campaigns from the Chalcidice to Thrace and into the Hellespont. However, they did not have sufficient land forces to hold onto their gains nor to take cities quickly enough or consolidate them with sufficient strength to hold onto anything for a length of time. They were simply overstretched and facing too many disparate adversaries in a very fluid geostrategic environment. Their sea power was never as dominant as it had been during the fifth century, and importantly they do not seem to have ever had land forces near enough to successfully conduct all the maritime operations they were engaged in. Their sea power provided them with still unsurpassed local mobility, but they never had enough troops to match their ambitions. This highlights the personnel pressures of maintaining a large expeditionary force of naval and land forces. The Athenians simply did not have the personnel to crew their fleet and conduct military operations ashore, especially time-consuming and labour-intensive sieges.

As a counterpoint to Athenian maritime operations, one of Athens' enemies, Alexander of Pherai, would prove more adept at launching amphibious operations than Athens could counter. In 362/1 Alexander sent a force of ships to attack the island of Tenos, deep in the Cyclades, and the island of Peparethos in the northern Aegean. His forces successfully enslaved many of the people of Tenos and then surprised an Athenian force, capturing six triremes – of which five were Athenian – as well as 600 men.[43] This was followed by an extremely curious and perhaps farfetched episode, in which apparently Alexander's ships sailed into the Piraeus unopposed and robbed the merchants along the waterfront before sailing off again.[44] If true, this last incident is an extraordinarily bold example of an amphibious raid, designed for the effect it would have on morale more than any material gain. In all the above examples Athens' response was desultory or non-existent, demonstrating how stretched their maritime resources had become and perhaps indicative of the strategic lethargy that a young Demosthenes would soon bemoan in the Assembly.

Finally, there is the Social War, where a coalition of poleis was able to keep Athenian sea power in check for several years. Unfortunately, it is a poorly documented war, especially considering how large a conflict it appeared to have been

---

[42] For a summary of all the different operations, see Heskel (1997) 140–53.
[43] Diod. 15.95.1–3; [Dem]. 50.4–5; Polyain. 6.2.1. Buckler (2003): 371–2.
[44] Polyain. 6.2.2. The incident is not mentioned anywhere else. Polyainos says that the Athenians mistook the ships for friendly ones, which is plausible if Athenian or other friendly ships were expected.

and how important the consequences were. Chios, Rhodes, Cos, and Byzantium conducted a series of maritime operations against the Athenians and successfully attacked Lemnos, Imbros, Samos, and a host of other Athenian-aligned islands.[45] According to Diodorus, both sides of the conflict wished to decide the war with a naval battle.[46] However, having gathered their forces in the Hellespont, battle was averted owing to poor weather conditions, which saw the Athenian *strategoi* break down into petty infighting.[47] The war ended with the breakaway poleis gaining their independence from Athens,[48] demonstrating that Athenian power could be resisted by a coalition of poleis in possession of their own sea power.

Athens and conflict with Philip

The Macedonian King Philip II was the most dangerous enemy Athens had faced in several decades. Few in Athens had any plan to deal with the rise of Macedonia, but some tried. Demosthenes delivered his *First Philipic* around the summer of 351, an attempt to spur the Athenians into action with a clear strategy of how to deal with Philip. It is important to highlight the context of the work. It was a speech given to the Athenian assembly, not a letter, pamphlet, or work of fiction. It was given in front of the public, in a political venue, as an actual proposal to be voted on. His strategy must have been comprehensible to the audience; the audience comprised of the general Athenian voting public. It is important to highlight this, for it shows how many ordinary citizens, not just politicians and military leaders, considered and were exposed to concepts of maritime strategy, and indeed made decisions regarding such matters. Demosthenes begins the speech by giving a summary of the geopolitical situation in northern Greece. Cities that Athens once controlled or were influential in, namely, Pydna, Poteidaia and Methone, as well as surrounding territories had fallen to Philip. Philip had won these through a combination of warfare, alliances, and friendship.[49] This was in part because they were willing to give their alliance to someone prepared and willing to do that which was necessary – in this case Philip and not the lax Athenians. This laxness is at the centre of Athenian problems, and he makes a point of

---

45 Diod. 16.21.1–2.
46 Diod. 16.21.1.
47 Diod. 16.21.3–4.
48 Dem. 15.26; Isoc. 8.16.
49 Dem. 4.6.

saying that those whom Philip has defeated had no recourse because of this Athenian dithering.[50]

Demosthenes then goes into the crux of his speech, a proposal for how Athens could act to counter Philip's advances. He proposes outfitting a force of 50 triremes, as well as transports and other vessels sufficient to carry half the force of Athenian cavalry.[51] Further, the Athenians themselves must be prepared to man these ships. He says this force is necessary to prevent Philip from striking out against Athenian interests, but especially Thermopylae, the Chersonese, or Olynthos. In this, the force is supposed to act as a deterrent, and he says that it would present in Philip's mind the consideration that the Athenians have shaken off their negligence and were willing to act, and thus he might stay his hand out of fear.[52] This is, as he says, possible because there were many people in Athens who regularly reported everything back to Philip. However, if Philip does act in spite of these Athenian preparations, he will be caught off guard because it will be a force strong enough to cause him harm. Demosthenes is very clearly outlining a deterrent force and understands the two key components of deterrence: the will to act and the ability to carry through with the threat. A force of 50 triremes and half of all Athenian cavalry certainly indicates a capable force. That the Athenians themselves, not mercenaries, should be prepared to go on campaign would demonstrate their will to carry through with this threat. One of the key attributes of this plan is the readiness level of the force that is higher than normal. Some scholars have criticised this plan as ineffective because it was not stationed in the north where it could react more quickly,[53] but Demosthenes makes the point that when previous expeditions had been ordered, everything was done from scratch – trierarchs had to be appointed, triremes outfitted, and troops mustered – taking considerable time and delaying Athenian action until it was too late. Demosthenes' plan would ensure that most of the preparations were completed ahead of time, greatly reducing the notice-for-sea of the force.

Importantly, there would also be a forward-deployed element as part of the strategy. Demosthenes proposes that the Athenians forward-deploy in northern waters a small contingent of troops and ships. It would consist of 2,000 infantry, with 500 of them being Athenians, and 200 cavalry, 50 of them being Athenians. They will serve for as long as necessary and would serve in a regular rotation. They would be provided with sufficient transport ships, and for protection, 10 triremes. These are necessary, for he says that Philip does possess a navy, requiring

---

50 Dem. 4.8.
51 Dem. 4.16.
52 Dem. 4.17–18.
53 Ellis and Milns (1970): 20.

Athenian escort warships.[54] This force was designed to carry out harassing attacks against Philip, not to face him in direct battle. Demosthenes uses a word most commonly used to refer to the activities of pirates and brigands.[55] This word describes a general type of activity and should not be taken as synonymous with piracy or brigandage. This would be a state-armed force conducting war against a power with which Demosthenes at least thinks Athens is at war. Indeed Demosthenes emphasises the point that citizens must be part of the force, especially as commanders.

Having addressed the force composition, Demosthenes then dives into the practicalities. First is logistics and he gives a brief rundown on how much this force will cost: 92 talents a month. He breaks down the costs between the triremes, the infantry, and the cavalry – 40, 40, and 12 talents, respectively.[56] Shortly after, comes a memorandum of ways and means – this proposal has had all the logistics calculated and all the accounting done in advance.[57] Interestingly, this is about half the pay such a force would normally receive, enough for rations and little else. Demosthenes expects that the force will make up for this by raiding Philip's territory. He is proposing a force that would, in order to survive, be inherently aggressive. Within the memorandum of ways and means, he gets into the second practicality – geography. Philip has very effectively taken advantage of weather to forestall the Athenians, attacking when the Etesian winds (the northerly winds) blow strongly, or during winter when weather was considerably worse for sailing thus delaying or slowing the transit of vessels.[58] Philip attacks when weather makes the dispatch of a force from Athens unlikely to arrive at a point where it could have an impact. For this reason, Demosthenes has proposed a force to be forward-based in the north, and he says that the Athenians have winter bases there ready to support his force – on Lemnos, Thasos, Sciathos, and the neighbouring islands, where harbours, provisions, and all that was required for operations could be found.[59] From these forward bases they could stand off the coast as needed and harass Philip and his allies. Aside from being friendly to Athens, these islands are in strategically significant positions that would allow the force to react speedily to situations across the northern area. Skiathos is 50 nautical miles from the Chalcidice; Thasos is just off the coast of Thrace; and Lemnos is a mere 45 nautical miles from the Hellespont. Demosthenes' grasp of geog-

---

54 Dem. 4.20–2.
55 Dem. 4.23.
56 Dem. 4.28.
57 Dem. 4.30–7.
58 Dem. 4.31.
59 Dem. 4.32.

raphy is solid, and it is also worth highlighting that this passage reveals just how well Philip also understood geography and weather and used them to his strategic advantage. Indeed, it is arguable that even if Philip himself did not possess a strong navy, he nevertheless had a solid grasp of maritime and naval considerations and was thus able to formulate an effective counter strategy to that of Athens.

Having said that the forward-deployed force would be engaged in raiding, Demosthenes becomes more specific about their proposed role. He mentions that Philip's forces have themselves been raiding the Athenian allies and that this forms the principal source of his revenue. More than this, he has caused direct damage to the Athenians, attacking Lemnos and Imbros, and at one point seizing a sacred Athenian trireme from Marathon.[60] Aside from raids on Philip, the forward-deployed force would have a vital defensive role, not only protecting direct Athenian interest but also depriving Philip of revenue. This gets to the heart of the matter as Demosthenes sees it, and has already hinted at: Athenian strategy, if it can be called that, had been totally reactive to that point in time. The Athenians had always left it too late to act, going so far as to tell the assembly that the Athenians take their orders from Philip.[61] Demosthenes has astutely identified Philip's strategy, correctly assessed the problems with current Athenians strategy – or lack thereof – and proposed a workable and well-reasoned counter strategy of his own.

In this speech we see a clear elucidation of a maritime strategy by Demosthenes. He has clearly and accurately identified the strategic situation in which the Athenian objective would be to halt Philip's advances and check his growing power. Demosthenes proposes the means by which the Athenians can achieve this objective. They must ready a large force – 50 triremes and half of all Athenian cavalry – to act either as a deterrent force or, in the worst case, as an amphibious readiness group that could react far more quickly than in previous instances when a fleet had to be outfitted from scratch. They must also send a smaller force to be forward deployed from the islands in the north. From there they could raid Philip's territory, protect trade and thereby reduce Philip's income, and directly protect Athenian interests in the region. This protection is not only direct but also indirect. He has already said that cities have fallen to Philip, in many cases, because of Athenian absence. The presence of an Athenian force, small but active, could potentially have a political effect in the region. This would prove a counter to Philip's strategy, which has involved only striking when Athenian sea power, based entirely out of

---

60 Dem. 4.34.
61 Dem. 4.41.

Athens, would always arrive too late to help. He is very clear about the resources available for this strategy and already has a well-conceived plan concerning funding and logistics. This is a clear example of maritime strategy in play: a direct relationship between means, ways, and ends, factoring in the opposition's strategy to that point. Both of the forces Demosthenes describes include warships and transport vessels – the naval component – as well as infantry and cavalry – the land component. They would work in conjunction with one another, and although there is scope for the naval component to conduct independent operations – intercepting enemy trade or engaging enemy warships – the majority of the operations envisaged would be joint, involving both naval and land components. The scope of projected operations included combat operations at sea, combat operations from the sea, and diplomatic operations, on the benign and coercive end of the scale. This is a fully prepared and conceived maritime strategy.

The Athenians, however, did not approve Demosthenes' proposal. Demosthenes was still young and early in his career and the Athenians' indifference to this plan seems to have fitted exactly with what Demosthenes admonished them for in his speech: dithering inaction. That Demosthenes' maritime strategy was not enacted is not a sign that the Athenians did not understand it or had lost their sense of maritime consciousness but that on a political level, the will was lacking for decisive action.

As a further source of tension, the issue of piracy was a flashpoint between Athens and Philip in the 340s. The pirate Sostratos had been using the island of Halonnesus as a base to launch pirate attacks into the Aegean. Little is known about the small island in this period, and it is not thought to have had a city during this time.[62] The island had apparently become a haven for pirates, who were expelled sometime in the mid-340s by Philip.[63] According to the speaker, Philip had considered it a joint burden of Athens and Macedonia to help guard the sea from pirates.[64] The danger in this, as the speaker then says, is that it would be a gateway for Philip's burgeoning sea power ambitions and a direct threat to Athenian sea power.[65] The speech is of course an anti-Philip polemic, but this should not detract from the core theme of piracy. While it is true that the speech demonstrates the weakening of Athenian sea power compared with other peer-competitors such as

---

[62] Evidence is slim, and the *Inventory of Archaic and Classical Poleis* cannot pin it down as having possessed an actual *polis*, though it may have. See Hansen and Nielsen (2004): 733.
[63] [Dem]. 7.2. The speech *On Halonessos* has been ascribed to Demosthenes; however, it appears certain that it was not written or delivered by him, but by another anti-Macedonian politician, Hegesippos. Trevett (2011): 113.
[64] Dem. 7.14.
[65] Dem. 7.15–16.

Macedonia,[66] it misses the point that piracy was clearly a threat and one which Athens was less able to deal with. Having disregarded the possibility that Athenian hegemony at sea was a stabilising factor providing good order at sea, he ignores the breakdown in this order that appears to have formed with the weakening of Athenian sea power and the apparent opportunities presented to pirates. That it was Philip who dealt with the pirate base on Halonnessus and not Athens should indicate how stretched Athens was at sea. Similarly, reference to a decree of Moirocles and a case where the Melians were fined ten talents for harbouring pirates around the same time demonstrates a continuing interest by Athens in doing all it could to supress piracy.[67] Though it is possible to see this as Athens flexing its political might against a weaker power, this need not be the prime motivation and there is no reason to assume that this was not primarily about piracy, as some do.[68] Maritime trade and the protection of it was of central importance to the Athenians, and it does seem as if the erosion of their sea power and the failure of any other state to take up the position of dominance at sea allowed for piracy to become more of a problem in the mid- and late fourth century. The increasing instability evident in the Aegean during this period surely contributed to the increased threat posed by piracy.

Finally, there is the little-understood final campaign of Athens against one of Alexander's successors, Antipater, in the Lamian War (323–322).[69] There appear to have been two engagements at sea, the first in the Hellespont and the second at Amorgos. However, the primary source, Diodorus, writes a very confusing account and does not specify that the final battle took place at Amorgos, this detail coming

---

66 De Souza (1999): 38.
67 The decree is mentioned in another speech of Demosthenes, 58 *Against Theokrines*, 56.
68 De Souza (1999): 39. He goes to great lengths to say that the two examples here were really about rivalry with Macedonia, and that piracy was only a pretext, despite saying that maritime commerce and trade was important to Athens. He even uses these incidents to conjecture how the right atmosphere was formed for the forgery of the Congress Decree, a rather circular way of arguing. This ignores the most likely explanation that piracy was a legitimate security concern and that Athens could and did take steps to counter piracy.
69 It seems as if the label of 'Lamian War' was given to the conflict in later times and that in the decades afterwards in Athens it was simply known as the 'Hellenic War'. The term Lamian War was seemingly popularised by the time Diodorus was writing, perhaps building upon Hieronymos of Cardia, a pro-Macedonian historian. The Athenians no doubt referred to it as the 'Hellenic War' as a means of legitimising their fight for Greek freedom from Macedonia, made clear by epigraphic references and the funeral oration of Hypereides, where the war is linking constantly to the cause of freedom. For a thorough discussion on the source tradition see: Ashton (1984): 152–7.

from a different work, the *Marmor Parium*.[70] Unfortunately there is not much to be said about this battle or even the naval campaign that led to it. Aside from reliably dating the battle to the Athenian year of 323/2 in the archonship of Cephisodorus and concluding that it was a decisive defeat for the Athenians, it is, as Ashton says, 'patently clear that no strategic or tactical analysis of the Amorgos conflict is feasible'.[71] What is evident is that the Athenians were defeated in a naval engagement, losing some ships but perhaps not suffering significant losses.[72] It is clear that 322 marked the end of Athenian hegemonic sea power, and although they appear to have been operating ships in the Hellespont in 321, even scoring some kind of victory,[73] their sea power was never the same. From that point on it was the navies of the *diadochoi* that would rule the Aegean until their usurpation by Rome.

The economic dimension

Even at the height of their respective sea power during this time, both Sparta and Athens seem to have been constantly stretched financially. The loss at Cnidos was not a death blow to Spartan sea power as a whole but without Persian funding it faded away over the next decade. The Athenians had many ships but were unable to ever bring all of them to bear and their campaigns in the northern Aegean, especially around Amphipolis, demonstrate how overextended they really were. Even without a peer competitor at sea, the Athenian naval resources could not cope with the scale of the demos' ambition to recover Amphipolis, Samos, and territory in the Thracian Chersonese. This continued into the period of the Social War where they were forced into compromise and later against Philip, who was constantly able to outmanoeuvre the Athenians, politically, diplomatically, and militarily. The poorly resourced Athenian fleet was always on the back foot trying to counter Philip, and as Demosthenes' proposal in his *First Philipic* demonstrates, even a small naval and military force would have had to rely on plundering Macedonian territory and seaborne trade in order to survive. In this respect it is un-

---

70 Ashton (1977): 1–2; IG 12.5.444 (+ Add. p. 315 + Suppl., p. 110). As Ashton points out, Diodorus' narrative at 18.5.9 does not make it clear whether there were two or three naval engagements.
71 Ashton (1977): 2.
72 Ashton comprehensively and painstakingly reconstructs ship numbers for before and after the battle. He concludes that there is nothing to suggest large naval losses around this time. Ashton (1977): 2–10.
73 On this see an analysis of a Panathenaic amphora by Hans Hauben (1974): 61–4. Ashton quotes Hauben's conclusion, that the victory in 321 meant 'a rehabilitation – meagre, to be sure – of the Athenian navy after the terrible setbacks of 322'. Ashton (1977): 1, n. 9.

surprising that despite a very large fleet, the Athenians who faced off against the *diadochoi* in the Lamian War had long lost their ability to conduct high-level military operations.

The members of the Second Athenian League were obviously and painfully aware of its predecessor, most notably in the way in which Athenian sea power had granted it such absolute control over the other member states – and reduced them to mere tributaries in most cases. Aside from a list of guarantees and protections listed in the Decree of Aristoteles,[74] a major factor limiting Athenian hegemony was the fact that Athenian sea power was not as pervasive as it had been in the fifth century. Further, as the Social War proved, this time the allies retained stronger naval and maritime forces with which they could in fact unite and challenge Athens. The allies had clearly learned from their experience of the Delian League. By contributing ships rather than money, the allied poleis were able to protect their own interests with their own warships, and thus retain a sovereign maritime defence capability. In the case of the Social War, it allowed several poleis to band together and challenge Athens outright. At the same time, this prevented Athens from monopolising naval skill and deprived them of a source of revenue with which to fund the fleet. Athenian sea power did regenerate after the end of the Peloponnesian War and as examples like Thrasybulus' Thracian cruise help illustrate, this sea power was effective. This of course was based on other Athenian successes in the 390s and 380s at sea that demonstrated Sparta was no longer ascendant at sea. This in turn reinforced the fact that the Athenian navy remained a potent force, even if not on the same level as the fleet of the Archidamian War.

Just as with the Delian League, Athens in the fourth century took steps to regulate the trade of allies. An interesting example is a regulation on the export of ruddle from three of the cities of Ceos. The regulation states that the ruddle is to be exported in whatever vessel the Athenians choose and no other.[75] It is hard to believe that the supply of ruddle was of great importance to Athens, and it is almost certainly an example of Athens tightly controlling the export of goods from an island as a means of wider control.[76] The islands of Lemnos, Imbros, and Skyros had been reacquired by Athens in 393 and confirmed as theirs in the King's

---

74 See Cargill (1981): 14–47, 131–45.
75 IG II² 1128, 12–13.
76 For discussion of this inscription, see Rhodes and Osborne (2004): 204–9. As the authors point out, it is reminiscent of the Athenian Decree that mandated the use of Athenian weights and measures. Originally dated to the 450s, a later date seems more likely. On the earlier date see: Meiggs and Lewis (1969): 111–17. On 'downdating' the decree, see: Mattingly (1993): 99–102 and (1996): 403–26.

Peace. They were strategically important as stepping stones to and from the Hellespont and thus vitally important for maintaining this economically vital sea lane. Athenian control over these islands was no small matter, and their retention of the islands is indicative of recognition by other powers, even enemies of Athens, that they represented a core interest of Athens, the loss of which might provoke a hostile reaction from Athens. Of further interest here is the Athenian tax of 374/3 on the islands, which levied a 1/12 tax on grain.[77] This is Athens controlling the production of a vital resource and ensuring the regular export of grain to Athens. This is a rare but very illustrative example of the non-naval use of sea power.

In a similar vein to the fifth century, the Athenians also collected money in coercive ways. In his oration, *On the Chersonese*, Demosthenes describes the actions of the Athenian *strategos* Diopeithes collecting money to fund his campaign in 341. One measure he took was to force merchant vessels to land,[78] presumably to either take some or all the cargo, or to extort money from the ships. The impression that Demosthenes gives is that it is all above board since the enemies of Athens cannot be arrested. Because of this, Athens has no choice but to send out ships and collect money.[79] Of note is that he says the Athenians have ways of dealing with their own people who do wrong, including decrees, impeachment, and the *Paralos*, one of the two state triremes. Clearly the *Paralos* was still a potent symbol of Athenian law and reach, unchanged since the plays of Aristophanes almost a century before.[80] Later in the speech, Demosthenes mentions in general terms the taking of money from different poleis for protection of their merchant vessels: not from the Athenians, but for protection in general.[81] He also says that those *strategoi* with more ships are able to collect more money. It may have been that the ships had little choice but to accept Athenian protection, but it also seems that they could rightly expect a proper defence if attacked. Who these merchant vessels need protection from is left unsaid, possibly pirates or perhaps the Macedonians, seeing that the speech is another chance for Demosthenes to rally against Philip. In either case, the Athenians were using their sea power to extract resources from neutrals and from allies. It is also possible that the Athenians were providing genuine protection to the trade vessels of other poleis, for, as discussed previously, maritime trade was a benefit to all and especially to Athens.

---

77 For discussion on the inscription, see Rhodes and Osborne (2007): 118–28.
78 Dem. 8.9.
79 Dem. 8.29.
80 *Birds*, 145–7, where the characters joke about being summoned by the other state trireme, the *Salaminia*. For more on this, see Chapter 4.
81 Dem. 8.25.

One need not be completely cynical of Athenian motives, and this very well could be a demonstration of Athens attempting to maintain 'good order at sea'.

As we saw with a few examples in the previous chapter, the Athenian law courts, in particular those dealing with merchant cases, the *dikai emporikai*, were an important part of Athenian and wider Mediterranean maritime affairs. The courts' first goal was obviously the protection of Athenian trade, but there seems to have been a flow-on effect of better regulated maritime commerce and trade for other poleis as well. Indeed, a key feature of these courts according to Edward E Cohen was their 'supranationality', the appearance of foreigners in these courts and even a case where both parties were foreigners.[82] In another maritime case, a failed attempt at defrauding a maritime loan led to the near sinking of a vessel, which managed to safely put into port at Cephalonia. There the local magistrates ruled that the ship should return to its home port, Athens, against the wishes of the Massaliots who had taken out the loan and attempted to sink their own ship, reluctant to face their creditors.[83] Whether or not the officials in Cephalonia were specialists in this sort of maritime case or just general magistrates, it shows a deferral of judgement to Athens and the specialist law courts there. Further, it may be that the Cephalonias did not want to antagonise the Athenians by unduly interfering in a trade matter, especially one dealing with the all-important grain trade. In these ways there is a duality in the nature of the *dikai emporikai*, a carrot and a stick. That the foreigners could access the courts for disputes shows that they must have been an attractive venue for the resolution of disputes, including when the dispute did not directly impact Athens. On the other hand, their existence must have signalled how serious maritime trade was to the Athenians, especially when concerned with the vital grain supply, and that they had a serious mechanism in place to deal with these cases. This is the benign, diplomatic way in which the Athenians sought to protect trade, including the trade of foreigners, and is another example of non-naval sea power being exercised across the Mediterranean.

Conclusion

The final decades of the fourth century, from Theban ascendency through to the rise of the Diadochi, were greatly influenced by sea power and maritime considerations. That there were no grand fleet engagements is of little consequence to this assertion. As the previous two centuries of naval warfare demonstrated,

---

[82] Euandros of Thespiai and Menippos of Caria. Dem. 21.176. Cohen (1973): 59.
[83] Dem. 32.8–9.

large-scale battle at sea, as it was on land, was quite rare. If anything, this period helps demonstrate the true reach of sea power. Athens may never have regained Delian League levels of power, but they remained an indomitable economic force in the Aegean and were still able to influence events in the Peloponnese and in northern Greece, even if it did not always go to plan. If anything, their ambition outweighed their ability, and although they maintained full sea control in the northern Aegean during their campaigns there, they overstretched themselves with their quixotic quest to retake Amphipolis. Although never a sea power in their own right, Macedonia under Philip clearly possessed some naval force and was invested in maritime trade across the region and into the Black Sea. Philip was clearly an astute strategist, able to effectively counter Athenian maritime manoeuvring by acting when the Athenians were least able to react. Finally, Alexander at least realised he needed the Athenian fleet for his campaign down the Levantine coast and used it to great effect, almost certainly commanded by someone with more sea power nous than him. The end of the Classical period may have seen Athens lose its position as the great sea power of the Aegean, but that mantle would be taken up by Hellenistic powers: Rhodes and Ptolemaic Egypt until Rome came along, and it was Roman citizens, not Greek, who were like frogs around a pond.

Chapter Eleven
The lessons of sea power

Having examined sea power throughout Classical Greek history, it is worth reflecting on the lessons that can be taken away. Going back to the theoretical model of maritime operations – military, diplomatic, and constabulary – we can gain an insight into how the Greeks utilised sea power in much the same ways as others throughout history and how this had a profound impact on the strategic environment. Something that has often gone overlooked is the sea power of smaller or less hegemonic poleis. A difficult topic, and one worthy of its own detailed treatment, it will nevertheless help broaden the scope of 'sea power' as something that was not just the sole purview of the rich and powerful poleis.

Non-hegemonic sea power

Having largely examined the operations of major 'hegemonic' sea powers, it is necessary to look at smaller poleis and how they used the maritime space. It is apparent that smaller poleis regularly contributed naval forces to maritime operations across the fifth and fourth centuries. At Salamis, in 480, there were ships present from 19 poleis, in addition to Athens and Sparta, from as far away as Croton in southern Italy.[1] In the 370s, long after their defeat at Cnidos, the Spartans were still able to gather a fleet with ships, with contributions by Corinth, Leucas, Ambracia, Elis, Zakynthos, Achaia, Epidaurus, Troezen, Hermione, and Halieis.[2] In the Social War of the mid-fourth century, Athens found itself on the wrong end of a coalition of allied poleis, with Chios, Rhodes, Cos, and Byzantium mustering a naval force strong enough to hold off Athenian sea power for several years, and eventually win their independence from Athens.

This examination will be, in large part, necessarily speculative. This is a source issue, the same issue that bedevils much of Classical scholarship. Ancient sources give us but the briefest glimpse of maritime thought and maritime operations outside of the hegemonic powers – Athens, Sparta, Thebes, and Macedonia. But it is possible to piece together a basic picture of how sea power may have operated in non-hegemonic poleis. The use of archaeological evidence, specifically the presence of ship sheds, can prove quite valuable. Ship sheds, as dis-

---

1 Hdt. 8.42–8.
2 Xen. Hell. 6.2.3.

cussed in Chapter Three, were a significant investment for any polis. This discussion will give a brief outline of some of the operations conducted by a few maritime poleis and speculate on how they might have used their sea power across the spectrum of maritime operations. It is by no means an exhaustive discussion of all Greek sea powers, but briefly covers the more notable ones.

Corinth

Corinth was an early sea power in the Greek world, a great early maritime trading polis and a prolific coloniser. 'Wealthy' Corinth commanded land and sea trade across the isthmus of Corinth and they pioneered shipbuilding, including of the first trireme, according to Thucydides.[3] Thucydides is explicit in saying that the Corinthians supressed piracy in what would have been the 'bad old days' of raiding, throughout the Aegean.[4] Indeed, Thucydides sets up the Corinthians as the hegemonic sea power, immediately preceding that of Athens. Corinth's position on the isthmus saw it develop maritime interests, both to the west through the Corinthian Gulf and to the south/south-east into the Aegean through the Saronic Gulf. It is this unique position that surely drove the construction of the *diolkos*, a large and significant investment in maritime infrastructure. This geography helped define Corinth's diplomatic relations, especially as they pertained to its all-important sea lanes. As we saw, the Saronic Gulf was a competitive area, especially with the island of Aegina.

The entente between Corinth and Athens that saw Corinth loan ships to Athens to defeat Aegina in 490 did not last. No doubt the deterioration in relations was, in large part, due to the growth of Athenian sea power. More than just a stoush over possession of the large Corcyraean navy, the fighting at Sybota indicates that by the 430s, the Corinthians saw the Athenians as encroaching into Corinth's sphere of influence in the west. As Phormio's successes in the early years of the Peloponnesian War demonstrated, Corinth could be cut off very easily by a hostile power operating in the vicinity of Naupactus. In Thucydides' narrative, it is the Corinthians at the outbreak of war who call for a decisive battle at sea against Athens. They maintained a fleet throughout the war – rather ineffective in the Archidamian War, though more effective in the later phases of the war. Some scholars attempt to defend Corinthian naval operations as being unfairly portrayed by Thucydides, referring especially to his rather condescending judge-

---

[3] Thuc. 1.13.2–5.
[4] Thuc. 1.13.5.

ment that: 'The Corinthians believed they were victors if they were only just defeated.'[5] Thucydides does not praise Corinthian effectiveness at sea, and in many cases, this is justified. Thucydides is criticised as being overly harsh when referring to the first engagement between the Corinthians and the Athenians under Phormio, where the Athenian *strategos* timed their attack with a favourable wind.[6] Yet, Thucydides is entirely fair in his judgement, for it demonstrates a woeful lack of local navigational knowledge on the part of the Corinthians in a geographic area that was vital to their own maritime operations. That the Athenian Phormio knew the pattern of local winds better than the regional sea power is an indictment of the Corinthians, and does prove the superiority of Athenian naval operations. Such navigational knowledge was fundamental to naval operations, not exceptional.

The Corinthians proved more effective in later engagements, especially during the Sicilian expedition, where a force of Corinthian warships engaged the Athenians at Naupactus and provided cover to merchant ships carrying hoplites to Sicily to fight the Athenians there.[7] Corinthian ships were also present with the Spartans at Aigispotamoi.[8] This loyalty to Sparta did not last long and the Corinthians used Persian money to rebuild their naval forces and contest Spartan control of the Corinthian gulf, after Cnidos, in 394.[9] However, two decades later, the Corinthians realigned themselves with Sparta and contributed ships to a fleet of 60, assembled in 373, by Sparta to attack Corcyra, and it may have been that Corinth could not resist joining an operation against their old nemesis.[10] In 344, the Corinthian Timoleon took a force of 10 ships, including 7 Corinthian ships, to fight in Sicily.[11] These later operations have Corinth contributing to a coalition and even though they took the lead in Timoleon's campaign to Sicily, it appears as if their capacity for independent naval action was diminished.

Corinth was a sea power during much of the Classical period, and certainly before this in the Archaic period. However, for the polis, which supposedly invented the primary warship of the age, little is known of the Corinthian navy or of their maritime interests in a broad sense. They contributed to many important naval operations in the fifth century, including Salamis, the Sicilian campaign – in both Greek waters and in Sicily – and at the final battle at Aegospotami. De-

---

[5] Thuc. 7.34.7. McKenzie and Hannah (2013): 206–27.
[6] McKenzie and Hannah (2013): 209–10.
[7] Thuc. 7.17, 19.5. See also Murray (2012): 19.
[8] Paus. 10.9.10.
[9] Xen. *Hell.* 4.8.10–11.
[10] Xen. *Hell.* 6.2.3.
[11] Plut. *Tim.* 8.4–5.

spite this, by the early fourth century, they were apparently reliant on Persian money to put together a fleet that was still no match for the waning navy of Sparta.[12] By the time of Timoleon's expedition in 344, they appear to have only been able to send seven ships on an expedition. Nevertheless, these seven ships were sent on a campaign to Sicily and so it is worth noting that they could still send ships on a campaign, outside of mainland Greece. Moreover, they still had political and military interests as far afield as Sicily that justified a naval expedition. Corinthian naval power may have waned over the course of the Classical period, but it is still in evidence to some degree, throughout.

On a final note, although the naval aspects of Corinthian sea power are often not well-defined, Corinth was undoubtedly an early and prolific coloniser and a trading hub of significance. Both are examples of the non-naval aspects of sea power. The strong ties that Corinth maintained with many of its former colonies in Italy and Sicily, as well as Poteidaia in the Aegean, and even second-order colonies like Epidamnus, demonstrates a clear policy of maintaining good overseas relations to preserve a network of allies and friends to aid in defence and trade. Having defined maritime strategy as 'the direction of all aspects of national power that relate to a nation's interests at sea'[13], Corinth is a great example of the non-naval side of 'interests at sea'. This would place the role of the Corinthian navy as an enabling force for these interests, not exclusively, as the Peloponnesian War clearly demonstrates, but to a large degree. Naval power was still important for Corinth, but its *sea power* was more than just triremes, even if the picture we see is largely that of warships. What is not seen are the trade networks and the political connections enabled and protected by this naval power. These connections had been built over a long time, so that although Corinth may have never regained the naval power it had in during the Archaic period, it still maintained powerful maritime interests into the Classical period. In this sense, naval power may have featured more prominently for its connection to trade protection to than hegemonic ambition.

Corcyra

Corcyra has come up many times as a prominent sea power in the decades leading up to and including the Peloponnesian War. As a colony of the maritime-minded Corinth and lying on the coastal sailing route from Greece to Italy and

---

12 Xen. *Hell.* 4.8.10–11.
13 As stated in the Introduction: Hattendorf (2013): 7.

Sicily, it seems unsurprising that Corcyra would develop strong maritime and naval interests. Hostility between the two sea powers led not only to the first naval battle in documented history, according to Thucydides, but also to the naval battle at Sybota, which precipitated the outbreak of war between Athens and Sparta.[14] Yet, the Corcyraean fleet only plays a minor role in the war that followed. In fact, the promise of Corcyra's sea power seems to exceed its usefulness. Despite mustering 60 ships to aid the Greeks at Salamis, they never made it past the Peloponnese.[15] The naval battle of Sybota saw the Corcyraeans lose 70 of their 110 ships, an appallingly high loss rate.[16] Although the island itself remained strategically important, including as the Athenian staging point for the Sicilian expedition, Corcyraean sea power itself is largely absent as an independent force. Even as late as 374/3, a party of Corcyraeans attempted to leverage their strategic position and convince the Spartans to send them aid, knowing, as they did, the importance of the island for those with sea power aspirations.[17] Nevertheless, just as at the outbreak of the Peloponnesian War, Corcyra is viewed by rival powers in the 370s as important chiefly because of its strategic position astride the coastal route from Greece to Italy. Corcyra's actual sea power does not figure prominently and is largely ineffective or absent.

This is despite the constant reference to Corcyra as a naval power. In the mid-fourth-century, Demosthenes referred to Athens as only having the weakest allies on its side and none of the powerful islanders, including Corcyra, in the list, along with Chios and Rhodes.[18] Even Appian, at one point, refers to Corcyraean thalassocracy.[19] Not just in literary sources, but archaeologically, it is also evident that Corcyra maintained its naval infrastructure into the Hellenistic and even Roman eras. Several ship sheds, dating from the early fifth century through to the Roman era, have been found on the island.[20] This upkeep indicates a conscious effort to maintain this infrastructure over several centuries. This would appear to suggest a strong maritime consciousness on the part of Corcyra.

Yet, with all the talk of Corcyra as a strong naval power, it never seems to play anything other than a supporting role or act as the pretext for conflict. I am not suggesting that Corcyraean naval and sea power was entirely ineffective or

---

14 Thuc. 1.13.4.
15 See Chapter Five.
16 Thuc. 1.54.2.
17 Diod. 15.46.1.
18 Dem. 18.234.
19 App. *B Civ.* 2.39.
20 The overall size of the naval facilities is yet to be fully revealed. See Blackman et al. (2013): 319–34.

non-existent, but I would suggest that Corcyra represents a polis that built warships but failed to implement an effective maritime approach to its strategy, beyond leveraging off what often appeared to be no more than a 'fleet-in-being'. Apparently, not everyone at the time thought they were worthy of sea power status, and although problematic, it is curious that Corcyra is not listed in the 'Thalassocracy lists', discussed in Chapter Four. Although I do not believe the list is a fully credible record of hegemonic Greek sea powers, it is notable in perhaps reflecting some fifth-century Greek attitudes towards historical sea powers.[21] Arguably, Sparta, a polis that to many, represents the land power *par excellence* of the time, had, at times, a stronger maritime consciousness than Corcyra. Sparta may have transformed itself into a temporary hegemonic sea power, but it never really changed structurally to the point where it could support sea power without outside financial aid. Nevertheless, when in possession of a fleet contributed by allies and/or paid for by outside (Persian) aid, the Spartans were able to wield it effectively. In this sense, despite having only a half-developed maritime consciousness, for the Spartans, it was certainly enough to rule the Aegean for a short time, when combined with resources not usually available to them – Persian money. The Corcyraeans quite simply never approached this level of effectiveness at sea. At the height of their naval power, before Sybota, the Corcyraeans could put to sea almost as many triremes as the Spartans commanded at Arginousai;[22] and yet, they were never in a remotely comparable position to Sparta in terms of hegemonic power at sea. This is a simplification of the relative power of the two poleis, but there is an undeniable difference in attitude that saw the Corcyraeans remain a supporting sea power rather than an independent one.

It is difficult to determine what operations the Corcyraean fleet engaged in, outside of the well-documented examples above. Considering their strong geographic position astride the coastal route from Greece to Italy, one may reasonably assume the Corcyraean fleet aided in suppression of piracy in the local area. Considering that Epidamnus was a Corcyraean colony, it seems likely that they had interests on the Illyrian littoral, and north, into the Adriatic. The frosty reception that the Corcyraeans gave the ambassadors from Epidamnus was seemingly not indicative of the Corcyraean capacity to act, for they were able to mobilise a

---

[21] Corinth does not appear on the list either, and this complicates matters. Considering that Aegina is listed as the final thalassocracy in 490–80, it seems likely that the natural successor would be Athens. This is not to make too much of an argument out of this list, but merely to highlight this particular observation.

[22] Corcyra with 110 at Sybota (Thuc. 1.47.1) and the Spartans with 120 at Arginousai (Xen. *Hell.* 1.6.26).

force rapidly and besiege the city of Epidamnos in a relatively short order.[23] It was, however, a very reactive operation on the part of the Corcyraeans. Perhaps, the primary purpose of the Corcyraean navy was to act as a 'fleet-in-being' and the mere existence of many warships was what influenced other major poleis to continually interfere in Corcyraean affairs to bolster their own sea power with that of Corcyra. This is not to say they did not conduct maritime operations, but that they may have usually conducted operations with a fraction of their navy on a regular basis, and that the full force of their fleet was only used in dire circumstances. Knowing almost nothing about Corcyraean naval infrastructure, it is plausible that putting 110 ships to sea, as they did at Sybota, was an exceptional circumstance. They may have had upwards of 120 ships but may not have had adequate personnel and material resources to crew that many on a regular basis. This could prove to be a good example where the possession of warships does not necessarily correspond with an effective navy.

Leucas

The island of Leucas is not usually associated with naval power; yet, it provides a tantalising glimpse of sea power in a smaller polis. The city committed to the building of naval infrastructure, and it is strongly suggested that it possessed several ship sheds.[24] The Leucadians were involved early in fifth-century naval operations. They provided three ships at Salamis, which is notable, considering the distance they travelled and the fact that they were not in immediate danger from the Persian invasion.[25] It is also worth noting that the Leucadian ships made it to Salamis, whereas the ships of their neighbour Corcyra were apparently held up by bad weather. Three ships may not have been a large contribution, but it was the mere fact that they were present at the great panhellenic naval victory of the Classical period that would have mattered to them and the other Greeks.

Just before the outbreak of the Peloponnesian War, Leucas sent 10 ships to fight with Corinth at Epidamnus and Sybota in 433.[26] They had 13 ships out on operations in 427 and provided two ships for the Corinthians to crew and send to Taras, Italy, in 414.[27] Finally, they and provided an unknown number of ships to

---

23 Thuc. 1.24.6–7; 1.26.3–4.
24 Blackman et al. (2013): 574–5.
25 Hdt. 8.45.
26 Thuc. 1.27.2, 46.1.
27 Thuc. 3.69.1; 6.104.

fight with the Spartans at Aegospotami, under the command of one Telycrates.[28] So, the Leucadians were present at two of the major naval battles of the fifth century, and on the winning side, no less. In this sense, their navy might have been small, but it was clearly more effective than not. They were present for several important battles and consistently called upon by allies to fight. This is not necessarily evidence of their effectiveness, but likewise they were not considered a drain on their allies, and their participation was deemed worthwhile.

There is less evidence of Leucadian operations in the fourth century, but we do know of a few instances where they conducted maritime operations. They sent ships to fight as part of a Spartan coalition in 373/2, and they provided a single ship for a Corinthian expedition, led by Timoleon's to Sicily, in 344.[29] This smaller contribution of a single ship may represent a diminishment in the size of their fleet, or it may represent hesitation at the campaign itself that it might be protracted and leave Leucas with fewer ships for local operations. What is noteworthy is that they were still willing to contribute to a maritime operation as part of a coalition, and as far afield as Sicily.

All of this adds up to more than just a catalogue of participation in maritime operations. It demonstrates the maintenance and growth of sea power over the fifth century. From three ships at Salamis to 10 at the outbreak of the Peloponnesian War shows a slow but steady growth. The outbreak of war clearly spurred more growth, as they went from contributing 10 at Sybota to 13 in operations in 427. An extra three ships built and crewed in five or so years may not seem like much, yet it is important to remember that this represented a significant investment in capital to build and outfit the ships and to find 600 more crew members. Further, it is reasonable to assume that it was unlikely they sent all their warships on campaign and surely would have left some in reserve for local defence. Even if this was only a few ships, their actual fleet size may have been bigger than the contributions above suggest. Leucas maintained their sea power throughout the war, and they were present at the final battle of Aegospotami. More than this, it is highly likely that their ships were in Lysander's fleet on campaign before the battle and so had been operating in the eastern Aegean for some time.

All this illustrates Leucas participating in a wide variety of coalition operations, sending warships to fight as part of an alliance. These were serious military campaigns; so they were clearly engaged in high-level combat operations. The primary role of their warships was to fight and so we may conclude that even if their navy was intended primarily to operate as part of an alliance force, their

---

28 Paus. 10.9.10.
29 Xen *Hell.* 6.2.3; Plut. *Tim.* 8.5.

ships were still expected to face combat. So even a polis, possessed of a relatively small navy, still trained its warships for military operations. What this represents is a polis that built a navy for war, not merely for prestige or only for combating piracy and low-level threats. This is not to say they did not use their warships for lower-level operations such as counter-piracy, for they almost certainly did, positioned in a valuable geostrategic position as they were. A navy capable of fighting in the line of battle at Salamis and Sybota was clearly able to fight pirates and more benign threats, and piracy must have been an issue of varying concern to an island that was reliant, to some degree, on maritime trade. Finally, we can assume that there existed in the city a strong maritime consciousness. The obvious commitment they showed to maritime operations over two centuries is illustrative of a polis that saw the importance of maritime pursuits and the utility of sea power. All of this taken together – two centuries of coalition operations documented by five different ancient sources and maritime infrastructure such as ship sheds – amply demonstrates that sea power was not something that only large, hegemonic powers could possess. That a smaller polis like Leucas maintained a highly active navy over hundreds of years illustrates that a maritime strategy was followed by a variety of poleis, large and small.

Aegina

The island polis of Aegina was a sea power from early times and had trade connections as far afield as the Black Sea during the sixth century. The polis was apparently a subject of Epidaurus on the mainland, but Herodotus says that Aeginetan superiority at sea let them break away.[30] After this began the enmity between Aegina and Athens, lasting several decades and leading to a deeply rooted dislike of the island in Athens. The Athenian statesman, Pericles, supposedly called Aegina, the 'eyesore of the Piraeus', an anecdote related by both Aristotle and Plutarch.[31] Labelling them a thalassocracy, as the 'Thalassocracy list' does for the years 490–480, is perhaps a stretch, but they doubtless had great sea power at this time and were a foil to both the Corinthians and the Athenians for some years.[32] We saw in Chapter Five that Aeginetan ships were sent to fight at Artemision and Salamis, and were considered the best of the Greeks that fought at Salamis. On the infrastructure side, Aegina had several ports and the remains of several ship sheds have

---

[30] Hdt. 5.83.
[31] Hdt. gives details of the hostility 5.83–91. See also Podlecki (1976): 396–403. Arist. *Rhet.* 1411a and Plut. *Per.* 8.5.
[32] Myres (1906): 95–6.

been found just to the south of Colonna Hill, seemingly dateable to the early fifth century.[33] Such an early date for ship sheds, if accurate, is indicative of a polis that took its navy and its sea power seriously and invested substantial capital in the fleet and its support.

As we have seen, the decline of Aeginetan sea power was the direct result of Athenian maritime ambitions. The shipbuilding program instituted by Themistocles after the silver strike at Laurion was, according to the politician, aimed at building ships to fight against Aegina, even before the threat of Persian invasion was raised.[34] During the *pentekontaetia*, after a naval battle and a siege the Athenians subdued Aegina, and apart from paying tribute to Athens, they were forced to surrender their ships and destroy their walls.[35] Aegina seems to have recovered after the Peloponnesian War and even flourished as a trading centre in the fourth century. Demosthenes refers to it as a flourishing marketplace, and Aeginetan merchants are specifically mentioned by Aristotle.[36] It is reasonable to expect that they maintained a fleet of some warships during the fourth century after the island's restoration. A fleet of even pentecontors would have been of great utility in protecting near seas against pirates as well as in low-level raiding operations in the local area.[37] As a trading hub, it would have been sensible for them to have maintained a small fleet capable of conducting constabulary operations. Such a fleet would also have been unlikely to antagonise its traditional rival, Athens. Despite the Athens-induced nadir in the latter half of the fifth century, Aegina was a maritime polis from earliest times and down to the end of the Classical period, at least.

Chios

The island of Chios was a strong sea power by the early fifth century. As an island known for the export of wine, the Chians required strong maritime trading links, and so possession of a large and capable navy is unsurprising. They provided 100 ships for the Ionian revolt at Lade in 494, with a large contingent of marines aboard each ship.[38] Chios was also one of the largest contributors to the Delian

---

[33] Three ports, though the northern most one most likely belongs to an earlier period and was not in use when the others were built. See Blackman et al. (2013): 284–93.
[34] Hdt. 7. 144.
[35] Thuc. 1.105.2–5, 108.4–5. See Chapter Six.
[36] Dem. 23.211; Arist. *Pol.* 1291b.
[37] Of the kind Figueira discusses Figueria (1990): 15–51.
[38] Hdt. 6.15.1. 40 citizen marines, to be specific.

League, providing a great number of ships until its eventual revolt in 412. They participated in all the major Athenian campaigns in the Peloponnesian War until this revolt.[39] They were present with Lysander's fleet at the battle of Aegospotami; however, two decades after this, they formed a renewed alliance with Athens and were a member of the Second Athenian League.[40] Finally, Chios was one of the four poleis that seceded from the League in 357 during the Social War.[41] All of these various alliances demonstrate active participation in the main naval alliances of the fifth and fourth centuries, both with and against Athens.

That the Chians retained a large and potent navy throughout most of the Classical period highlights that their policy and their strategy had a maritime focus. Their experience during the Ionian revolt clearly made them an early candidate for membership of the Delian League, and the fact that they always contributed ships demonstrates that they took an active role in the League and were unwilling to diminish their own navy. That they made an alliance with Athens in the 380s and joined the Second League also shows a strong commitment to maritime security in the Aegean, during the fourth century.

Thucydides has Alcibiades call the Chians the wealthiest of all the Greeks.[42] This is important for three reasons. As we have seen, wealth was one of the greatest enablers of naval power. Fleets were expensive to build, maintain, and operate. This wealth is evident in the number of ships Chios contributed to a vast array of operations before, during, and after the Peloponnesian War. Secondly, that Chios was one of the few poleis in the Delian League that contributed ships rather than money is indicative of a strong maritime consciousness. They retained a sovereign naval capability throughout the existence of the League, and this must have been part of their overall strategy. It was a strategy that paid off in the fourth century during the Social War, where combined with the fleets of Byzantium, Cos, and Rhodes, they were able to successfully break away from the control of Athens. It is not just the fact that they had ships, but that they had been operating a navy in the previous century that is important. This means that they retained the capability to conduct maritime operations to a level that was able to prevail against entrenched Athenian sea power. Finally, it is worth speculating about how Chios became and stayed so wealthy, and the obvious answer is through the export of wine, a bulk cargo that had to traded by sea. Chian's wealth

---

39 Raiding the Peloponnese (Thuc. 2.56.2), Pylos (Thuc. 4.13.2), Melos (Thuc. 5.84.1), and the Sicilian expedition (Thuc. 6.43, 7.20.2).
40 Paus. 10.9.10. Alliance in 384/3: Tod 118. Second Athenian League: IG II^2 43.24, 79. See also Cargill (1981): 24–5, 52.
41 Dem. 15.3; Diod. 16.7.3.
42 Thuc. 8.45.4.

was thus built on maritime trade. This again returns us to sea power as a holistic concept, and Chios is an example of a Classical Greek polis that had a strong maritime consciousness, a large and capable navy, participated in the predominant maritime leagues of the fifth and fourth centuries, and had an economy built on the export of goods (wine) through maritime trade. In the very truest sense of the term, Chios was a model of a non-hegemonic sea power.

This is by no means an exhaustive list of non-hegemonic sea powers. In exploring the ones that I have, it becomes clear that sea power did not follow a universal model in the ancient world, much as it does not follow one model today. Rather, there is a great variety in the ways in which different poleis approached the maritime domain. Some poleis, like Corcyra and Chios, built and maintained large navies, but with vastly different strategies and outcomes. The Chians remained a potent naval power throughout the Classical period, whereas the promise of Corcyraean sea power was always greater than the reward. Not all focused on their navy as a central factor in their maritime approach, but instead looked to trade, like Aegina. It is not remarkable that maritime hegemony was only ever achieved by two poleis in the Classical Greek world, Athens and Sparta: there have been few hegemonic sea powers throughout all of history. What must be highlighted here is that hegemony is not the same as sea power. As Thucydides says in the beginning of his great work, navies of the ancient Greek world may not have been large, but they were still a source of strength to those poleis that cultivated them.[43] Leucas and Chios may never have 'ruled the waves', but to them at least, their sea power was something they could not live without and it shaped the way they interacted with the world.

Enablers and the trinity of maritime operations

Having rounded out the examination of maritime operations in the Classical Greek period, albeit a far from comprehensive examination, we can see several lessons that have emerged. Aside from the above point that hegemony was not the same as sea power and that poleis of all shapes and sizes had maritime interests, there are several key lessons from this study.

Wealth underlies maritime operations, far more than with land operations, especially when combining the two. Warships were capital-intensive, both in acquisition and in upkeep. They required appropriate berthing arrangements, usually in the form of ship sheds, which themselves were significant investments for any

---

[43] Thuc. 1.15.1.

polis. The average trireme required a trained crew, in the order of 200 sailors, rowers, and marines. They needed to be kept supplied and paid while on campaign – campaigns that could range far and wide and last for months on end. It is no surprise then to find the largest sea powers possessed great natural wealth – lucrative mines in Athens and Thasos – or significant maritime trade interests – Corinth, Corcyra, Chios, and Aegina, in particular, although Thasos was also a great exporter of wine and so had dual wealth streams. Except for Athens' lucky silver strike, these poleis did not become so wealthy overnight, and it is likely that some wealth drove investment in warships, which aided the poleis in protecting its trade, expanding its territory, damaging its rivals, and altogether helping build more wealth to drive further investment in maritime infrastructure, ships, and qualified and experienced crews. No doubt, the suppression of piracy and the maintenance of 'good order at sea' helped maritime trade flourish. Finally, by the late fifth century and into the fourth, there was the Persian option. Sparta would have had almost zero chance in the second half of the Peloponnesian War were it not for the vast coffers of the Persian empire. That they were willing to throw money at the Spartans, even after losses like those at Arginousai, was crucial to wearing down the Athenians. When Sparta became too powerful, the Persians were happy to do the same for the Athenians, funding the downfall of Sparta's short-lived maritime empire. Money fuelled maritime operations, which in turn could fuel the growth of even greater wealth.

A more intangible factor was that of maritime consciousness. It was not enough to build warships, train rowers, and then go on campaign. Sea power was only effective when a polis could use it in concert with other state mechanisms and have an appreciation of the capabilities and limitations of engagement in the maritime realm. This does not mean citizens of a polis needed any specific love of the sea to have saltwater flowing through their veins or any other such notions. Rather, it is the ability to see how the maritime realm could be engaged with, be it through trade and all that it required: ships, regulations, overseas markets, protection from piracy, alliance with a neighbour, or access to specific bodies of water. It would be the knowledge of how maritime forces could be used to destroy a rival, through military action, trade usurpation, intimidation through 'gunboat diplomacy', promising your naval forces to a bigger alliance, and drawing upon combined maritime forces, or a combination of all. The comic, Aristophanes', joking about Athens' triremes appearing all over the Aegean to summon allies for war was funny because it reflected reality. Tragic heroes leading their cities as if they were steering a ship was evocative because people knew of the skill required – and the dangers faced – by a ship's captain, if only as a subordinate. Sadly, we rarely get a glimpse of this maritime consciousness outside of Athens, where a wealth of sources gives us intense detail about how the maritime world shaped Athens. From stories of the gods and goddesses through to tragedy and comedy and down to the bitter ramblings of Plato's Atlantis myth, we get many views on the place of the sea in a city that for a long time strived to become an island.

We come now to maritime operations themselves. This is not to categorise maritime operations in the Greek world, though admittedly that is what the database at the Appendix does. It is to have an informed discussion on how these different operations demonstrate the uses of sea power across the board. These labels need not be proscriptive and, in any case, many operations cannot be defined as only military or only diplomatic simply because they were both. Rather, it is a trigger for thinking of these operations as more than just warships sailing about landing troops or going into battle.

Military operations

Naval forces conducted combat operations at or from the sea, and often in combination. Examples of combat operations at sea include battle, cover, and the protection or interdiction of trade. Combat operations from the sea primarily consisted of amphibious landings against a hostile or neutral shore. This could be on a large scale, such as the Athenian attack on Sicily in 415, or a much smaller raid, such as when Alexander of Pherai launched a raid against the Piraeus in 361. An important point is that combat operations at sea were a key enabler of combat operations from the sea. Power projection operations relied on the attacking force being in possession of sea control, or at least being able to operate in a contested environment, what might be termed 'working sea control'. The ability to fight and win at sea is what allowed for the deployment of force ashore, although battle at sea itself could have a definitive effect on the wider strategic situation.

There are several points to note when discussing naval battle, applicable to the ancient as well as the modern world. Combat operations against an enemy's combat or logistics units were and are a key role for navies. These operations can be on a large or small scale and to varying effect, on a strategic or a tactical level. As seen with the battle of Arginousai, not every large-scale naval engagement was the result of a desire to engage the enemy fleet in battle, but might come about because of some other maritime operation, a blockade in this case. Scale is an issue that often obscures the combat role of navies and their effect on events. Large battles such as Salamis or Arginousai – or Lepanto, Trafalgar, Jutland, Midway – are rare, and most naval combat operations are not of this scale. Operations by a few ships could have a large impact on a particular campaign, such as the Athenian navy's operations under Phormio, in the Corinthian Gulf in 429. Just as single-ship actions in the modern world of naval combat could be of strategic consequence, so too were small-scale combat operations in the Greek world of great importance.[44]

Another issue concerns ships fighting near land. Technological limitations are the standard reason given by scholars for this, and although this was surely a factor, it obscures a key point about sea power. As discussed from the very beginning, sea power is concerned with influencing events ashore and as such, it should be expected that naval battles would often take place in close vicinity to land – 'close vicinity' or 'near' being very relative terms. Naval forces often engaged in battle to protect or defend important geographical features such as a strait, gulf, harbour, or a landing spot. Key modern naval battles have taken place near land, including the Battle of the Nile in 1798 – a battle conducted at anchor – Trafalgar, the Dardanelles campaign in 1915, and Midway in 1942.[45] There are various reasons for this, but the determining factor was not technology – it was strategic or tactical considerations. Though some scholars have recognised modern parallels, there is still misunderstanding over the issue. Scholars use examples like Trafalgar and Midway to say admirals, ancient and modern, liked calm seas and nearby refuges, but neither was a key consideration for these battles.[46] A storm the day after Trafalgar proved the nearby coast extremely dangerous, rather than any kind of refuge, sinking many ships. The island of Midway was merely the bait provided by the US Navy to lure the Japanese into a trap. Strategic and tactical considerations are of primary importance. The battles of Artemision and Salamis were fought close to land because of the tactical consideration that confined waters would negate the superior numbers of the Persians. An example from Sicily shows that proximity to land and a force of friendly soldiers might be of no help at all. In 396, the Sicilians fighting the Carthaginians engaged in a battle near Catane. Dionysius had his troops arrayed along the shore, in case the fleet got into trouble, something Diodorus calls the most important consideration.[47] It was all to no avail, for after the Carthaginians prevailed in the battle, they had their lighter vessels range just offshore and kill any Sicilian sailors swimming for shore, who 'perished in great numbers not far from land, while the troops of Dio-

---

[44] A good example is the two World Wars where German commerce raiders, such as *Emden* and *Kormoran*; the former tied up vast naval resources in the Indo-Pacific theatre during 1914, until destroyed by the Royal Australian Navy cruiser *Sydney*. For an excellent recent examination, see Stevens (2015): 68–81.
[45] Proximity being a relative term, as in the case of Midway where carrier and land-based aircraft extended the range at which ships could influence and be influenced by land features.
[46] Hanson (2005): 258.
[47] Diod. 14.59.6.

nysius were unable to help them in any way'.⁴⁸ Proximity to land meant little when that shore was hostile. Navies, ancient and modern, are not concerned with the control of the open ocean: they are concerned with influencing events ashore, and so it is to be expected that naval battles were mostly conducted 'near' land. Battles, close to land, are not an exceptional feature of ancient naval operations that set them apart from naval operations in later times.

Blockade in the ancient world was a much different and more limited affair than in more recent naval operations. Firstly, there was no legal aspect to it, as there is in the modern world.⁴⁹ Secondly, technology was a limiting factor in this case, and ancient ships did not have the endurance of later ships that would allow for a distant blockade. Nevertheless, despite what some scholars would say, there are clear instances of naval forces engaged in a close blockade of a port or city. This is perhaps best encapsulated by the term 'naval siege warfare', as William Murray has called these actions.⁵⁰ Similar to a blockade is a barrier operation, whereby a naval force uses geography to close an area or passage.⁵¹ Phormio's operations to block the entrance to the Corinthian Gulf are an excellent example.

One of the core functions of maritime forces is the ability to project power ashore and conduct combat operations from the sea. To conduct combat operations from the sea, whether raiding or a large amphibious operation, a naval and military force may need protection from enemy interference from the sea. Cover is a key operation conducted at sea to protect a friendly land force. Without this cover, it would be possible for land forces to find themselves outflanked from the sea or entirely cut off, as in the example of the fleet covering the hoplites fighting at Thermopylae in 480. These operations were of critical importance to the conduct and outcome of many different conflicts. Obviously, in the Classical context, the projection of power ashore by maritime forces refers to the deployment, or threat of deployment, of land forces. This ranged from a raid to a large force and, in some cases, even direct assaults on enemy positions or cities. In some cases, the role of the maritime forces involved was to provide 'sea lift', moving large numbers of troops or supplies. In a few instances, their role was as part of an amphibious withdrawal, the evacuation of land forces from a hazardous situa-

---

48 Diod. 14.60.5–6.
49 Such as in the First World War or more recently, UN Sanctions and embargoes that allow naval forces to board and inspect all vessels leaving or entering a country. A recent example of this would be against Iraq after the first Gulf War, when ships were authorised to check vessels for illicit cargo, including oil being smuggled outside of the UN-mandated regime of monitored exports.
50 Murray (2012). Chapter 3, 'The Development of Naval Siege Warfare'.
51 For further explanation, see *Australian Maritime Doctrine*, 103; Till (2013): 178–83.

tion. The vast coastlines of the Mediterranean littoral gave Greek maritime forces a large operating theatre for conducting these sorts of operations.

Diplomatic operations

The use of navies as a tool of diplomacy is evident throughout the Greek Classical period. Many poleis used navies to further their foreign policy interests. Most of the time, this was on the coercive end of the scale, what is often referred to as 'gunboat diplomacy'.[52] Navies were, and are, quite capable of projecting force over long distances while remaining removed from directly engaging in conflict: lying offshore but not encroaching onto a polis' actual territory. Armies are inherently intrusive, whereas navies can remain at a distance, threatening or reassuring, as desired, without physical encroachment into foreign territory. A key feature that distinguishes this from other maritime operations is the absence of the use of force, although the threat of force is often implied at some level. This is harder to detect in the Greek Classical world where ancient sources often do not give a high level of detail, and it is possible that many of these diplomatic operations, especially tribute collection, did involve the application of force that goes unmentioned. Nevertheless, the primary aim of these operations was not to engage in combat or cause widespread harm or destruction. Low-level violence aside, naval forces, acting in a diplomatic role, demonstrated the potential power that could be brought to bear. Sometimes, the mere existence of a navy could be of diplomatic value. In the case of Corcyra before the Peloponnesian War, it was more than a dispute over who was right and who was wrong over the issue of Epidamnus. The issue was the large Corcyraean fleet, a fleet that could significantly bolster the sea power of either Athens or Corinth. As a 'fleet-in-being', the Corcyraean navy was a powerful diplomatic tool.

Maritime diplomatic operations should be viewed on a spectrum, from benign through to coercive. A fleet appearing in the port of one polis might be a reassuring presence to allies and in the very same cruise, convey a threat to a more recalcitrant ally. Likewise, a polis might send a few or many ships, depending on the level of reassurance or threat they wished to convey. The presence of two or three triremes sends a much different message than the presence of 20. In

---

52 Though this term has fallen out of usage in modern parlance, with practitioners, politicians, and scholars preferring terms such as 'coercive' or merely, 'naval' diplomacy, or more broadly, 'sharp power': 'Gunboat diplomacy' conjures up too many images of western imperialism/colonialism.

this respect, categorising a maritime operation as diplomatic is usually quite subjective.

As the Theban example from the previous chapter highlights, navies were only useful as diplomatic tools if they were respected or feared as a fighting force. Thebes had no naval tradition, with no record of combat victories at sea, and thus they were neither feared nor respected. The Athenian navy, on the other hand, was widely feared, with a long history of victory in combat and notoriety in tribute collection across the Aegean. Poleis were rightfully sceptical of throwing their lot in with Thebes when Athens had a proven capability to fight and win at sea. Thus, the most important enabler of naval diplomatic operations is a proven ability to conduct combat operations, both at and from the sea.

In the matter of resourcing, naval diplomacy is flexible and very much a matter of scale. Obviously, a larger naval force could threaten a wider range of poleis than a small navy. Athens could bully almost any other poleis in the Greek world, save peer competitors, and likewise, for Sparta, during its short naval ascendency. The navies of smaller and less capable poleis, such as Leucas, could still conduct coercive naval diplomacy, just on a smaller scale. They might send a small force of warships and soldiers to conspicuously sail past or land in the vicinity of a bothersome polis as a demonstration, or on the more coercive end of the scale, they might detain the fishing or trading vessels of other poleis for 'customs/tax' enforcement. On the other side of the coin, it did not necessarily take a large fleet to provide comfort and/or deterrence. The 10 ships sent by Athens to aid Corcyra at the outbreak of the Peloponnesian War were enough to signal Athens' intent, to friend and potential foe alike. Finally, navies could be a powerful bargaining tool on the diplomatic front, and poleis such as Corcyra could leverage off the existence of a large fleet to gain attention and protection from more powerful poleis.

Naval diplomacy did of course have its limits. Despite the presence of Athenian triremes with strict non-confrontational orders alongside the fleet of Corcyra, Corinth still engaged in battle and precipitated the outbreak of war between Athens and Sparta. As in all matters related to diplomacy, sometimes deterrence is not enough, and war is the outcome. Another limitation, painfully learned by Athens and Sparta, is that the use of navies for tribute collection may be effective, but it can be extremely abrasive and cause severe resentment on the tributaries. Many Aegean poleis had long memories when it came to the appearance of Athenian warships in their harbours, and into the later years of the fourth century, there was widespread mistrust of Athenian fleets on ostensibly peaceful business. Finally, some poleis were simply immune to naval diplomacy, being either isolated from the sea or with few interests at sea. Thebes is a case in point, and although sea power was not a trivial factor in the Spartan and Athenian conflicts with Thebes, the diplomatic aspect of sea power was of little significance when dealing with Thebes. Navies could be powerful diplomatic tools, but there were distinct limits.

Constabulary operations

The weakest link in the trinity of maritime operations, when looking at the Classical Greek world, is that of constabulary. This is, as discussed, primarily a source issue. These types of operations are often low-key and not worthy of the attention of the extant ancient sources. As the title implies, these operations often fall outside the normal realm of military operations and into the realm of police or paramilitary forces. We do, however, get glimpses of naval constabulary operations. On the other side of piracy is obviously counter piracy, and it is clear from Thucydides and others that a polis would often supress piracy since it was bad for the business of maritime trade. The suppression of piracy in the Aegean by Athens benefited other poleis, despite not falling within the parameters of any international law. On the legal side, without the strict delineation of legal jurisdictions at sea, a polis presumably policed its local seas or fishing grounds as it saw fit, excluding or taxing the activities of foreign vessels.[53] Certainly, possession of a few small warships would be extremely useful to a state enforcing sovereign rights in local waters. Moreover, such a task was probably better suited to warships smaller than a trireme, especially ships like pentecontors, and so less glorious to discuss than fleets of triremes in action.

Then, there are other operations that are also recognisable to us in the modern world: the use of navies in 'humanitarian and disaster relief' operations, to borrow a very modern term. To the Greeks, it would have just been prudence. What is important to remember is that these operations had a profound significance, remembering that they were conducted to evacuate civilians, not combat forces. We witnessed two such evacuation operations, the evacuation of Athens to Salamis in the face of the Persian invasion in 480, and the partial evacuation of the Sicilian city of Himera in 409, in the face of the Carthaginian invasion. The first operation is what allowed Athens to fight at the battle of Salamis, and consequently led to the defeat of the Persian invasion. The second case was perhaps more desperate, for the Carthaginians killed or sold into slavery those who re-

---

[53] For more on this, see Lytle (2012): 1–55; Bresson (2016): 11–184. It is hard to disagree with Bresson's conclusion that cities enforced their claims with whatever sea power they possessed, otherwise not at all.

mained in Himera; so the evacuation of half the population spared them such a fate. What these examples show is that possession of a navy, of any size, could impart benefits outside of war and diplomacy. In the case of counterpiracy, it is a good investment for a polis worried about maritime trade and piracy. *In extremis*, warships could be used to protect the civilian population of a city. Navies then were not just for line of battle but were useful in many different types of maritime operations. This was the true utility of sea power.

Conclusion

The history of Greece in the Classical period was driven by maritime concerns. The practice of sea power, true sea power: 'the capacity to influence the behaviour of other people or things by what one does at or from the sea' is evident throughout.[1] Such an elegant and timeless definition reflects the reality of how various Greek poleis used the maritime domain in the fifth and fourth centuries, across the Mediterranean.

Greek maritime pursuits obviously went back a millennium or more before the Classical period. The Mycenaeans and Minoans were certainly interested in the sea and maritime pursuits. Historical or not, a Minoan sea power was such that they could be called a thalassocracy by the likes of Herodotus and Thucydides. In this respect, the Classical Greeks themselves considered it historical, or at least mythical, and therefore could connect the idea of thalassocracy in their day with a storied past. Epics like the *Iliad* and *Odyssey* both explored the maritime world in different ways, and as foundational works these are exceptionally important. The *Iliad* is after all a tale of the Trojan War, which in essence was one great expeditionary operation carried out across the Aegean, and its 'order of battle' was related in a catalogue, not in numbers of soldiers, but of ships. The *Odyssey* was a maritime epic through and through, illustrating a vast world of the oceans, wondrous and scary. Along with other stories like Jason and the Argonauts, and even many of the adventures of the great hero Heracles, they gave a sense of the Greeks exploring the world, both in metaphysical and in actual space.

As the Greek world expanded through colonisation around the shores of the Mediterranean east to west and even into the Black Sea, maritime connections were of great importance. This Greek world was reinforced by shared religion and cults, language, culture, and most importantly, through trade. It was the seas that often connected the Greeks as they built their cities across the region. It was not just that the Greeks settled near the shoreline, enjoyed views of the pellucid sea, and ate of its bounties. They established stories of the sea and its inhabitants, from sea creatures to gods and goddesses. They had heroes cross the seas, taming the clashing rocks and opening the Pillars of Heracles. The opening of the seas made the Greek world wider.

Naturally with these more open seas came conflict, within the Greek world and with others as well. As poleis became wealthier through maritime trade, they were able to use the seas for conquest. Piracy became a means of making a living, and if not entirely respectable, somewhat legitimate in the eyes of many. That

---

1 Till (2013): 25.

was until a hegemonic power like Minos, Corinth, or Athens came along and decided piracy was bad for business and suppressed it by naval force. Although the origins of navies as government entities rather than private affairs is shrouded in mystery, the process began sometime in the sixth century and was fully formed by the dawning of the fifth. Thalassocracy – rule of the sea – became a fully formed and realisable concept.

As we have seen, war on and across the seas was endemic to the Greek world of the fifth and fourth centuries. Used in conjunction with a land force, navies were able project power across the Aegean and have a defining impact on a polis' fate. Sea power as strategy was a powerful force, as the Athenians and Spartans were both able to demonstrate. Navies were used for military, diplomatic, and constabulary tasks, in ways recognisable to a naval practitioner from any period. Most importantly, this work has only scratched the surface of some aspects of sea power and maritime strategy in the ancient world. Events in Sicily over the period have only been covered in the barest detail, and there is much more that could be studied from the wars of the Sicilians and the Carthaginians there. The sea power of non-hegemonic poleis was touched on in brief, and there is great potential to delve into the sea power of any one of the poleis of Corinth, Corcyra, Leucas, Chios, and Aegina, let alone others: Samos, Thasos, Byzantium, a whole host of other places that clearly took a maritime view of the world. The study of their sea power has only just begun.

It is with no small delight to quote Plato – who hated maritime pursuits so much that he invented an entire mythological city to demonstrate its poisonous influence – but also managed to so aptly describe the Greeks surrounding the Mediterranean like frogs around a pond. From the mouth of its harshest critic is revealed the true place of sea power as the driving force of the ancient Greek world. Far from being just about the hoplites, the '300' at Thermopylae, and the land power/sea power dichotomy of the Peloponnesian War, the history of strategy and warfighting in this age saw ships play a critical role. Hoplites, archers, and cavalry had their place, but it was as an integral part of what we call sea power. It was often on and across the 'wine dark sea' that the fates of nations were determined.

Appendix 1
Glossary of terms

The following terms are defined as they are used in this work, following their normal usage in discussing issues of sea power and maritime strategy. Definitions are always tricky, subject to differences of opinion and the vagaries of time. As stated in the introduction, there is no suggestion that the Greeks used these terms; rather, they are a conceptual tool for examining the history of the period. It is a vocabulary, like that used when looking at issues of the economy, or literature, or any number of other studies examining the ancient world.

Maritime power projection

In the modern world this includes strikes from the sea using naval gunfire, missiles, or ship-launched helicopters and aircraft, conducted against targets ashore or in the littoral environment such as port facilities or offshore infrastructure.

Considering the lack of weapons capable of being wielded from ship to shore, maritime power projection in the context of the Greek Classical period refers to the use of maritime forces to land, or threaten to land, combat troops onto the shore. This could include raids, attacks on the countryside, or attacks on cities. Walled cities were often more vulnerable to attack from the sea, where the port precluded the construction of walls down to the waterfront.

It can also include the establishment of forward bases, such as the Athenian base established at Pylos in Spartan territory, which was used for years to harass and attack the Spartans and their Peloponnesian allies.

Maritime strategy

A maritime strategy is best described as 'the direction of all aspects of national power that relate to a nation's interests at sea'.[1] In the Classical Greek world this involved diplomacy, the safety and defence of merchant trade, fishing, and coastal defence. Navies obviously have a central role to play in any maritime strategy, but it goes beyond the use of warships and combat. For instance, Athens could use its vast trade network to coerce another polis by cutting off vital sup-

---

[1] Hattendorf (2013): 7.

plies/goods. As a maritime trading polis, the island of Chios maintained good diplomatic relations with other island poleis in the region.

Naval operation – military

Military operations are at the core of what a navy does. Without the ability to conduct effective military operations, a navy cannot protect the state. It also enables a navy to be effective at diplomatic or constabulary operations. This involves combat operations at sea and combat operations from the sea.

Combat operations at sea include things such as battle; trade interdiction and trade protection; providing cover to a land force ashore so they might operate without interference from a hostile naval force; and blockade.

Combat operations from the sea primarily consist of amphibious operations, landing troops on a friendly or hostile shore. (See above, maritime power projection)

Naval operation – diplomatic

Often referred to as 'Gunboat Diplomacy' in the past, it is the use of a naval force for diplomatic purposes. This could be coercive – the sense of 'gunboat diplomacy' where a warship or group of warships is dispatched to intimidate an enemy, neutral state, or even a non-cooperative ally. Non-coercively, a naval force might be sent to an ally to reassure them of a polis commitment to their protection – a positive signal to an allied polis and deterrent to a hostile polis.

As stated above in military operations, a naval force is only useful diplomatically if it is a credible military force. The Athenian Navy could sail around the Aegean threatening and reassuring as needed because it was an effective, feared naval force. When Thebes attempted such a feat, they influenced few poleis because the Theban navy had no reputation in military operations.

Naval operation – constabulary/policing

Constabulary, or policing operations are operations that, in the modern world, have more of a law-enforcement or non-military feel to them. Despite the existence of police and coast guard forces in the modern world, navies are at times called upon for operations that those other forces might be expected to conduct.

The greatest example in both the ancient and modern world of constabulary operations is that of combating piracy.

Naval strategy

Naval strategy commonly refers to the purely military aspect of naval power: a navy develops a strategy to defeat another navy and thus develops a naval strategy. A naval strategy is how one navy will defeat another – it is restricted to the military realm. It is thus a subset of maritime strategy. This is not to be confused with 'military' in a purist sense of referring only to the activities of armies. This work uses military in the broader sense of meaning the actions of any force engaged in armed conflict, be it on land or at sea.

Operational level of war

The level of conflict which sits between strategy and tactics. It deals with campaigning, such as the movement of forces and supplies as part of the conflict. 'It is particularly concerned with the operational ways to achieve strategic ends by tactical means.'[2]

Piracy and privateering

Piracy in the Greek world was not as specific a term as it is now. In the modern world, Article 101 of *The United Nations Convention on the Law of the Sea 1982* (UNCLOS) strictly defines piracy. Prior to this 'pirate' was often a pejorative term used to describe any maritime activity a state deemed to be unsavoury.

The simplest definition for the Classical Greek context is that piracy is an armed attack conducted by a ship or ships of a non-state actor. The navy of a polis might raid a port or seize a merchant vessel, but so long as this activity is being conducted at the behest of the controlling polis, this is more properly designated as 'raiding' or 'trade interdiction'. An army on land that pillages or raids enemy territory is not said to be engaged in 'banditry', and so a navy does not engage in 'piracy' while under the orders of its polis.

Privateering in the ancient context is also difficult to define. In the age of sail Letters of Marque could be issues by a state to a private ship, which legalised their attacks on that state's enemies. As we have seen, there are examples of a polis hiring private ships for attacks on their enemies. Sparta during the Peloponnesian War took this approach to make up for their lack of warships. In this, the ships in question might be privately owned and operated, but they are paid for

---

2 *Australian Maritime Doctrine* (2010): 202.

and directed by a polis, and thus we can think of them as privateers rather than pirates, though as in any age of naval warfare, an adversary might not see it this way and still label the offending ships 'pirates'.

Sea control

Sea control is a nebulous and oft-debated term, subject to constant revision over time and the vagaries of academic thinking.

Simply put, sea control is a state by which a naval force can conduct operations as desired at a certain time and in a certain place with no or minimal interruption by an opposing force. Simultaneously, the opposing force is unable to utilise the sea as they would wish in that particular space at that particular time.

It is possible for the state of sea control to be in contest, with neither side in control of the sea. Julian Corbett believed the normal state of affairs was a sea which was 'uncommanded' – control of the sea has to be fought for and won; it is neither gained nor lost by default.

Admiral Raoul Castex said of sea control that: 'The mastery of the sea is not absolute but relative, incomplete, and imperfect.'[3] Hence one may speak of such things as 'working sea control' whereby one side has freedom to operate, but an enemy still has the potential to operate at sea, but only at high risk. For a good summation of sea control, including a table breaking it down into five different levels, see Geoffrey Till's 2013 guide on sea power.[4]

Sea denial

Sea denial is where an adversary is unable to use the sea for their desired purposes. A power might not have sea control but may still be able to deny the use of the sea to an adversary.

Sea power

We came across two definitions of sea power in the introduction. Admiral Sir Herbert Richmond is the first to explicitly give a definition of sea power:

---

3 Castex (1994): 53.
4 Till (2013): 150–2.

> Sea Power is that form of national strength, which enables its possessor to send his armies and commerce across those stretches of sea and ocean, which lie between his country or the countries of his allies and those territories to which he needs access in war; and to prevent his enemy from doing the same.[5]

A simple one-line definition of sea power is provided by Geoffrey Till: 'the capacity to influence the behaviour of other people or things by what one does at or from the sea'.[6]

Sea power is not just naval power, but refers to a state's use of the sea taken as a whole and although naval power is at its core, can also include maritime trade, diplomacy, and legal aspects. Most importantly it is a relative term and not something limited only to hegemonic powers.

Strategy

Strategy is one of the most defined terms in the study of warfare and diplomacy. Strategy is a term used to describe the relationships between means and ends, concerned with identifying national objectives as well as the resources and methods available for meeting such objectives.[7] Critically, strategy comes into play where there is actual or potential conflict between opposing powers. Strategy is much more than a 'plan' because it is required when an opposing force's own interests and objectives must be considered.

Simply put, it is the interplay between ends, ways, and means, where the desired end state is reached through particular 'ways' – the operational level of war – and enabled by the 'means' – the resources and tactics used in the conduct of operations. As an example, the Peloponnesian War strategy of Athens under Pericles saw the *end state* being the status quo *ante bellum*; the *ways* in which this was achieved was a campaign of maritime power projection aimed at Sparta and Sparta's allies, wearing down their will to fight while protecting the Athenian empire; the *means* was sea power, the naval forces of Athens and her allies combined with the economic dominance of the Delian League, which could pay for constant campaigning and keep Athens fed and supplied in the face of Sparta attacks on Athenian territory.

---

5 Richmond (1946): ix.
6 Till (2013): 25.
7 Freedman (2013): xi; Strachan (2013): 211.

Appendix 2
Database of maritime operations

Military operations

Year	Area/location	Notes	Reference
546–528	Thrace/Naxos	Athenian tyrant, Peisistratus, establishes Athenian influence over the River Strymon in Thrace and conquers the island of Naxos.	Hdt. 1.64.1–2
548/7	Samos	Samians (allegedly) intercept Spartan vessel on its way to Sardis. Samian's motive is unknown.	Hdt. 1.70
546	Sparta/Lydia	Spartans prepare a force to sail to Lydia and help their ally, Croesus. Croesus is captured before Spartans can sail.	Hdt. 1.83
545	Phocaea	Phocaeans return to their city and destroy the Persian garrison there.	Hdt. 1.165.2
539	Corsica	60 Phocaean ships battle a combined force of 60 Etruscan and Carthaginian ships. 'Cadmean' victory for Phocaeans.	Hdt. 1.166
525?	Samos	Polykrates, tyrant of Samos, conquers many islands and attacks 'everyone without exception'.	Hdt. 3.39
525?	Samos/Egypt	At request of Cambyses, Polykrates sends 40 triremes in aid to the expedition to Egypt. Crews consist of citizens of questionable loyalty to Polykrates.	Hdt. 3.44.2
525	Samos	Spartans and Corinthians attack Samos.	Hdt. 3.47–48, 3.54, 3.56
524	Siphnos	Samians sail to Siphnos and request a loan. When denied, Samians ravage the island and defeat the Siphnians in a land battle.	Hdt. 3.58
524	Cydonia/Crete	Samians, settled at Cydonia in Crete, are defeated in a naval battle by the combined force of Cretens and Aeginetans.	Hdt. 3.59
511/510(?)	Sybaris/Italy	Spartan prince, Dorieus, leads expedition to Italy and fights with Croton against Sybaris.	Hdt. 5.43–45

(continued)

Year	Area/location	Notes	Reference
505(?)	Attika	Aeginetans raid the coast of Attica in an 'undeclared war'.	Hdt. 5.81
505	Aegina	Athens sends ships to Aegina. Conflicting story on events.	Hdt. 5.85.86
498	Hellespont/Caria	Ionians sail to the Hellespont and take Byzantium and other cities. Sail to Caria and secure 'the greater part of Caria' as their ally.	Hdt. 5.103
496	Cyprus	Ionians fight the Phoenicians, off Cyprus. Ionians sail off after the Persians are victorious on land.	Hdt. 5.108–116
494	Byzantium	Ionian Histiaios crews 8 triremes from Lesbos and sails to Byzantium where he intercepts ships sailing out of the Pontos.	Hdt. 6.5
494	Lade/Miletus	Battle of Lade. 353 Greek triremes vs 600 Persian ships. Persians victorious.	Hdt. 6.7–15
494	Sicily	Dionysius of Phocaea sails to Sicily and becomes a '*leistes*', but never attacking the ships of the Hellenes.	Hdt. 6.17
490	Attika	Aeginetans ambush and seize Athenian ship carrying religious and political officials.	Hdt. 6.87
490	Aegina	Athens buys 20 ships from Corinth, sails to Aegina with a force of 70 ships. Athens wins sea battle; defeated in a second sea battle.	Hdt. 6.89–93
490	Aegina/Attika	Aiginetan exiles settled by Athens at Cape Sounion. From there, they launch raids against Aegina.	Hdt. 6.90
490	Paros	Athenian leader, Miltiades, with 70 ships besieges island of Paros, but fails.	Hdt. 6.132–135
496	Lemnos	Miltiades conquers the island of Lemnos.	Hdt. 6.137–140
480	Sicily	Gelon of Syracuse readying force to sail to Greece and aid in their defence against Persia.	Diod. 11.26.4–5
480	Thessaly	Combined naval/land force goes north to defend the pass at Tempe. Navy acts as a 'covering force'. No contact made.	Hdt. 7.173

(continued)

Year	Area/location	Notes	Reference
480	Artemision	Combined naval/land force defends Artemision and Thermopylae. Greek navy holds off Persian force, retreats after Greek defeat on land.	Hdt. 7.175–8.21
480	Salamis	Battle of Salamis. Greeks win decisive victory.	Hdt. 8.84–96
480	Aegean	Greek fleet begins pursuit of defeated Persian fleet towards the Hellespont. Decides against destroying Hellespontine bridges.	Hdt. 8.108
480	Andros	Greek fleet besieges island of Andros, having demanded money and been refused.	Hdt. 8.111
479	Samos/Mycale	Greek fleet pursues Persians, who decline battle. Persians land at Mycale and are defeated in battle.	Hdt. 9.90–106
479	Hellespont	Greek fleet sails to Hellespont. Peloponnesians retreat, but Athenians stay and besiege Sestos.	Hdt. 9.114–118
478	Hellespont	Pausanias leads 20 Peloponnesian, 30 Athenian, and number of allied ships, and subdues most of Cyprus; then takes Byzantium from the Persians.	Thuc. 1.94
474	Italy	Cumae in Italy asks Hieron of Syracuse for aid against the Tyrrhenians, who were rulers of the sea at that time. Tyrrhenians defeated in a great naval battle.	Diod. 11.51.1–2
476–467	Aegean	Delian league takes Eion, Skyros, and Carystos on Euboea, and retake Naxos after a revolt.	Thuc. 1.98
467(?)	Eurymedon River	Athenians win decisive victory over Persians at Eurymedon River. Entire Phoenician fleet of 200 ships destroyed.	Thuc. 1.100.1
466	Syracuse	Thrasybulus attempts to gain tyranny in Syracuse; defeated in a battle and loses a number of triremes.	Diod. 11.68.3
465?	Thasos	Thasos revolts. Athenians win a naval battle and eventually take Thasos.	Thuc. 1.100.2–1.101
461	Syracuse	Syracusans fighting against mercenaries in revolt, defeat the rebels in battle.	Diod. 11.76.1
460–454(?)	Cyprus/Egypt	200 Athenian and allied ships on an expedition in Cyprus agree to aid in Egyptian revolt.	Thuc. 1.104

(continued)

Year	Area/location	Notes	Reference
459(?)	Troezen	Athenian amphibious assault on Halieis defeated. Afterwards, Athenians defeat Peloponnesian fleet, off Cecryphalia.	Thuc. 1.105.1
458?	Aegina	Athenians defeat Aeginetans and take 70 ships. Athens lands force and begins siege.	Thuc. 1.105.2
457	Peloponnese	Athenians, under Tolmides, sail around the Peloponnese, attacking Gythion, taking Chalcis, and attacking and defeating Sikyon.	Thuc. 1.108.5
454(?)	Egypt	Persians defeat Egyptian and Athenian forces; relief force of 50 Athenian ships also defeated in battle.	Thuc. 1.109–110
454	Sicyon	Pericles leads amphibious force and defeats Sicyons; besieges Oeniadai but fails to take it.	Thuc. 1.111.2–3; Plut. *Per*. 19.2–3
451	Cyprus/Egypt	200 Athenian and allied vessels sail to Cyprus. 60, detached to Egypt. Remaining force defeats Phoenicians, Cyprians, and Cilicians by land and sea.	Thuc. 1.112.1–4
444	Sth. Italy	Thurii and Tarantum engaged in constant raiding and skirmishing by land and sea. Inconclusive.	Diod. 12.23.2
441/0	Samos	44 Athenian ships under Pericles defeat 70 Samian vessels – 20 transports – off the island of Tragia. 16 other Athenian ships on scouting mission.	Thuc. 1.116.1
441–440	Samos	Athenians reinforced by 40 Athenian and 25 Chian and Lesbian vessels, and conduct successful 9-month siege of Samos.	Thuc. 1.116.2–1.117
435	Epidamnus	Corcyraeans send 25 ships to Epidamnus and make demands. Upon being refused, commence operations with 40 ships.	Thuc. 1.26.3–4
435	Epidamnus	Corinthians and allies with 75 ships sail to Epidamnus. Defeated by 80 Corcyraean ships as remaining 40 ships continue siege of Epidamnus.	Thuc. 1.27–29
435	Ionian Gulf	Corcyraeans ravage Leucas and Cyllene. Corinthians rebuild fleet and sail to Actium to protect and reassure their allies.	Thuc. 1.30

(continued)

Year	Area/location	Notes	Reference
432	Macedonia	30 Athenian ships operating in the area.	Thuc. 1.59
431	Peloponnese	100 Athenian ships, later joined by 50 ships from Corcyra.	Thuc. 2.23; 2.25; 2.30
431	Locris	30 Athenian ships; concurrent attack on the Peloponnese above.	Thuc. 2.26
430	Peloponnese	Pericles leads 100 Athenian ships, with horse transports plus 50 ships from Chios and Lesbos. They attack five different cities in the Peloponnese.	Thuc 2.56
430	Zakynthos	Sp. and unnamed allies with 100 ships.	Thuc. 2.66
430/429	Naupactus	20 Athenian ships intercept trade.	Thuc. 2.69
429	Akarnania	Sp. combined land and sea attack against Akarnania, with hope of subsequently taking the islands of Zakynthos and Cephalonia, and hindering Athenian movements in the area.	Thuc. 2.80
429	Crisaian Gulf	Phormio's ships intercept large contingent of Corinthian ships carrying troops and routs them.	Thuc. 2.83–5
429	Naupactus	Vastly superior Sp. fleet challenges Athenian fleet stationed at Naupactus. Athens victorious.	Thuc. 2.86–92
429/8	Salamis	Spartans with 40 vessels plan attack on the Piraeus; attack island of Salamis instead.	Thuc. 2.94–5
428	Mytilene/Lesbos	Athenians blockade Mytilene in revolt.	Thuc. 3.6
428	Peloponnese	Athenians with 30 ships raid along the coast.	Thuc. 3.7
428	Peloponnese	100 Athenian ships attack Peloponnese, while also maintaining siege of Mytilene as a demonstration of power, explicitly aimed at Sp., but implicitly at Athenian Allies considering revolt.	Thuc. 3.16
427	Eastern Aegean	Sparta sends 42 ships to relieve Mytilene. City surrenders before they reach it. Spartan Admiral attacks several different places in the eastern Aegean.	Thuc. 3.26–33

(continued)

Year	Area/location	Notes	Reference
427	Minoa/Megara	Athenians captures and garrisons island to blockade Megara and prevent the sailing out of Sp. privateers.	Thuc. 3.51
427	Corcyra	Corcyraeans launch disorganised attack against Sparta and are routed. Spartans flee when Athenian relief fleet arrives.	Thuc. 3.77–81
427/6	Sicily	Athenians and 30 Rhegian ships attack Aeolian islands in the winter.	Thuc. 3.88
426	Melos	Athenians, with 60 ships, attack the island since it would not submit to the Athenian alliance.	Thuc. 3.91
426	Peloponnese	Concurrent with the attack on Melos, 30 ships attack the Peloponnese; reinforced by 15 Corcyraean ships.	Thuc. 3.91; 3.94
426	Locris/Italy	Athenian ships in Sicily take fort on the river Halex.	Thuc. 3.99
426	Aetolia	Demosthenes, with allies, establishes base at Oineion.	Thuc. 3.95–98
426	Naupactus	Demosthenes, with 1,000 hoplites, reinforces the city of Naupactus by sea and saves it.	Thuc. 3.102
426/5	Peloponnese	20 Athenian ships said to be cruising off Peloponnese; no further details given.	Thuc. 3.105
426/5	Himera/Sicily	Athens attacks Himera in Sicily as well as the Aeolian islands. 40 additional ships sent by Athenian to aid the Sicilian expedition and bring it to an end.	Thuc. 3.115
425	Messana/Sicily	Force from Syracuse and Locris reinforces Messana, at their invitation. Messana revolts from Athens; improves strategic position and enables them to control Strait of Messana.	Thuc. 4.1
425	Corcyra	Both sides send ships to Corcyra to influence events there. Athenians given permission to use fleet against the coast of the Peloponnese, enroute.	Thuc. 4.2–3
425	Pylos/Messenia	Amphibious campaign by both sides around Pylos and the island of Sphacteria. Sparta offers peace terms, Athens refuses. Athenian victory.	Thuc. 4.3–41

(continued)

Year	Area/location	Notes	Reference
425	Sicily	Syracuse and their allies attack Rhegium. Naval battle, Athens victorious.	Thuc. 4.24–25
425	Corinth/Argolid	80 Athenian ships attack Corinthian territory and the Argolid.	Thuc. 4.42–45
424	Kythera	60 Athenian Ships attack and garrison the island of Kythera.	Thuc. 4.53–54
424	Megara	Athenians land on the island of Minoa, off Megara, and launch combined land and sea attack.	Thuc. 4.67
424/3	Boiotia	40 Athenian ships plan attack on the city of Siphas; plan betrayed and operation cancelled. Ships then unsuccessfully raid Sicyonian coast.	Thuc. 4.76–77, 89, 101.3
424/3	Chalcidice	Seven Athenian ships under the command of Thucydides fail to relieve city of Amphipolis in time from Sp. attack. Athenians save the city of Eion.	Thuc. 4.104–107
423	Chalcidice	40 Athenian and 10 Chian ships attack and take the city of Mende.	Thuc. 4.129
422	Thrace	30 Athenian ships attack Scione and Torone.	Thuc. 5.2
419/8	Argolid	Spartans elude Athenian patrols and transport 300 men to the city of Epidaurus.	Thuc. 5.56
416	Melos	38 Athenian and allied ships attack the island of Melos (scene of the Melian dialogue)	Thuc. 5.84
415	The Argolid	30 Athenian ships and a force of Argives besiege Orneai.	Thuc. 6.7.2
415	Macedonia	Concurrent with the above operation, Athenians and Macedonian allies sail to Macedonia and attack the country of Perdikkas.	Thuc. 6.7.3–4
415	Italy/Sicily	Athens launches the Sicilian expedition. Musters in Corcyra and sails for Rhegium in Italy.	Thuc. 6.42–43
415	Syracuse	Athenians raid Syracuse territory.	Thuc. 6.52
415	Sicily	Athenian fleet splits into two contingents, sail around Sicily, and conduct limited raiding.	Thuc. 6.62

(continued)

Year	Area/location	Notes	Reference
415/4	Syracuse	Athenians launch first attack on the city of Syracuse by land and sea.	Thuc. 6.65
414	Sicily	Athenians raid along the coast near Katana.	Thuc. 6.94
414	Syracuse	Athenians launch second attack on Syracuse.	Thuc. 6.97
414	Peloponnese	30 Athenian ships go to the relief of Argos, breaking the treaty between Sparta and Athens.	Thuc. 6.105
414	Italy	20 Athenian ships sent to interdict Corinthian ships sailing for Syracuse.	Thuc. 7.4.7
414	Syracuse	12 Peloponnesian ships arrive in Syracuse to reinforce the city.	Thuc. 7.7
414	Amphipolis	Athenians blockade Amphipolis.	Thuc. 7.9
414/3	Naupactus	Athenians attempt to interdict Corinthian merchant vessels sailing to Sicily. Corinthians send escorts and successfully prevent the Athenians from attacking the transports.	Thuc. 7.17; 7.19.5
413	Peloponnese	60 Athenian ships attack the Peloponnese enroute to Sicily. Concurrent with Argos operation.	Thuc. 7.20
413	Syracuse	First naval battle in the Great Harbour of Syracuse. Athens victorious at sea but Syracusans capture important land fortification.	Thuc, 7.22–24
413	Italy	11 Syracusan ships attack and destroy Athenian transports in Italy.	Thuc. 7.25.1–2
413	Sicily	Athenian ships near Megara and Sicily fail to intercept all but one ship bound for Syracuse.	Thuc. 7.25.3–5
413	Peloponnese	Athenians fortify an isthmus in Laconia, opposite the island of Cythera.	Thuc. 7.26
413	Thebes	Mercenaries from Thrace, sent back to their homeland by Athens, raid along the coast in Thebes on the return journey.	Thuc. 7.27, 29
413	Naupactus	Athens and Corinth engage in battle near Naupactus.	Thuc. 7.34

(continued)

Year	Area/location	Notes	Reference
413	Syracuse	Second naval battle in the Great Harbour of Syracuse.	Thuc. 7.36–41
413	Syracuse	Third naval battle in the Great Harbour of Syracuse.	Thuc. 7.52–55
413	Syracuse	Fourth naval battle in the Great Harbour of Syracuse. Athens finally defeated.	Thuc. 7.70–72
413/2	Attika	Athenians fortify and garrison ships at Cape Sounion to protect grain ships.	Thuc. 8.4
412	Saronic Gulf	Athenian intercept and destroy Spartan ships bound for Chios.	Thuc. 8.10–11
412	Leucas	Athenians intercept Spartan ships sailing back from Sicily.	Thuc. 8.13
412	Aegean	Athenians intercept and take small Chian squadron.	Thuc. 8.19
412	Speiraios	Spartans break Athenian blockade and sail out.	Thuc. 8.20
412	Lesbos	Chians and Sparta incite revolt in Methymna and Mytilene on Lesbos.	Thuc. 8.22
412	Lesbos	Athenian counterattack puts down revolt on Lesbos.	Thuc. 8.23
412	Miletus	Athenian forces blockading Miletus, attack the surrounding territory.	Thuc. 8.24
412	Chios	Athenians defeat and blockade the Chians.	Thuc. 8.24
412	Miletus	48 Athenian ships sail to Miletus and are victorious; subsequently retire after declining battle with 55 Spartan ships.	Thuc. 8.25–27
412/1	Miletus	Athenian reinforcements allow for renewed blockade of Miletus and to conduct amphibious ops.	Thuc. 8.30
412/1	Chios	Spartan forces sail from Chios and unsuccessfully raid along the Asian coast of Ionia.	Thuc. 8.31
412/1	Chios	Small Athenian forces intercepts and unsuccessfully pursues Chian ships.	Thuc. 8.34
412/1	Cnidos	Spartans intercept merchant ships near Cnidos. Athenian counterattack and defeat the Spartan ships.	Thuc. 8.35

(continued)

Year	Area/location	Notes	Reference
412/1	Aegean	Spartan ships sail to Melos and defeat small Athenian force. Second Spartan force raids on its way to reinforce them. Another battle, off Syme; both sides take losses.	Thuc. 8.39–42
412/1	Rhodes	94 Spartan ships sail to Rhodes and convince two cities of Lindos and Ielusos to revolt from Athens.	Thuc. 8.44
412/1	Rhodes	Athenians raid Rhodes.	Thuc. 8.55
412/1	Chios	Chians unsuccessfully attempt to break the Athenian blockade.	Thuc. 8.61
411	Samos	Spartans sail to Samos to engage the Athenian in battle, refuse when they learn of Athenian reinforcements.	Thuc. 8.79
411	Hellespont	Spartans sail to Byzantium and induce it to revolt. Small naval battle.	Thuc. 8.80
411	Euboea	Large naval battle, off Eretria; Sparta win decisive victory. Euboea revolts from Athens.	Thuc. 8.94–96
411	Lesbos	Athenians attack city of Eresos.	Thuc. 8.100
411	Hellespont	Battle at the entrance to the Hellespont. Sparta victorious.	Thuc. 8.102
411	Hellespont	Athenians win decisive victory over Spartans at Cynossema.	Thuc. 8.103–106
411	(Unknown)	Spartans defeat Athenians in a naval battle. Location unknown.	Xen. *Hell*. 1.1.1
411	Hellespont	Two battles fought between Spartans and Athenians near Rhoiteion and Abydos.	Xen. *Hell*. 1.1.2–7
411	Hellespont	40 Athenian ships levying money.	Xen. *Hell*. 1.1.8
410	Hellespont	Two groups of 20 ships levying money.	Xen. *Hell*. 1.1.12
410	Cyzicus	Athenians defeat Spartans in a battle, off Cyzicus. Subsequently, levy much money.	Xen. *Hell*. 1.1.16–21
410	Hellespont	Athenians intercepts and destroy three Spartan transports.	Xen. *Hell*. 1.1.36

(continued)

Year	Area/location	Notes	Reference
409	Lydia	Athenians attack the land around Pygela and other places in Lydia.	Xen. *Hell*. 1.2.1–5
409	Pylos	Spartans' land and sea attacks; retake Pylos.	Diod. 13.64.5–7
409	Lesbos	Athenians intercept 25 ships from Syracuse near Methymna.	Xen. *Hell*. 1.2.11–13
408	Bosporus	Athenians attack and besiege Byzantium and Chalcedon.	Xen. *Hell*. 1.3.1–22
407	Andros	100 Athenian ships attack and defeat forces of Andros.	Xen. *Hell*. 1.4.21–23
406	Notion	Athens defeated in battle of Notion.	Xen. *Hell*. 1.5.11–14
406	Samos	Athenians on Samos reinforced; raid enemy territory.	Xen. *Hell*. 1.5.18–20
406	Lesbos	Spartans captures Methymna. Defeat Athenians in a battle, off Mytilene, and besiege the city.	Xen. *Hell*. 1.6.12–18
406	Arginousai	Athenians win a decisive victory at the battle of Arginousai.	Xen. *Hell*. 1.6.22–35
406	Sicily	Syracusans intercept Carthaginian invasion force headed for Sicily and capture 15 ships.	Diod. 13.80.5–7
406	Acragas	Syracuse collects allies and goes to the relief of Akragas, under siege by Carthaginians. 30 ships act as a covering force.	Diod. Sic. 13.86.5
406	Acragas	Carthaginians attack and sink eight Syracusan triremes escorting grain ships. Syracusans complacent in convoying their supplies.	Diod. 13.88.3–5
405	Gela	Dionysius sends relief force to Gela, including 50 ships.	Diod. 13.109.1–5
405	Samos	Athenians raid Persian territory.	Xen. *Hell*. 2.1.16
405	Hellespont	Spartans sail to Hellespont to intercept trade.	Xen. *Hell*. 2.1.17
405	Hellespont	Spartans attack and capture Lampsacus.	Xen. *Hell*. 2.1.18–19

(continued)

Year	Area/location	Notes	Reference
405	Hellespont	Battle of Aegospotami. Athenian fleet annihilated.	Xen. *Hell.* 2.1.20–29
405	Saronic Gulf	Spartans liberate Aegina and raid Salamis. Spartans then blockades Athens by sea.	Xen. *Hell.* 2.2.9
404	Samos	Lysandros and the Spartans besiege and take Samos.	Xen. *Hell.* 2.3.6
404	Syracuse	Syracusan rebels sent to Messana and Rhegium; receive support of 80 triremes to help blockade Dionysius.	Diod. 14.8.2
403	Athens	Lysandros besieges the Piraeus by land and his brother Libys blockades the port by sea.	Xen. *Hell.* 2.4.28–29
401	Asia	Sparta sends a fleet to the Persian Cyrus. Unknown numbers.	Xen. *Hell.* 3.1.1
397	Motye	Dionysius leaves his admiral, Leptines, with the naval force, in command of the siege of Motye.	Diod. 14.48.3–4
397	Motye	Battle between Carthaginian and Syracusan forces, as skirmishing increases the Carthaginians refuses battle.	Diod. 14.50.1–4
397	Sth. Sicily	Syracusan admiral, Leptines, keeps watch for Carthaginian reinforcements sailing to Sicily. Also besieges Aegesta and Entella.	Diod. 14.53.5;54.4
396	Sth. Sicily	Leptines sails out with 30 triremes and intercepts Carthaginian transports, sinking 50 before wind allows others to escape.	Diod. 14.55.2
396	Catana	Battle between Carthaginian and Syracusan forces. Devolves into boarding action, Greeks defeated and pursued, losing 100 ships.	Diod. 14.59.5–60.7
396	Syracuse	Dionysius and Leptines sail out with warships to escort supply vessels.	Diod. 14.64.1
396	Syracuse	Whist Dionysius and Leptines are on escort mission, remaining Syracusan forces set out with five ships and seize a supply ship. Carthaginians sail out with 40 ships and lose 24 in the subsequent naval battle.	Diod. 14.64.1–2

(continued)

Year	Area/location	Notes	Reference
394	Cnidos	Spartan fleet defeated in battle, off Cnidos, and Spartan admiral Peisander killed.	Xen. *Hell.* 4.3.10–12
393	Corinthian Gulf	Using Persian money, Corinth builds a fleet and confronts Sparta in the Corinthian Gulf, but is defeated.	Xen. *Hell.* 4.8.10–11
393	Rhegium	Dionysius crews 100 triremes and launches surprise night attack on Rhegium. Fails to take city, ravages the land and sails home.	Diod. 14.90.4–7
391	Argos	Combined Spartan naval/land force attacks Corinth and (approx.) 12 Spartan triremes seize ships and the dockyards.	Xen. *Hell.* 4.4.19
389	Acarnania	Athenian squadron, based out of Oiniadai, blockading entrance to the Corinthian Gulf, forcing Spartans to cross the gulf at Rhion.	Xen. *Hell.* 4.6.14
390	Samos/Rhodes	Teleutias encounters 10 Athenian triremes that were enroute to Cyprus and captures them all.	Xen. *Hell.* 4.8.24
390	Hellespont	Athenians send 40 ships to the Hellespont and extend their influence, set up democracy in Byzantium. Collect tax from ships sailing in from the Black Sea.	Xen. *Hell.* 4.8.25–27
390	Rhegium	Dionysius sets out against Rhegium with 120 ships. Italian Greeks send 60 ships to help Rhegium. Battle ensues but storm forces Dionysius to flee, losing 7 ships.	Diod. 14.100.1–5
389	Lipari Islands	30 Syracusan ships sail to Lipari islands and take 10 ships from Rhegium.	Diod. 14.103.2–3
389	Lesbos	Athenians sail to Lesbos and land a force which defeats the Spartans.	Xen. *Hell.* 4.8.28–29
389	Hellespont	Spartans, with three triremes, attack Abydos and gather three more ships. Then, attempt to capture boats of the Athenians and their allies.	Xen. *Hell.* 4.8.33
389	Hellespont	Athenians counter the above Spartan force with eight ships. Athenians utilise ruse involving his ships, sailing off as if going to collect tribute, as was the normal practice.	Xen. *Hell.* 4.8.34–35

(continued)

Year	Area/location	Notes	Reference
389(?)	Aegina	Reciprocal raiding between Athens and Aegina. Athenian naval squadron driven off.	Xen. *Hell*. 5.1.1–2
389	Aegina	Athenians on Aegina blockaded by 12 Spartan triremes. Athenians outfit ships and rescue the force trapped on Aegina.	Xen. *Hell*. 5.1.5
388	Tenedos/Abydos	Spartans ravage Tenedos and extract money. Sail to Abydos in the Hellespont, where their 25 ships are blockaded by 32 Athenian ships.	Xen *Hell*. 5.1.6–7
388	Aegina/Attika	Naval battle by moonlight as Athenians sail back into the Piraeus and lose four ships.	Xen. *Hell*. 5.1.8–9
388	Aegina	Ten Athenian triremes, with 800 peltasts, land on Aegina and defeat the Spartans on land.	Xen. *Hell*. 5.1.10–12
387	Attika	Spartans sail by night and raid Piraeus at dawn. 3–4 triremes escort the captured merchant vessels to Aegina. Remaining ships stay and interdict Athenian shipping.	Xen. *Hell*. 5.1.19–24
387	Abydos	12 Spartan ships ambush and capture the relief force of eight Athenian ships sailing from Thrace to the Hellespont.	Xen. *Hell*. 5.1.26–27
387	Hellespont	Spartan Antalcidas' force 80 triremes, including 20 from Syracuse; establishes sea control in Hellespont. Interdicts Athenian trade from the Pontos.	Xen. *Hell*. 5.1.28
381	Pharos	'Barbarians' attack colony of Pharos. Governor of Lissus sails with triremes and intercepts the light craft of the Illyrians.	Diod. 15.14.1–2
381	Tyrrhenia	Dionysius, in need of money, sets out to plunder a rich temple in Tyrrhenia under the auspices of suppressing piracy.	Diod. 15.14.3–4
377	Pagasai/Oreos	Thebans, short of grain, send two triremes to Pagasai for grain. Spartans, with three triremes, ambush and capture triremes and grain.	Xen. *Hell*. 5.4.56
377/6	Aegean	Spartans plan attack on Athenian grain ships. Athenians learn of this and successfully escort the grain back to Athens.	Diod. 15.34.3–5

(continued)

Year	Area/location	Notes	Reference
376	Aegean	Spartan fleet of 60 ships preventing grain ships from reaching Athens. Athenians man fleet and defeat the Spartans, allowing grain ships into the city.	Xen. *Hell*. 5.4.61
375	Peloponnese	With Theban encouragement, Athenians open second front on Spartans by raiding the Peloponnese with 60 ships.	Xen. *Hell*. 5.4.62–63
375	Alyzeia	55 Spartan ships engage 60 Athenian ships and are defeated. Athenian fleet then grows to 70 ships.	Xen. *Hell*. 5.4.65–66
375–373	Attika	Attica still subject to raids from Aegina, wearing them down.	Xen. *Hell*. 6.2.1
373	Corcyra	60 ships from Sparta and their allies attack Corcyra and blockade the port.	Xen. *Hell*. 6.2.5–7
373	Cephalonia/Corcyra	Athenian force of 70 ships under Iphikrates raid Cephalonia; then, ambush and capture 10 ships from Syracuse.	Xen. *Hell*. 6.2.33–35
373	Corcyra	Spartans, worried by Athenian fleet, evacuate Corcyra, taking slaves and valuables.	Xen. *Hell*. 6.2.24–26
372	Cephalonia & Peloponnese	Taking over a fleet of 90 Corcyraean ships, Iphicrates coerces money from Cephalonia. Raids Spartan and allied territory.	Xen. *Hell*. 6.2.38
369	Corinth	20+ triremes, with Celtic and Iberian infantry, from Dionysius of Syracuse come to the aid of Sparta and allies fighting the Thebans. Return to Sicily after much success.	Xen. *Hell*. 7.1.20–22
368	Arcadia	Second force from Dionysius of Syracuse arrives in Sparta and helps Spartans in the campaign in Arkadia.	Xen. *Hell*. 7.1.28
362	Peloponnese	Athenian reinforcements to the Peloponnese avoid Epaminondas' force at Nemea by going by sea.	Xen. *Hell*. 7.5.4–7
368/7	Eryx	Dionysius leaves 130 ships at Eryx and dismisses the remaining 170. Carthaginians attack and are victorious.	Diod. 15.73.3–4

(continued)

Year	Area/location	Notes	Reference
366/5	Samos	Timotheus successfully takes Samos after a 10-month siege.	Isoc. 15.111; Polyain. 3.10.9
364/3	Thrace/Hellespont	Timotheos besieges Torone and Potidaia and relieves Cyzicus, which had been under siege by Theban force.	Diod. 15.81.6
361/0	Cyclades	Alexander, tyrant of Pherai, attacks Cyclades. Athens counterattacks.	Diod. Sic. 15.95.1–2
360/59	Thrace/Macedonia	Athens sends 3,000 hoplites and considerable naval force to oppose Philip, by restoring Argaeos to the throne.	Diod. 16.2.6
358/7	Aegean	Social War. Athens attacks Chios.	Diod. 16.7.3–4
357/6	Syracuse	Dionysius, short of grain, raids the countryside, being in control of the sea (but, see below).	Diod. 16.13.3
357/6	Syracuse	Syracusans interdicting supplies bound for Dionysius.	Diod. 16.13.3
356/5	Syracuse	Battle between the Syracusan force of 60 ships and 60 ships of Dionysius. Syracusans victorious.	Diod. 16.16.3–4
356/5	Syracuse	Syracusans interdict supplies bound for Dionysius.	Diod. 16.18.4
356/5	Aegean	Social War. Allies sack Imbros and Lemnos, and move to Samos.	Diod. 16.21.2
356/5	Hellespont	Social War. Allies and Athens face off at Hellespont. Weather prevents battle.	Diod. 16.21.3
347/6	Corcyra	Iphicrates loitering near Corcyra with a naval force, and seizes Syracusan ship with gold and ivory statues bound for Olympia and Delphi.	Diod. 16.57.2–3
344	Sicily	Corinthian aristocrat Timoleon sails to Sicily with 10 ships, including 7 from Corinth, 2 from Corcyra, and 1 from Leucas.	Plut. *Tim.* 8.5
322	Amorgos	Naval battle at Amorgos between Athens and Macedonians. Athenians outnumbered, and after losing a few ships, retreat, conceding defeat.	Plut. *Mor.* 338a; Demetr. 11.3 FrGH 239b, 9

Diplomatic operations

Year	Area/ location	Notes	Reference
546	Phocaea	Spartans send a pentecontor to Phocaea to warn Cyrus against attacking Hellenic territory.	Hdt. 1.152.2
500/499	Athens/Ionia	Athens sends 20 ships to help the Ionians in their revolt from Persia.	Hdt. 5.97.3
480	Corcyra/ Peloponnese	Corcyraeans send 60 ships to help Greeks at Salamis; claim contrary winds kept them back; possible diplomatic posturing, awaiting battle outcome.	Hdt. 7.168
480	Aegean Islands	Themistocles threatens other islands and extorts money from Carystians and Parians.	Hdt 8.112
479	Delos	Greek fleet of 110 ships assembles at Aegina before the army sails to help the Ionians but refuses to sail further east than Delos out of fear.	Hdt. 8.131–132
479	Sparta	Athenians threaten to sail their fleet away unless the Spartans march north of the isthmus of Corinth to fight. Isthmus indefensible without Athenian fleet.	Hdt. 9.8–11
441/0	Samos	40 Athenian ships sail to Samos and set up a democracy.	Thuc. 1.115.3
440	Byzantium	Byzantium agrees to be subject to Athens as before. No further details given by Thucydides.	Thuc. 1.117.3
436(?)	Black Sea	Pericles, with a large force of ships, conducts a 'flag-showing' expedition through the Aegean and up into the Black Sea.	Plut. *Per.* 20.1
433	Sybota/ Corcyra	Athenian aid Corcyra against Corinth before the outbreak of hostilities. Athens sends 10 ships and three *strategoi*, with orders to avoid breaking the treaty with Sparta; hence diplomatic nature of operation.	Thuc. 1.45–55
430/429	Caria/Lycia	Six Athenian ships sent out to collect tribute and deter *leistai*.	Thuc. 2.69
429	Cydonia/ Crete	20 Athenian ships bound for Naupactus, as reinforcements diverted to Crete to aid Athenian *proxenos* against a neighbour.	Thuc. 2.85
427	Corcyra	Athens sends 12 ships to help arrange a truce in Corcyraean civil war.	Thuc. 3.75
427	Corcyra	Sparta sends 53 ships to Corcyra, both as a diplomatic gesture as well as winning over the island from Ath.	Thuc. 3.76

(continued)

Year	Area/location	Notes	Reference
427	Sicily	Athens sends 20 ships to Sicily to aid the city of Leontinoi against Syracuse.	Thuc. 3.86
425/4	Thrace	Athenians collecting allied tribute.	Thuc. 4.50
424	Lesbos	Athenian squadron collecting tribute, diverted to Antandros, Lesbos and defeat Mytilenian rebels.	Thuc. 4.75
416	Argolid	20 Athenian ships take 300 pro-Spartans from Argos to neighbouring islands.	Thuc. 5.84.1
415	Katana/Sicily	60 Athenian ships coast from Rhegium to Naxos then to Katana. Sail to reconnoitre Syracuse. Athenian ships and men bully Katana into accepting them into the city.	Thuc. 6.50–51
413	Argos	30 Athenian ships sail to Argos and demand a troop commitment from the city, in accordance with their treaty.	Thuc. 7.20
412	Chios	Small Spartan fleet persuades Chios to revolt from Athens.	Thuc. 8.12, 14
412	Samos/Teos	Spartan ships sail to Samos and take one vessel, sail to Teos and get the Teians to remain silent.	Thuc. 8.16
412	Miletus	Spartan ships sail to Miletus and incite it to revolt.	Thuc. 8.17
411	Hellespont	Athenians sail against Cyzicus, recover the city and levy money.	Thuc. 8.107
407	Caria	20 Athenian ships levy money in the Cerameios gulf in Caria.	Xen. *Hell.* 1.4.8–9
405	Bosporus	Spartans sail to Byzantium and Chalcedon. The two cities surrender to Sparta.	Xen. *Hell.* 2.2.1–2
405	Lesbos	200 Spartan ships 'order the affairs' of Lesbos. 10 ships sent to Thrace and bring the cities over to the Spartan side.	Xen. *Hell.* 2.2.5–6
404	Aegean	Lysandros appointed admiral and ordered out to set up harmosts throughout the Aegean.	Diod. 10.1
399	Sth. Italy/Sicily	Rhegium, angered by the growing power of Dionysius, sends expeditionary force, which gathers aid from Messana – 50 triremes from Rhegium and 30 from Messana. Force eventually turns back but convinces Dionysius to conclude a peace.	Diod. 14.40.1–7

(continued)

Year	Area/location	Notes	Reference
398	Locri	Dionysius sends lavishly furnished quinquereme to Locri to pick up his new bride-to-be.	Diod. 14.44.7
397	Eryx	People of Eryx awed by Dionysius' forces, including 200 warships and 500 merchant vessels.	Diod. 14.47.7–48.1
396	Syracuse	Spartan admiral, Pharacidas, and 30 warships arrive in Syracuse to aid Dionysius.	Diod. 14.63.4
396	Ephesus	Spartan Agesilaos confronts the Persian satrap, Tissaphernes, demanding autonomy for the Greek cities.	Xen. *Hell.* 3.4.4–5
393	Ionia	Athenian Thrasyboulos sent to Ionia with 40 triremes and collects money from allies. Makes an alliance with two kings of the Thracians.	Diod. 14.94.1–2
391	Rhodes	Fearful of Athenian influence in Rhodes, Sparta crews eight ships and aids Rhodian exiles.	Xen. *Hell.* 4.8.20–22
390	Samos & Rhodes	Spartan Teleutias, with 12 ships, sails for Rhodes. Stop at Samos and obtain (?) ships that were there.	Xen. *Hell.* 4.8.23
375	Corcyra	Athenian fleet sails to Corcyra and brings it under their influence, favourably.	Xen. *Hell.* 5.4.64
365	Sparta	Third force of 12 triremes from Dionysius of Syracuse (the younger) assists Spartans in taking the city of Sellasia (inland Peloponnese city).	Xen. *Hell.* 7.4.12
377/6	Cyclades	Athenian, Chabrias, sails to the Cyclades and wins over Peparethos an Skiathos and some of the islands, formerly subject to Sparta.	Diod. 15.30.5
368/7	Thessaly	Alexandros, tyrant of Pherai, asks for aid from Athens against Thebans. Athens sends 30 ships and 1,000 ships under Autocles. Thebans march home without battle.	Diod. 15.71.3
340/39	Byzantium	Athenians vote that Philip's siege of Byzantium breaks truce and sends large fleet, picking up allies along the way. Philip abandons the siege.	Diod. 16.77.1–2
367	Aegean	Theban navy sent out into the Aegean. Athenians avoid battle.	Diod. 15.78–79

Constabulary operations

Year	Area/location	Notes	Reference
c.540/30s	Athens	In the reign of Peisistratus, the Athenians conducted regular or semi-regular sweeps for pirates in the Saronic Gulf.	Polyaenus 5.14
480	Attika/Salamis	Greek fleet evacuates Athenian personnel and goods from Athens to Salamis before the arrival of the Persian army.	Hdt. 8.40
470	Skyros	Athenians under Cimon supress pirates attacking from Skyros.	Plut. *Kim.* 8.3–5
431	Opous	Ath. fortifies unoccupied island of Atalanta to prevent 'privateer' raids on Locris and Euboea.	Thuc. 2.32
410	Bosporus	Athens establishes 'customs-house' on the Bosporus and taxes vessels sailing into the Pontos.	Xen. *Hell.* 1.1.22
447	Chersonese	Pericles leads an expedition to the Chersonese. Takes 1000 Athenian colonists and builds defences against the 'robber bands' in the area.	Plut. *Per.* 19.1–2
453	Tyrrhenia	Syracusan admiral, Phayllos, sent to put down Tyrrhenian piracy. Takes bribe to leave, and exiled. Apelles replaces him, and sent with 60 triremes.	Diod. 11.88.4–5
409	Himera/Sicily	Syracusans and Himeraeans forced to evacuate Himera. Half the force of triremes present used to evacuate women and children.	Diod. 13.61.4–5
373	Corcyra	Spartans, worried by Athenian fleet, evacuate Corcyra, taking slaves and valuables.	Xen. *Hell.* 6.2.24–26
359/8	Apulia	Dionysius, the Younger, establishes two cities in Apulia to make safe, the route across the Adriatic, from pirate attacks.	Diod. 16.5.3
357/6	Adriatic	Syracusan Philistus recalled to Syracuse by Dionysius. Had been cruising the Adriatic – anti-piracy.	Diod. 16.11.3
342	Halonnesos	Pirate Sostratos expelled from the island by Philip.	Dem. 7.14–16
325/4	Adriatic	Athenians set up colony to protect trade against 'Etruscan' pirates.	IG II2 – 1629

Bibliography

Ancient sources

The following is a list of ancient sources used throughout this work, though by no means exhaustive. It is a list of the works themselves, and in many cases, there are numerous versions and translations available, and sometimes with different, modern names given for their works. The most common names are given below. Many of these works are available online at such places as the Loeb Classical Library. Some of the texts, as well as some commentaries, are listed in the 'Modern sources' section of the Bibliography.

Historical works

Diodorus Siculus, 'Bibliotheca Historica'.
Herodotus, *A History of My Times*.
Thucydides, *History of the Peloponnesian War*.
Xenophon, *Hellenica; The Anabasis; Oeconomicus; Poroi (Ways and Means)*.
(Unknown author, fragmentary) *The Hellenica Oxyrhynchia*.

Athenian law court speeches

Antiphon.
Demosthenes, law court speeches and speeches given to the Athenian Assembly. (N.B.: Many of the speeches that have been attributed to Demosthenes have now been assessed as works of different authors. In this case, convention is to list this as [Dem.])
Lysias.

Philosophers

Aristotle, *The Athenian Constitution; Meteorologica; Politics; Poems; Testimonia*.
Isocrates.
Plato, *Critias; Laws; Phaedrus; The Republic; Timaeus*.

Playwrights

Aeschylus (Tragedy)
Aristophanes (Old Comedy)
Euripides (Tragedy)
Sophocles (Tragedy)

Poets and other works

Apollonius of Rhodes, *Argonautica*.
Hesiod, *Works and Days*.
Homer, *Iliad; Odyssey*.
The 'Old Oligarch', *Constitution of the Athenians*.
Pausanias, *Description of Greece*.
Pindar, *Odes*.
Plutarch, *Parallel Lives: Alcibiades; Cimon; Demosthenes; Lysander; Nicias; Pericles; Philopoemen; Themistocles; Theseus*.
Polyaenus, *On Stratagems*.
Theophrastus, *Characters*.
Vegetius, *Concerning Military Matters*.

Modern sources

Abulafia, David. *The Great Sea. A Human History of the Mediterranean*. Allen Lane, London: 2011.
Allmand, Christopher. *The De Re Militari of Vegetius. The Reception, Transmission and Legacy of a Roman Text in the Middle Ages*. Cambridge University Press, New York: 2011.
The American Practical Navigator. An Epitome of Navigation. Originally by Samuel Bowditch, prepared and published by the National Imagery and Mapping Agency, Bethesda Maryland: 2002.
Amit, M. *Athens and the Sea: A study in Athenian Sea-Power*. Latomus, Bruxelles: 1965.
Andrewes, Antony. 'The Arginousai Trial', *Phoenix*, Vol. 28, No. 1 (1974), pp. 112–122.
Aperghis, Gerassimos. 'Athenian Mines, Coins and Triremes', *Historia: Zeitschrift für alte Geschichte*, Vol. 62, No. 1 (2013), pp. 1–24.
Ashton, N.G. 'The Naumachia near Amorgos in 322 B.C.', *The Annual of the British School at Athens*, Vol. 72, (1977), pp. 1–11.
Ashton, N.G. 'The Lamian War – stat magni nominis umbra', *The Journal of Hellenic Studies*, Vol. 104, (1984), pp. 152–157.
Asmonti, Luca. 'The Arginusae Trial, the Changing Role of Strategoi and the Relationship Between Demos and Military Leadership in Late-Fifth Century Athens', *Bulletin of the Institute of Classical Studies*, Vol. 49, (2006), pp. 1–21.
Asmonti, Luca. *Conon the Athenian. Warfare and Politics in the Aegean, 414–386 B.C.* Franz Steiner Verlag, Stuttgart: 2015.
Australian Maritime Doctrine, published by the Sea Power Centre – Australia, Canberra: 2010.
Baika, Kalliopi. 'Sounion', in David Blackman and Boris Rankov (eds.) *Shipsheds of the Ancient Mediterranean*. Cambridge University Press, Cambridge: 2013.
Ball, R. 'The Carians' Place in Diodorus' Thalassocracy List', *The Classical Quarterly*, Vol. 27, No. 02 (1977), pp. 317–322.
Beaulieu, Marie-Claire. *The Sea in the Greek Imagination*. University of Pennsylvania Press, Berlin, Boston: 2015.
Bekker-Nielsen, Tønnes. 'The Technology and Productivity of Ancient Sea Fishing', in Tønnes Bekker-Nielsen (ed.) *Ancient Fishing and Fish Processing in the Black Sea Region*. Aarhus University Press, Aarhus, DNK: 2006.

Beresford, James. *Mnemosyne, Supplements, History and Archaeology of Classical Antiquity. Ancient Sailing Season*. Brill, Leiden, NLD: 2012.
Berkey, David L. 'Why Fortifications Endure. A Case Study of the Walls of Athens during the Classical Period', in V.D. Hanson *Makers of Ancient Strategy: From the Persian Wars to the Fall of Rome*. Princeton University Press, Princeton and Oxford: 2010, pp. 58–92.
Bers, Victor. *Demosthenes, Speeches 50–59*. University of Texas Press, Austin: 2003.
Bilić, Tomislav. 'The Myth of Alpheus and Arethusa and Open-Sea Voyages on the Mediterranean – Stellar Navigation in Antiquity', *The International Journal of Nautical Archaeology*, Vol. 38, No. 1 (2009), pp. 116–132.
Blackman, David, Rankov, Boris, Baika, Kalliopi, Gerding, Henrik and Pakkanen, Jari. *Shipsheds of the Ancient Mediterranean*. Cambridge University Press, New York: 2013.
Blondel, Jaques, Aronson, James and Bodiou, Jean-Yves. *The Mediterranean Region. Biological Diversity in Space and Time (2nd ed.)*. Oxford University Press, Oxfrod: 2010.
Boegehold, Alan L. 'The Date of Theophrastus' Characters', *Transactions and Proceedings of the American Philological Association*, Vol. 90, (1959), pp. 15–19.
Booth, Ken. *Navies and Foreign Policy*. Croom Helm, London: 1977.
Bosworth, A.B. *A Historical Commentary on Arrian's History of Alexander. Volume I. Commentary on Books I-III*. Clarendon Press, Oxford: 1980.
Bosworth, A.B. *A Historical Commentary on Arrian's History of Alexander. Volume II. Commentary on Books IV-V*. Clarendon Press, Oxford: 1995.
Bowie, A.M. (ed.) *Herodotus, Histories, Book VIII*. Cambridge University Press, Cambridge and New York: 2007.
Braswell, Bruce Karl. *A Commentary on the Fourth Pythian Ode of Pindar*. Walter de Gruyter, Berlin, New York: 1988.
Braudel, Fernand. *The Mediterranean and the Mediterranean World in the Age of Philip II*. (trans. Siân Reynolds) University of California Press, Berkley: 1995. Originally published in French as *La Méditerranée et le monde méditerranéen à l'époque de Philippe II* (1972).
Braudel, Fernand. *The Mediterranean in the Ancient World*. Penguin Books, London: 2001.
Bresson, Alain. *The Making of the Ancient Greek Economy. Institutions, Markets, and Growth in the City-States*. (trans. Steven Rendall) Princeton University Press, Princeton and Oxford: 2016. Original French edition published in 2 vols., Armand Colin, c2007 and c2008.
Broodbank, Cyprian. *The Making of the Middle Sea. A History of the Mediterranean from the Beginning to the Emergence of the Classical World*. Thames and Hudson, London: 2013.
Buckler, John. *The Theban Hegemony, 371–362 BC*. Harvard University Press, Cambridge, Massachusetts: 1980.
Buckler, John. *Aegean Greece in the Fourth Century BC*. Brill, Leiden; Boston: 2003.
Burke, Edmund M. 'Athens after the Peloponnesian War: Restoration Efforts and the Role of Maritime Commerce', *Classical Antiquity*, Vol. 9, No. 1 (1990), pp. 1–13.
Burke, Edmund M. 'Finances and the Operation of the Athenian Democracy in the "Lycurgan Era"', *The American Journal of Philology*, Vol. 131, No. 3 (2010), pp. 393–423.
Burn, A.R. 'Greek Sea-Power, 776–540 B.C., and the 'Carian' Entry in the Eusebian Thalassocracy-List', *The Journal of Hellenic Studies*, Vol. 47, Part 2 (1927), pp. 165–177.
Burn, A.R. *Persia and the Greeks. The Defence of the West, c.546–478 B.C.* Edward Arnold (Publishers) Ltd., London: 1962.
BR 45 vol. 1 – Admiralty Manual of Navigation. 1987.
Braswell, Bruce Karl. *A Commentary on the Fourth Pythian Ode of Pindar*. De Gruyter, Berlin and New York: 1988.

Bresson, Alain. *The Making of the Ancient Greek Economy. Institutions, Markets, and Growth in the City-States*. (trans. Steven Rendall) Princeton University Press, Princeton, NJ: 2016.

Brock, Roger. *Greek Political Imagery from Homer to Aristotle*. Bloomsbury, London and New York: 2013.

Cable, James. *The Political Influence of Naval Force in History*. Macmillan Press Ltd., Hampshire and London: 1998.

Cairns, Francis. 'The "Laws of Eretria" ("IG" XII. 9 1273 and 1274): Epigraphic, Legal, Historical, and Political Aspects', *Phoenix*, Vol. 45, No. 4 (1991), pp. 296–313.

Cargill, Jack. *The Second Athenian League. Empire or Free Alliance?* University of California Press, Berkeley and Los Angeles: 1981.

Campbell, Penny. 'A Modern History of the International Legal Definition of Piracy', in Bruce A. Ellerman, Andrew Forbes and David Rosenberg (eds.) *Piracy and Maritime Crime: Historical and Modern Case Studies*. Naval War College Press, Newport, RI: 2010.

Campbell, Peter B. and Koutsouflakis, George. 'Aegean Navigation and the Shipwrecks of Fournoi archipelago in Context', in Stella Demesticha and Lucy Blue (eds.) *Under the Mediterranean I. Studies in Maritime Archaeology*. Sidestone Press, Leiden: 2021.

Carey, Christopher. *Trials from Classical Athens* (2nd ed.). Routledge, London and New York: 2012.

Cartledge, Paul. *Agesilaos and the Crisis of Sparta*. Duckworth, London: 1987.

Casson, Lionel. *Ships and Seamanship in the Ancient World*. Princeton University Press, Princeton: 1971.

Casson, Lionel. *Travel in the Ancient World*. George Allen and Unwin, London: 1974.

Casson, Lionel. 'Review: STARR (C . G.) The Influence of Sea Power on Ancient History', *The Journal of Hellenic Studies*, Vol. 112, (1992), pp. 198–199.

Casson, Lionel. 'A Trireme for Hire (Is. 11.48)', *The Classical Quarterly*, Vol. 45, No. 1 (1995), pp. 241–245.

Castex, Raoul Admiral. *Strategic Theories*. (ed. & trans. Eugenia C. Kiesling) Naval Institute Press, Annapolis, Matyland: 1994.

Caven, Brian. *Dionysius I. War Lord of Sicily*. Yale University Press, New Haven and London: 1990.

Cawkwell, G.L. 'Eubulus', *The Journal of Hellenic Studies*, Vol. 83, (1963), pp. 47–67.

Cawkwell, G.L. 'Athenian Naval Power in the Fourth Century', *The Classical Quarterly*, Vol. 34, No. 2 (1984), pp. 334–345.

Charles, John F. 'The Anatomy of Athenian Sea Power', *The Classical Journal*, Vol. 42, No. 2 (1946), pp. 86–91.

Clausewitz, Carl. *On War*. (trans. Michael Howard and Peter Paret) Oxford University Press, Oxford: 2007. Translation published 1976.

Cohen, Edward E. *Ancient Athenian Maritime Courts*. Princeton University Press, Princeton, New Jersey: 1973.

Chronopoulou, Christina and Mavrakis, A. 'Ancient Greek Drama as an Eyewitness of a Specific Meteorological Phenomenon: Indication of Stability of the Halcyon Days', *Weather, Royal Meteorological Society*, Vol. 69, No. 3 (2014), pp. 66–69.

Constantakopoulou, Christy. *The Dance of the Islands: Insularity, Networks, the Athenian Empire, and the Aegean World*. Oxford University Press, New York: 2007. Access via ANU: https://ebookcentral-proquest-com.virtual.anu.edu.au/lib/anu/detail.action?docID=415851#

Cook, R.M. 'Archaic Greek Trade: Three Conjectures', *The Journal of Hellenic Studies*, Vol. 99, (1979), pp. 152–155.

Corbett, Sir Julian S. *Some Principles of Maritime Strategy*. Reprinted by Dodo Press, UK: 2009. Originally published 1911.

Corbett, Sir Julian S. *England in the Seven Years' War. A Study in Combined Strategy*, 2nd edition. Longmans, Green and Co., London: 1918.

Corner, Sean. 'Transcendent Drinking: The Symposium at Sea Reconsidered', *The Classical Quarterly, New Series*, Vol. 60, No. 2 (2010), pp. 352–380.

Crane, Gregory. 'Power, Prestige, and the Corcyraean Affair in Thucydides 1', *Classical Antiquity*, Vol. 11, No. 1 (1992), pp. 1–27.

Csapo, Eric. 'Parade Abuse, From the Wagons', in C. W. Marshall and George Kovacs (eds.) *No Laughing Matter: Studies in Athenian Comedy*. Bristol Classical Press, London: 2012. pp. 29–43.

Csapo, Eric. 'The Dionysian Parade and the Poetics of Plenitude', in *UCL Houseman Lecture, 20 February 2013*. Booklet published by the UCL Department of Greek and Latin, London: 2013.

Curtis, Robert I. 'Sources for Production and Trade of Greek and Roman Processed Fish', in Tønnes Bekker-Nielsen (ed.) *Ancient Fishing and Fish Processing in the Black Sea Region*. Aarhus University Press, Aarhus, DNK: 2006.

Danzig, Gabriel. 'Why Socrates was Not a Farmer: Xenophon's Oeconomicus as a Philosophical Dialogue', *Greece & Rome*, Vol. 50, No. 1 (2003), pp. 57–76.

Davies, Mark I. 'Sailing, Rowing, And Sporting in One's Cups on the Wine-Dark Sea', in *Athens Comes of Age. From Solon to Salamis*. Princeton University Press, Princeton: 1978.

DeSantis, Marc G. *A Naval History of the Peloponnesian War. Ships, Men and Money in the War at Sea, 431–404 BC*. Pen and Sword Maritime, South Yorkshire: 2017.

de Romilly, Jacqueline. *Thucydides and Athenian Imperialism*. (trans. Philip Thody) Arno Press, New York: 1979. Original French edition, *Thucydides et l'imperialisme athénien*, 1963.

de Romilly, Jacqueline. *The Mind of Thucydides*. (trans. Elizabeth Trapnell Rawlings) Cornell University Press, Ithaca and London: 2012. Original French edition, *Histoire et raison chez Thucydide*, 1967.

de Ste. Croix, G.E.M. *The Origins of the Peloponnesian War*. Duckworth, London: 1972.

de Souza, Philip. 'Chester G. Starr: The Influence of Sea Power on Ancient History (Book Review)', *The Classical Review*, Vol. 40, No. 2 (1990), pp. 506–507.

de Souza, Philip. *Piracy in the Graeco-Roman World*. Cambridge University Press, Cambridge: 1999.

de Souza, Philip. 'The Athenian Maritime Empire of the Fifth Century BC', in Philip de Souza, Pascal Arnaud and Christian Buchet (eds.) *The Sea in History – The Ancient World*. The Boydell Press, Woodbridge: 2017.

de Souza, Philip and Sabin, Philip. 'Battle' in Philip Sabin, Hans van Wees and Michael Whitby (eds.) *The Cambridge History of Greek and Roman Warfare Volume 1: Greece, The Hellenistic World and the Rise of Rome*. Cambridge University Press, Cambridge: 2008. Access via ANU: http://universitypublishingonline.org.virtual.anu.edu.au/cambridge/histories/ebook.jsf?bid=CBO9781139054157

de Wet, B.X. 'The So-called Defensive Policy of Pericles', *Acta Classica*, Vol. 12, (1969), pp. 103–119.

Dougherty, Carol. *The Raft of Odysseus: The Ethnographic Imagination of Homer's Odyssey*. Oxford University Press, Cary USA: 2001.

Eddy, Samuel K. 'Athens' Peacetime Navy in the Age of Pericles', *Greek, Roman and Byzantine Studies*, Vol. 9, No. 2 (1968), pp. 141–156.

Ellerman, A. and Paine, S.C.M. (eds.) *Commerce Raiding. Historical Case Studies, 1755–2009*. Naval War College Press, Newport, RI: 2013.

Ellis, J.R. and Milns, R.D. *The Spectre of Philip: Demosthenes' First Philipic, Olynthiacs and Speech On the Peace; A Study in Historical Evidence*. Sydney University Press, Sydney: 1970.

Engels, Donald W. *Alexander the Great and the Logistics of the Macedonian Army*. University of California Press, Berkley and Los Angeles: 1978.

Fagan, Brian. *Fishing. How the Sea Fed Civilization*. Yale University Press, New Haven and London: 2017.

Fagan, Garrett and Trundle, Matthew (eds.) *New Perspectives on Ancient Warfare*. Brill, Boston: 2010.
Figueira, Thomas J. 'Aegina and the Naval Strategy of the Late Fifth and Early Fourth Centuries', *Rheinisches Museum für Philologie*, Vol. 133, (1990), pp. 15-51.
Finley, M.I. *The Ancient Economy (2nd ed.)*. University of California Press, Berkeley: 1985.
Freedman, Lawrence. *Strategy. A History*. Oxford University Press, New York: 2013.
Frost, Frank J. *Plutarch's Themistocles. A Historical Commentary*. Princeton University Press, Princeton: 1980.
Fuchida, Mitsuo and Okumiya, Masatake. *Midway. The Battle that Doomed Japan, The Japanese Navy's Story*. United States Naval Institute, Annapolis, Maryland: 1955. With introduction by the United States Naval Institute, 1992.
Gabrielsen, Vincent. *Financing the Athenian Fleet. Public Taxation and Social Relations*. The John Hopkins University Press, Baltimore and London: 1994.
Gabrielsen, Vincent. 'Rhodes and the Ptolemaic Kingdom: The Commercial Infrastructure', in Kostas Buraselis, Mary Stefanou and Dorothy J. Thompson (eds.) *The Ptolemies, the Sea and the Nile. Studies in Waterborne Power*. Cambridge University Press, Cambridge: 2013.
Gaddis, John Lewis. *On Grand Strategy*. Penguin Press, New York: 2018.
Gal, David, Saaroni, Hadas and Cvikel, Deborah. 'A New Method for Examining Maritime Mobility of Direct Crossings with Contrary Prevailing Winds in the Mediterranean During Antiquity', *Journal of Archaeological Science*, Vol. 129, (2021), pp. 105369. https://www.sciencedirect.com/science/article/pii/S030544032100039X?via%3Dihub
Gallant, T.W. *A Fisherman's Tale*. Belgian Archaeological Mission in Greece and State University of Gent, Gent: 1985.
Gallo, L., 'Athens and the Pontic Poleis in the Tribute List of 425/4 BC'. In Tsetskhladze, G.R., Atasoy, S., Avram, A., Dönmez, Ş. and Hargrave, J. (eds.), *The Bosporus: Gateway between the Ancient West and East (1st Millennium BC-5th Century AD)*, Oxford, (2013), pp. 159-61.
Garland, Robert. *The Piraeus. From the Fifth to the First Century B.C.* Cornell University Press, Ithaca, New York: 1987.
Garnsey, Peter. *Famine and Food Supply in the Greco-Roman World*. Cambridge University Press, Cambridge: 1988.
Garvie, A.F. *Aeschylus Persae. With Introduction and Commentary*. Oxford University Press, Oxford and New York: 2009.
Gauthier, Philippe. *Un Commentaire Historique des Poroi de Xenophon*. Librairie Droz, Paris: 1976.
Gerding, Henrik. 'Syracuse', in Blackmen, et al. *Shipsheds of the Ancient Mediterranean*. Cambridge University Press, New York: 2013.
Goheen, Robert F. *The Imagery of Sophocles' Antigone. A Study of Poetic Language and Structure*. Princeton University Press, Princeton, New Jersey: 1951.
Gomme, A.W. *A Historical Commentary on Thucydides. Vol. I*. Oxford University Press, London: 1945.
Gomme, A.W. *A Historical Commentary on Thucydides. Vol. III*. Oxford University Press, London: 1956.
Garcia, Gonzalez, Javier, Francisco, de Quiroga, Barja and Lopez, Pedro. 'Neocon Greece: V.D. Hanson's War on History', *International Journal of the Classical Tradition*, Vol. 19, No. 3 (2012), pp. 129-151.
Gordon, Andrew. *The Rules of the Game. Jutland and British Naval Command*. Naval Institute Press, Annapolis, Maryland: 1996.
Grainger, John D. *Hellenistic & Roman Naval Wars 336-31 BC*. Pen & Sword Maritime, South Yorkshire: 2011.
Graninger, Denver. 'Plutarch on the Evacuation of Athens ("Themistocles 10.8-9")', *Hermes*, Vol. 138, Jahrg., H. 3 (2010), pp. 308-317.

Gray, Colin S. *The Leverage of Sea Power. The Strategic Advantage of Navies in War*. The Free Press, New York: 1992.
Green, Peter. *Diodorus Siculus, Books 11–12.37.1: Greek History 480–431 B.C., the Alternative Version*. University of Texas Press, Austin TX: 2006.
Green, Peter. *Diodorus Siculus, the Persian Wars to the Fall of Athens. Books 11–14. 34 (480–401 BCE)*. University of Texas Press, Austin: 2010.
Grove, Eric. *The Future of Sea Power*. Routledge, London: 1990.
Hägg, Robin and Marinatos, Nanno. *The Minoan Thalassocracy. Myth and Reality. Proceedings of the Third International Symposium at the Swedish Institute in Athens, 31 May-5 June, 1982*. Svenska Institutet i Athen, Stockholm: 1984.
Hale, John R. *Lords of the Sea. The Epic Story of the Athenian Navy and the Birth of Democracy*. Penguin, New York: 2009.
Halpern, Paul G. *A Naval History of World War I*. UCL Press, London: 1994.
Hamel, Debra. *The Battle of Arginusae. Victory at Sea and Its Tragic Aftermath in the Final Years of the Peloponnesian War*. Johns Hopkins University Press, Baltimore: 2015.
Hamilton, Charles D. *Sparta's Bitter Victories. Politics and Diplomacy in the Corinthian War*. Cornell University Press, Ithaca and London: 1979.
Hamilton, Charles D. *Agesilaus and the Failure of Spartan Hegemony*. Cornell University Press, Ithaca and London: 1991.
Hammond, N.G.L. *Philip of Macedon*. The John Hopkins University Press, Baltimore: 1994.
Hansen, Mogens Herman. *The Athenian Assembly in the Age of Demosthenes. Structure, Principles and Ideology*. (trans. J.A. Cook) Basil Blackwell, Oxford and New York: 1987.
Hansen, Mogens Herman. *The Athenian Democracy in the Age of Demosthenes. Structure, Principles and Ideology*. (trans. J.A. Cook) Blackwell, Oxford, UK and Cambridge, USA: 1991.
Hansen, Mogens Herman and Nielsen, Thomas Heine. *An Inventory of Archaic and Classical Poleis*. Oxford University Press, Oxford: 2004.
Hanson, Victor Davis. *The Western Way of War. Infantry Battle in Classical Greece, 2nd ed*. University of California Press, Berkley: 2000. Originally published 1989.
Hanson, Victor Davis, *Warfare and Agriculture in Classical Greece*, University of California Press, Berkley: 1998.
Hanson, Victor Davis. *Carnage and Culture. Landmark Battles in the Rise of Western Power*. Anchor Books, New York: 2001.
Hanson, Victor Davis. *A War Like No Other. How the Athenians and Spartans Fought the Peloponnesian War*. Random House, New York: 2005.
Hanson, Victor Davis (ed.) *Makers of Ancient Strategy: From the Persian Wars to the Fall of Rome*. Princeton University Press, Princeton and Oxford: 2010.
Hattendorf, John B. 'What is Maritime Strategy?', Published by the Sea Power Centre – Australia, October 2013. Accessed at: http://www.navy.gov.au/media-room/publications/soundings-papers-october-2013
Hauben, Hans. 'An Athenian Naval Victory in 321 B.C.', *Zeitschrift für Papyrologie und Epigraphik*, Bd. 13, (1974), pp. 61–64.
Hawes, Greta. *Rationalizing Myth in Antiquity*. Oxford University Press, Oxford and New York: 2014.
Herzogenrath-Amelung, Tristan. 'Naval Hoplites. Social Status and Combat Reality of Classical Greek *epibatai*', *Historia*, Vol. 66, No. 1 (2017), pp. 45–64.
Heskel, Julia. *The North Aegean Wars, 371–360 B.C*. Franz Steiner Verlag, Stuttgart: 1997.
Hignett, C. *Xerxes' Invasion of Greece*. Clarendon Press, Oxford: 1963.

Horden, Peregrine and Purcell, Nicholas. *The corrupting sea: a study of Mediterranean history*. Blackwell, Oxford: 2000.

Hornblower, Simon. *A Commentary on Thucydides. Volume I, Books I-III*. Clarendon Press, New York: 1991.

Hornblower, Simon. *A Commentary on Thucydides. Volume II, Books IV-V.24*. Oxford University Press, New York: 1997.

Hornblower, Simon. *A Commentary on Thucydides. Volume III, Books 5.25–8.109*. Oxford University Press, New York: 2008.

Hornblower, Simon. 'The Old Oligarch (Pseudo-Xenophon's *Athenaion Politeia*) and Thucydides. A fourth-century date for the Old Oligarch?', in P. Flensted-Jensen, et al. (eds.) *Polis and Politics. Studies in Ancient Greek History Presented to Mogens Herman Hansen on his Sixtieth Birthday, August 20, 2000*. Museum Tusculanum Press, Copenhagen: 2000.

Jacobsen, Anne Lif Lund. 'The Reliability of Fishing Statistics as a Source for Catches and Fish Stocks in Antiquity', in Tønnes Bekker-Nielsen (ed.) *Ancient Fishing and Fish Processing in the Black Sea Region*. Aarhus University Press, Aarhus, DNK: 2006.

Jeffery, L.H. *Archaic Greece. The City-States c.700–500 B.C.* Methuen & Co., London: 1976.

Jordan, Borimir. *The Athenian Navy in the Classical Period. A Study of Athenian Naval Administration and Military Organization in the Fifth and Fourth Centuries B.C.* University of California Press, Berkeley and Los Angeles: 1975.

Jordan, Borimir. 'The Sicilian Expedition Was a Potemkin Fleet', *The Classical Quarterly*, Vol. 50, No. 1 (2000), pp. 63–79.

Kagan, Donald. *The Outbreak of the Peloponnesian War*. Cornell University Press, New York: 1969.

Kagan, Donald. *The Archidamian War*. Cornell University Press, New York: 1974.

Kagan, Donald. *The Peace of Nicias and the Sicilian Expedition*. Cornell University Press, New York: 1981.

Kagan, Donald. *The Fall of the Athenian Empire*. Cornell University Press, New York: 1987.

Kagan, Donald. 'Athenian Strategy in the Peloponnesian War', in Williamson Murray, et al. (eds.) *The Making of Strategy. Rulers, States, and War*. Cambridge University Press, New York: 1994.

Kagan, Donald. *Thucydides. The Reinvention of History*. Viking Penguin, New York: 2009.

Kallet-Marx, Lisa. *Money, Expense, and Naval Power in Thucydides History 1–5.24*. University of California Press, Berkeley and Los Angeles: 1993.

Kapellos, Aggelos. 'Adeimantos at Aegospotami: Innocent or Guilty?', *Historia: Zeitschrift für Alte Geschichte*, Bd. 58, H. 3 (2009), pp. 257–275.

Keen, Antony G. 'Athenian Campaigns in Caria and Lykia during the Peloponnesian War', *The Journal of Hellenic Studies*, Vol. 113, (1993), pp. 152–157.

Keen, Antony G. 'Grain for Athens: The Importance of the Hellespontine Route in Athenian Foreign Policy Before the Peloponnesian War', in G.J. Oliver, R. Brock, T.J. Cornell and S. Hodkinson (eds.) *The Sea in Antiquity*. BAR International Series 899. Archaeopress, Oxford: 2000.

Kelly, Thomas. 'Thucydides and Spartan Strategy in the Archidamian War', *The American Historical Review*, Vol. 87, No. 1 (1982), pp. 25–54.

Kelly, Justin and Brennan, Michael. 'Alien: How Operational Art Devoured Strategy,' Published by the Strategic Studies Institute, U.S. Army War College, 2009. Accessed at: www.strategicstudiesinstitute.army.mil/pubs/display.cfm?pubID=939

Kirkwood, G.M. 'Eteocles Oiakostrophos', *Phoenix*, (*Studies Presented to G. M. A. Grube on the Occasion of His Seventieth Birthday*), Vol. 23, No. 1 (1969), pp. 9–25.

Kirshner, Jonathon. 'Handle Him with Care: The Importance of Getting Thucydides Right', *Security Studies*, Vol. 28, No. 1 (10 September 2018), pp. 1–24.

Knight, Donald W. 'Thucydides and the War Strategy of Pericles', *Mnemosyne*, Fourth Series 23, Fasc. 2 (1970), pp. 150–161.
Kopp, H. 'The "Rule of the Sea": Thucydidean Concept or Periclean Utopia?', in C.R. Thauer and C. Wendt (eds.) *Thucydides and Political Order*. Palgrave Macmillan, New York: 2016.
Kowalski, Jean-Marie, Claramunt, Christophe and Zucker, Arnaud. 'Thalassographein: Representing Maritime Spaces in Ancient Greece', in Stephan Winter, Matt Duckham, Lars Kulik and Ben Kuipers (eds.) *Spatial Information Theory. 8th International Conference, COSIT 2007, Melbourne, Australiia, September 19–23, 2007. Proceedings*. Springer, Berlin Heidelberg: 2007.
Kyriakou, Poulheria. *The past in Aeschylus and Sophocles*. De Gruyter, Berlin and Boston: 2011.
Lambert, Andrew. *Seapower States*. Yale University Press, New Haven and London: 2018.
Larson, Jennifer Lynn. *Ancient Greek cults: a guide*. Routledge, New York: 2007.
Lazenby, J.F. *The Defence of Greece 490–479 BC*. Aris & Phillips, Oxford: 1993.
Lazenby, J.F. *The Peloponnesian War. A Military Study*. Routledge, London: 2004.
Lendon, J.E. *Soldiers and Ghosts. A History of Battle in Classical Antiquity*. Yale University Press, New Haven: 2005.
Lendon, J.E. 'Athens and Sparta and the Coming of the Peloponnesian War', in Loren J Samons II (ed.) *The Cambridge Companion to The Age of Pericles*. Cambridge University Press, Cambridge: 2007.
Lentini, Maria Costanza, David, Blackman and Pakkanen, Jari. 'The Shipsheds of Sicilian Naxos: A Second Preliminary Report (2003–6)', *The Annual of the British School at Athens*, Vol. 103, (2008), pp. 299–366.
Lonsdale, David J. *Alexander the Great. Lessons in Strategy*. Routledge, London and New York: 2007.
Loraux, Nicole. *The Invention of Athens. The Funeral Oration in the Classical City*. (trans. Alan Sheridan) Zone Books, New York: 2006. Originally Published in French as *L'Invention d'Athènes. Histoire de l'oraison funèbre dans la cité Classique*, 1981.
Loraux, Nicole. 'Thucydides is not a Colleague', in John Marincola (ed.) *Greek and Roman Historiography*. Oxford University Press, Oxford and New York: 2011, pp. 19–39.
Lund, John and Gabrielsen,. 'A Fishy Business: Transport Amphorae of the Black Sea Region as a Source for the Trade in Fish and Fish Products in the Classical and Hellenistic Periods', in Tønnes Bekker-Nielsen (ed.) *Ancient Fishing and Fish Processing in the Black Sea Region*. Aarhus University Press, Aarhus, DNK: 2006.
Lytle, E. 'Fish Lists in the Wilderness: The Social and Economic History of a Boiotian Price Decree', *Hesperia: The Journal of the American School of Classical Studies at Athens*, Vol. 79, No. 2 (2010), pp. 253–303.
Lytle, E. "Ἡ θαλασσακοινή: Fishermen, the Sea, and the Limits of Ancient Greek Regulatory Reach', *Classical Antiquity*, Vol. 31, No. 1 (2012), pp. 1–55.
MacDonald, Brian R. 'The Authenticity of the Congress Decree', *Historia: Zeitschrift für Alte Geschichte*, Bd. 31, H. 1 (1982), pp. 120–123.
MacDonald, Brian R. 'The Diolkos', *The Journal of Hellenic Studies*, Vol. 106, (1986), pp. 191–195.
MacDowell, Douglas M. *Aristophanes and Athens: An Introduction to the Plays*. Oxford University Press, Oxford and New York: 1995.
MacDowell, Douglas M. 'Epikerdes of Kyrene and the Athenian Privilege of Ateleia', *Zeitschrift für Papyrologie und Epigraphik*, Bd. 150, (2004), pp. 127–133.
Mahan, Alfred Thayer. *The Influence of Sea Power Upon History 1660–1783*. Dover Publications, New York: reprint 1987. Originally published 1890.
Mair, A.W. 'Oppian, *Halieutica*', in A.W. Mair (ed. and trans.) *Oppian, Colluthus, Tryphiodorus*. Loeb Classical Library 219. Harvard University Press, Cambridge, MA: 1928.

Malkin, Irad. *Myth and Territory in the Spartan Mediterranean*. Cambridge University Press, New York: 1994.
Malkin, Irad (ed.) *Greek and Roman Networks in the Mediterranean*. Routledge, London: 2009.
Malkin, Irad. *A Small Greek World: Networks in the Ancient Mediterranean*. Oxford University Press, Oxford: 2011.
Mark, Samuel. 'The Earliest Naval Ram', *The International Journal of Nautical Archaeology*, Vol. 37, No. 2 (2008), pp. 253-272.
Marr, J.L. *Plutarch Life of Themistocles. Introduction, Text, Translation and Commentary*. Aris & Phillips Ltd, Warminster: 1998.
Marr, J.L. and Rhodes, P.J. *The 'Old Oligarch'. The Constitution of the Athenians Attributed to Xenophon*. Aris & Phillips, Oxford: 2008.
Martin-Mcauliffe, Samantha A. and Papadopoulos, John K. 'Framing Victory: Salamis, the Athenian Acropolis, and the Agora', *Journal of the Society of Architectural Historians*, Vol. 71, No. 3 (2012), pp. 332-361.
Massie, Robert K. *Dreadnought. Britain, Germany and the Coming of the Great War*. Vintage Press, London: 2007.
Mattingly, Harold B. 'New Light on the Athenian Standards Decree (ATL II, D 14)', *Klio*, Vol. 75, (1993), pp. 99-102.
Mattingly, Harold B. *The Athenian Empire Restored: Epigraphic and Historical Studies*. University of Michigan Press, Ann Arbor: 1996.
McGrail, Seán. *Boats of the World. From the Stone Age to Medieval Times*. Oxford University Press, New York: 2001.
McKechnie, Paul R and Kern, Stephen J. (ed. and trans.) *Hellenica Oxyrhynchia*. Aris & Phillips, Warminster: 1988.
McKenzie, Nicholas J. and Hannah, Patricia A. 'Thucydides' Take on the Corinthian Navy. οἵ τε γὰρ Κορίνθιοι ἡγήσαντο κρατεῖν εἰ μὴ καὶ πολὺ ἐκρατοῦντο, 'The Corinthians believed they were victors if they were only just defeated'', *Mnemosyne*, Vol. 66, No. 2 (2013), pp. 206-227.
Mead, Walter Russell. 'Thucydides, Polybius, and the Legacies of the Ancient World', in Hal Brands (ed.) *The New Makers of Modern Strategy. From the Ancient World to the Digital Age*. Princeton University Press, Princeton: 2023.
Meiggs, Russell. *The Athenian Empire*. Clarendon Press, Oxford: 1972.
Meiggs, Russell and Lewis, David. *A Selection of Greek Historical Inscriptions to the End of the Fifth Century B.C.* Clarendon Press, Oxford: 1969.
Messina, Paul F. 'The Elephant vs. The Whale: Bringing National Forces to Bear During the Second Peloponnesian War', *Small Wars Journal*, (12 August 2019).
Momigliano, Arnaldo. 'Sea-Power in Greek Thought', *The Classical Review*, Vol. 58, No. 1 (1944), pp. 1-7.
Morgan, Kathryn A. 'Designer History: Plato's Atlantis Story and Fourth-Century Ideology', *The Journal of Hellenic Studies*, Vol. 118, (1998), pp. 101-118.
Morison, Samuel Eliot. *The Two-Ocean War. A Short History of the United States Navy in the Second World War*. Naval Institute Press, Annapolis, Maryland: 1963.
Morrison, J.S. 'Hyperesia in Naval Contexts in the Fifth and Fourth Centuries BC', *The Journal of Hellenic Studies*, Vol. 104, (1984), pp. 48-59.
Morrison, J.S. 'Athenian Sea-Power in 323/2 BC: Dream and Reality', *The Journal of Hellenic* Studies, Vol. 107, (1987), pp. 88-97.
Morrison, J.S., with Coates, J.F. *Greek and Roman Oared Warships*. Oxbrow Books, Oxford: 1996.

Morrison, J.S and Coates, J.F. (eds.) *An Athenian Trireme Reconstructed. The British sea trials of Olympias, 1987*. BAR International Series 486: 1989.

Morrison, J.S, Coates, J.F. and Rankov, N.B. *The Athenian Trireme. The History and Reconstruction of an Ancient Greek Warship*. Cambridge University Press, Cambridge: Second Edition 2000.

Morrison, James V. 'Preface to Thucydides: Rereading the Corcyraean Conflict (1.24–55)', *Classical Antiquity*, Vol. 18, No. 1 (1999), pp. 94–131.

Murphy, Thomas M. 'The Vilification of Eratosthenes and Theramenes in Lysias 12', *The American Journal of Philology*, Vol. 110, No. 1 (1989), pp. 40–49.

Murray, William M. 'Do Modern Winds Equal Ancient Winds?', *Mediterranean Historical Review*, Vol. 1, (1987), pp. 139–167.

Murray, William M. *The Age of Titans. The Rise and Fall of the Great Hellenistic Navies*. Oxford University Press, New York: 2012.

Mylona, Dimitra. *Fish-Eating in Greece from the Fifth Century B.C. to the Seventh Century A.D. A Story of Impoverished Fishermen or Luxurious Fish Banquets?* BAR International Series 1754: 2008.

Myres, John L. 'On the 'List of Thalassocracies' in Eusebius', *The Journal of Hellenic Studies*, Vol. 26, (1906), pp. 84–130.

Nash, John. 'Sea Power in the Peloponnesian War', *Naval War College Review*, Vol. 71, No. 1 (2018), pp. 119–139.

Nellopoulos, Emmanuel D. *The Greek Trieres*. (trans. Philippa Currie) John Floros Publishing House, Athens: 1999.

Nolan, Cathal J. *The Allure of Battle. A History of How Wars Have Been Won and Lost*. Oxford University Press, New York: 2017.

NP 136: Ocean Passages of the World. United Kingdom Hydrographic Office, 2004.

O'Brien, Phillips Payson. *How the War was Won. Air-Sea Power and Allied Victory in World War II*. Cambridge University Press, Cambridge: 2015.

Ober, Josiah. 'Views of Sea Power in the Fourth-Century Attic Orators', *The Ancient World*, Vol. 1, No. 3 (1978), pp. 119–130.

Ober, Josiah. 'Thucydides and the Invention of Political Science', in Antonis Tsakmakis and Antonios Rengakos (eds.) *Brill's Companion to Thucydides*. Brill Online, 2006, pp. 131–159. Accessed at: http://booksandjournals.brillonline.com.virtual.anu.edu.au/content/books/b9789047404842s007

Ober, Josiah. *The Rise and Fall of Classical Greece*. Princeton University Press, Princeton and Oxford: 2015.

Ormerod, Henry A. *Piracy in the Ancient World. An Essay in Mediterranean History*. Argonaut Inc., Publishers, Chicago: 1967. Originally published 1924.

Oron, Asaf. 'The Athlit Ram Bronze Casting Reconsidered: Scientific and Technical Re-examination', *Journal of Archaeological Science*, Vol. 33, (2006), pp. 63–76.

Osborne, Robin. *The Old Oligarch. Pseudo-Xenophon's Constitution of the Athenians. Introduction, Translation and Commentary*. London Association of Classical Teachers, London: 2nd edition 2004.

Paine, Lincoln. *The Sea and Civilization: A Maritime History of the World*. Knopf, New York: 2013.

Palmer, Michael A. *Command at Sea. Naval Command and Control since the Sixteenth Century*. Harvard University Press, Cambridge, Massachusetts: 2005.

Papalas, Anthony. 'Polycrates of Samos and the First Greek Trireme Fleet', *The Mariner's Mirror*, Vol. 85, No. 1 (1999), pp. 3–19.

Papillon, Terry L. *Isocrates II*. University of Texas Press, Austin: 2004.

Peter Paret with Gordon A. Craig and Felix Gilbert (eds.) *Makers of Modern Strategy: From Machiavelli to the Nuclear Age*. Princeton University Press, Princeton, N.J.: 1986.

Parker, Robert. *Miasma. Pollution and Purification in Early Greek Religion*. Clarendon Press, Oxford: 1983.

Parry, Chris. *Super Highway. Sea Power in the 21st Century*. Eliot and Thompson Books, London: 2014.

Parshall, Jonathan B. and Tully, Anthony P. *Shattered Sword. The Untold Story of The Battle of Midway*. Potomac Books, Washington, D.C.: 2005.

Pertsinidis, Sonia. *Theophrastus' Characters: A New Introduction*. Routledge, Milton: 2018.

Pettegrew, David K. 'The Diolkos of Corinth', *American Journal of Archaeology*, Vol. 115, No. 4 (2011), pp. 549–574.

Platias, Athanassios and Koliopoulos, Constantinos. *Thucydides on Strategy. Grand Strategies in the Peloponnesian War and their Relevance Today*. Hurst & Company, London: 2010.

Podlecki, A.J. 'Athens and Aegina', *Historia: Zeitschrift für Alte Geschichte*, Bd. 25, H. 4 (1976), pp. 396–413.

Polakowski, Mateusz. *Warships of the First Punic War: An archaeological investigation and contributory reconstruction of the Egadi 10 warship from the battle of the Egadi Islands (241 b.c.)*, Master's Thesis, East Carolina University, ProQuest Dissertations Publishing, 2016.

Pomeroy, Sarah B. *Xenophon Oeconomicus. A Social and Historical Commentary*. Clarendon Press, Oxford: 1994.

Pritchard, David M. *The Fractured Imaginary: Popular Thinking on Citizen Soldiers and Warfare in Fifth Century Athens*. PhD Thesis, Department of Ancient History, Division of Humanities, Macquarie University: 1999.

Pritchard, David M. 'Aristophanes and de Ste. Croix: The Value of Old Comedy as Evidence for Athenian Popular Culture', *Antichthon*, Vol. 46, (2012), pp. 14–51.

Pritchard, David M. 'Public Finance and War in Ancient Greece', *Greece & Rome*, Vol. 62, No. 1 (2015), pp. 48–59.

Pritchard, David M. 'The Standing of Sailors in Democratic Athens', *Dialogues d'Histoire Ancienne*, Vol. 44, No. 2 (In Press 2018), pp. 1–21.

Rahe, Paul A. *The Grand Strategy of Classical Sparta: The Persian Challenge*. Yale University Press, New Haven: 2015.

Rankov, Boris. *Trireme Olympias: The Final Report*. Oxbow, Oxford: 2012.

Rawlings, Louis. *The Ancient Greeks at War*. Manchester University Press, Manchester, GBR: 2007.

Rhodes, P.J. *The Athenian Boule*. Clarendon Press, Oxford: 1972.

Rhodes, P.J. *A Commentary on the Aristotelian Athenaion Politeia*. Clarendon Press, Oxford: 1981.

Rhodes, P.J. 'The Alleged Failure of Athens in the Fourth Century', *Electrum*, Vol. 19, (2012), pp. 111–129.

Rhodes, P.J. and Osborne, Robin. *Greek Historical Inscriptions, 404–323 BC*. Oxford University Press, Oxford and New York: 2004.

Richardson, L.J.D. 'ΥΠΗΡΕΤΗΣ', *The Classical Quarterly*, Vol. 37, No. 1/2 (1943), pp. 55–61.

Richmond, Herbert Admiral Sir. *Statesman and Sea Power*. Oxford University Press, Oxford: 1946.

Robinson, Eric W. 'What Happened at Aegospotami? Xenophon and Diodorus on the Last Battle of the Peloponnesian War', *Historia: Zeitschrift für alte Geschichte*, Vol. 63, No. 1 (2014), pp. 1–16.

Roisman, Joseph. 'Alkidas in Thucydides', *Historia: Zeitscchrift für Alte Geschichte*, Bd. 36, H. 4 (1987), pp. 358–421.

Rovner, Joshua. 'Sea Power versus Land Power: Cross-Domain Deterrence in the Peloponnesian War', in Eric Gartzke and Jon R. Lindsay (eds.) *Cross-Domain Deterrence: Strategy in an Era of Complexity*. Oxford University Press, Oxford: 2019, pp. 163–186.

Royal, Jeffrey G. and Tusa, Sebastiano. 'The Warship Rams: Depositional Contexts and Descriptions', in Jeffrey G. Royal and Sebastiano Tusa (eds.) *The Site of the Battle of the Aegates Islands at the end of the First Punic War. Fieldwork, Analyses and Perspectives, 2005–2015*. L'Erma di Bretschneider, Rome: 2020.

Rubin, Alfred P. *The Law of Piracy*. Naval War College Press, Newport RI: 1988.
Rusten, Jeffrey. 'Theophrastus, *Characters*', in I. C. Cunningham Jeffrey Rusten (ed. and trans.) *Theophrastus, Herodas, Sophron. Characters. Herodas: Mimes. Sophron and Other Mime Fragments*. Loeb Classical Library 225. Harvard University Press, Cambridge, MA: 2003.
Sabin, Philip and de Souza, Philip. 'Battle', in Philip Sabin, Hans van Wees and Michael Whitby (eds.) *The Cambridge History of Greek and Roman Warfare Volume 1: Greece, The Hellenistic World and the Rise of Rome*. Cambridge Histories Online, 2008.
Salmon, J.B. *Wealthy Corinth. A History of the City to 338 BC*. Clarendon Press, Oxford: 1984.
Scott, Lionel. *Historical Commentary on Herodotus Book 6*. Brill, Leiden, Boston: 2005.
Seager, Robin. 'The Congress Decree: Some Doubts and a Hypothesis', *Historia: Zeitscchrift für Alte Geschichte*, Bd. 18, H. 2 (1969), pp. 129–141.
Sharp, *Andrew, Ancient Voyagers in the Pacific*, Polynesian Society,Wellington: 1956.
Shaw, Timothy (ed.) *The Trireme Project. Operational Experience 1987–90 Lessons Learnt*. Oxbrow Monograph 31: 1993.
Shipley, Graham. *Pseudo-Skylax's Periplous: the Circumnavigation of the Inhabited World. Text, Translation and Commentary*. Oxford University Press, Oxford: 2nd edition 2020.
Sidwell, Keith. *Aristophanes the democrat: the politics of satirical comedy during the Peloponnesian War*. Cambridge University Press, Cambridge and New York: 2009.
Slater, W.J. 'Symposium at Sea', *Harvard Studies in Classical Philology*, Vol. 80, (1976), pp. 161–170.
Smith, David G. 'The Reception of Aeschylus in Sicily', in Rebecca Futo Kennedy (ed.) *Brill's Companion to the Reception of Aeschylus*. Brill, Leiden and Boston: 2017.
Spence, I.G. 'Pericles and the Defence of Attika during the Peloponnesian War', *The Journal of Hellenic Studies*, Vol. 110, (1990), pp. 91–109.
Sprawski, Sławomir. 'Alexander of Pherae: Infelix Tyrant', in Sian Lewis (ed.) *Ancient Tyranny*. Edinburgh University Press, Edinburgh: 2006.
Stadter, Philip A. 'The Motives for Athens' Alliance with Corcyra (Thuc. 1.44)', *Greek, Roman and Byzantine Studies*, Vol. 24, No. 2 (1983), pp. 131–136.
Stadter, Philip A. *A Commentary on Plutarch's Pericles*. The University of North Carolina Press, Chapel Hill and London: 1989.
Starr, Chester G. 'Thucydides on Sea Power', *Mnemosyne*, Vol. 31, Fasc. 4 (1978), pp. 343–350.
Starr, Chester G. *The Influence of Sea Power on Ancient History*. Oxford University Press, New York: 1989.
Steinsson, Sverrir. 'The Cod Wars: A Re-analysis', *European Security*, Vol. 25, No. 2 (2016), pp. 256–275.
Stevens, David. *In All Respects Ready: Australia's Navy in World War One*. Oxford University Press, Melbourne: 2015.
Stevens, Gorham Phillips. 'The Periclean Entrance Court of the Acropolis of Athens', *Hesperia: The Journal of the American School of Classical Studies at Athens*, Vol. 5, No. 4 (1936), pp. 443–520.
Strachan, Hew. *The Direction of War. Contemporary Strategy in Historical Perspective*. Cambridge University Press, Cambridge: 2013.
Strauss, Barry A. 'Aegospotami Reexamined', *The American Journal of Philology*, Vol. 104, No. 1 (1983), pp. 24–35.
Strauss, Barry A. 'Democracy, Kimon, and the Evolution of Athenian Naval Tactics in the Fifth Century BC', in P. Flensted-Jensen, et al. (eds.) *Polis and Politics. Studies in Ancient Greek History Presented to Mogens Herman Hansen on his Sixtieth Birthday, August 20, 2000*. Museum Tusculanum Press, Copenhagen: 2000.
Strauss, Barry A. *Salamis. The Greatest Naval Battle of the Ancient World, 480 BC*. Arrow Books, London: 2004.

Strauss, Barry A. 'Sparta's Maritime Moment', in Andrew S. Erickson, Lyle J. Goldstein and Carnes Lord (eds.) *China Goes to Sea. Maritime Transformation in Comparative Historical Perspective*. Naval Institute Press, Annapolis, Maryland: 2009, pp. 33–61.

Stylianou, P.J. *A Historical Commentary on Diodorus Siculus Book 15*. Clarendon Press, Oxford: 1998.

Talbert, Richard J.A. (ed.) *Barrington Atlas of the Greek and Roman World*. Princeton University Press, Princeton: 2000.

Tammuz, Oded. 'Mare clausum? Sailing Seasons in the Mediterranean in Early Antiquity', *Mediterranean Historical Review*, Vol. 20, No. 2 (2005), pp. 145–162.

Thompson, Christina. *Sea People. The Puzzle of Polynesia*. William Collins, London: 2019.

Thorne, James A. 'Warfare and Agriculture: The Economic Impact of Devastation in Classical Greece', *Greek, Roman and Byzantine Studies*, Vol. 42, No. 3 (2001), pp. 225–253.

Till, Geoffrey. *Seapower: A Guide for the Twenty-First Century*. Routledge, New York: Third edition 2013.

Tilley, Alec. *Seafaring on the Ancient Mediterranean. New Thoughts on Triremes and Other Ancient Ships*. BAR International Series 1268: 2004.

Trevett, Jeremy. *Demosthenes, Speeches 1–17*. University of Texas Press, Austin, TX: 2011.

Tritle, Lawrence A. *A New History of the Peloponnesian War*. Wiley-Blackwell, Malden, MA: 2010.

Van Wees, Hans. '"Those Who Sail are to Receive a Wage": Naval Warfare and Finance in Archaic Eretria', in Garrett Fagan and Matthew Trundle (eds.) *New Perspectives on Ancient Warfare*. Brill, Boston: 2010.

Van Wees, Hans. *Greek Warfare. Myths and Realities*. Bloomsbury, London and New York: Reprint 2014. Original, 2004.

Van Wees, Hans. *Ships and Silver, Taxes and Tribute. A Fiscal History of Archaic Athens*. I.B. Tauris, London and New York: 2015.

Vidal-Naquet, Pierre. 'Athènes et l'Atlantide. Structure et signification d'un mythe platonicien', *Revue des Études Grecques*, tome 77, fascicule 366-368 (1964), pp. 420–444.

Vidal-Naquet, Pierre. *The Atlantis Story. A Short History of Plato's Myth*. (trans. Janet Lloyd) University of Exeter Press, Exeter: 2007. Original French edition, *L'Atlantide: Petite histoire d'un mythe platonicien*, 2005.

Wachsmann, Shelly. 'Panathenaic Ships: The Iconographic Evidence', *Hesperia: The Journal of the American School of Classical Studies at Athens*, Vol. 81, No. 2 (2012), pp. 237–266.

West, Martin L. 'Odyssey and Argonautica', *Classical Quarterly*, Vol. 55, No. 1 (2005), pp. 39–64.

Westlake, H.D. 'Seaborne Raids in Periclean Strategy', *The Classical Quarterly*, Vol. 39, No. 3/4 (1945), pp. 75–84.

Westlake, H.D. 'Ionians in the Ionian War', *The Classical Quarterly*, Vol. 29, No. 1 (1979), pp. 9–44.

Wheeler, Everett L. 'Review: A War Like No Other: How the Athenians and Spartans Fought the Peloponnesian War', *The Journal of Military History*, Vol. 70, No. 3 (2006), pp. 816–818.

Wilkins, John. *The Boastful Chef. The Discourse of Food in Ancient Greek Comedy*. Oxford University Press, New York: 2000.

Wilkins, John. 'Fish as a Source of Food in Antiquity', in Tønnes Bekker-Nielsen (ed.) *Ancient Fishing and Fish Processing in the Black Sea Region*. Aarhus University Press, Aarhus, DNK: 2006.

Williams, Charles Kaufman. 'Corinth, 1978: Forum Southwest', *Hesperia: The Journal of the American School of Classical Studies*, Vol. 48, No. 2 (1979), pp. 105–144.

Woodhead, A. Geoffrey. *Thucydides on the Nature of Power*. Harvard University Press, Cambridge, Massachusetts: 1970.

Worthington, Ian. *Alexander the Great Man and God*. Routledge, London and New York: 2004.

Worthington, Ian. *Demosthenes of Athens and the Fall of Classical Greece*. Oxford University Press, Oxford: 2013.

Index

Abydos 162, 164, 168, 169, 189, 240, 243, 244
Achaia 182, 203
Acragas 59, 172, 173, 241
Admiral 12, 19, 35, 134, 168, 170, 173, 182, 186, 235, 242, 243, 248–250
Adriatic Sea 9, 10, 12, 16, 117, 182, 207, 250
Aegina
– As a thalassocracy 78, 82, 85, 97, 207, 210, 211
– Conflict with Athens 90, 109, 110, 167, 168, 171, 181, 203, 210, 211, 232, 234, 244, 245
– Peloponnesian War 126, 127, 242
– Persian Wars 93, 96, 97, 210, 247
– Poseidon 58
– Trade 213, 214
Aegospotami, battle of 150, 157–159, 161, 175, 177, 204, 209, 212, 242
Aeschylus 35, 54, 61–65
Agesilaus 163–167
Alcibiades 76, 138, 149, 152, 161, 177, 212
Alcibiades the Younger 176, 177
Alexander of Macedon 1, 7, 181, 196, 201
Alexander of Pherai 183, 190, 215, 246
Ambracia 95, 130, 182, 203
Amphipolis 42, 103, 137, 138, 140, 147, 159, 183, 187–190, 197, 201, 237, 238
Antipater 196
Apollodorus 43, 44, 49, 189, 190
Appian 121, 206
Arginousai, battle of 39, 154–157, 159, 162, 175, 207, 214, 215, 241
Argonauts *see Jason*
Argos/Argolid 138, 141, 237, 238, 243, 248
Artaphrenes 87
Artaxerxes 162, 163, 169
Artemision 1, 42, 72, 92–96, 100, 120, 210, 216, 233
Athens
– Aegina *see Aegina, conflict with Athens*
– Acropolis 17, 96, 99
– Archaic period 7, 36, 104, 232, 250
– As an 'island' 6, 69, 107, 122, 215
– Colonies 4, 189, 250
– Delian League 50, 76, 85, 101–103, 105–107, 112–115, 146, 149, 159, 198
– Evacuation (480) 93, 94, 121, 220, 250

– Lamian War 196, 197, 246
– Law courts 2, 3, 23, 107, 174–180, 200
– Myths 58–60, 79, 80
– Naval administration 34–38, 104, 177–179
– Naval depictions in comedy 45, 46, 64–66, 214
– Naval depictions in tragedy 61–63
– Naval funding 48–51, 103, 152, 197–200
– Naval infrastructure 46, 47, 49, 101, 102, 109, 158, 164
– Naval tactics 39, 40, 144, 145
– Outbreak of Peloponnesian War 118–120, 124, 219, 235, 247
– Peloponnesian War strategy 4, 103, 107, 108, 117, 119 *see also Pericles, Peloponnesian War strategy*
– *Pentecontaetia* 11, 102, 104, 108–112, 233, 234, 247
– Persian Wars 88, 90, 91, 94–97, 109, 121, 220, 232–234, 247, 250
– Second Athenian Confederation 166, 167, 170, 179, 180, 185, 187–191, 198, 199, 202, 246
– Sicilian expedition (427) 135, 136, 172, 236, 237, 248
– Sicilian expedition (415) 141–146, 237–239
– State triremes 65, 199
– Trade 2, 4, 11, 23, 56, 66, 69, 70, 106, 112, 113, 115, 131, 137, 138, 150, 151, 168, 179, 198–200, 225, 244, 245
Alcidas 134, 135, 153, 154
Andros 87, 171, 233, 241
Ariobarzanes 189
Aristophanes 45, 48, 64–66, 199, 214
Aristotle 15, 30, 35, 74, 210, 211

Black Sea 4, 10, 12, 13, 23, 32, 41, 55, 56, 112–115, 117, 123, 137, 142, 150, 151, 157, 168, 201, 210, 222, 243, 247
Blockade 98, 108, 111, 112, 120, 128, 132, 134, 153, 154, 157, 158, 167–170, 173, 215, 217, 226, 235, 236, 238–240, 242, 245
Boeotia 11, 58, 110, 164, 169, 181, 184
Bosporus 13, 55, 68, 112, 152, 241, 248, 250
Brasidas 137–140, 159

Byzantium 41, 45, 66, 76, 89, 115, 157, 167, 185, 186, 189, 191, 202, 212, 223, 232, 233, 240, 241, 243, 247

Callicratidas 153, 154
Cape Sounion 16, 17, 150, 165, 232, 239
Carthage 37, 42, 57, 70, 82, 89, 171–174, 216, 220, 223, 231, 241, 242, 245
Caspian Sea 68
Cavalry 125, 126, 128, 130, 145, 171, 177, 178, 187, 192–195, 223
Ceos 16, 42, 54, 171, 198
Cephalonia 126, 127, 200, 235, 245
Chalcidice 136–138, 140, 159 167, 186, 189, 190, 193, 237
Chersonese 183, 186–189, 192, 197, 199, 250
Chios 15, 32, 47, 85–88, 111, 114, 148, 149, 153, 164, 170, 184, 185, 191, 202, 206, 211–214, 226, 235, 239, 240, 246, 247–249
Chrysopolis 152
Cimmerian Bosporus 151
Cimon 96, 98, 99, 110, 111, 114, 118, 250
Cleon 65, 128, 138
Cnidos, battle of (394) 75, 162, 180, 197, 202, 204, 243
Conon 153, 154, 161–164
Corcyra
– Conflict with Corinth 81, 82, 85, 117, 118, 182, 204, 206, 218, 234, 247
– Fishing 31, 32
– Fourth century 182, 204, 206, 245, 246, 249, 250
– Geographic significance 127, 150, 182, 205, 206
– Navy 86, 95, 114, 119, 203, 205–208, 213, 219
– Peloponnesian War 114, 117–120, 126, 207, 218, 219, 235–237, 247
– Persian War 95, 208, 247
Corinth
– As a thalassocracy 78, 81, 82, 203, 207, 223, 232
– Conflict with Corcyra 81, 85, 117, 118, 182, 204, 206, 218, 234, 247
– Conflict with Sparta 165, 166, 169, 243
– Corinthian Gulf 12, 47, 110, 127, 130, 132, 133, 134, 150, 168, 184, 215, 217
– Isthmus of 11, 91, 93, 98, 148, 187, 203, 247 *see also Diolkos*

– Navy 82, 85, 86, 90, 119, 20–205, 232, 245, 246
– Peloponnesian War 110, 118–120, 130, 132, 133, 143, 148, 203, 204, 208, 219, 235, 237, 238
– Persian War 96, 121
– Trade 31, 90, 203, 205, 214
Cos 164, 179, 191, 202, 212
Crete 15, 56, 82, 103, 133, 231, 247
Croesus 81, 87, 231
Cyme 162
Cyprus 25, 26, 54, 88, 98, 106, 109–111, 232–234, 243
Cyrene 57, 58
Cythera 54, 127, 164, 238
Cyzicus 152, 153, 189, 240, 246, 248

Dardanelles *see Hellespont*
Decelea 16, 65, 117, 125, 147, 150, 153, 155, 158
Delian League *see Athens, Delian League*
Delos 58, 81, 247
Demosthenes (5th century strategos) 128, 129, 236
Demosthenes (4th century politician)
– Death 58
– Law court Speeches 23, 32, 42, 43–45, 77
– Political speeches 15, 84, 121, 167, 177–179, 189, 190–199, 206, 211
Diodorus Siculus 13, 37, 46, 56, 57, 68, 70, 71, 80, 93, 98, 99, 108–112, 126, 134, 145, 146, 151–154, 156, 159, 164, 171–174, 184, 185, 191, 196, 197, 216
Diolkos 34, 47, 48, 148, 203
Dionysius of Phocaea 89, 232
Dionysius, Tyrant of Syracuse *see Syracuse*

Egypt 4, 17, 18, 23, 24, 106, 109, 127, 149, 150, 201, 231, 233, 234
Elephantine Palimpsest 24, 28, 46
Elis 182, 202
Epaminondas 183–187, 245 *see also Thebes*
Epidamnus 117, 118, 205, 207, 208, 234
Epidaurus 58, 182, 202, 210, 237
Eratosthenes 175–177
Eretria 34, 35, 85, 240
Erythrain Sea *see Red Sea*
Euboea 13, 22, 34, 35, 85, 87, 92, 93, 131, 132, 147, 150, 153, 171, 233, 240, 250
Euripides 54, 57, 60, 113

First World War 52, 120, 185, 217
Fisher, Admiral Jackie 131
Fishing 4, 9, 11, 29–33, 43, 46, 165, 219, 220, 225
Fourni Islands 24, 25, 33

Grain trade 4, 24, 28, 37, 42, 107, 109, 112, 113, 115, 137, 143, 150, 151, 168, 171–173, 189, 199, 200, 239, 241, 244–246

Halieis 182, 202, 234
Hellenica Oxyrhynchia 125, 153
Hellespont 12, 68, 72,
- Fourth Century 44, 45, 164, 166–168, 188–193, 196–199, 243, 244, 246
- Peloponnesian War 115, 137, 138, 147, 150, 154, 157, 158, 240–242, 248
- Persian War 91, 98, 232, 233
Heracles 53, 55–57, 60, 72, 79, 222
Hermione 58, 182, 202
Herodotus 18, 39, 42, 68, 79–83, 88–99, 102, 121, 210, 222
Hesiod 22, 23, 53, 55, 61, 73
Himera 172, 220, 221, 236, 250
Histiaios 87, 89, 90, 232
Homer 56, 61, 72, 73, 141,
- *Iliad* 30, 55, 56, 58, 74, 95
- *Odyssey* 20, 21, 30, 54–56
Hoplite 39, 43, 44, 72, 74, 75, 90, 105, 107, 110, 117, 121, 124, 129, 130, 137, 141, 167, 184, 204, 217, 223, 236, 246

Imbros 191, 194, 198, 246
Iphicrates 170, 188, 245, 246
Isocrates 74–77, 151, 169, 184

Jason 21, 55, 56, 58, 78, 184, 222
Jellicoe, Admiral Sir John 120

King's Peace *see Persia*

Laches 185, 186
Lade 88, 211, 232
Lemnos 20, 191, 193, 194, 198, 232, 246
Leonidas 1, 92
Leptines 173, 174, 178, 242
Lesbos 27, 42, 43, 81, 89, 111, 114, 115, 134, 158, 170, 232, 235, 239–241, 243, 248

Leucas 95, 149, 182, 202, 208–210, 213, 219, 223, 234, 239, 246
Long Walls *see Athens, Naval infrastructure*
Lysander 35, 156–158, 163, 177, 242, 248
Lysias 175–177, 179, 180

Mantineia 187
Marathon 46, 72, 75, 90, 100, 194
Marines 40, 44, 74, 99, 170, 211, 214
Maritime power projection 6, 123, 131, 182, 187, 225, 226, 229
Maritime Strategy definition 3, 4, 225, 226
Maroneia 44, 45
Megara 11, 132, 143, 236–238
Melos 15, 16, 77, 105, 138, 139, 212, 236, 237, 240
Methymna 153, 170, 239, 241
Midway, battle of 215, 216
Miletus 87–89, 111, 149, 232, 239, 248
Minos, King 57, 61, 78–80, 83, 84, 86, 223
Mytilene 41, 47, 89, 134, 135, 153, 154, 158, 170, 235, 239, 241, 248

Naupactus 19, 130–133, 143, 145, 203, 204, 235, 236, 238, 247
Naval Strategy definition 3, 4, 226, 227
Naxos 45, 80, 81, 87, 231, 233, 248
Naxos, Sicily 47
Nicias (Athenian *strategos*) 37, 132, 141–143
Nicias (Athenian ally in Crete) 133, 134
Nisyros 164

Oeniadai 167, 234
'Old Oligarch' 49, 69, 71, 75, 101, 104–108, 115, 128, 129
Olympias 40
Olynthos 187, 188, 192
Operational level of war 96, 123, 129, 227, 229

Paros 26, 27, 87, 232
Pausanias (Spartan) 108, 233
Pausanias (writer) 17, 31, 57, 58, 175–177, 184
Peace of Nicias 16, 119, 124, 137, 138, 140
Pentecontor 39, 42, 81, 211, 220, 247
Pericles
- As a *strategos* 6, 111–113, 142, 234, 235, 247, 250
- On Aegina 210

- Peloponnesian War strategy 50, 66, 75, 107, 113, 121–124, 126–129, 135, 140, 148, 229
Persia
- Ionian Revolt 80, 87–89, 100, 102, 232, 247
- King's Peace 169, 170, 181, 189
- Support for Athens 48, 161–164, 166, 180, 189, 214
- Support for Corinth 204, 243
- Support for Sparta 48, 50, 119, 155–157, 159, 197, 205, 207, 214
- Support for Thebes 48, 183
- War with Greeks 5, 12, 76, 81, 90–100, 102, 109, 114, 163, 232, 233, 241, 249, 250
Persians (tragic play) 62
Pharnabazos 162, 164
Philip II 15, 76, 84, 137, 181, 191–197, 201, 246, 249, 250
Phocaea 82, 86, 89, 162, 231, 232, 247
Phoenicia 56, 81, 89, 98, 102, 132, 163, 232, 234
Phormio 12, 19, 132–134, 203, 204, 215, 217, 235
Pindar 55, 63, 93
Piracy 5, 29, 67, 83–86, 89, 90, 114, 131, 193, 195, 196, 203, 207, 210, 214, 220–223, 226, 227, 244, 250
Plato 6, 71–77, 215, 223
Plutarch 12, 55, 61, 71, 78, 93, 94, 96, 98, 99, 103, 104, 111–114, 118, 126, 127, 143, 158, 163, 184, 210
Polycrates, Tyrant of Samos 79–83, 86
Pompey 121
Pontus 68, 89, 106, 115, 152, 167, 169, 179
Poseidon 16, 22, 54, 58, 60, 72, 73
Privateer 127, 131, 132, 157, 227, 228, 236, 250
Proconnesus 189
Pydna 188, 191
Pylos 117, 128–130, 136, 137, 140, 148, 149, 151, 153, 159, 166, 212, 225, 236, 241

Red Sea 68
Rhodes 23, 25, 66, 153, 170, 184, 185, 191, 201, 202, 206, 212, 240, 243, 249
Richmond, Sir Herbert 2, 228

Salamis, battle of 12, 35, 61, 62, 72, 75, 88, 90, 91, 93–100, 120, 121, 202, 204, 206, 208–210, 215, 216, 220, 233, 247

Samos 79–82, 86, 111, 112, 149, 189, 191, 197, 223, 231, 233, 234, 240–243, 246–249
Sardis 81, 87, 231
Sea control 6, 87, 88, 95, 97, 110, 112, 113, 118, 119, 128, 133, 145, 155, 149, 162, 165–168, 183, 186, 201, 215, 228, 244
Sea denial 6, 228
Sea Power definition 2, 228, 229
Sea Power Theory 2–4, 228, 229
Sestos 45, 98, 190, 233
Sicyon 11, 110, 234, 237
Skyros 198, 233, 250
Smyrna 162
Social War 75, 190, 191, 197, 198, 202, 212, 246
Sophocles 63
Sostratos 195, 250
Span of maritime operations 3, 6, 226
Sphacteria 128–130, 136, 137, 140, 159, 166, 236
Sparta
- Archaic period 80–82, 231, 247
- Archidamian War strategy 119, 124, 128, 135, 136–138
- Defeat by Thebes 76, 170, 182
- Fourth century 75, 76, 161–171, 181–183, 202, 204, 209, 243–245, 249, 250
- Invasions of Attica 16, 65, 117, 121, 124–127, 129, 130, 139, 147, 150 see also *Decelea*
- Ionian War strategy 146–149, 155–159, 214, 229, 239, 240, 248
- Naval funding 48, 50, 121, 153, 162, 197, 214, 219
- Naval organisation 7, 34–36, 186, 207
- *Pentecontaetia* 11, 102, 108–110, 113
- Persian Wars 87, 88, 92, 95, 202, 247
- Privateers 132, 157, 227
- Support to Syracuse 142, 144, 145, 238
Strategy definition 4, 5, 123, 229
Sybota 39, 203, 206–210, 247
Syracuse
- Conflict with Carthage 42, 70, 172, 173
- Dionysius 46, 173, 174, 216, 241–246, 248–250
- Fourth century 168, 242, 244–246, 249, 250
- Infrastructure 46
- Peloponnesian War 119, 135, 142–145, 147, 149, 154, 236–239, 241, 242, 248
- *Persians* performed 61
- Sea power 171, 232, 233

Teleutias 48, 165, 243, 249
Teos 164, 248
Thalassocracy 78–80, 83, 86, 103, 206, 207, 210, 222, 223
Thalassocracy List 80, 82, 207, 210
Thasos 28, 42–45, 102, 153, 166, 167, 179, 193, 214, 223, 233
Thebes 48, 62, 63, 76, 169–171, 181–188, 202, 219, 220, 226, 238 see also *Epaminondas*
Themistocles 6, 7, 12, 34, 88, 90, 94, 96, 102–104, 108, 121, 164, 176, 211, 247
Theophrastus 66, 67
Thera 26, 59, 60
Theramenes 176, 177
Thermopylae 9, 92, 93, 100, 116, 130, 192, 217, 223, 233
Theseus 55, 58, 61, 78, 79
Thirty Tyrants 71, 158, 175, 177
Thrasybulus 166, 167, 198
Thucydides
– As a *strategos* 237
– As a source 5, 35, 67, 101, 124, 128, 129, 136, 138, 139
– 'Thucydides Trap' 5, 124
– Persian War 99, 100
– Views on sea power 50, 67, 75, 79, 80, 83–85, 102, 103, 106, 107, 113–115, 118–120, 122, 123, 204, 213, 220, 223
Timoleon 204, 205, 209, 246
Timotheus 188, 189, 246
Tirpitz, Admiral Alfred von 120
Trireme 17, 25, 35, 38–41, 43, 44, 48, 49, 68, 69, 79, 85, 108, 203, 214, 220
Troezen 58, 79, 93, 130, 182, 202, 234

United Nations Convention on the Law of the Sea (UNCLOS) 84, 227

Vegetius 23

Xenophon 35, 41, 48, 68–70, 151, 152–154, 156, 158, 161, 163–167, 169–171, 174, 181, 182
Xerxes 62, 91

Zakynthos 127, 182, 202, 235

www.ingramcontent.com/pod-product-compliance
Lightning Source LLC
Chambersburg PA
CBHW050519170426
43201CB00013B/2007